Hobbies

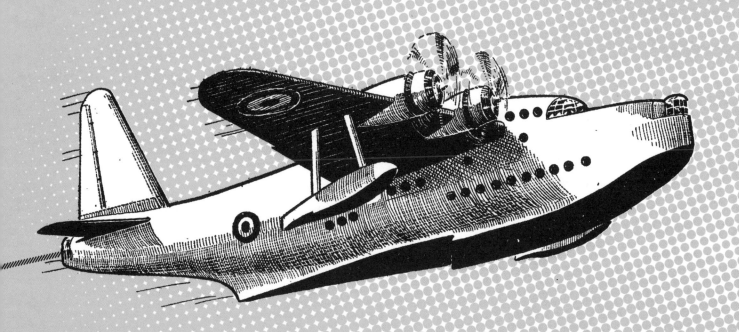

USEFUL OCCUPATIONS FOR PRACTICAL CHAPS

AMMONITE
PRESS

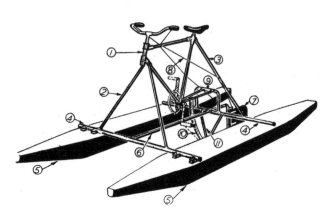

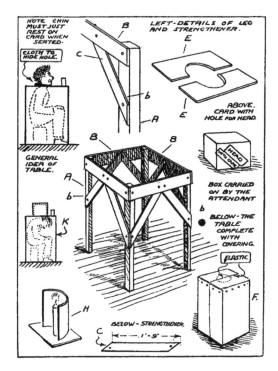

First published 2009 by

AMMONITE PRESS
Castle Place, 166 High Street,
Lewes, East Sussex BN7 1XU

© in the Work AE Publications Ltd., 2009

ISBN 978-1-906672-20-1

A catalogue record for this book is available from
the British Library.

Editor Huw Pryce
Design Gilda Pacitti, Rebecca Mothersole and Robert Janes

Colour origination by GMC Reprographics
Printed and bound in India by Replika Press PVT Ltd

This book is a nostalgic compilation of old articles originally
published in the *Hobbies* magazines between 1920 and 1964.
As such, they are published for reading pleasure only. They are
not intended for use. You should not follow any instructions
or formulae to make any of the fireworks, weapons or firearms
which are illustrated in these articles. Whilst all reasonable
care has been taken in the preparation of this book, to the
fullest extent permitted by law, we do not accept or assume
responsibility to you or any third party for any direct or
indirect loss, injury, illness or damage caused by following any
formula or instruction contained in the articles. Any contact
details, prices, product information or competitions advertised
in the articles are out-of-date and, as such, you should not
respond to them. Any views expressed in the articles should
be taken as those of the original authors and AE Publications
Ltd. does not give its endorsement to any such views. This
book is intended to be read by readers over the age of 16 only.

Whilst every effort has been made to obtain permission from
the copyright holders for all material used in this book, the
publishers will be pleased to hear from anyone who has not
been appropriately acknowledged, and to make the correction
in future reprints.

Show a copy of *Hobbies* to your friends.

Show a copy of *Hobbies* to your friends.

WHAT DID WE DO

Those long winter evenings in front of the fire, nothing to do but bicker and flirt, drink, fight and fornicate? In antiquity boredom was a luxury permitted only to the upper classes, the rest of us worked from dawn 'til dusk and slept the sleep of the just. Just exhausted probably.

By the end of the 19th century however, leisure time was becoming a thing of the masses. Gas and then electric light extended the waking day late into the evening and automation made work easier and even began to shorten shifts. Disposable income became the rule for the middle classes and even workers' pay extended to a couple of bob per week to spend on luxury items.

WORK FOR IDLE HANDS

Back in those days Victoria was on the throne, the UK was called Great Britain, and much of the rest of the globe was coloured Empire pink. The devil really did find work for idle hands during this period, alcoholism was rife and the temperance movement set out to warn people of the demon drink. While crime was actually falling, with improvements in policing and the general human condition in the late 19th century, an increasingly literate populace read more about crime in the Penny

Dreadfuls – the red-top tabloids of their time, and were more frightened of it. There was a will to improve society.

Marx and Engels both resident in the UK when not stirring up trouble in mainland Europe, had published their opinions on society during the middle of the century and their brand of social improvement certainly did not go down well with the establishment, or amongst that section of the middle classes known as 'trade'. A large proportion of trade came from non-conformist protestant stock and they had a religious obligation to reform society and had replaced old-fashioned Catholic guilt with the work ethic.

What better way to improve society and get people out of the pubs, clubs, music halls, brothels and revolutionary meetings than to encourage home crafts? These were slowly dying out in Victorian Britain, as mass

BEFORE TELEVISION?

production and industrialisation took more work away from cottage industries such as spinning, weaving, bodging and shoemaking. With factories turning out inexpensive, high quality goods the impetus to make your own, either out of necessity or for profit, was lost. Mass produced tools, an Empire of materials and a national obsession with worthy pastimes combined to make carpentry the rock and roll of the day, and embellishing was the new black. Victorians loved highly decorated, ornate furnishings and ornaments. Nobody said the work done to fill up that dangerous leisure time, need be at all useful. It should be worthy, patriotic, decorative, broadening.

Carving, pokerwork, modelling, stencilling, picture framing, woodturning and even small furniture-making could all be done in a small space, with little mess or noise, and a great deal of virtue. Much of Britain's Tudor and Jacobean furniture was wrecked during this period, by enthusiastic carvers intent on improving plain old wooden surfaces.

EMBROIDERY FOR MEN

King of the hobby craftsmen in these heady, early days was the fretworker. Fretwork is the art of cutting intricate patterns through panels of wood with little saws, leaving a lace-like effect. It is a technique which lends

itself well to Victorian and Art-Nouveau decorative styles. A sort of high-tech whittling, or embroidery-for-men.

It was from fretwork that the company of J H Skinner in Dereham, Norfolk took its first taste of the hobbies market. John Henry Skinner was born in 1860 in Wisbech. As a young man, he worked for his uncle William Stebbings, a timber merchant in Dereham. By 1887 Skinner had taken over his uncle's timber yard and had set up John Henry

Be Constructive...

Make and Do with Handframe or Machine!

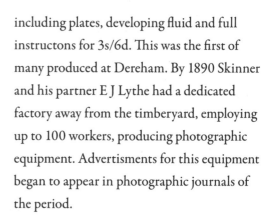

Skinner & Co. to import fretwork tools and materials. Fret machines weren't produced in Britain in the 1880s, so Skinner imported them from the US and Germany.

Fretwork machines were made of cast iron, often elaborately ornate in design, and were usually powered by a treadle, much like an old fashioned sewing machine. Skinner's sold a range of these with names like The Fleetwood, The Lester Improved, The Cricket and The Roger. These are all featured in the company's 1887 catalogue, alongside patterns for fretwork projects and materials. The machines sold for as much as £5/12s/6d but the New or Improved Roger could be obtained for as little as 16s/6d. While these prices look low in this day and age the £5 note of 1897 would be worth £390 today. Seen as a proportion of average income however it's more like £2,170! So paying 17 bob for an Improved Roger was an expensive business.

The catalogue also featured a camera, part of the Eclipse complete photography kit

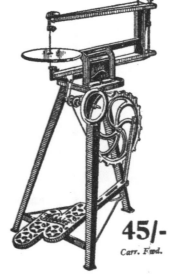

45/-

Carr. Fwd.

including plates, developing fluid and full instructons for 3s/6d. This was the first of many produced at Dereham. By 1890 Skinner and his partner E J Lythe had a dedicated factory away from the timberyard, employing up to 100 workers, producing photographic equipment. Advertisments for this equipment began to appear in photographic journals of the period.

INTO PRINT

Hobbies Magazine later known as *Hobbies Weekly* first saw the light of day in October 1895, around the same time as *The Woodworker Magazine* was first published. *Hobbies Magazine* was the brainchild of John Henry's brother Frank Skinner a journalist based in London, who became *Hobbies'* first editor. There were rumours in later years that the magazine was actually produced in a pair of old railway carriages in the back of Stebbings' old timber yard, but that was a myth born out of Skinner's claim that 'JHS & Co. give away no middle profits. They turn their own brasswork, make their own bellows, cut up the mahogany logs in their own saw mills, and season the wood themselves.'

While the tale of the magazine's railway car origins is wishful thinking, Skinner's policy of doing everything in-house was to be a guiding principle behind the success of the venture in later years.

Hobbies, A Weekly Journal For Amateurs of Both Sexes, No.1 Vol.1 was published on 10th of October. It cost a penny, contained features on fretwork and inlaying, photography, hobbies that pay, philately, magic lanterns, bazaars and how to decorate them, an electric scarf pin(?!), cycling, football, athletics, a free fretwork design, bent ironwork, prizes competitions, correspondence and details of

a fretwork model of St Paul's Cathedral, plans for which were given to subscribers. Each successive generation of readers would grow to know the St Paul's model, it was the first of many recurring projects which graced the pages of *Hobbies* week on week for the next 80 years.

By this time Skinner's were producing treadle machines of their own, copied fairly openly from the American and German machines they used to import. *Hobbies'* issue 1 carried a fretwork competition, the first prize was a very good treadle fretwork machine. Future competitions would usually feature a fretwork machine. Fretwork was the cornerstone of a growing empire; once a reader had a machine, he could produce fretted items quickly and frequently enough to sell them for a profit. Skinner's sold patterns and fretwood by post, and these represented a far greater market than the machines themselves.

The *Hobbies'* bicycles; a gentleman's roadster and a lady's open frame sold in subsequent issues were made for *Hobbies* by another company, but they were the first goods sold bearing the *Hobbies* logo. The Men's Light Roadster, the basic men's bike sold without brakes or mudguards to lighten it, weighed 80lbs. Both bicycles cost eleven pounds, the equivalent of a small family car today. Cycling was a mainstay outdoor activity in the *Hobbies Weekly* repertoire.

WIDER STILL AND WIDER

Hobbies Weekly was generating considerable business for J H Skinner & Co. which became a limited company in April 1896.

In April 1897, Hobbies Publishing Company Ltd. and J H Skinner Ltd. merged under the name of Hobbies Ltd. People buying material advertised in *Hobbies Weekly* were now often buying products from Hobbies Ltd., the magazine was a formidable marketing tool and the Skinners were paying themselves for their own advertising space.

The magazine covered anything which might be deemed a hobby. Subjects featured over the next few years included the usual fretwork, bent iron work, carving, photography, sports, bazaars (useful for selling finished projects) and cycling, but they also featured livestock rearing, horticulture, smallholding, chemistry, electrical experiments and tales from around the world.

The *Hobbies* factory grew apace with the expanding circulation of the magazine. Marketing was consistently aggressive; photographic competitions were often restricted to pictures taken with *Hobbies'* cameras, threepenny discount coupons were printed in the magazines redeemable for up to 5% of the cost of a *Hobbies'* product. Each was only valid for three months from the cover date of the magazine. This allowed *Hobbies Weekly* to rightly claim that a penny spent on the magazine was actually worth 7d; the cover price of the magazine, the coupon and the cost of the free fretwork design which was included in every issue.

Postal transactions were cumbersome affairs in those days. Payment was raised by postal order, so small amounts of money were tiresome things to take care of. *Hobbies* helpfully provided The Hobbies Deposit Coupon Scheme, whereby a book of coupons worth a shilling each could be bought in advance at a 5% discount, this worked to the advantage of the company, in that once purchased, the coupons could not be spent on anything other than *Hobbies'* products, and they might of course never be redeemed. There was also a monthly payment scheme for the purchase of large machines.

By 1898 Hobbies Ltd. had opened two Hobbies Supply Stores in Salisbury Square and Aldersgate Street, London. These displayed and sold items made by *Hobbies* and their principle advertisers, and made a point of locating and procuring items not sold by Hobbies Ltd. for customers. *Hobbies Weekly* had a circulation of 50,000 including subscribers as far afield as Afghanistan, with plenty more in the dominions of Canada and Australia. The London editorial office in Paternoster Square claimed to receive 1000 letters a week.

Hobbies Ltd.'s factory now featured sawmills including a large vertical band saw, reckoned to be the first of its kind in Britain, this could cut planks from logs at 1000 feet per hour. Planks and boards were then fed through

a rolling planer, which gave them a high quality finish. This was also something of an innovation, the only other two such machines being owned by the British Government. Hobbies Ltd. could boast a stock of fretwood amounting to more than a million feet.

The Eastern Daily Press at this time describes a considerable site on both sides of the railway at Dereham Station featuring the timber yard, a seasoning kiln, sawmills, storerooms, packing areas, and large machine shops producing tools. The engineering department could produce 250 complete treadle machines per week, plus 1000 hand fretsaws. The factory also produced cameras and electrical goods

including electric motors and shocking coils. There was even an electroplating plant, presumably set up to nickel plate the more expensive treadle machines, surplus capacity was used to replate old cycle parts and frames for customers.

In 1899 Hobbies Ltd. bought the nursery next door to the Dereham works and launched the Hobbies Horticultural Department, selling bulbs, seeds, raspberry canes, shrubs and fruit trees. The magazine printed an eight-page horticultural supplement, which would become a regular fixture in years to come. That year saw the opening of a third Hobbies Supply Store, in Lime Street, Liverpool, a fourth in Argyle St, Glasgow and a fifth in Bishopsgate, London.

That year also saw the introduction of the A1 Fret Machine, which became the first prize of choice in fretwork competitions and descendents of which were still in production in the early 1960s. Steam engines made an early appearance in the *Hobbies Catalogue*. The company became a major supplier of model steam engines and boats, eventually resulting in the offshoot Mamod which still makes model steam engines.

Profits around the turn of the century give an idea of how well the company was performing; 1899 saw profits of £2,895, increasing in 1900 to £3,778 and £4,545 in 1901. John Henry Skinner left the company he founded in 1903, to make plywood and veneer in Durban, South Africa. Frank Skinner took over from his brother as managing director and staff and directors turned out at 5.30pm on Christmas Day to wave their former employer off from Dereham Station.

As the business grew it opened stores in major cities all over the British Isles, and set up a distribution network that extended to agencies and stores around the world. All these Hobbies Supply Stores had large shop windows, which were used to display items for sale, but also for displays of items made by local hobbyists and even for live shows of fretwork by paid demonstrators. One such display at the Manchester branch was closed down by the police after a crowd of onlookers started blocking the road.

Displays weren't confined to the High Street, in the 1930s Hobbies made up a van which opened out to create a demonstration area. The Hobbies van toured the country demonstrating at fairs and fêtes and taking part in carnivals and parades. The driver Frank Mayfield Toyne was a regular contributor to *Hobbies Weekly*, writing about his experiences under his initials, FMT.

THEIR FINEST HOUR

Hobbies served a dual purpose in times of war. The magazine published patriotic tracts and sported the Union Flag on much of its merchandising and promotional material. Many of the fretwork projects were on a military or patriotic theme and advertisements for the fret machines stressed their British origins and derided the quality of the German machines (on which many of them were based). The Dereham plant was bombed and partially burned down during a Zeppelin attack in 1915 but survived unscathed through the Second World War. This was fortunate and surprising because behind the scenes during both world wars Hobbies Ltd. was manufacturing munitions.

Hobbyists who had just completed the 'Build Your Own Caravan' project in 1939 probably never got to take them to the seaside. World War Two saw *Hobbies Weekly* reduced in size as paper became scarce, but the number of projects was still very high. The issue of the week of the outbreak of war carried a project for an air-raid shelter. Subsequent issues offered various designs for blackout lanterns, gas-mask cases, improvised substitutes for tools and other scarce items. As the Hobbies factory churned out bomb racks for bombers and machined cone-heads for the bombs, *Hobbies Weekly* did its bit for the home front. This was certainly their finest hour.

Of course the striking images of *Hobbies Weekly* in the war were of the military models. Planes featured more prominently than anything else, partly because they're the best looking (and most often seen by civilians), and partly because printing and distributing the designs for working naval ships might give U Boat crews an unfair advantage. 'Ach Dieter! Hand me mien copy of Hobbies September 1942 und arm tubes funf und sechs ...'

DEATH AND RESURRECTION

After the war the company continued to perform well through the austerity of the 40s, but by the mid 1950s things were starting to lose momentum. The factory plant was old, the board of directors was older and television and pop music started to eat away at the market. Modern, 'clean lines', which had people boxing in their panelled doors and banisters, made fretwork a thing of the past, a forgotten art. New pattern lathes in the factories of other defence contractors, could produce in a couple of minutes, the number of nose cones the Hobbies lathes could manage in a day. Contracts began to dry up and things started to look slow.

The Hobbies board was set for retirement – Joint Managing Director, Major J A Pratt, had joined Hobbies in 1926 – and they accepted a takeover bid while the workforce were on their annual holiday in 1964. The new management introduced new products and practices, frequently cutting away more than just the dead wood. Over the next couple of years the company was broken up and sold on. The *Hobbies Weekly* of the 60s covered subjects such as home brewing, pop music and recipes as well as the usual run of projects. But, the magazine closed in December 1965 immediately after a complete redesign and the appointment of a new editor.

The redesign was very in keeping with the styles of the period and it would be nice to think that, given a little nurturing care and the infusion of new blood, *Hobbies Weekly* could have made it through the turbulent 60s into the relative calm and self sufficiency of the 70s, where make-do-and-mend, build-your-own, and do-it-yourself became fashionable alternatives to the excesses of modern life. Hobbies Ltd. was liquidated in 1968 having stagnated under the old guard and then lost with them its guiding principles of prudence and showmanship.

The brand was far from dead however. Ivan Stroulger a *Hobbies* reader and later employee, made redundant in 1968 when Hobbies closed, had little option at the age of 51, but to set up in the crafts trade. Using his redundancy to buy up old *Hobbies'* materials and distributing through their network (which was being used to liquidate the existing stock), he set up in the dolls'-house business. In 1978 he persuaded the directors of the holding company which had bought and closed the old company, to assign the trademark to him. Hobbies Ltd. was born again!

A Frying pan for a clock!
A SWASTIKA BOOK CASE

FOR *Pleasure* & **PROFIT**

HOW TO HIDE A BENCH IN A LIVING ROOM

AN ELECTRIC EXTENSION LEAD!

RENOVATING A BATH

THE amateur who likes to do things about the house will find it quite an easy matter to renovate the bath when it begins to look shabby. The little time it takes and the small cost of materials will be well repaid, for a clean white bath certainly adds considerably to the good appearance of the bathroom.

The materials required, apart from the brush, are a pound tin of flat white paint and a tin of bath enamel.

Before commencing to apply any paint it is essential to make the bath as clean as possible.

The First Job

First of all wash thoroughly with soap and water, and when dry remove any grease with a rag moistened in turpentine. The surface should then be smoothed up with fine glasspaper, finally dusting down and cleaning out all particles of dust. The bath is then ready to receive the preliminary coat of flat white paint.

The taps, of course, will have to be turned off securely, and if they are likely to drip they should be stopped up with corks or have pieces of flannel tied over them. The whole business of re-enamelling must naturally be undertaken at a time when the bath can be out of use for at least ten days.

Painting

Two coats of the flat white paint should be given, following with two coats of the bath enamel.

Two fairly thin coats of paint are always preferable to one thick application, but each must be allowed to dry quite hard before putting on the next.

After the final coat of enamel has dried for a couple of days, fill the bath with cold water and leave it to stand for five or six days, after which the bath will be ready for use.

If the bath is surrounded with woodwork, the top of this will very likely be worn in parts, but it can soon be made to look as good as ever. The materials required in this case are a quarter of a pound of matt seine stain, a gill of french polish, and a little linseed oil.

Clean the Woodwork

To clean the woodwork proceed in the same way as you did with the inside of the bath.

The parts that are particularly worn are then painted with matt seine, and when these are dry the whole surface receives an application. Give this time to dry, then apply one coat of french polish with a soft brush.

Almost immediately—say, a couple of minutes afterwards—polish the surface with a wad dipped in linseed oil, the wad consisting of a piece of soft rag in which cotton wool has been wrapped. A light brisk motion should be used, and the longer it is polished the better.

The above applies only to the top of the bath, any woodwork surrounding the sides being painted to match the rest of the woodwork in the room in the usual way.

The Metal Parts

Having renovated the bath and woodwork to satisfaction, you may now feel inclined to turn your attention to brass taps, plugs, and so on.

For taps in the bathroom white glossy bath enamel again provides a suitable treatment. First of all the taps, fittings, etc. should be well cleaned with metal polish or turpentine, rinsed with water, and dried.

Painted Taps

Two thin coats of the enamel should then be put on, leaving the first to dry for a couple of days before the next is applied.

If the taps do not then appear as white as desired a third coat may be necessary. A soft flat brush about an inch wide will be found most suitable.

Bathroom taps always look well when finished white in this way, only requiring an occasional wash with warm soapy water to make them look fresh and attractive. An interesting alternative is to use aluminium paint, the silvery surface looking very modern and pleasing.

Cleaning Brass or Paint

The brass should be cleaned as before, and two coats of the paint given. If the taps have been previously enamelled white there is no need to clean this off, as the aluminium will take quite well on top after they are washed and dried.

Whichever way they are done, the fittings should always be allowed to dry quite hard—give them at least two days—before using.

A Bath Enamel Recipe

SOME readers may like to make their own bath enamel, and the following, if prepared from pale durable copal varnish answers admirably. Obtain 5 lb. of pure zinc white ground in varnish, 6½ pts. of extra-pale copal varnish, ½ pt. of Japan gold size (pale), ½ pt. pale terebine, and ½ pt. turpentine. Mix the zinc white with the varnish, the whole when finished being free from lumps. Warm the preparation over a fire until very fluid, then add the gold size, terebine and turpentine in order, stirring thoroughly during the operation. If on cooling the enamel should thicken, add equal parts of varnish and turpentine.

TROPHY SHELVES FOR JESS

POPULAR Rock 'n Roll Star, Jess Conrad, who made such a hit when he took the lead in the ITV show 'Wham!' and was groomed to take lead parts in serials such as the popular 'Odd Man Out', has a problem.

He wrote to me (says Ed Capper), 'As you know I play football with the Television All Stars and over the years have collected quite a variety of cups, shields, trophies, etc and I would be glad if you would design for me some shelves on which I could display them. As they are at the moment, they are littered all over my room.'

There is no better home for such a collection than on shelves built into the chimney recess in the room. Most of you know the way to fix shelves. There are two methods: (1) Supporting battens to carry the shelves are fixed to the wall by screws Rawlplugged into holes drilled in the wall or (2) fitting side pieces of timber, of the same width as the depth of the recess, and then screwing the battens to the side pieces to take the shelving.

Use good knot-free timber at least 1 in. thick. If you wish, instead of the rather tedious job of painting or polishing the finished shelves you can cover them with Fablon or Contact adhesive sheeting bearing an imitation wood pattern. This has the advantage of easy cleaning.

The finished shelves need some front treatment to give that unit effect finish instead of just another set of shelves. Plywood or hardboard is best. The top pelmet can be shaped to any form you prefer. Incidentally, many hardware dealers now stock hardboard pelmets ready cut.

The pelmet should be held by fixing to a length of 1 in. square battening screwed into the concealed ceiling joists. To locate the position of the unseen joists, tap the ceiling lightly with a hammer. A hollow resounding note will indicate the ceiling itself; a dull, solid note will indicate you are striking immediately below a joist into which you can screw.

Side strips, also of hardboard or plywood should be fitted right down the entire length of the unit, as shown. The lowest shelf looks best around 6 in. from the floor with the front filled in.

If you can afford it, and your collection of trophies justifies the expense, the shelves can be illuminated with concealed strip lighting. The lights are fitted behind the hardboard facings as indicated by the dotted lines in the drawing. The current consumption need not be expensive as 15 watt lamps are ample.

If you are fitting strip lights, make the hardboard facing at least 6 in. wide so that the lights are completely concealed, otherwise the whole effect will be spoilt.

Finally, to make a really classy fitment you can fit plate glass shelves. Stronger lighting can then be used behind the top pelmet, which will illuminate the whole unit admirably.

HOW TO DO CARD TRICKS AND ENTERTAIN PEOPLE
By Harry Baron

WOULD you like to be able to do the Three Card Trick or deal yourself out a hand of trumps, or tell what card a person is thinking of? Would you like to make cards pass mysteriously from one place to another, cause them to change colour, multiply, and disappear?

Harry Baron, who is a member of the Magic Circle, the London Society of Magicians and the International Brotherhood of Magicians, has set out in this very interesting book some of the secrets of handling cards so that even novices are enabled to mystify their friends.

Published by Nicholas Kaye Ltd. 194–200 Bishopsgate, London, E.C.2. Price 15s. 0d.

A Frying Pan is needed for this
NOVEL CLOCK CASE

HERE is a novelty for the home which can be made up easily by the amateur who can use a few very ordinary household tools.

It is a clock in the form of a frying pan, and the novelty of course lies in the fact that it is made from an ordinary galvanized iron pan such as is used in any household. The movement is an ordinary cheap alarm-clock fitting.

Before work can be started on the frying pan, the movement should be prepared, as certain holes have to be made in the former and their exact positions cannot be ascertained until the movement has been taken in hand.

Preparing the Clock

So the first thing to do is to remove the feet from the clock case then the bell gong, and any little screws which hold the frame to the casing. Draw away the movement and remove the hands and metal face. Cut through as close as possible to the wire which forms the hammer of the bell.

The next thing to do will be to bend down the three lugs which at present stand up at right angles with the circular frame. In Fig. 1, which is a diagram of the movement when fixed in the pan, the three lugs are shown as A, B and C.

The holes in the lugs are enlarged to take a scant 3/16in. bolt. This enlarging can be done with a file using the handle end as a rimer or, of course, a rat-tail file could be used.

An ordinary 10in. frying pan of stout metal with a black japanned handle is needed. The first work upon it will be the drilling or punching of a hole exactly in the centre for the hands. The centre can be found and marked by measurement.

By laying the pan flat on a soft surface the hole can be punched with an ordinary stout wire nail and afterwards enlarged and finished smooth each side with a file. Stand the movement in place in the pan with the hand projections pushed through the hole and with the clock frame therefore resting flat on the inner surface of the pan. The three lugs should now be so arranged that the one farthest from the escapement wheel is pointing towards the handle marked A in Fig. 1.

Bolted Firmly

In the plan (Fig. 2) the dimensions are given for the three holes, but the positions of the latter should be checked by actual trial with the movement.

Three holes are made and three ½in. long 3/16in. diam. bolts with rounded and slotted heads will be put through from the face and through the lugs in the movement and the nuts put on and all tightened up. The round heads of the bolts will not look at all unsightly, as they can be enamelled the same colour as the rest.

Colouring Hints

A blue enamel with yellow figuring looks exceedingly well and brilliant, but almost any colour scheme can be arranged.

The style of figuring most suitable and one that is easily traced and transferred to the ground colour is shewn in Fig. 3. A small, fine camel-hair brush will be found useful for painting in the figures. The two hands are made from thin composition such as xylonite, the outline of them

(Continued foot of opposite page)

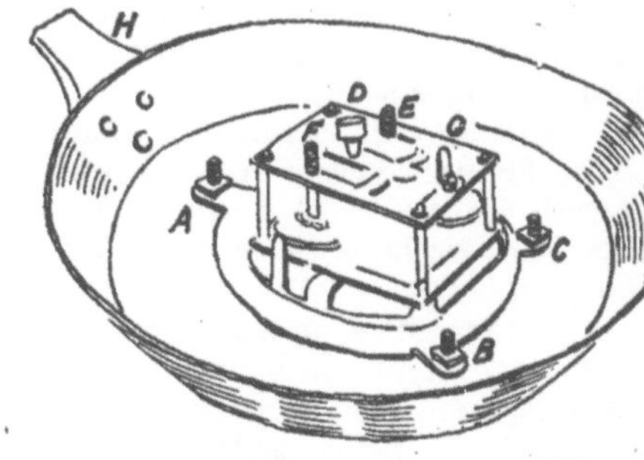

Fig. 1— Back view showing the works

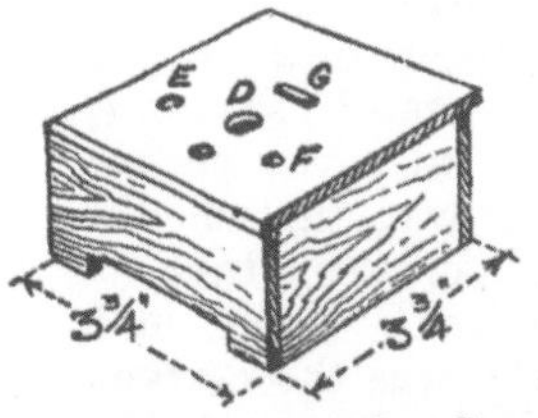

Fig. 4—The Wooden Case

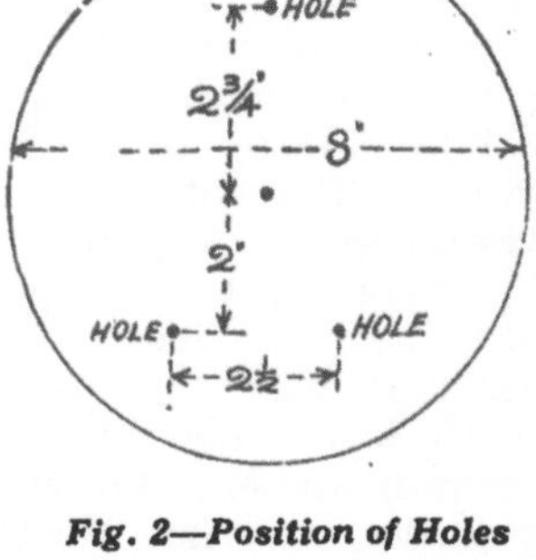

Fig. 2—Position of Holes

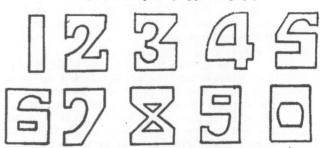

Fig. 3—Full size drawing of the figures needed

A BELGIAN WATERWAY.   *Photo by J. H. Little.*

THE TROUBLES OF A MARKET GARDENER.

A SKETCH.   BY BEN CRAVEN.

"WOULD you like to live rent free, old fellow?" asked neighbour Hopkins.

Of course I said I would, providing it was not at Government expense.

"Well, Daisy Bower is to let; you could easily sell enough out of the garden to cover the rent, and what you could get for the paddock would be a nest egg towards buying the place."

I afterwards became the tenant of Daisy Bower.

My wife, with her usual forethought, made a meat pie, which immediately on our arrival was placed in the pantry, and at night, when we felt we had done enough work to justify a dinner at the Cecil, Keturah, the little maid, was bidden to bring it in. Alas! the rats had given the order first, the crust of the pie had all gone, and with it a small tablecloth. We supped off bread and cheese, comforting ourselves with the thought that even though we had rats for neighbours, they were of the aristocratic species, particular as to linen.

The garden was so overrun with weeds you had to consult a map to find the whereabouts of the paths; it would be necessary to have a boy to help with the weeding. Charley was engaged. On the first Monday I had a half day off from the office, determined to get things under weigh.

"Where's that boy, Charlie?"

"What I want to know," said the missis, "is where's my clothes line?—it's quite a new one. You can put handkerchiefs to dry on currant bushes, but you can't sheets. Do look for the clothes line?" Yes, I found the clothes line, and Charley, too, both in the same place. The line was in the form of a swing in the loft; and Charley the swinger.

Charley made a still further acquaintance with the clothes line after that.

While Charley weeded—and I could not understand why Keturah could not be allowed to weed, too—I borrowed a scythe to mow the lawn with. It was beautifully shaded with oak trees, and the plan was to have all our meals *al fresco*, but the scythe must have been the wrong shape, for it did the work of a spade rather than a mower, so there was nothing for it but to go on my knees and cut the rank grass with a pair of shears.

"Miriam," said I, that night, in a faint voice, "there'll be no need for you to buy a timbrel just yet."

"No," she said, with a snap, "I think it's a case of having put ourselves into slavery, rather than getting out of it."

I had no difficulty in letting the paddock, but it took the first year's rent to put the fence in order. However, as I said to Miriam, things were sure to be a little expensive for us the first year.

Old Mrs. Bowen sent a message by Charley, "Could she have some rhubarb?" "Yes," said I, thinking here was already the sign of better things, "two pence a bundle." Mrs. Bowen came herself for the rhubarb. "That there Chawley o' your's been tryin' to do me—says as how the rhubarb's twopence a bunch. I've had as much rhubarb an' apples as I can eat from Daisy Bower for nothin' this thirty year, so I'm not likely to begin now on yer twopences. 'No, young man,' says I, 'you can't get my coppers into yer pocket like that.'" What could I say to the wheezy old dear after that, but, "Certainly take as much as you like, Mrs. Bowen." Later on I found it was Mrs. Bowen who was the market gardener, and not Miriam's husband at all.

What wrong parts we do play in the world!

My first serious piece of business was to prepare a deep trench for celery. Plants and manure cost seven and sixpence. "But we shall never eat all that celery!" exclaimed the missis. "Of course not, I should not allow you to do so," I said, loftily. "Charles will take them to Romford market." Charles never did; the plants all rotted away, not even one "head" came to perfection. The birds stripped

The Cherry Trees,

naughty boys, doubtless headed by Charles, relieved us of the eating pears. The question of "bottom fruit," as Charles described gooseberries, currants, and raspberries, was solved for us by a neighbour. Romfort market had been again mentioned, but as there was likely to be a family quarrel as to who was to find the customers there, that idea was dropped. Just at the critical moment the suggestion came, that after home had been fully supplied with jam, and relatives, too, gratis, the remainder of the fruit should be passed on to a bazaar jam maker, and as pride forbade even the mention of "rent," the plan was agreed to, Charles being paid to pick the fruit, and Keturah told off to watch over him.

I came across during my early explorations at Daisy Bower a bed of broad, green leaves. "Lilies of the Valley!" I murmured. "In the spring they can be sent to market."

"Lilies!" sniggered Charles,

"That's Garlic."

And all along it was just like that!—every lily leaf proved to be garlic.

I did not even have the satisfaction of venting my anger on neighbour Hopkins. Fortunately for him, he had to leave the neighbourhood. When I did set eyes on him and he asked how we were getting on, I gave him a bit of my mind. "You had better have sent us to Timbuctoo, or Jericho. 'Getting on,' indeed! The missis has had to start a poultry farm, and take in summer lodgers, to keep me off the list of bankrupts, till we can get rid of the lease. Daisy Bower, indeed! a fine old sort of Daisy she's been to me! I call the place 'Thorney Corner,' that's more like the proper sort of name for it." And would you believe it!—he only smiled, and said something about "the mare 'being' the better horse."

A New Muff Suspender.

—:o:—

The convenient and ornamental muff chains, with which we have been amply satisfied for the last few years, are, it is said, losing their hold on those who are particular in following the vagaries of Fashion.

The most approved substitutes at present are bands of velvet and of kid, the latter of which are plain to ugliness, and certainly cannot be accused of possessing any tawdry appearance. A velvet muff suspender can easily be made by any worker who can make neat, strong stitches, and smart, crisp bows. The requirements are about a quarter of a yard of silk cord, the same colour as the lining of the muff, and from a yard and a-half to two yards of very narrow ribbon velvet—that is, not exceeding three-quarters of an inch in width. A couple of steel or paste slides must be procured, or one more important looking brooch, the choice depending upon whether the suspender is to be worn crossed upon the chest or brought straight down on each side of the muff. Take the cord first and turn down each end to make a loop, binding the ends very firmly round with strong silk twist, after having secured them wit stitches. The loops need not be very larg only ample enough, indeed, to enable the velve to pass through them easily. Cut off a piece the velvet long enough to pass round the nec and down to the side of the muff, to reach th cord which is to rest inside it. Slip the end of the velvet through the loops and sew ther neatly and strongly in place. The slides o buckles should be passed on to the velvet befor it is sewn to the second end of the cord. On should set on each side of the suspender whe this is in use. Finally, make up three littl jaunty bows of the velvet and sew one at th back of the neck and the others on each sid close to the muff. The cord should be finishe at the ends without making a loop, but small metal ring should be sewn ther instead. The velvet, instead of being attache by stitches to the cord, should be provided a each end with a patent hook which will faste into the ring provided for it. The suspende can then be easily shifted and attached to an other muff when required.

A HOBBY ALPHABET

V STANDS FOR:— VEGETABLE GROWING

"GROW More Food" is a slogan with most gardeners today, for vegetables are a necessity with us more than ever at the present time.

Vegetable growing makes a grand, useful hobby. Experience soon shows one what to do, and there is an attempt to save you time and money by imparting hints and tips on the planting, growing and cultivation of different vegetables. These are set out in a simple way as follows :—

Turnips

While turnips will grow in almost any soil, they thrive best in moist, friable, sandy loam. Sow not too early in drills and thin to single plants ; turnips may be sown in March, April and May.

In cold districts, growers are often troubled with late frosts which nip the crops. There are early and winter varieties, however. A good, general cropper is Golden Ball, while Swede stands up well to frosts.

Soil must always be kept moist. For a winter crop, sow in July, continuing until September. Seed could be broadcast after potatoes, if any, have been lifted.

Round galls (A) are sometimes seen on the roots of turnips, this being due to a weevil (a tiny black beetle pest) which lays eggs in a hole in the turnips. The eggs produce a yellowish larvae which feeds on the roots and causes the swellings. Infected plants must be pulled up and immediately burned, and the soil must be dressed with gas lime or quick lime.

Potatoes

These grow best in sandy loam. It is advisable to use the seed potatoes that come from Scotland, there being several varieties, most of which have to be passed by the Board of Agriculture before they can be grown in private gardens.

Sets sprouted in a dark place give better results. Plant well apart, earlies being set 24ins. between drills and 12ins. apart. Late and maincrop kinds having more haulm are set 30ins. between drills and about 16ins. apart. Three sprouts should be left on each set ; it is best—if no increase of stock is required—not to cut the spuds in pieces.

Never cut kidneys. Earthing up is proceeded with as the plants grow. Haulms are lifted and stored in a clamp when they turn yellow ; lift earlies whenever required for the table.

Brown patches on leaves are the first signs of potato blight (B). The disease occurs from the beginning of June to the middle of July, if the weather is warm and damp. Patches spread over the leaves and stems, and unless checked by spraying with Bordeaux Mixture, the haulms die right back and checks the development of the roots.

Spraying should be done in June, early in the morning or evening ; the sun must not be shining on the crop. Spray a second time at the end of July. In bad cases, do not spray, but cut the haulm away and leave the potatoes in the ground to ripen. The illustrations at C and D shows the sprouts of potatoes emerging wrongly and correctly, respectively.

Brussels Sprouts

These miniature cabbages originated in Belgium. Three sowings may be made, (1) in the heat in March ; (2) outside in April, and (3) during the months of July or August.

While good, rich soil is essential, avoid over-feeding with horse manure or artificials as the sprouts become coarse and loose. Loose soil means more leaves than sprouts, so when planting, make the soil firm, this resulting in more sprouts.

These should not be picked before the first frosts occur ; afterwards, pick them from the bottom as shown (F).

There are different varieties of Brussels sprouts, such as Dwarf Gem, Aigburth, Darlington and Covent Garden. The Aigburth is excellent for early or late sowing.

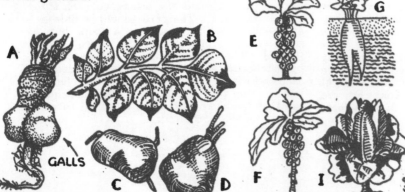

Any housewife would like this fine
HOUSEMAID'S BOX

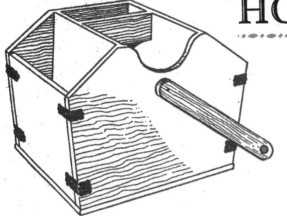

THIS pattern of household or, as some call it housemaid's box, is a most useful domestic article. It differs from the familiar pattern in not having a lift-out tray. In some way this is an advantage as everything is at hand for removal when wanted.

The side compartments can hold floor and furniture polishing cloths; the tray in the centre is intended for tins of polish, and the middle compartment for brushes, etc. White deal, ½in. finished thickness, will do nicely for construction.

The Main Portions

A perspective view, with one side removed, is shown in Fig. 1 to explain how the box is fitted together. Cut the sides to the dimensions given in Fig. 2, the grooves A and B for the divisions being ⅛in. deep.

One side, that opposite the tray, has a portion cut out for easy access to the compartment. This is shown by dotted lines.

Cut the two end pieces and nail the sides to the ends. Plane the bottom edge of the latter pieces level with that of the sides. Cut the bottom to overlap ¼in. all round, then nail the bottom on. If the overlap is neatly rounded it looks better.

The Tray

The divisions A and B are cut ¼in. wider than the ends, the extra, of course, to fit in the grooves. Cut grooves for the tray bottom and front to fit in as in Fig. 3.

Cut the bottom piece of the tray, glue between

the divisions and push the latter pieces in the grooves cut in the sides. Apply a little glue to the grooves first.

Now cut the tray front and glue that in. When dry, and not before, drive a few nails through the side into the tray bottom.

The Handle

For the handle cut two 1½ins. strips of wood as shown in Fig. 4. Bore the larger hole for a length of ½in. dowel rod and near the bottom end a hole with a bradawl to take the threaded part of a stout 1in. round-headed screw.

At a spot indicated at C, Fig. 2, bore in each side piece a hole large enough to permit the easy entry of the shank part of the screws.

Now drive these screws from the inside into the handle strips, to fix the handle in place. Do not drive the screws in too tight, let there be just enough freedom to allow the handle to fall down sideways when released without scraping the sides of the box.

The handle grip is a length of ½in. dowel rod, glued between the strips. After gluing, drive a

CUTTING LIST						
All ½in. thick.						
					Length.	Width.
Sides (2)	..	..	..	..	1ft. 3ins.	9ins.
Ends (2)	..	..	..	..	9ins.	6½ins.
Bottom	..	..	..	..	1ft. 3½ins.	10½ins.
Divisions (2)	..	..	..	..	9½ins.	9ins.
Tray bottom	..	..	..	..	6½ins.	3½ins.
Tray front	..	..	..	..	6½ins.	2ins.
Handle strips (2)	..	..	..	..	10ins.	1½ins.
For handle grip, 12ins. of ½in. dowel rod.						

small nail through each strip into the dowel rod to further fix it.

The box is now complete with the exception of the metal corner plates shown in the general view.

These are optional but they do strengthen the box a lot, and as such an article sometimes gets rather rough usage they are well worth fixing. They can be bought at most hardware stores.

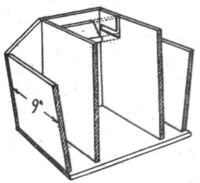

Fig. 1—Showing general construction

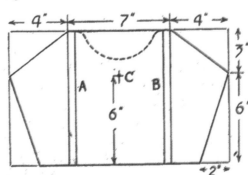

Fig. 2—How to mark out the sides

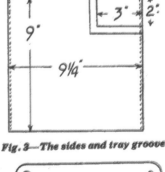

Fig. 3—The sides and tray groove

Fig. 4—The handle sides

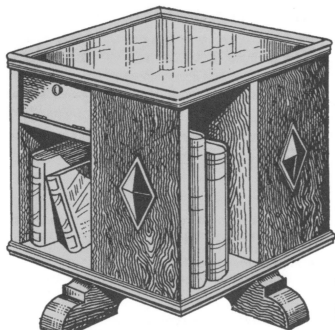

four separate compartments irrespective of the little cupboards previously mentioned. The front elevation at Fig. 1 will give most of the dimensions whilst the view at Fig. 3 would almost suffice to clearly explain the mode of assembly.

In view of younger workers, however, we would add that the central division sections (measuring 13ins. long by 15ins. wide by ½in. thick) are first squared to size, centred, and ½in. wide channels (half checks) cut half and half in each with tenon saw and chisel. This is in order that they may "lock" together as indicated by the cut away view

Fixing the Wings

When this has been done, the "wing" portions—they measure 13ins. long by 7¾ins. wide by ½in. thick—are glued and nailed (use flat nails) to the edges carefully, after which the cupboard shelf divisions (7¼ins. by 7¾ins. by ½in.) are glued and nailed 3ins. down from the top. The top and bottom covering pieces are 16ins. square and must be attached similar to the divisions, keeping same flush with the edges.

All nail heads must, of course, be punched a trifle below the surface and filled in with plastic wood or coloured wax. It will not be necessary to do this to the nails at the top and bottom. These will be effectively hidden with the mouldings.

Corner Moulding

When the glue has set, glasspaper all parts to be seen, neat and smooth. The corner moulding (No. 301) could be mitred and affixed to the top edges, the other moulding (No. 18) going to the bottom as in the picture.

WE illustrate herewith one of the latest pieces of furniture yet designed for the modern home. Every home-craftsman will enjoy making it, for apart from its simple construction, we have here "something" novel and really worth while.

There's another point about it too, that many will like—that's its plainness and size. Why, the whole thing just stands 18ins. high by 16ins. square—ideal for that bare-looking corner of the sitting room or beside that "isolated" armchair!

A Combination

It is, in fact, almost a "combination" of everything. As well as being a revolving bookcase, you can utilize it as a smoker's cabinet, wine or invalid cabinet or as a card table, etc.

What makes this possible is the two small hinged doors of the top compartments. There is sufficient accommodation inside for the smoking outfit, playing cards, and any other odds and ends. The doors are fitted with ball catches and are, of course, quite easy to open and close.

It is constructed throughout from ½in. and 1in. thick satin walnut—a deservedly popular wood and cheap in respect to grain value and durability. This and the fittings are supplied by Hobbies Ltd., a price for which will be given on request.

Building the Case

The case is constructed in the well-known "swastika" fashion, i.e., we have the formation of

MATERIALS SUPPLIED

6 pieces satin walnut, 16ins. by 16ins. by ½in. thick.
1 piece satin walnut, 12ins. by 8ins. by ½in. thick.
1 piece satin walnut, 16ins. by 3ins. by ½in. thick.
1 piece satin walnut, 16ins. by 8ins. by ½in. thick.
2 pieces satin walnut, 16ins. by 3ins. by 1in. thick.

4 lengths No. 301 corner moulding, 18ins. long.
4 lengths No. 18 moulding, 18ins. long.
4 diamond ornaments No. 206.
2 brass knobs No. 5373.
4 brass hinges (strong) 1in. long.
2 ball catches No. 5480. 3/16in.
1½ doz. ⅜in. by 3 brass flat head screws.
1 doz. ⅜in. by 4 iron flat head screws.

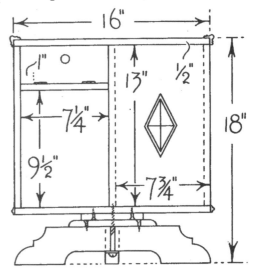

Fig. 1—Front elevation with dimensions

Owing to the unusual shape of the former moulding, the mitring will not prove difficult if a piece of planed scrap wood is set in the mitre block and the length of moulding placed along the foremost corner.

Making the Feet

A half section of the base stand feet parts will be found at Fig. 2. This could be marked on on thin card, cut out, and used as a template for pencilling the complete shape onto the wood which, in this case, measures 16ins. long by 3ins. wide by 1in. thick. Still, as the design shape is composed

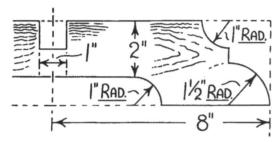

Fig. 2—Half section of feet

mostly of "compass" work, it should be easy to strike the shape direct to the wood with the compasses and set square. This will also ensure accuracy, and when doing so, don't forget to make the central half checks opposite to each other.

Regarding the thickness, many workers might find the work of cutting out the shape rather a tough proposition, especially as the usual home implements available are only the bow saw or scroll saw. The next best thing, therefore, is to take the prepared wood to the local machine shop,

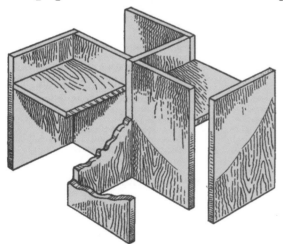

Fig. 3—A view of the case construction

or alternatively, use a good sharp chisel, a ½in. gouge, the mallet and a tenon saw. If you adopt this effective means, be sure to clamp the material singly to a scrap piece of wood on the bench and chip away a little at a time and, in view of outside curves, with shoulder pressure on gouge or chisel. The roughed out shape should be finally levelled off with a rasp, file, and glasspapered all over prior to assembling with glue.

The Pivot Discs

It will be seen by the drawing detailed at Fig. 1

and again at Fig. 4 that the feet are further strengthened by circular pivot plates. These are discs of ½in. wood cut 7ins. and 5ins. respectively, the edges of the forementioned being rounded over. Both are drilled and then countersunk to suit ¼in. by 8 flat head iron screws.

As the pivot used is a 3½in. by 10 round head screw, it would be advisable to find the centre of the feet half checks, and—working from top and bottom alternately—drill out a suitable hole to accommodate the screw shank with an exact amount of freedom. The larger disc only remains to be screwed on and the drilling continued from the reverse side.

Ease of Movement

Screw the other disc to the centre of the case bottom, and indicate the centre with a bradawl. As ease of movement and balance depends largely on these two discs, make positive that the screw heads do not interfere by rubbing across the surface with a flat file. A smearing of candle tallow will do a lot to ensure grace of movement.

Turn the work upside down when pivoting the feet, and have a small metal washer coming between the screw head and foot rail as shown.

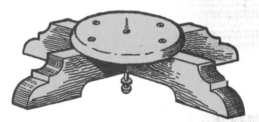

Fig. 4—The feet assembled

The small drop doors of the cupboards are cut from ½in. stuff and planed to fit neatly in the apertures which measure 7¾ins. long by 3ins. in width. Two 1in. long brass hinges (Hobbies heavy variety) are sunk flush with the lower edges about 1in. inwards from the ends.

Allow the "knuckles" to project a little forward, and before screwing in position, drill a 3/16in. hole of adequate depth in the middle of the top edges of both doors for the ball catches supplied. Grip the doors in a vice to do so. Knock the catches in with a mallet, or failing this, use a hammer and provide yourself with a piece of scrap wood to prevent damage to the casing.

Doors and Catches

The doors should be screwed to show a slight break at the front. Pieces of plywood about 1in. by ½in. serve as door stops. These must be "pinned" before gluing and pressing against the case top inside. To obtain an even break, close the doors gently, open, and drive in the nails without shifting the position if possible.

The true position of the ball catch plates are another point of importance. Same is usually found by blackening the ball with oil-stone grease and closing the door. This will give the "spoor" ending. The "inlet" hole for the catch plate can thus be made with a bradawl and the plate screwed directly over the same.

A HOUSE BUILT IN A MONTH.

I REMEMBER, when I was a child, what delight we used to take in building with toy bricks. I little thought then that when I grew up I might be tempted to build a house actually to live in on the same plan. We hear all sorts of solutions to the housing problem, but certainly the most practical is the method I've just seen. Fancy, a bungalow built by a man in a month!

The house I saw put up arrived very much like the box of bricks of old—all in pieces of proper sizes, shapes and thicknesses, carefully numbered and bundled for the grown-up youngster to put together.

The Builder and Owner.

All these things I saw at Elmham, Norfolk, and a natural curiosity finally drove me into conversation with Mr. Alan Calver, the happy owner.

His pride of possession was contagious, and soon I was having a look at this neat little three-roomed bungalow. Its front door opened from a verandah into a comfortable living room from which one could enter the two bed rooms. There was also a small scullery-kitchen in one corner of the living room with an exit by a side door. The whole establishment, indeed, looked most cosy and comfortable.

The Scheme Explained.

Mr. Calver explained the simplicity of it all which was a revelation to me—the standardised parts fitted together so quickly that it was fascinating to see the house grow under one's eyes. You who have watched a house that is being built, standing for months without apparent progress, will appreciate the difference. Our friend was enthusiastic about it, and was sure he had sunk his spare cash in a remunerative manner. He told me the whole of the material —including the wood, doors, windows, felt for the roof, nails, etc.,—only cost him £86. The wonderful part was, too, that it was all erected in a month—a feat accomplished quite easily by this man and a young girl, with the occasional help of a friend in the evenings.

He told me all about it from a diary he had kept. "Having been under notice for twelve months or more," he said, "I have now built my own house, and can say it is a splendid success. I was able to buy a plot of land about 40ft. wide and 108ft. deep. This is a useful size to hold a bungalow, and leaving a nice piece of ground for a garden back and front. Then I simply ordered a set of A2 Bungalow wood, etc., from Messrs. Hobbies Limited, of Dereham, who supply the material for building bungalows. In a

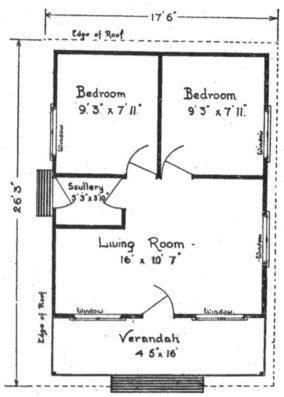

Ground Plan

A PICTURE SHOWING THE FRONT DOOR.

few days the land looked like a sale yard; timber, all numbered and bundled, lay everywhere.

How the Work was Accomplished.

Some interested people wondered where I should use it all, but I told them I had a schedule showing all the wood numbered, where it was to be used, and what nails required.

On the first day I unloaded and stacked the wood, and the following (Wednesday) morning early I started to lay the foundations out with the creosoted blocks supplied by Hobbies Limited, and level out for floor joists the same day. The floor joists were laid on roughly with the sleeper plates, and some of the end stud work was started. On Thursday I finished the stud work at the end, and also fixed on some of the feather-edge boards to keep work square and upright, whilst the two next days were taken up with both sides and building in the windows and one door."

"On Saturday afternoon," continued our diarist friend, "with the help of friends (two of them) I fixed up and made the principal, and had them all in position before night. On Monday the purlins were all fixed and the ridge and some match-boarding fixed on the roof. As this was all cut to size it was no trouble, and on Tuesday I finished the boards and put some of the felt on the roof. By Wednesday night the felt was all on my future

home, and covered in from rain. The gable end and capping and the two sides occupied two days to cover with feather-edge weather boards.

"On Saturday I fixed one door and two windows in front. My first delay caused by rain came on the Monday, but I was able to lay the floor down inside the building. Tuesday, being fine and dry, I creosoted all round outside, and started forming the ceiling inside with ½in. matchboarding; the whole of which was finished by Wednesday. On Thursday the walls were similarly treated, and some partition studs fixed, the doors being built in as usual. On Saturday I laid the floor on the verandah and creosoted it at once while dry, and painted the front windows.

"The painting and creosoting inside and out occupied about a week, with odd jobs of fixing shelves, railings to verandah, setting the stove and chimney. This was a happy completion to the building of my bungalow,

ANOTHER STAGE OF THE BUILDING
OPERATIONS.

and soon the furniture was in and being set out. Indeed, within a month of starting work, I was living in a bungalow of my own building."

So our friend concluded on the same note of enthusiasm. Indeed, so ardent was his manner, that I am now very much of a mind to build a bungalow for myself.—F. C.

If YOU require a House.

THE above is a contributor's account of an interview he had with the owner of a Hobbies A2 Bungalow. These are supplied for £86 complete, carriage forward, and reference to the plan given shows the dimensions and positions of the rooms. The Bungalow is sent, as explained, in parts, with the materials cut, shaped and numbered ready for building. A complete list of material and a schedule of the various pieces are supplied with the plan, so that any handyman can emulate Mr. Calver, and build his own house. If you are one of those unfortunate people who cannot find a house, you cannot do better than obtain a piece of land and then get Hobbies Ltd. to send you the materials along so you can construct your own. A four-roomed Bungalow is also obtainable in the same way, and this, too, can be erected with very little labour or trouble.

Make an attractive 'Dice' Table Lamp

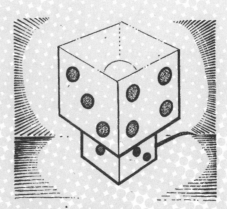

A DICE-SHAPED table lamp looks very attractive in almost any setting, and is fairly simple soldered to the corners of one of the squares (B). The upper wire square is then soldered to the tops of the up-

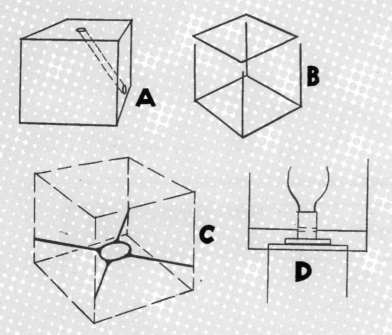

rights. The supports for the shade are made by laying two lengths of wire diagonally inside the frame from corner to corner. A ring of wire, large enough to fit over the lampholder, is placed where the diagonals cross. They are cut where the ring crosses them and soldered to it to give the shape shown at C. This is soldered to the uprights, 1 in. above the lower wire square (D). The complete frame is washed and given a coat of white paint.

The shade sides are covered with four 8 in. squares of plain plastic or acetate sheeting, preferably white or a pale colour. The spots on each of these sides are penny-sized circles of red plastic or felt, which are glued in place. If they are painted, the light shining through the shade may show the brush marks.

The covering material can be bound to the frame with plastic thonging or silk braid, but to emphasize the square lines of the shade and its resemblance to a dice, thin white cotton or linen thread, which is unobtrusive if neatly done, should be used. (A.L.)

and inexpensive to make.

The base of the lamp is a 4 in. cube of wood, which must be glass-papered to a very smooth finish. A hole for the flex is drilled from the top at an angle, coming out at the bottom of the rear face (A).

A white plastic lampholder, with flex attached, is screwed to the top of the cube after the flex has been led through the hole.

The base is then painted. After the undercoats have been applied, it is given a coat of white enamel. When this is dry, the spots are put on. Use a sixpence as a guide, drawing the circles round it in pencil, and painting them in red enamel with a small water-colour brush.

The shade is also made in the form of a cube. First, two squares with 8 in. sides are made from lampshade wire, and four 8 in. long wire uprights are

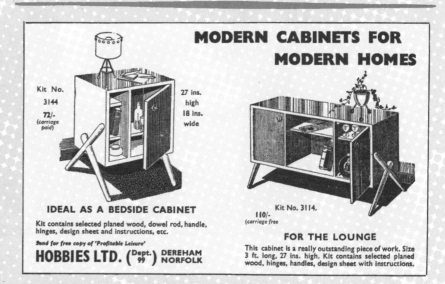

An Electric Extension Lead

FOR owners of the various types of portable electric drills, this extension lead will prove a very useful item.

You will need a length of 3-core rubber-covered flexible cable (about 20ft.), a standard 230 volts, 3-pin 5 amp. plug and socket, a wooden switch block (4ins. square) and a piece of 3 ply to suit.

First cut the plywood to fit the base of the switch block and drill it with four countersunk holes for screwing on. In the centre of one side of the block drill a hole of sufficient size to allow the cable to pass through. Remove any sharp edges each side of the hole.

The 3-pin socket is now fitted to the block. This is done by removing the cover, placing it in the centre of the block and marking through the fixing holes. Three holes about $\frac{3}{16}$in. diameter should be made for the wires to the socket. These can be marked through in the same way as for the fixing screws. Screw the socket into position.

The cable is now passed through the hole in the side of the block and the ends stripped back for connecting to the appropriate sockets.

To prevent the wire from pulling out it is cleated as shown in Fig. 1. This cleat is made from 20 S.W.G. copper wire and twisted up tight with pliers.

Now connect the leads as follows:—Red to 'L' terminal, Black to 'N' and Green to 'E'. At the other end of the lead the 3-pin plug is fitted in a similar manner.

Finally fit the plywood base to the block with small brass countersunk screws. (J.A.H.)

3 CORE CABLE

230 V. 3 PIN 5 AMP PLUG

230 V. 3 PIN. 5AMP SOCKET (SHUTTERED TYPE)

PLYWOOD BASE

4 INCH WOODEN SWITCH BLOCK.

FIG 1

ANDY DIDITT by FROSTIE.

"THE MAN NEXT DOOR WOULD LIKE TO KNOW IF YOU WANT THE OTHER END OF THAT NAIL BENDING DOWN?"

A handyman can make this practical and sensible
ADJUSTABLE ASHTRAY

SOME ashtray stands are too high, others not high enough, so here is a simple adjustable type that will suit anyone.

There is the chain and hook-eyes to consider. You need only two of the latter, one serving as the adjusting pin. Picture chain should be used; and is obtainable from Hobbies Ltd., in suitable sizes. A piece 12ins. long serves the purpose.

Column and Base

Start off by making the column and base parts. The column consists of two side pieces (16ins. long by 1¾ins. wide by ½in. thick) and two end pieces (same length and thickness, but ⅞in. wide) which are glued and nailed together.

Use 1½in. oval nails, and be certain that the width of the end pieces is truly parallel, otherwise you will experience difficulty in fitting and working the adjustable post. This is supposed to slide up and down easily and not rock too unsteadily when near the top end of the column, i.e., at the highest point.

It will be seen from the sectional elevation (Fig. 1) that the column is plugged at the bottom. Do this with a block 1½ins. by ⅞in. by ⅞in.

Base Blocks

Three base blocks (see Fig. 4) are now cut out from ⅞in. stuff. The largest base piece has a 5in. hole cut in its centre as detailed; the smallest base piece is checked ½in. deep to take the bottom end of the column.

Drill and countersink a hole to suit a 2in. or 2½in. by 8 flathead iron screw. Insert the column and screw it in place, having applied glue, as well as having attached the other two base parts, using glue and nails, although flathead screws would be the best.

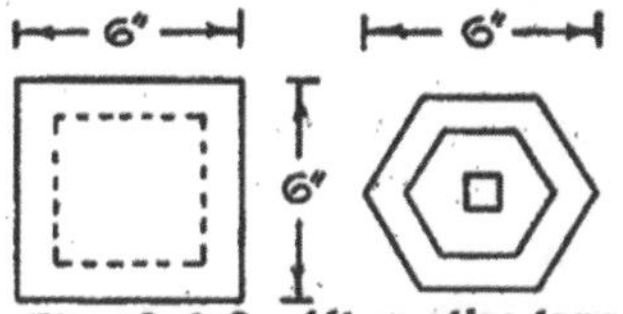

The post and stand top parts are prepared. For the post, you need a piece of ⅞in. square wood 12½ins. long. It is sunk into and screwed to a supporting piece of ⅞in. stuff 4ins. square.

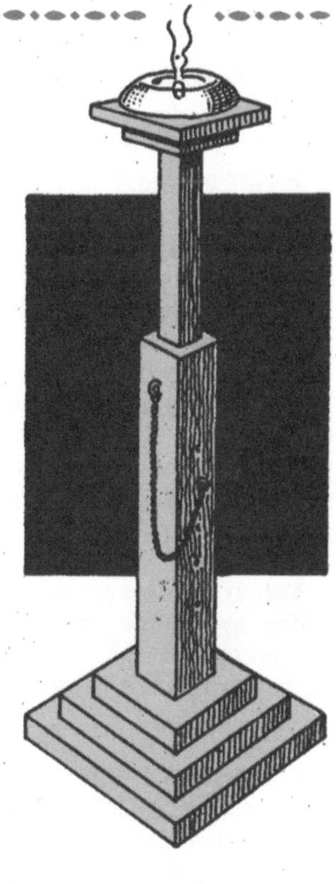

Screws or nails are driven through this into the top piece, same being cut from ½in. wood. The top (Fig. 2) can be square or hexagonal (Fig. 3) in shape, which also applies to the base parts.

The Sliding Column

Naturally, prior to attaching the stand top parts to the post, you will have tested it in the column to see that it slides up and down easily.

Allow some freedom, remembering that the post will be enamelled and there will be a slight swelling of the wood in consequence. The post should be given only one light coat of paint. The inside of the column should not be touched. The adjusting holes in the column can be made to your own judgment. Keep them about 1½ins. apart, and instead of using a hook-eye as an adjusting pin, a piece of brass wire ⅛in. thick could be bent suitably.

Weighting the Base

To conclude, we might add that you could do without cutting a 5in. hole in the large column base piece. It is to enable you to make it heavy, if desired, by pouring in melted lead piping to about ½in. deep.

In order to keep the lead in place, nail or screws could be driven into the base (the underside of the middle one) to project about ¼in. Alternatively, the moulded weight could be bored, and screw in place. Regarding the assembly of the three base pieces, have them attached together so that the grain of each runs crosswise with each other much in the way that plywood is built up. This will prevent the wood warping. There is no necessity to fix feet to the base unless desired.

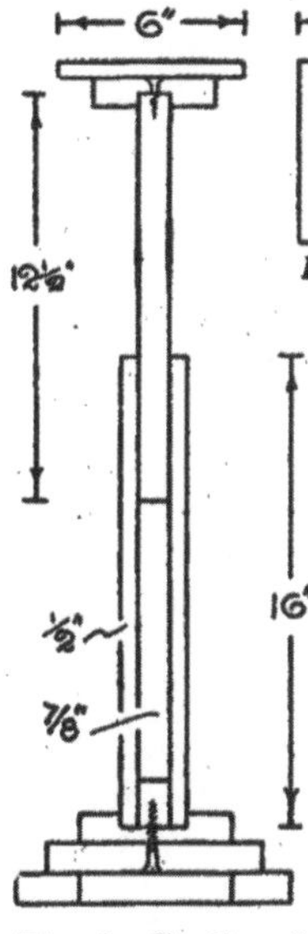

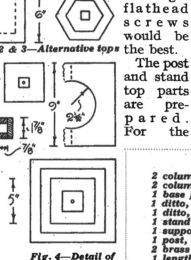

Figs. 2 & 3—Alternative tops

Fig. 1—Sectional Elevation

Fig. 4—Detail of parts

MATERIALS

2 column sides, 16ins. by 1¾ins. by ½in.
2 column ends, 16ins. by ⅞ins. by ½in.
1 base piece, 5ins. by 5ins. by ⅞in.
1 ditto, 7ins. by 7ins. by ⅞in.
1 ditto, 9ins. by 9ins. by ⅞in.
1 stand top, 6ins. by 6ins. by ½in.
1 support piece, 4ins. by 4ins. by ⅞in.
1 post, 12½ins. by ⅞in. by ⅞in.
2 brass hook-eyes
1 length of picture chain, 12ins. long.

NOVEL "TIGER" CIGARETTE DELIVERY BOX

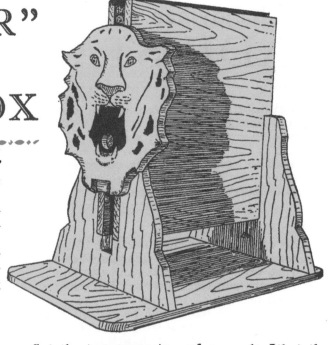

THIS novel cigarette box delivers a 'smoke' through the mouth of the tiger each time the lever is pressed. To help you understand the simple mechanism, a general view is shown at Fig. 1, one side of the box being omitted to reveal the "works."

The cigarettes lie, one on top of another, just above the cross slip glued to the side shown. At the rear of the cigarettes you will see a shaped piece of wood to the bottom of which a length of twine is attached, the other end of the twine passing over a pulley and then secured to the lever below.

When the lever is depressed, the piece of wood slides along the cross slips and ejects a cigarette. An elastic band, attached to the opposite end, pulls the ejector back when the lever is released.

The Various Parts

Patterns for the various parts are given in the accompanying illustrations. The sides are cut from 3/16in. fretwood. When cut, place both together and at the spots marked by a small black dot, bore tiny holes to fit ⅛in. thin wire nails. The one at the top right hand corner is for the lid; those just below the guide slips are for the pulleys; and the bottom one is for the lever to pivot on.

The guide slips, strips of ¼ by ⅛in. wood, are glued where shown. Rub these strips with glass paper to reduce their thickness a trifle.

The piece, marked as block B, should be cut from fretwood a full 5/16in. thick and glued where shown between the sides so as to keep them that distance apart.

As 5/16in. is not a standard thickness of wood, you must either plane a piece of thicker wood down or glue two pieces of thinner wood together. Before gluing make sure the space between the sides will allow the cigarettes to enter easily and not stick.

Cut the two supports, and remember that the one intended for the front only needs the smaller slot, the 5/16in. one; the back support needs only the big slot. Glue the sides in the slots of the supports.

The ejector shown at Fig. 2, measures ⅜in. sq., and is cut from ¼in. fretwood. Grooves are cut either side, and should be glasspapered to smoothness until the ejector can slide freely between the guide slips. Fix a tiny wire hook each end and connect a thin rubber band to the rear hook and a piece of fine twine, or gut, to the front hook.

Cut two ½in. discs from ¼in. wood for the pulleys, and file a small groove round the edges. Bore holes in the centres then pivot the rear pulley by a nail through the sides.

The Ejector Band

The elastic band, at the rear of the ejector should be passed over the pulley and secured to a small hook driven in below.

Fix the front pulley in the same manner, and cut the lever from ¼in. fretwood. Drill a hole in this at about the spot marked by a cross and near the opposite end drill a fine hole for the twine. Pivot the lever between the sides by driving a

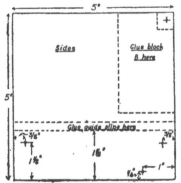
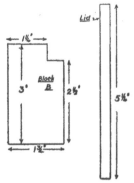
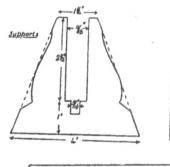

Details and dimensions of the various parts required

wire nail through the bottom holes ; pass the twine over the front pulley, through the hole in the lever and tie off. Arrange this so that when the lever is up the position of the ejector will be as shown in Fig. 1.

The lid is a piece of ⅛in. fretwood just 5/16in. wide ; a small piece of wood is cut semi-circular and glued to one end of the lid. This is bored, then a nail is driven through the top corner holes of the side so that the lid is hinged as shown by the detail sketch, Fig. 3.

The base is not shown being simply a rectangular

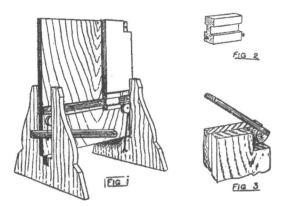

piece of fretwood, measuring 6ins. by 4ins. The supports are glued to this, the front support being about ⅛in. from the edge. The perspective view of the completed article shows this.

You can now fill the box with cigarettes, and if you have made everything A1, the cigarettes will be partly ejected, one by one, each time the lever is depressed.

The Tiger's Face

Apart from finishing, all that now remains to be done is to cut the tiger face. A drawing for this is given, drawn over 1in. squares.

Copy this, full size, on to a piece of thin white paper, paste on to a piece of fretwood and cut to the outline. The hole in the mouth should be bored a full ⅜in. and the face glued to the front of the box with the hole directly over the place the cigarettes emerge from.

For a finish, the face can be painted or enamelled, and the remainder of the box polished in the usual manner. Small tins of enamel can be purchased for 2d. each, and the whole box might well be enamelled and would look well.

As a suggestion to this end, enamel the face of the tiger yellow. When dry, trace the features and other markings, and enamel them in black ; the iris of the eyes green and the pupils black. Enamel the supports green, and the remainder of the box black. The whole will then look very effective.

A Novel pastime telling how to cut
SILHOUETTES FOR PROFIT

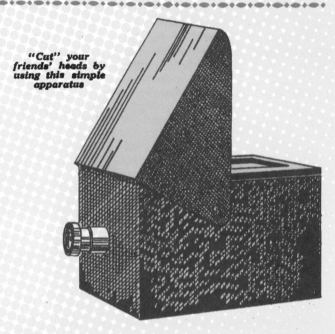

"Cut" your friends' heads by using this simple apparatus

SILHOUETTES are an attractive form of portraiture because one's profile, cleared of all minor detail, is so characteristic with its handsome aquiline nose and firm chin, or, maybe, with just that funny tuft of hair that will sprout on the back of one's head.

With the tracer to be described here a record of one's friends can be made, and, after a little practice, it can be used very profitably as a side-show at, say, a bazaar or Scouts' Fair.

The case is made of ¼in. ply and may be covered with a leatherette paper. Cardboard (not paste-board which cracks when bent) is used for the focussing tubes; while the hood can be made in one piece out of a sheet of tin or zinc.

Material Needed and Obtainable

You will also require a plano-convex lens, diameter 1in., with a focal length of 6½ins., a Hobbies mirror (No. 5753, price 1/1), and a Hobbies clear glass (No. 5802, price 2d.) both 5½ins. by 3½ins., a pair of ¾in. by ¼in. hinges and a pair of small ball-catches. The cost of the lens is only 1/3 post free and the address from which it can be obtained is obtainable from the Editor.

The construction of the focussing tubes is shown in Fig. 1. Make the lens tube first by bending a strip of thin cardboard 1¼ins. wide round a former or circular wooden rod ¾in. in diameter. Mark where the edges should meet, trim to size, draw the edges together round the rod and fix with a strip of gummed paper.

The Tubes

Now glue a second strip of card round the first keeping the joins on opposite sides of the tube and bind down with string. When set remove the string and build up a flanged seating for the lens with several

Two examples of finished pictures and how to cut out the shape

more narrow strips of card.

The first few strips, their number depending on the thickness of the card, should be ¼in. wide and put on so that their edges come flush with the end of the tube.

The remaining strips must be ⅜in. wide, ¼in. projecting beyond the end of the tube to form the

seating in which the lens is glued. Rough edges should be taken down with fine glasspaper and the whole tube painted dull black.

Now make a second tube out of 1½in. strips in the same way, forming it over the first tube, but so that the two are free to slide. Before gluing and pinning the shorter tube into the hole in the front of the case cover it with leatherette paper.

The Case Construction

The construction of the case can be seen in Figs. 2, 3 and 4. The measurements shown give a medium sized image when the lens is pulled out half way so that a small error in the total length A, B, C, can be taken up in the focussing.

It is important, however, to centre the lens truly on the mirror with its axis parallel to the sides

and top and bottom of the case. The mirror, too, must be set squarely across the case at an angle of 45 degrees with the bottom.

A little care taken over these points will ensure that it is equally reflected on to the screen to give an undistorted image.

The mirror is mounted by sliding it into the grooves formed by the strips S. S., Fig. 4. These strips must be exactly opposite one another on either side of the case. A reference to Fig. 2 will show where they must be placed so that the edge of the back of the mirror lies along the line X Y.

The frame supporting the clear glass screen must be so fixed that when the latter is glued down its surface will be flush with the edges of the case.

After painting the inside of the case dull black, slip the mirror into place and glue and pin on the back. Next cover with the leatherette paper, turning it in over the edges as far as the frame. Ease the edges a little with glasspaper so that the extra thickness of the paper does not prevent the screen fitting.

The hinged lid shown in Figs. 3 and 4 should be glasspapered and painted dull black all over which makes a neater job than papering it. It is then hinged to the front of the case. Quarter

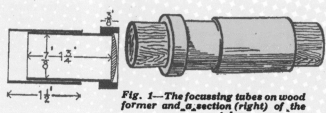

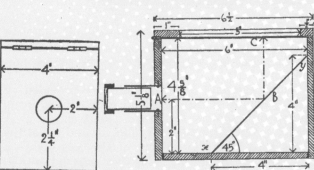

Fig. 1—The focussing tubes on wood former and a section (right) of the tubes

To use the Tracer, place your sitter before a bright window or artificial light in front of which you have stretched a sheet of tissue paper. (A child's hoop or piece of cane bent into a circle makes a serviceable frame for the paper).

Then, with the Tracer firmly supported on a table, two or three feet from the sitter, focus up his image on a piece of tracing, or thin bank paper, held in position over the glass screen by the four pins in the hinged lid.

The image will be seen facing in the opposite direction, but it will be the right way up and is quite easy to trace round with a sharp pencil.

Never rub out. Have half a dozen fresh shots if necessary until you can run round any profile in a few seconds. This is the only way to get crisp, lively portraits.

If you have to work in a room where there are other lights in addition to the screened one behind the sitter's head, use a focussing-cloth to brighten the image, although with practice you will find that the hood by itself usually casts enough shade.

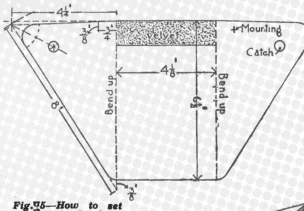

Fig. 5—How to set out the hood

Fig. 2—Front view and section of case

inch ply will carry hinges quite satisfactorily if thin screws are used, removed, dabbed with glue and screwed home again.

Fig. 5 shows how to set out the hood on a single piece of tin or zinc. The small holes on the side pieces engage with the ball catches to hold the hood open. Mount the hood with two small roundheaded screws and two washers.

Place it so the edge is flush with the front of the case, but raised a little above it. This is to give clearance when the hood is lifted and comes forward as shown in the finished article. The strip of velvet inside the hood (Fig. 5), excludes the light. Now adjust the hood to a suitable angle and find where the ball catches must be screwed into the case.

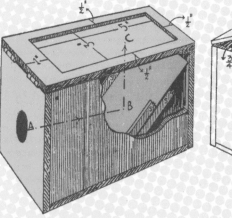

Fig. 3—Broken view to show mirror

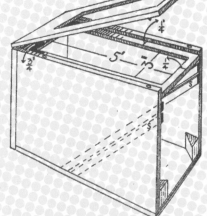

Fig. 4—End removed to show mirror and screen supports

Having done a number of tracings fill them in with a small sable-hair brush and process black, which can be obtained from most artist's colourmen. It is an intense black which covers larger areas without streaking or flaking as Indian ink may do.

Finally cut out the silhouettes with a pair of sharp scissors—curved nail scissors will be found useful here—and mount on a white card.

A MODEL GRAND PIANO POWDER BOX

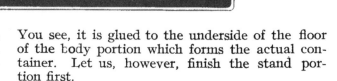

Just the thing for a lady. Full size patterns are given on pages 380 and 381

WHEN you are looking for novelties to make up, remember this little model of the grand piano. It is completed in fretwood from a few odd pieces (the whole parcel only costs 1/-) and full size patterns are given in the centre pages of this issue.

As can been seen, it is a realistic little piece of work, and is intended as a small powder box. Indeed, it can take the place of the usual flap-jack because the whole of the top piece of the "piano" is a separate box which contains the powder box and a mirror in the lid which raises.

The whole thing can be carried in the handbag for use when necessary, but can be kept on the dressing table by standing it on the lower portion of the piano model. A picture is given of it open, and we also show the box container portion in use.

The Wood

The thicknesses and sizes of the wood required are given on each pattern, and it is a simple matter to cut out the paper patterns, paste them down to whitewood or ordinary fretwood, and cut them out carefully with a fine fretsaw.

Notice that the base of the model has a circular opening which forms a disc to be glued to the underside of the actual body. In order to make a better fit, this disc is cut with the saw on the bevel. If you have a handframe it may not be possible to do this, but it does not really matter. If you have a machine, however, it is a simple matter to loosen the nuts beneath the table and tilt the latter slightly. The saw then cuts at an angle to the wood, and provides the bevel required.

This bevel, by the way, is merely to make the disc fall into position later.

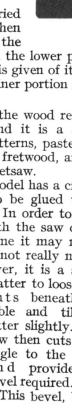

You see, it is glued to the underside of the floor of the body portion which forms the actual container. Let us, however, finish the stand portion first.

Three legs and a pedal stand are provided on the underside of the base, and each is fixed in by means of a mortise and tenon joint shown at A and B. Cut these to get a tight fit, and see at the same time that the bottom of the legs makes a flat stand on the table. Glue these legs in position, then clean everything up carefully.

Do not at the moment add the little pedals D, because they are apt to become broken off in the handling during construction.

The Body Work

The body is cut in ⅜in. thick material. The central circle is cut right out, then a thinner floor provided by a circle of 3/16in. wood. This should fit nicely into the circle of the body, and can be fixed there by gluing round the edges and also gluing on the underside a larger circle of tough brown paper to hold it in place.

Then immediately in the centre of the circle made by the floor, the disc is added. A good plan is to put the body in place on the base, turn the whole thing upside down, then glue the disc in the actual position on the underside of the floor.

The box in use

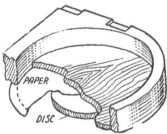

PAPER

DISC

A cut-away view of the box

This will ensure the box being returned to its proper place afterwards. A cut-away view of the box is given to show how it is made up.

The lid of course, is an overlapping piece. It is cut from 3/16in. material and a mirror is held in place by a narrow overlay rim of ⅛in. wood. The under and inner edge of this rim must be bevelled slightly all round with a file, in order to allow it to be glued to the inside of the top and hold the mirror in place. A suitable piece of glass is provided by Hobbies, and the bevelled mirror is No. 5704 which costs only 3d.

The whole top is hinged by means of a pair of small ½in. hinges fixed in the position shown. Recess them slightly into the body and the lid in order to get the part down flat.

All that now remains is to add the smaller portions to finish the model off.

The keyboard is cut from ⅛in. wood and the pattern drawn can be left on after the wood has been glued. It is glued to the actual base but not, of course to the body, although it rests close against that part. The ends of the keyboard are two small fancy pieces glued on as shown at C.

Now we can add the tiny ⅛in. pedals, and it is advisable to run a nail carefully through the pedal stand from behind, to provide further strength.

The whole model would look best if made quite dark with stain or, indeed, it can be treated wth Hobbies Ebony Polish to provide a highly glossy black surface. This would look quite striking. Or, of course, you could darken it down to the normal rosewood or even walnut.

The keyboard also can be varnished with clear varnish to prevent the paper being rubbed off or becoming disfigured.

The completed article is just the sort of thing to make for a Sale of Work or Scout Exhibition because it would have a ready sale and can be offered at 1/6 or 2/- to show an excellent profit.

What you have to do if you want to make
PROFIT FROM PLASTICS

"IF I make some articles in Perspex, what are my prospects of selling them at the present time?". Many readers are asking themselves and us this question, so let us examine it more closely.

Firstly, it is obvious that Perspex has come to stay, for we see items made of this material featured more and more frequently in shop window displays. But we must realise that a considerable number of 'amateur' workers are turning out such items for sale, which means that we shall be entering a competitive market with our goods.

Quality Essential

On the whole, the items we see displayed are of high quality, some of them, of course, are excellent, but there is also a fortunately small sprinkling of poor quality, badly designed pieces on show. This should teach us our most important lesson, that if we are to sell our goods, they must be well designed and of high quality.

There will, of course, always be a market for cheap and shoddy goods, provided that the price is cheap enough. To obtain this, the work has to be skimped, with the result that the article deteriorates rapidly, and usually falls to pieces.

Take the case of the well-made article. The price to the buyer is, of course, higher, but the article is correspondingly better. The design must be good, otherwise the item, though well made, will not be a success. So avoid unnecessary frills in the design.

Study the Windows

The next time you pass a first class jewellers, study the design of such things as silver cigarette boxes. Notice how the box is invariably simple in shape—there are no fancy bits stuck all over it. But the workmanship is excellent. It is this which sells the box. Even the decoration is simple, but executed in faultless style.

The workmanship we put into our goods must, therefore, be of our best. To achieve this, see the tools are properly sharpened and in good condition. Two minutes work with the oilstone may make all the difference between a well cut joint which will cement without difficulty—(and thus save valuable time)—and one which will come apart at the first knock.

All edges must be cleanly cut and free from unsightly nicks and scratches. This can only be ensured by careful work. Rushing the job will never produce good results.

When we buy our material, we shall usually find it covered on both sides with paper. This is to protect the delicate surfaces from scratches which are so easily caused by grit, particularly on the workbench. So we must be sure to keep the bench really clean—in fact a good plan is to use a piece of brown paper pinned to the bench top on which to work.

We can also put the paper covering of the Perspex to good use by marking out the shapes we want, and then cutting out before we remove the paper. You will find that it is quite easy to plane and even polish the edges without taking off the paper.

Therefore, by doing this, no harm will come to the highly polished surfaces during the making up stages, and this will be rewarded by the high finish we will be able to obtain.

High Class Work

You may say that all this takes time, and time means money. Quite true, but remember that you will always find a market for a well-made article, provided that you do not expect an unreasonable profit. High class work for a reasonable price means a satisfied customer and a good recommendation. These will show you a profit from Perspex.

Smokers will find added enjoyment by using
A HOOKAH

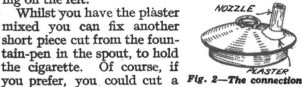

Fig. 1—Padded lid

Fig. 2—The connection

A HOOKAH, or hubble-bubble, is a pipe in which tobacco smoke is drawn through water, and thus cooled. Well, here is a hookah in which you can smoke your favourite brand of cigarette; and you can make it yourself out of an old tea-pot and a few odds and ends.

The tea-pot can be any shape or size, and in any condition, so long as it holds enough water to come above the spout holes inside. The lid must fit tight. If it is at all loose a circle of felt (from an old hat) can be glued over it, as in Fig. 1.

Most lids have a ventilation hole through the knob, and if yours has, fit the end of a two-foot length of rubber-tubing over the knob. The diameter of the tubing is gauged by the size of the knob.

If the hole, however, is on the surface of the lid, you will have to fix a nozzle over it on which to attach the tubing. An inch cut from an old vulcanite fountain-pen will suffice. This should first be glued over the hole (as in Fig. 2) and strengthened with plaster (made with size) heaped neatly round the base. This should be done before sticking on the felt.

Whilst you have the plaster mixed you can fix another short piece cut from the fountain-pen in the spout, to hold the cigarette. Of course, if you prefer, you could cut a real cigarette-holder in half, and fix on end in the tea-pot spout. The mouthpiece is afterwards fixed in the free end of the rubber tube.

To smoke the hookah you fill the pot with water to come about half an inch above the spout holes. Then insert a cigarette in the holder, and light in the ordinary way, drawing through the rubber tube. If you draw only air there must be a leak somewhere, and this must be stopped up.

You will enjoy your cigarette all the more because it is cool and refreshing, and no smoke can irritate the eyes. It is also economical as the cigarette will last half as long again, and can be smoked down to the last shred.

As you draw the smoke you will hear it bubbling through the water—which is how the pipe got its alternative name of 'hubble-bubble.'

Straightforward Woodwork

MODERN BUREAU-BOOKCASE

THIS typically modern fitment is simple in outline and not at all difficult to make. Any good hard wood would be suitable, but either oak, or mahogany is the best choice. Two useful diagrams are given in Figs. 1 and 2, the former supplying all the necessary measurements for assembly, while the latter clearly shows the construction.

Commence by preparing the sides (A). These will be dovetailed at the top to the cross rails (C) (see detail Fig. 3), and either rebated or dovetailed to the floor (B). The two shelves (E) can be grooved into the sides, or better still, dovetailed.

One of two methods may be followed for fixing the back (H). It may be simply screwed direct to the edges of the sides (A), the shelves (E) and the floor (B), or the inside edges of the sides may be rebated so that the back fits in flush.

hand door at the top to fit into a wood block, which is glued to hold the doors flush when they are closed. A ball catch is fitted to the right-hand door and also to the falling front of the bureau. To the latter a pair of quadrants must be fixed to support the front when lowered.

CUTTING LIST

(A).	(2).	4ft. 1in. by 14½ins. by ⅞in.
(B).	(1).	1ft. 11½ins. by 14ins. by ⅞in.
(C).	(2).	1ft. 11½ins. by 2½ins. by ¾in.
(D).	(1).	1ft. 11½ins. by 14ins. by ⅝in.
(E).	(2).	1ft. 10½ins. by 14ins. by ¾in.
(F).	(2).	1ft. 1½ins. by 3ins. by ⅝in.
(G).	(2).	2ft. by 3ins. by ⅞in.
(H).	(1).	4ft. 1in. by 23½ins. by ⅛in. ply.
(I).	(2).	1ft. 1in. by 1½ins. by ⅜in.
(J).	(1).	1ft. 10½ins. by 11ins. by ⅞in. overall size.
(K).	(2).	2ft. 1in. by 12ins. by ⅞in. overall size.

for the shelves, but a neater job should be to have grooved bearers as shown on Fig. 5.

The finish will differ according to the wood and personal taste; oak would be best left its natural colour. or, perhaps, lightly stained, with the base of the bureau ebonised and polished. Mahogany would

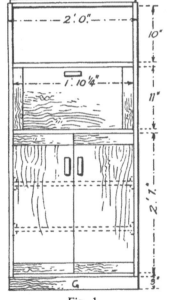

Fig. 1

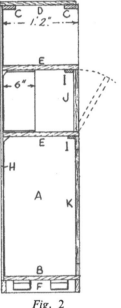

Fig. 2

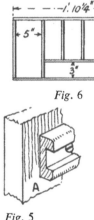

Fig. 5

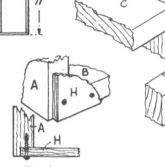

Fig. 6

Fig. 4

Fig. 3

Both methods are given in Fig. 4. The shelves (E) and the floor (B) will be ¼in. less wide if the second method is adopted. In assembling the various parts connect the top of the sides by the cross rails, and add the floor (B).

The base of the fitment consists of the rails (G) and two rails (F). They are rebated and screwed to the floor, as shown, with blocks glued behind them. The hinged front of the bureau is solid, and is partly framed by the two upright rails as seen in the detail Fig. 3. The two doors are made in similar manner as seen in the front view, Fig. 1. The doors and the bureau front are fitted with 2½ins. brass or chromium plated hinges, and a small bolt is put behind the left-

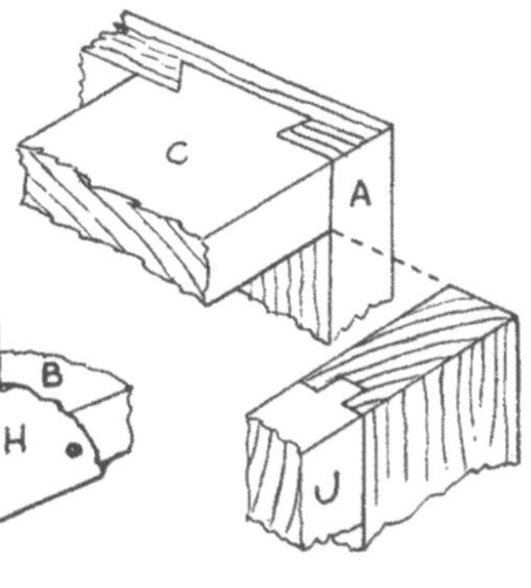

A small block of wood should be glued underneath the top shelf (E), against which the flap will rest. A lock can be fitted if necessary.

The main top of the bureau is fixed to the rails (C) by screws from beneath. In Fig. 6 the plan is shown for making the pigeon hole fitment. This is constructed from ¼in. wood and then slipped into place and screwed. A separate back is not required for this fitment, as it fits snugly against the main back of the bureau. A triangular fillet may be added to enable it to be screwed firmly into place. Two shelves can be fitted in the cupboard as suggested by the dotted lines in Fig. 1. Plain strip wood bearers screwed to the sides would act as supports

look most pleasing if stained and waxed-polished. Plain wood block handles would suit the piece, but black bakelite handles would look effective with oak. The cutting list will be found to be a useful aid to construction.   (S.W.C.)

V.—Opening Out and Shaping Bulbs.

TO open out a bulb successfully requires considerable pains. It is one of the processes in this art that when once the knack of accomplishing it has been obtained it seems simple enough, but until then one will have many failures. The simplest method of procedure and the chief causes of non-success we will briefly detail, so as to endeavour to assist the reader as far as we can to a short cut to success. In most ornamental forms made from bulbs it will be necessary to open them, so that the process becomes one of importance and merits particular attention.

Figs. 1 and 2 show the difference in appearance of the end of the two bulbs, the one shown by Fig. 1 being blown at the end of a tube that has been closed by heating the tube until it closes itself, and the other having been closed by drawing it out. The former is the superior bulb, for the reason that it is of a thicker glass, as we mentioned in a previous chapter, but the knob on the end is of a very fair size, while that in Fig. 2 is a mere point. As a bulb usually requires to be opened out at the place where the projection is, the first process

consists in removing it, at any rate, as far as possible. This is done by applying heat to the point to soften it, and then bringing a hot glass rod or closed up tube against it to draw away the surplus (Fig. 3 *a*). This is simple enough, but there are two things to guard against. One is to be sure and heat the projection only, not the whole end of the bulb, or it will become distended, as in Fig. 3 *c*, which is not required in the present instance. The other point is to ensure that the projection is hotter than the rod brought against it, for the reason that should the end of the rod be hotter and therefore softer than the projection, the point of the bulb will draw away some of the glass rod, instead of vice versa. With due care taken in these two points the projection can be almost entirely removed, although with all one's pains to confine the heating to the projection only, there is usually a slight extending of the bulb at the end, as in Fig. 3 *c*, but this is a help rather than otherwise in the succeeding operations.

It can be seen from the foregoing remarks that the need for effective local heating is of paramount importance, and this has led the writer to devise a very simple arrangement, costing only a few pence, to secure this. It is shown in Fig. 4, and consists of an ordinary brass blow-pipe, the nipple on the end of which has been removed. This is passed through an ordinary cork in which a hole has been burnt with an iron skewer. The cork fits the end of the burner, which we described in

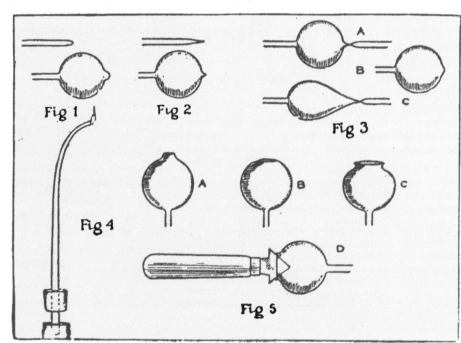

Fig 1

Fig 2

Fig 3

Fig 4

Fig 5

our first chapter, or could be connected with a length of india-rubber tube with an ordinary burner. If the gas supply is turned low the result will be a tiny jet, which can be focused with greater precision on the particular part being worked upon.

Now proceed to heat the bulb at the slight projection at the end (Fig. 3 b), twirling the tube slowly in the fingers whilst doing so, in order that it may be equally softened. Then when it becomes bright red, blow into the tube hard to burst it. It depends on the amount of heat applied what sort of burst is obtained, but with careful local heating Fig. 5 a is the most usual, there being loose fragments of fine glass round the opening. If a little larger area is heated, of course a larger aperture is obtained. Now rotate the opening in a larger flame, and it will gradually enlarge and flatten down, as in Fig. 5 b, and the sharp edge will become

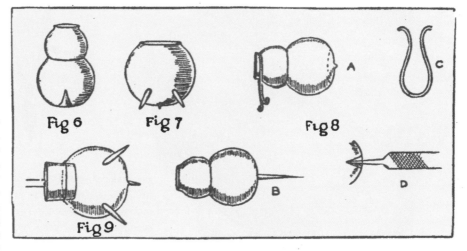

Fig 6   Fig 7   Fig 8   Fig 9

nicely rounded off and slightly thicker. If the copper tool is worked into it at this stage the well-known thistle funnel form (Fig. 5 c) will be produced, the tube being spun round as rapidly as possible to obtain a perfectly round opening (Fig. 5 d). In opening out bulbs in this way with the copper former, an important point is not to overheat the opening. The thin glass of a bulb becomes very quickly softened, especially at the opening, and if the heat is continued many seconds longer it will quickly fall about and become unmanageable, and the introduction of the copper former will only tend to make matters worse by doubling it up. Therefore only apply just enough heat to cause the glass round the opening to slightly glow, then quickly remove from the flame and spin adroitly against the former, the whole process only taking a few seconds.

Figs. 6 and 7 show two glass ornaments, on a very small scale of course, standing about 1½in. to 2in. in height. Fig. 6 consists of two bulbs, a larger and a smaller one, blown against one another, as described in the preceding chapter, the smaller one being opened out at the end. Allow to cool, and then heat the other end where the tube is joined on, and draw away as close up to the bulb as possible, with a slight twisting motion, so as to cause it to detach itself quickly (Fig. 8 a), otherwise the narrowing tube is likely to become unduly

extended (Fig. 8 b). A convenient method of gripping the other end has to be provided, for which a piece of bent iron wire, as shown in Fig. 8 c, serves well, the rim in the upper part of the ornament preventing it slipping. The fine projecting portion left when the tube is detached has next to be removed, and it is not a bad plan to heat it and snip it off with a pair of scissors; it will cut very easily—like twine, when it is soft. Now heat a small area of the base, as indicated by the dotted lines (Fig. 8 a), and when softened push inwards by pressing the tang of a small file or similar sharp instrument into the glass (Fig. 8 d), which should give sufficient flatness for the ornament to stand. If not, heat base again and bring down quickly upon a warm metal plate to flatten it.

Fig. 7 consists merely of a bulb opened out at the top, standing upon three glass feet, which introduces a fresh process to the reader —that of jointing glass tubing to bulbs. In reheating bulbs very considerable care is requisite, or the thin glass soon sags in and takes the most unseemly shapes that cannot be rectified. In the present instance the whole bulb must not be heated, but only a very small area where it is desired to attach the short lengths of tube that form the legs. For this purpose the blow-pipe connection previously described will be necessary

The various stages of the work, in making this ornament, will consist of first blowing a bulb and opening it out. The central tube is then drawn out as close up to the bulb as possible, the resultant knob being softened and gradually drawn away in the manner which we have described. A cork pushed in the aperture at the other end, with a piece of glass through it, does not make a bad method of support for this end of the vessel during the operation, as shown (Fig. 9), but be careful not to put it in contact with the flame. Then take a short length of narrow tubing, and close one end by heating it in the flame. Now with a small flame endeavour to heat the end sufficiently to cause it to glow, and at the same time a very small area of the bulb where it is required to be attached. The softening of the bulb will only take a second or two, being of such thin glass, but be sure that the tube is heated to a red, to thoroughly soften it. The two are then brought together, which should result in a neat join. If not the tube has not been heated sufficiently, and the process must be repeated. In heating the bulb it will slightly sag inwards at the place where it is heated, but in jointing with the tube it can be drawn gently outwards while the glass is still soft, when a join has been effected. The other two feet are attached similarly (see Fig. 9), and then the tubes are each in turn drawn out a short distance from the join with the bulb. Upon cooling they are snipped off to an equal length.

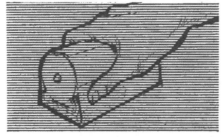

SIMPLE THINGS TO MAKE WITH WIRE

How to make an egg whisk, a gridiron, a toast rack, a glove shaper, a toasting fork, and a cake stand.

WIREWORK is quite easy, and very useful articles can be made in very little time and at very little cost. Suitable wire of the right gauge must be selected for the article in question, and the only tool needed for making the articles mentioned is a pair of flat nosed wire cutting pliers.

To Make an Egg Whisk

Fairly fine gauge nickelled steel wire should be used. Shape three loops as shown and bind in the manner indicated. The entire work can easily be carried out by hand it only being necessary to measure off equal lengths for looping, the longer ends of the centre loop being used for binding.

Curved bends can be shaped over a piece of round wood. A strengthening piece of wire is fitted arc shape across the loop ends. The handle

Any number of sections can be shaped.

It is essential carefully to measure off each distance as each bend is made. All the square bends are made with the pliers. It is as well to calculate roughly the length of wire required to make a given article before you start to ensure against finishing the work short.

This is an easy matter once you have determined dimensions. The shaping of any of these articles is dependent upon the accuracy of the bending and the measuring off of distances. Work with a rule and a small square for testing purposes.

A Glove Shaper

This is a glove shaper, not a glove stretcher. To make, place the hand on a piece of white paper and draw the outline. Use this as a guide for shaping, keeping well inside the line.

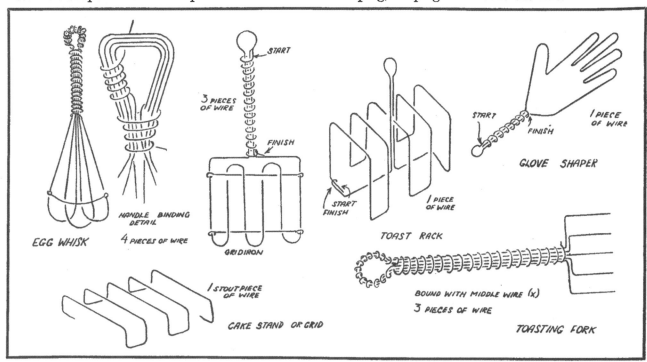

EGG WHISK

HANDLE BINDING DETAIL

4 PIECES OF WIRE

3 PIECES OF WIRE

START

FINISH

GRIDIRON

START FINISH

I PIECE OF WIRE

TOAST RACK

START

FINISH

GLOVE SHAPER

I PIECE OF WIRE

I STOUT PIECE OF WIRE

CAKE STAND OR GRID

BOUND WITH MIDDLE WIRE (X)

3 PIECES OF WIRE

TOASTING FORK

may be tape of thong wrapped to give added thickness.

A Gridiron

Bound, or preferably square section iron wire should be used for this article. Shaping is simple. The round ends are shaped over a round piece of wood and the square bends made with the pliers. Distances to each bend should be carefully measured as the work proceeds. Two strengthening wires are fixed as shown.

A Toast Rack

Use the same wire as for the gridiron, preferably square section. This article looks a little more complicated but it is quite simple and easy to shape up if the method shown is carefully followed.

To make the pair, simply repeat the process for the other hand. Use stout copper wire.

A Toasting Fork

A useful five-prong toasting fork with a handle any length you like can easily be made as shown. Use nickelled steel wire. Bending is carried out with pliers and round wood shaper for the handle loop The prong end can be sharpened off with a file.

A Cake Stand

This useful article is simply shaped in the manner indicated, one continuous wire being used. Use for preference, square section iron wire and do all the shaping with the pliers, carefully measuring off distances between each bend. Test the bends with the square.

ONE-PIECE MOCCASINS

By J. MacIntyre

MOCCASINS are very comfortable to wear about the house and they have the added advantage of being easily tucked away in the corner of a suitcase when needed for holidays. Leather workers will experience little difficulty in making up the moccasins. In fact even the inexperienced worker should find no trouble provided the necessary tools are at hand.

Any strong flexible leather will make the moccasins. If in any doubt about choice, the leather storeman will advise.

A paper pattern is drawn first around the foot and cut to shape shown. Next, it is transferred to the leather and neatly cut. An inner sole is optional but if required a pattern may easily be cut from the foot outline. If used, the inner sole should be cemented when the moccasin is flat.

The enlarged sections of the drawings show how the leather is punched round the edges. Punch at both sides of each heel seam and insert metal eyelets with a punch. The holes around the toe are roughly $\frac{1}{4}$" apart and metal eyelets are inserted in the last hole at each side only. Carefully fold all the edges to the inside of the moccasin and cement together with leather adhesive.

Laces can be cut from leather scraps of a contrasting colour or ordinary thonging is ideal. The lace is run through the holes around the toe and the string drawn and tied. The heel is adjusted to size and tied in the same manner.

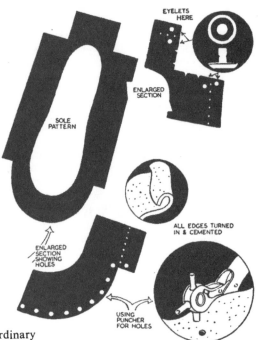

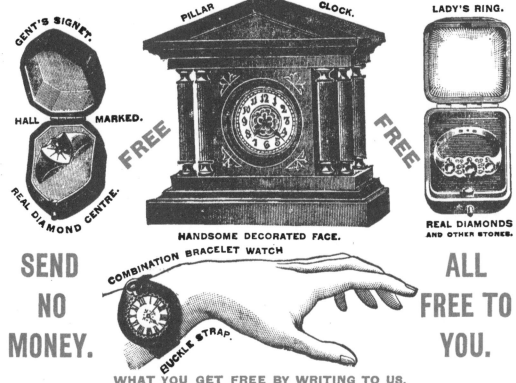

No blame can be cast on the flue when the draught is adversely affected by insufficient ventilation, as if the fire is not provided with a good supply of air the chimney cannot be expected to draw properly.

The discomfort which is experienced from sitting in a room with the door open in cold weather is familiar to most people, and generally arises when the doors and windows fit so closely as to be almost airtight. In most rooms the crevices under the doors and around the window sashes permit the entrance of a sufficient volume of air for the purpose, but in the absence of such facilities a sluggish draught is almost sure to result, as the velocity of the ascending current will be reduced by the failure of the supply of air to the fire.

Ventilation of Room.

The question of the ventilation of the room as it affects the working of the fire must not be lost sight of as an active agent in producing a smoky chimney, and in doubtful cases, experiments should be carried out in order to ascertain whether the trouble originates from deficiency in this respect. All doors and windows and other possible means by which air can obtain admission should be tightly closed, so that the effects can be noted while the fire is burning slowly. If this results in the issue of smoke from the fireplace the doors and windows should be opened, and some improvement will probably be obtained. Each door and window should be opened separately, to discover which one has the greatest effect in accelerating the draught, but if neither gives the desired result, the seat of the trouble must be looked for in some other direction.

It will be a comparatively simple matter to rectify the trouble when it has been definitely proved to arise from lack of ventilation, the remedy lying in the provision of a free

CHIMNEY STACK REBUILT IN
ZIGZAG FORM.

and unobstructed current of air to the fire at all times. To ensure this, a ventilating air brick should be inserted in the wall as near as possible to the door or window giving the best results in the preliminary test, an outside wall being selected for the purpose. The superficial area of the inlet opening should be large enough to guarantee that a sufficient volume of air shall be admitted, to enable the fire to burn brightly, and with a fairly quick draught. The inlet should be situated near the floor, and the current of air can be directed towards the ceiling by means of a "Tobin's" tube, which is fixed on the wall immediately over the opening. The tube is a long narrow casing made of wood, sheet iron, or zinc; it is about 9ins. wide, and is secured by means of screws or nails to the wall in a vertical position. The casing should project about 4ins. or 5ins. from the wall, and with its lower end enclosing the air brick, it will direct the cold air upwards until it is discharged into the room 5ft. or 6ft. above the floor, thus preventing the access of cold draughts to the feet of the occupants, and assisting in the ventilation of the room at the breathing level. The volume of the incoming air is regulated by means of the butterfly.

Straight Flues.

No flue should be constructed to rise in a straight vertical line directly off the fire, as this method is not conducive to a quick disposal of the products of combustion. It is an established principle in building construction that the sky should not be visible when looking up the chimney from below, the line of vision being broken by the introduction of a sharp bend in the direction of the flue. This bend is located immediately above the chimney arch, the brickwork being gathered over from one side so that the throat is not situated midway between the chimney breasts; this encourages a quicker draught, and incidentally, it prevents the precipitation of rain and soot on to the fire below, to a great extent. In modern houses the fireplaces on the upper floors are usually planned directly over the one in the room below, and the bend in the lower—flue caries it—round the fireplace above, but in the older buildings, where they are arranged indiscriminately, the chimney is more often than not built in a perfectly straight line.

The difficulty can sometimes be surmounted by reconstructing the throat of the flue, but when this is not practicable or is insufficient to remedy the trouble, an improvement will probably be effected by taking down the chimney stack above the roof, and rebuilding it in zig-zag form, as illustrated, contracting the dimensions of the flue to 9in. square at the same time to increase its efficiency. Kitchen ranges require a flue not less than 9in. by 14in., the smaller size being suitable for the ordinary register stove or interior. The stepped portion of the brickwork should be weathered by running a fillet of cement mortar along the set offs, as shown at A in the illustration.

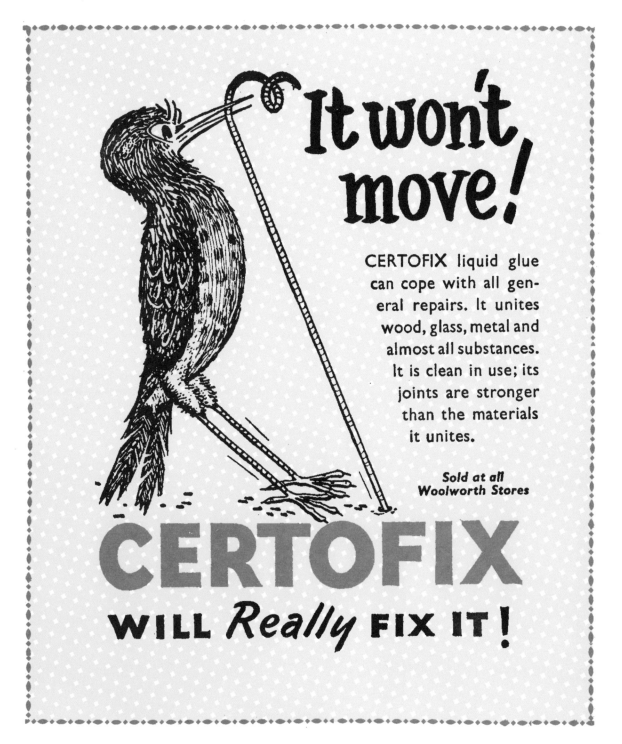

HOW TO HIDE A BENCH IN THE LIVING ROOM

IT is the ambition of every amateur woodworker to possess a well equipped workshop ; but unfortunately few have a room which they can set aside for use exclusively in connection with their hobby. The inestimable value of a sturdy bench to work on is also well recognised, and Hobbies Ltd., have several inexpensive models which are within the means of most workers.

But many, and especially those who live in modern houses, have no place which they can use as a workshop, except a living room. Such a room may be utilised for this purpose without much inconvenience if some large sheets of brown paper, or a sheet of balloon fabric, are placed on the floor to catch the sawdust and shavings. If, however, the bench is camouflaged by the method described it will become an ornament and not an eyesore.

A Suitable Bench

An excellent bench of suitable size can be obtained for as little as 21/-, and for a small extra outlay this can be given the appearance of a handsome cabinet when not in use. The chief material used is Venesta plywood which, whilst cheap and strong, can be stained and polished to a Jacobean Oak shade and ornamented with beading.

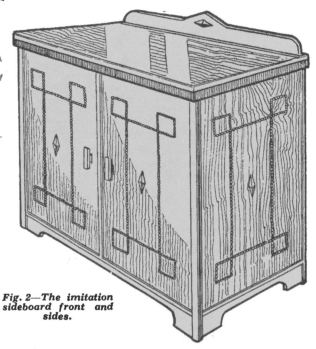

Fig. 2—The imitation sideboard front and sides.

Work carefully executed with these materials has a most pleasing appearance, though those who desire a specially good finish and do not mind a little extra expense, will use oak or mahogany veneered plywood instead of the cheaper variety,

The camouflage takes the form of a screen, which folds flat when not in use, and a lid which covers the top and holds the screen in position. Fig. 1 shows the bench ready for use and Fig. 2 with the screen in position ; whilst Figs. 3 and 4 give particulars of how the latter is constructed.

The Screen

To form the screen, three pieces of plywood are shaped and hinged together, as shown in the diagrams. The sizes will, of course, have to be varied to suit the particular bench in question, but the finished screen should fit closely round the bench so as to entirely hide the front and sides.

Fig. 1—The bench with its false top raised

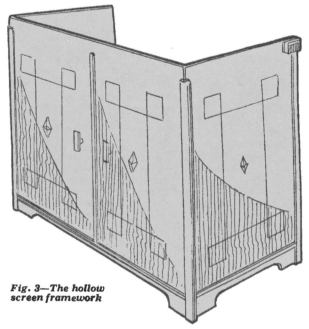

Fig. 3—The hollow screen framework

When setting out the side pieces due allowance must be made for the vice which projects some inches in front of the main carcase.

The lid (see Figs. 1 and 2) is constructed from a sheet of plywood with ornamental moulding No. 139 or 135 for the sides, and hinged to the bench at the back. A shaped pediment for the back of the bench should also be prepared and fitted as shown.

The lid should be of such a size that when the screen is in position it may be shut down to fit closely round the top of the screen and hold it in place. As the lid does not go quite to the back of the bench, two small pieces of the moulding used for the sides of the lid should also be glued on the sides of the screen for the sake of appearance. The position of these pieces on the screen is in the top back corners and will be seen from Fig. 3.

A strut should be fixed to hold the lid in a vertical position when the bench is in use, and several suitable types will be found illustrated on page 194 of Hobbies Handbook.

Fig. 4—The hinged front and corners, in section

Attention must next be given to the process of converting the screen into a sham cabinet carcase. First lengths of moulding No. 300 are fitted to the two front corners (see Fig. 4). A third piece is cut down its length and one half glued to each of the back edges so these will match the front. Stripwood or plain moulding fixed in position as shown will give the illusion of panelled sides and doors, and dummy handles should also be added.

If additional ornamentation is required, this may be achieved by the application of half-round beading and Jacobean diamonds as shown. The benches supplied by Hobbies Ltd. are fitted with a receptacle for tools in the top, and extra shelves and racks for wood and tools can easily be fitted underneath if desired.

Finally the whole should be stained and polished. If the work is carefully executed, the result will be a piece of furniture which will enhance the appearance of any living room ; and yet may, at a moment's notice, be converted into a serviceable woodworking bench.

MAKING A DADO.
— By A. P. Luxon. —

WOOD mosaic built up to form a dado for fixing around the walls of the hall or a room will look extremely well. We illustrate such a dado at Fig. 36; it should not be very deep, about six inches being quite sufficient, and should be fixed to the wall at the point where the backs of the chairs come into contact with the paper.

The design shown for the mosaic is of a rather pleasing nature; woods of three colours are introduced, and the whole will not be very difficult to make up. A full size design of a length of the mosaic (as shown at Fig. 37) should be made up first. Fig. 38 will show more clearly the details of the design; it will be seen that the edges consist of two rows of chequer pieces, each row being ½in. wide. Inside this is a row of dark figures, measuring ¼in. wide, and the centre of the design is 3ins. wide, making the mosaic a total width of 5½ins.

Setting out the Design.

In setting out the design on paper, first draw two parallel lines 5½ins. apart; inside each of these lines set off two rows of a chequer design, each of the chequers measuring exactly ½in. square, and a row of figures measuring ½in. long by ¼in. wide. The centre of the design is composed of 3in. squares, these squares are alternately light and dark, and a row of chequer pieces, edged with a row of dark figures interpose between each square. The wood used in making up the mosaic should be selected to give the effect shown in the illustration, that is the parts shown black should be of a dark wood, that shown plain of a light wood, and that lined in of a wood which will form a contrast between the dark and light.

In cutting out the mosaic it will be best to first cut out and make up the squares of which

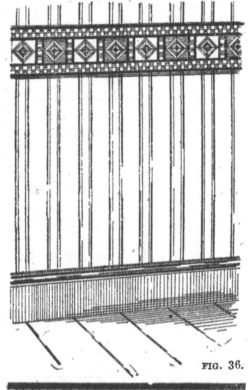

FIG. 36.

FIG. 37.

the centre is composed. The centres of these squares are made up from four strips of wood. Four strips of a suitable width and colour should be glued together (as shown at Fig. 39), and from these, pieces of the required size are cut at an angle of 45 degrees, as indicated by the dotted lines in Fig. 39. It will be noticed that the pieces cut from one edge will be suitable for the light squares, and those cut from the other edge will be suitable for the dark squares. A sufficient number of these pieces should be cut, and then glued up into the squares required. These squares are surrounded by four triangular pieces of light or dark wood, as the case may be, to make the whole up to 3ins. square. The method of cutting these triangular pieces is shown at Fig. 40; the strips of wood should be 1½ins. wide, and the triangles are cut as indicated by the dotted lines.

Having obtained a sufficient number of these squares, lengths of the chequered strips, which intervene between them should be made up. These chequered strips consist of six chequers, which are each ½in. square, they may be easily made up by glueing together three light and three dark strips of wood, each being ½in. wide, and from the end of these cutting off strips exactly ½in. at each cut. The rows of dark figures which are fixed to the edges of the chequered strips, consist of six figures in each row, each figure measuring ½in. long by ¼in. wide. These may be cut by glueing up six pieces of dark wood, each piece being ½in. wide, and from the ends of these, strips measuring ¼in. wide are cut; the chequered and dark strips may be then glued together.

The edges of the design may then be made up into short lengths. The rows of the chequered design should first be prepared;

this may be easily done in the manner described in the opening chapters. To the inner edge of the chequered pieces a row of dark figures are fixed; these figures, as already stated, measure ½in. long, by ¼in. wide.

A wood backing will be required, to which the mosaic may be fixed. It may be of three-ply wood, 3-16th inch thick, and should be 6¼ins. wide. The backing may be the correct length required for the side of the room, or for convenience may be cut off into

The face of the mosaic is then cleaned off, and the ends of the pieces are fitted together and cut to form the correct length for the wall.

The pieces of the dado are then fixed to the wall with screws (as shown at Fig. 41), the screws being driven through the overhanging edges of the wood backing. If it is impossible to find any woodwork in the wall into which the screws may be driven, wood plugs will have to be resorted to. The dado.

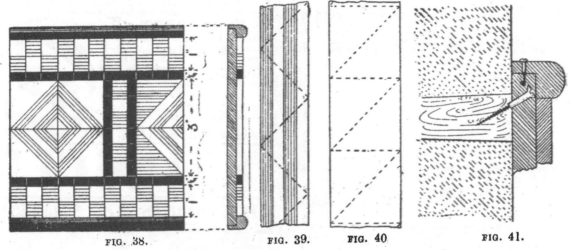

FIG. 38.   FIG. 39.   FIG. 40   FIG. 41.

lengths of about five feet. We recommend the latter method, as it will be found much better to deal with. The pieces of mosaic are then finally fixed in position on the wood backing. It should be noted that the backing overhangs the mosaic on each edge. Start by glueing the centre squares in position exactly in the centre of the backing, place the pieces of the chequered design between each square, and cramp in position until the glue is dry. The chequered pieces which form the border are then glued and cramped in position to form the complete design.

should be fixed so that the bottom edge is about 2ft. 9ins. above the floor of the room. The edges of the dado are finished with pieces of moulding, as shown in the illustration. Dark mahogany will be very suitable for the purpose. The moulding is ⅝in. wide, by ¼in. deep, and is shaped as shown at Fig. 41; the front edge is rounded, and the back edge is rebated over the overhanging edge of the wood backing. The moulding is fixed in position with a few round head brass screws, as shown. In our next article we will describe the method of making a frieze for a room.

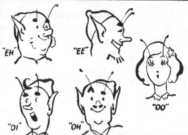

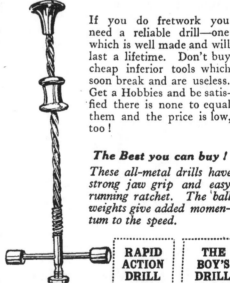

MENDING THE VENETIAN BLINDS.

Within Everyone's Reach.

ANY excuse, however slight or pointed, as to being unable to clean or repair the venetian blinds is, to say the least of it, perfectly unwarranted, for it is within the range of all at home, old and young, to see that this useful work is carried out, and no better time could be chosen for its execution than during the early weeks of Spring, for this particular piece of work can be then completed before the more serious business of the annual "clean and clear up" takes place.

The Sentinels of Home Privacy.

This remark is perfectly original (I hope I shall not be thought sentimental), for are the venetian blinds not worth every inch of the space they occupy? Do they not add effect to the windows, and with clean panes, and a properly hung and choice pair of curtains, do they not make a pretty, clean and comfortable piece of work? This effect is not confined to the outside of the house, but the inside as well, and it carries with it a reflection of credit and good taste of which no one need be ashamed.

IN A BAD STATE OF REPAIR.

What is Required to be Done and How to Do It.

Why it comes within the grasp of anyone old enough at home to do this work is easily explained. A small hammer and screwdriver are about the only tools required, and as the average work of mending and cleaning is by no means intricate, a little care and attention to the work will see the blinds properly repaired and as clean as the proverbial "new pin."

A Broken Cord.

This should by no means be knotted, or it will refuse to run in the pulleys. A ladder, however, may sometimes be repaired by sewing with a strong thread.

On no account attempt to mend a blind while in position on the window. First remove the few screws which fasten the blind to the top of the window frame. Clear a space on the floor underneath and lay the blind out flat.

Fitting New Cords.

Before removing the old cord, take a careful note how it passes through the small pulleys at the top of the blind, and how it threads between the strips. A small piece of copper wire twisted tightly round the end of the cord, and acting as a needle, will assist the threading process. After threading the cord, and knotting it, take the canvas back over the knots and replace the blind, being careful to fix it squarely and firmly.

Renewing Broken Laths.

If a new lath is required, the same method should be adopted. Take out the cords, examine the pulleys, and give the spindles some French chalk. Take off the old laths, noting how much extra tape is required for turning and retacking.

Before cutting off the new tape, make quite sure that there are enough spaces to receive the full number of laths, the bottom heavy lath, and a margin for retacking. When finished the blinds sometimes seem a trifle short, but after a few days' hanging the ladders stretch to the length of the old ones.—L.

BASKET MAKING.—VIII.—WASTE PAPER BASKET.

WASTE PAPER BASKETS form one of the best selling lines in the fancy basket trade. There is a steady demand and plenty of opportunity of making up different shapes and varieties. There are about three distinct varieties, first the fancy basket, mainly worked with platted rush or straw ; secondly, the straight bar, and then the crossbar ; the two latter forms contain new strokes and will be described later.

The fancy basket shown at Fig. 1 is made very similarly to the round baskets already described, but there is more work in it, not only because the dimensions are greater, but there is stronger construction. The design is about as simple as it is possible to make a substantial basket, and the finished price depending on the appearance, may range from 1s. 9d. to 2s. 6d.

The difference in the construction is hardly evident from the sketch of the finished basket, but it will easily be seen, when looking at the detail drawings given at Figs. 2 to 7.

FIG. 1.

The base should be 10in. diameter when finished, so first of all the sticks should be prepared. It will be necessary to provide eight 12in. or 14in. lengths of well-soaked osier, white or buff, about 5-16in. diameter, and bind them together (as shown at Fig. 2). This will be found a little more difficult than the small bottoms of the fancy baskets and it will be necessary to place the pieces together, after sliping them, on the workboard and then placing the foot on top. The bending is done in exactly the same way, but the breaking out is rather different (as shown at Fig. 3). The end of the binding rod (as shown at a, Fig. 2) is carried under Nos. 10 and 11 sticks, which are left close together ; it is then taken over Nos. 12 and 13, which are bent considerably, as will be noticed at Nos. 4 and 5. The rod is then carried under the next two over the next and so on until No. 10 is reached again, when it is carried underneath it and over No. 11, under No. 12 and so on until all the sticks have been opened

out. It is now necessary to work in another rod and then carry both weavers one over and one under, piecing them as shown before, until the required diameter is reached. As the weaving progresses, it will be seen that there is a tendency for the work to spring upward. This should be allowed and encouraged within reason, as the arched or domed bottom is very much stronger than a plain flat one. When the bottom is finished, prepare thirty-one stakes, sharpen the ends, and drive them in one alongside each rudial, the odd one, of course, pushed in by one stick, where three happen to be closer together than the others. The stakes should now be turned up with the domed bottom crown upwards, each stake being turned up against the picking knife and then driven in tight against the outside weaving of the bottom. (This is done best with the flat side of the iron).

The stakes should be gathered into a heap considerably larger than the outside diameter of the top of the basket, which is 14in.

The next stage is upsetting and this is done with four rods. Choose four long and straight osiers as thin as possible, and cut off a few inches at the top of each with a slicing cut. Drive the sliced top alongside four stakes (as indicated at Fig. 4). Work the first rod, "a" in front of stakes 2, 3 and 4, behind 5, and out again in front of 6. Do the same with the next one, "b," carrying it in front of 3, 4 and 5, behind 6 and out in front of 7, and continue the process around the basket, taking care to work the rods as closely as possible. When arriving at the starting point in each case and it is very convenient if the rods are long enough to go round without piecing, work in four more rods, but commence with the butt ends and work right around to the tops. This will give the basket a good foundation and form a neat and strong base.

The method of filling in the sides is indicated at Fig. 1. It will be seen that following the upsetting is a few rows of slewing. This should be in colour, using some dyed osiers, as explained in the article treating of the materials. On top of the slewing is worked a pair of white or buff rods and this is followed by a few rows of platted rush. The upper portion is the reverse of the lower, with the exception that the waling is substituted for the upsetting. As already mentioned in the case of the small fancy baskets, there is

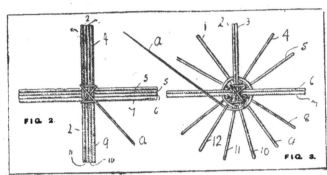

FIG. 2. FIG. 3.

practically an unlimited opportunity of designing different arrangements for filling up the sides. Many baskets of this character are made with platted straw, purchasable from the same people who supply rush. It does not matter much about the strength of the material used in weaving up the sides, providing that the upsetting, waling and bordering is properly done. The strength of the basket depends mainly on this part of the construction. The wale shown at Fig. 5 is very similar to upsetting; four rods are used, commencing with the tops and placing a top in front of a stake. Carry the first rod behind the next two and left in front of the next two. Now pick up the second rod, place it behind the next two and leave in front of the next two and so on until the four have been started and then work them alternately until they are used up, piecing them, if necessary and working a second four from butt to top, as in upsetting, bringing up the height of the sides to 15in.

We are now ready for bordering. This is illustrated in plan at Fig. 6, but using a much smaller number of stakes for the sake of clearness. First of all lay down five stakes and start by taking No. 1 behind Nos. 2 and 3 and in front of Nos. 5, 6, 7 carry it behind No. 8 and leave it in front of No. 9. This method is continued and is quite straightforward, the first three stakes finished being shown, a, b, and c, the last rods being finished by the process known as cramming, that is as each top is brought forward, in front of the respective stakes, it is pointed with the knife, bent at right angles, and tapped down beside the fifth stake (Fig. 7). This method of bordering gives a full border and greatly adds to the appearance of the basket.

The handles may be on the lines of those made in clothes baskets, and are made simi-

larly and on a reduced scale to the large bow handle on the small oval basket, or if desired, round drop handles, may be made by twisting some platted rush round a ring, made of osier and about 3in. to 4in. in diameter. The finished ring is attached to the sides by means of a twisted osier, fixed in to form a loop. One often finds this kind of handle on a waste paper basket, and they are very simple to make. To finish the basket, carefully pick all projecting ends with the picking knife and then give the basket a coat of varnish.

Fancy baskets similar to the above type are generally provided with a foot, that is the basket work is carried out again in the opposite direction to the sides at a considerable angle and then, when weaved for a few inches, the ends of the new stakes are bordered in the ordinary way.

To arrive at the actual cost of a fancy basket is not an easy task. It does not follow that a basket containing a lot of work and difficult strokes is going to sell for more than one containing simple strokes and easy work for the latter may be very attractive in design, both in the shape and the weaving, sort really pays to work up baskets which are easily made and yet have an artistic appearance.

Square baskets are usually commenced by

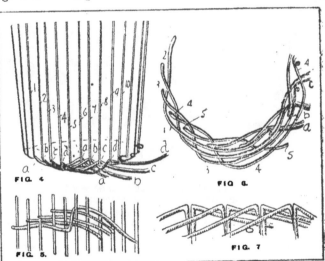

FIG. 4. FIG. 6.
FIG. 5. FIG. 7.

making the bottom in the screw block, but an interesting form of construction is to form the square on similar lines to the method used in making a round bottom. Commence in the usual way with six sticks, bind them together, and when breaking out, keep the middle sticks at right angles and insert an extra stick in the middle of each right angle, making sixteen radials in all. When weaving, bend the weavers sharply at the right angle sticks and gradually work to form parallel sides. The method is not an easy one to commence with, but it is very useful, owing to the practice it gives in manipulating the weavers.

IF YOU DO CARPENTRY
YOU NEED A HANDSAW

Fun! Fun! Fun!

WITH THESE TWO COLOURFUL ACCESSORIES

The cat and the snake

FUN WITH A FORMICARIUM

The rooke season

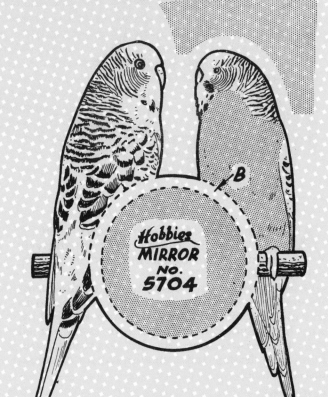

Hobbies
MIRROR
NO.
5704

What a baboon can be taught to do!

Animal Husbandry

Lets raise silkworms

Modern method of poultry keeping is in
HOME-MADE HEN BATTERIES

A NEW method of keeping poultry—housing the birds in cages—has comparatively recently come to the fore and is proving very successful.

These cages, or batteries as they are called, take up very little room and can, in fact, be housed in any old shed, providing it is dry, airy and well lit. Any handyman can make his own cages, for all that he needs is some 1in. by 1in. timber, 1in. mesh wire netting and a small quantity of galvanised sheeting.

In Pairs Best

The batteries can be built to any individual measurements, though a good idea is for each cage to be about 18in. cube. Also, it is advisable they should be built in pairs or multiples of two. For the purpose of this article we will deal in pairs.

Make the front of the cages first; a study of Fig. 1 will show how. The top piece of 3ft. 3ins. timber is fastened, at the ends, to two 2ft. 3ins. uprights. A 20ins. centre upright is also fitted.

Use any joint you like, but do have the edges flush—it looks so much neater. More important, and this applies to all the framework, make the job firm—screws are better than nails.

Now screw on another length piece, 16ins. below the top one. This will leave 8ins. legs with the centre upright overlapping 2ins. Do not make this bottom piece flush, simply screw it on.

The Framework

The rear part of the battery is exactly the same as the front with the exception that all the joints are flush. Also, the centre upright has no overlap. Now fix the two parts together, at the joints of the length pieces and uprights, with six pieces of timber 16ins. long. Small angle brackets are advisable here since they give the whole structure a rigid finish.

You will now want three 2ft. 1in. lengths of wood. These carry the floor and must be very firmly screwed. Fix the middle one first, underneath the centre uprights, with the overlapping portion at the front. The bottom of the front centre upright and the rear of the floor support must be cut at an angle to allow correct fitting.

Do not worry because the floor slopes, it must, so the eggs will roll down away from the birds. Otherwise they would eat them.

Screw on the two end pieces next, at a corresponding slope, on the inside of the legs. Along the fronts of these floor supports fasten a 3ft. 1in. length piece.

Fixing the Floor

You now encounter the most difficult part of the proceedings, fixing the floor. For this it is advisable to use the stoutest gauge of 1in. netting you can afford. The stronger the wire the tighter you can fix it, thus reducing the danger of sagging.

You need a piece 3ft. 1in. long and 2ft. 6ins. wide. Start at the back first by stapling the wire to the outside of the bottom length piece of the framework. Work the netting underneath the floor joists and fix it at the front.

On the inside of the timber to which you have just fastened the netting—the one which runs along the fronts of the floor supports—there should now be fastened a little felt. This will prevent the eggs from breaking as they roll down the wire.

Any gauge of 1in. netting will do for the top, back and sides of the cages. Do not forget to fasten a piece in the middle, since you are making two compartments.

The Doors

For the doors you need a small quantity of plasterer's laths. Cut two pieces 17ins. long and five pieces 15ins. long for each door. Fasten the shorter lengths to the others at corresponding intervals as shown in Fig. 3. Hook the doors to the top of the cages, making sure that they swing backwards and forwards without interference.

To hold the droppings tray, screw on the insides of the legs, 2ins. from the bottom, two pieces of 18ins. timber. If these are grooved the tray will slide better.

Any form of sheeting will serve for the tray itself but have it 2ins. wider than the width of the cages. Turn the sheeting up 1in. at the rear to prevent the droppings falling off. The other rin. can be turned down at the front. Besides preventing the tray from sliding too far back, this also facilitates withdrawal.

All that remains to be done now is the fixing of

on the insides to hold the troughs and to prevent them slipping.

Make the food troughs of wood, to any measurements you wish, remembering that the bigger they

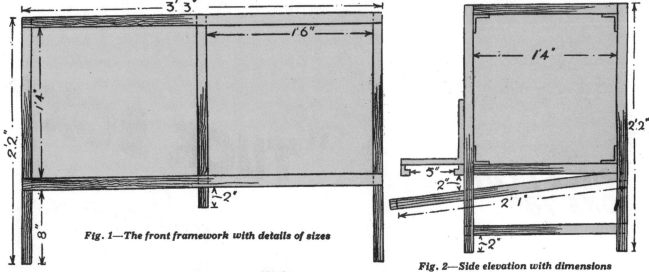

Fig. 1—*The front framework with details of sizes*

Fig. 2—*Side elevation with dimensions*

Fig. 3—*A front view of the completed house with constructional details*

the food trough rack. With the aid of two angle brackets attached to the two end front uprights, fix a 3ft. 3ins. length of wood 5ins. in front of, and at the same level, as the bottom front length piece.

These two pieces, incidentally, should be grooved

are the more food they will hold. Do not have them too deep, though, or the birds will not be able to clear up the contents—4ins. is ample here. Place ½in. lips all round the troughs to stop the birds from spilling their food.

One water trough, 8ins. long, placed in the centre of the food rack is sufficient for the two compartments. It can be made of galvanised sheeting or, at a pinch, a two pound jam jar will suffice. When you place the troughs in position you will notice that the doors cannot swing outwards, thus the birds cannot escape.

You can, if you wish, place these batteries in tiers of two or even three high. The legs of the bottom cages can also be of any length you desire.

BRIGHTEN YOUR 'BUDGIE' C

"TUCK BOX"

PIECE I. CUT ONE 1/8"

2
2
2

2
2
2
3

3

PIECE 3 CUT ONE 1/8"

2

PIECES 2 CUT THREE 1/2"

COLOURS CAN BE TAKEN FROM YOUR OWN PET BUDGI

GE WITH THESE TWO COLOURFUL ACCESSORIES

"VANITY MIRROR"

PIECE.C. CUT ONE 1/8"

B

PIECE.B. CUT ONE 1/8"

Hobbies MIRROR NO. 5704

B

PIECE A. CUT ONE 1/8"

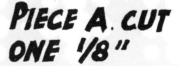

• PRINTED IN ENGLAND. •

Huxley's Pet Cat.

AT one time Professor Huxley was asked for some remarks on his pets, remarks that might be of use in an article upon the "Home Pets of Celebrities." Following is the letter which he sent in response :

"To Mr. J. G. Kitton, Hodslea, April 12th, 1893.

"A long series of cats has reigned over my household for the last forty years, or thereabouts, but I am sorry to say that I have no pictorial or other record of their physical and moral excellencies.

"The present occupant of the throne is a large, young, gray tabby, Oliver by name. Not that he is in any sense a protector, for I doubt whether he has the heart to kill a mouse. However, I saw him catch and kill the first butterfly of the season, and trust that this germ of courage, thus manifested, may develop with age into efficient mousing.

"As to sagacity, I should say that the judgment respecting the warmest place and the softest cushion in a room is infallible—his punctuality at meal-times is admirable; and his pertinacity in jumping on people's shoulders till they give him some of the best of what is going indicates great firmness."

Of this same kitten Huxley writes to his youngest daughter :

"I have seen handsomer kittens, but few more lively and energetically destructive. Just now he scratched at something that M— [his wife] says cost thirteen shillings and sixpence a yard, and reduced more or less of it to combings.

"I have argued that it is as immoral to place thirteen shillings and sixpence a yardnesses within reach of kittens as to hang bracelets and diamond rings in the front garden. But in vain. Oliver is banished, and the protector (not Oliver) is sat upon. In truth and justice aid your pa."

This letter is embellished with fancy portraits of Oliver when most quiescent (tail up, ready for action). Oliver as polisher (tearing at the table leg). Oliver as plate basket investigator. Oliver as gardener (destroying plants in a pot). Oliver as stocking-knitter (a wild tangle of cat and wool). Oliver as political economist, making good for trade at thirteen shillings and sixpence a yard (pulling at a hassock.)

The Cat and the Snake.

IN "A Midsummer Trip to the Tropics," Lafcadio Hearn gives the most attractive descriptions of St. Pierre, Martinique Island, which has so recently been destroyed by volcanic action. The charm of the tropical forest was lessened by the presence of the *fer-de-lance*. This snake reigned absolute king over the mountains and the ravines. At night he extended his dominion over the public roads, the parks and pleasure resorts. Mr. Hearn writes as follows :—

"Domestic animals are generally able to discover the presence of their deadly enemy long before a human eye can perceive it. If your horse rears and plunges in the darkness, trembles and sweats, do not try to ride on until you are assured the way is clear. Or your dog may come running back, whining, shivering; you will do well to accept his warning. The animals kept about country residences usually try to fight for their lives; the hen battles for her chickens; the bull endeavours to gore and stamp his supple enemy; the pig gives more successful combat; but the creature who fears the monster least is the brave cat.

"Seeing a snake, she at once carries her kittens to a place of safety, then boldly advances to the encounter. She will walk to the very limit of the serpent's striking range and begin to feint, teasing him, startling him, trying to draw his blow. A moment more and the triangular head, hissing from the coil, flashes swift as if moved by wings. But swifter still the stroke of the armed paw that dashes the horror aside, flinging it mangled in the dust.

"Nevertheless, pussy does not yet dare to spring; the enemy still active, has almost instantly reformed his coil; but she is again in front of him, watching, vertical pupil against vertical pupil. Again the lashing stroke; again the beautiful countering; again the living death is hurled aside; and now the scaled skin is deeply torn, one eye socket has ceased to flame. Once more the stroke of the serpent; once more the light, quick, cutting blow. But the *trigonocephalus* is blind, is stupefied; before he can attempt to coil pussy has leaped upon him, nailing the horrible flat head to the ground with her two sinewy paws. Now let him lash, writhe, twine, strive, to strangle her! In vain! he will never lift his head; an instant more and he lies still; the keen white teeth has severed the vertebra just behind the triangular skull."

A Rare Bird.

BRITISH army pets are of necessity limited in number by regulation; otherwise each regiment would be cumbered with a menagerie. But when Tommy Atkins wants a new pet very much, he generally finds a way round rules even if it involves a little cutting of red tape, and he is often assisted by his official superiors, if they are kind-hearted.

A troop-ship lately put in at Malta for a few hours, and one of the sergeants went on shore to pay a visit to a soldier son who was stationed there. When he returned he carried a small woolly dog under one arm. It was an engaging young thing, but the quartermaster steeled his heart and shook his head.

"Official number of dogs already on ship," said he, uncompromisingly.

The sergeant tried palaver, but it availed nothing, so after looking perplexed for a space he re-entered the boat in which he had come off to the ship, and returned to shore. When he came back he carried a bird-cage, containing a strange-looking creature. It was covered with gay feathers, but it had four legs.

"Can't pass that there dog on board ship," said the sentry, and the quartermaster bore out this verdict.

"Dog, sir?" echoed the sergeant, in surprise and disgust. "Can't you tell a Maltese bird of Paradise from a dog? And you that up in feathers that perfessers consult with ye!"

"Pass John Smith and one Maltese bird of Paradise!" sang out the quartermaster, with a broad grin.

"There isn't any order against taking birds on board as I knows on," remarked John Smith, as he came over the side. And his expression of triumph did not fade even when, in the course of a few days, the feathers on the rare bird came off in the wash.

What the Baboon Can be Taught to Do.

IF the baboons were not generally liable to become bad-tempered when they grow old (says "The Living Animals of the World"), they could probably be trained to be among the most useful of animal helpers and servers; but they are so formidable, and so uncertain in temper, that they are almost too dangerous for attempts at semi-domestication. When experiments have been made, they have had remarkable results. Le Vaillant, one of the early explorers in South Africa, had a chacma baboon which was a better watch than any of his dogs. It gave warning of any creature approaching the camp at night long before the dogs could hear or smell it. He took it out with him when he was shooting, and used to let it collect edible roots for him.

The latest example of a trained baboon only died a few years ago. It belonged to a railway signalman at Uitenhage station, about 200 miles up-country from Port Elizabeth, in Cape Colony. The man had the misfortune to undergo an operation in which both his feet were amputated, after being crushed by the wheels of a train. Being an ingenious fellow, he taught his baboon, which was a full-grown one, to pull him along the line on a trolley to the "distant" signal. There the baboon stopped at the word of command, and the man would work the lever himself. But in time he taught the baboon to do it, while he sat on the trolley, ready to help if any mistake were made.

A fine Animal Jointed Toy Design Sheet next week

HOW TO SKIN MAMMALS

IN Hobbies Weekly of January 26th, 1935, we described a way by which anyone interested in natural history can skin and preserve small birds.

By employing much the same method it is possible to make specimens of the various mice, shrews, moles, etc., which you may find dead, or perhaps catch in traps in your own gardens. The same implements as those employed for skinning birds can be used, but in addition a pair of forceps and an old tooth-brush are required.

For the actual skinning process, having first plugged its mouth with cotton-wool, lay the mouse (or whatever animal it is you are going to skin, for anything up to the size of a rabbit can be prepared in this way) on its back on a sheet of paper. With the scissors

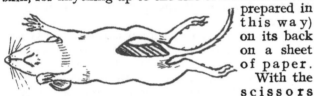

Fig. 1—The incision with knee pushed up

make an incision from the root of the tail upwards for about a third of the length of the body, taking care to cut only the skin. Should you accidentally cut the flesh below, and find moisture leaking out, cover the wound plentifully with dry sawdust.

Next separate the skin from the flesh all round the incision. Sever the tail-bone at its junction with the body, and, by pushing up the hindlegs towards the body, cut off the legs from inside at the "knee." (Fig. 1). The hind-legs and the tail should now be hanging loose, held only by the skin.

Now, with the points of the forceps, grasp the base of the spine where you severed it from the tail, and begin carefully to peel the skin down towards the head. You will find it comes away easily enough and is turning inside out as you go. On reaching the forelegs, cut them off at the "elbows," and continue downwards towards the head.

The Skull

Great care should be taken over the skull as the skin round the ears and eyes is very tender. However, by using the forceps and your thumbnails you should be able to work the skin over the ears and eyes right down to the lips, where it should be carefully cut away from the skull.

The animal's skin is now turned completely inside out. Remove all flesh and fat from the skin and all flesh from the fore-legs as far as the "wrist" and from the hind-legs as far as the "ankle." After treating with preservative (alum or boric acid powder) wrap a small piece of cotton wool round each bone.

With large animals the entire tailbone should be removed and a piece of straight wire, wrapped in wool, substituted, but with smaller animals, the tail-bone can be left intact, after the base has been dusted with preservative.

Next turn the skin back again, but before doing so, carefully sew the upper and lower lips together.

The specimen is now ready for stuffing. With the knitting needle push up the cotton wool into the head until you have filled it out to its natural size and shape. This is important. Do not give an animal with a naturally pointed face a round one and vice versa. Also fill out the eye sockets.

If you do not like white cotton-wool eyes, black headed pins make good substitutes for the real thing.

A Natural Shape

In the same way stuff the whole of the body to its natural shape and finally, when you are quite satisfied with the appearance of the specimen, sew up the incision, finishing at the tail.

With a tooth brush—any other small brush will do equally well—give the animal a thorough brushing to remove any knots in the fur and to bring out the gloss. Also brush the fur of the underparts over the wound.

Lastly, take a piece of flat board and some pins and laying the specimen on its front, pin out the fore-paws flat on either side of the head. The hind feet are put close together on either side of the tail. Straighten the tail and to keep it in position, pin a loop of paper over it. (Fig. 2).

Once more brush out the fur and see that your

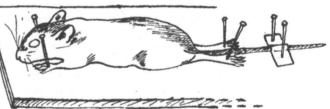

Fig 2—A complete specimen pinned out to dry

specimen is symmetrical and of natural shape. Now put it aside to dry somewhere where it is not likely to be interfered with and after a week or ten days it can be removed from the board and stored away.

Here are a few hints which a beginner may find useful : Always skin a mammal while fresh, as if it is stale the fur on flanks and underparts frequently falls out and spoils the looks of the specimen. If the fur of a specimen has become soiled with dirt or blood, it can easily be washed with soap and water and stuffed while wet and the fur brushed out smooth when it is dry.

Bats can be skinned in the same way as other mammals, but the wings should be pinned out flat as they are in flight. If, when you come to stuff it, you find difficulty in remembering the original shape of an animal, make a rough sketch or tracing of it before you begin.

Curing Skins for Mats, &c.

—:o:——

To prepare roughly-dressed skins such as are used for rugs, nothing is better than to damp them well and evenly. This can be done by rolling them in damp cloths, then, when well moistened, stretch them tightly, and rub down the flesh side (that which was inside when on the animal) with pumice stone, using at the same time a good supply of chalk in powder. This must be continued until the whole skin is even and uniform. Of course, if there are lumps of flesh and fat round the edges, these must be removed with a sharp knife.

The reason for using the chalk is for the purpose of cleansing the skin, as the chalk combines with, and takes up, the natural grease and dirt. Skins of whatever kind can be made soft and pliable by thoroughly working oil or yolk of an egg into its pores. By the use of the latter the softness to be found in kid gloves is produced, the skins having been previously cured with alum. After the yolk or oil has been well worked in, draw the skin many times over a semi-circular knife. This is known as "staking," which action brings the skin to as pliant a condition as it was when taken off the animal, no matter how long since the skinning process took place. This information will serve to show the *general* method of treating animal skins. There are, however, *special* methods according to the kind of skin to be treated. Sheepskins, for house mats, need careful curing to be satisfactory. Amateurs are not generally careful enough in removing every fragment of flesh which adheres to the skin. In using the knife, the inner skin must not be cut or bruised.

After this work has been done, dry the skin, lay it out on a flat board, and with hot water and soft soap rub well the inside of the skin, then wash again, and prepare a mixture of salts of tartar, 2 ozs., ammonia, 1 oz. When quite crushed, sprinkle this over the skin, in order to remove the grease. After this has been done rub thoroughly with dry sawdust, and allow it to remain for a short time.

The next operation is to tan the skin. For this purpose procure oatmeal, 16 ozs., corrosive sublimate, 8 ozs., saltpetre, 4 ozs., vinegar, 1 gallon. The vinegar must be boiled, and in its hot condition poured over the other ingredients, stirring as the liquid is poured in. This mixture must be allowed to stand until cold, when the skin can be placed within, and left for two or three days, according to the size. After which, take it out, and stretch it until dry. During the drying process, comb out the wool with a large-toothed comb, and, if carefully done, the work will be a success.

For the skins of rabbits and cats, which have hair instead of wool, the preliminary work, as stated, must be done, but the curing liquid had better be different. There are very many methods, but the following is as good as any :— Whiting, 2½ lbs. ; soft soap, 1 lb. ; chloride of lime, 2 ozs. ; tincture of musk, 1 oz. Boil the soap and whiting together in one pint of water, powder the chloride of lime and well stir it in. When nearly cold, add the musk. Dress the skins well with this mixture, and dry them. Finally finish by combing, brushing the hair, and trim as desired.

Mammals.

—:o:—

CHAPTER VI.—SQUIRRELS AND STOATS.

THIS is a branch of the subject which will very likely have fewer votaries than the preceding one, the work not being quite so fascinating, the results on the whole not so varied, nor will good results be arrived at so quickly. In fact, only long practice will enable the student to reach the point where a semblance to nature of his specimens will be apparent.

On the other hand, there is this advantage. If the results are not satisfactory at first, the work can be undone easily, and without the same damage happening to the specimen as would be the case with a bird.

Let us then procure a specimen, a rather small one, say a squirrel or a stoat. Take its measurements carefully—length and girth at different points. Note the colour of the eyes. *Black*, did you say? Look again. Take in its contour generally. If it is still stiff, pull the limbs gently, and manipulate it into flexibility. If it is bleeding from nose or mouth, or from shot or other wounds, or if there is any exudation whatever, dust with plaster of Paris and plug with wadding.

Lay the specimen squarely in front of you, head towards you (the reverse of the bird in Chapter I). Hold the fore limbs well apart to put a tension on the skin of the breast; make a little incision with the scalpel just in the line between the fore limbs. Put in the point of the scalpel with its back downwards, so as to cut *outward*. Run the cut straight along the median line as far as the hind limbs, taking care not to cut deeper than the skin. If the fur was not soiled when you began, so as to necessitate future washing, sprinkle some plaster of Paris and go on skinning. By the application of plaster as the work proceeds you may retain the fur quite clean throughout.

As the junction of the hind limbs with the body come into view, sever them close to the body, taking care not to cut the skin (always begin by the hind legs), skin back to the base of the tail, and cut off at the stump. Use plenty of plaster of Paris if exudation threatens when you cut through the rectum. Hold the denuded portions up with one hand and let the skin fall back. Go on skinning down the dorsal side, cutting off the fore limbs close to the body when they appear. Cut very gently the attachment of the ears with the skull. Do this with short little strokes of the very point of the scalpel. Exercise the same care with the eyes,

letting the point of the knife come into actual contact with the ridge of bone around the orbits. The corners of the mouth will present some difficulty (in a larger animal the articulations of the upper and lower jaws should be severed, which would facilitate the thorough removal of flesh, but in this little animal they can be left attached), but care will overcome it. With the point of the scalpel remove every vestige of flesh you see, and go on skinning down to the tip of the nose. If you stop short of this so as to be unable to introduce some stuffing into this region, your specimen will wear a "weazened" expression when done, caused through the shrinkage of what tissues may have been left in. Give attention to the limbs, push from without, or pull from within, until you have skinned down to the toes. Scrape off all the flesh (you may leave the large tendon at the back of the hind limbs—"the tendon of Achilles"—it will facilitate getting the limb into good form). Now for the tail. Denude the enclosed vertebræ all you can, turning the skin inside out, and then get as good a grip upon them as you can (in the case of a larger animal, say a monkey, an assistant is desirable for holding on while you pull), and pull steadily; the tail should slip from its sheath cleanly and completely. If it should part and leave some of the vertebræ in the skin, then you had better open the tail from the under side, and skin this portion, sewing up the skin neatly.

If any part be left in, in this way, it is difficult for the preservative to penetrate, and sooner or later the hair will fall off around the part. As a compromise, a little solution of corrosive sublimate spirit may be poured down the tail sheath, helping its penetration into the part with a pointed wire.

Pull the limbs now out into their natural position. Paint with arsenical soap the inside and the outside of the skull; fill the cavity with chopped tow. (Never put wadding in such parts as you will have to pass wire through; for the reason why, try a bit in your hand). Put balls of wadding in the eye sockets, then push the skull into its natural position.

If the fur is soiled, wash well with tepid water, using a little mild (*i.e.*, not alkaline) soap, if necessary. Rinse well, squeeze out superfluous water, and apply dry plaster of Paris, one application after another, shaking and beating well between each application, until quite dry. Never allow plaster to set to hardness on either hair or feather, otherwise you will have trouble, and little balls of it will remain among the soft fur or down, which even if out of sight in themselves, will cause a rough appearance, instead of the sleekness required in the coat. Put one hand inside the skin and brush the fur until quite bright and smooth.

For setting up, we again have the choice of the hard and the soft methods, and for these little animals, at least, the latter is easiest. Paint all the inside with arsenical soap. Fill the neck with chopped tow, also place a good layer along the back down as far as the tail, leaving the tail sheath empty. Cut a wire of suitable thickness a little longer than the animal, tail and all. Point one end, and working it through the very centre of the forehead, guide it well down the very centre of the neck and along the median line of the body. At about half-an-inch or so from the point of the wire, start winding some long fine tow very tightly around it, to equal in thickness and in length the tail you have taken away. Push this wrapped up portion of the wire into the tail sheath until its point comes out at the end. (If you have left much of the tail in the sheath, the wire must have that much less tow along it). Push the legs in so that the whole of the bones you have left in can be seen—*i.e.*, back as far as the toes. Push pointed wires of sufficient length through the feet, well central. Coat the bones with the arsenical soap, and with fine long tow wind bone and wire together, regulating the thickness of the tow to equal as nearly as possible the muscle that has been removed, in order to give the same outline.

For such portions of the work as this, some professionals use a *paste* made of paper pulp, mixed with a little preservative, such as a portion of arsenical soap, and worked into a consistency about as stiff as putty. This has advantages, especially when the animal is one that has slender limbs and short hair—for instance, a "Toy Terrier," where the sinews can be traced through the skin. This *paste* allows of good modelling, for with the skin wet and this yielding paste within, it is very obvious that any "bosses" of muscle, tendons, etc., can be impressed, and their form will remain.

For ordinary work, the tow answers very well, always attending, of course, to the important point that the skin is still wet, and that evenly—not one part wet and supple and another as stiff as parchment. In this latter case good results will not be possible.

Having gone so far as getting the wires through the legs and modelling the muscles of them, coat the skin of the legs with the soap and pull back into place. Wind the inside free ends of the wires tightly around the longitudinal wire, or *backbone*, exactly as in the case of the bird described in a previous chapter. Place the animal squarely in front of you once more, and regulate the wires—the dorsal one quite straight, the leg wires proceeding from it symmetrically right and left. Complete the filling of the body with chopped tow, seeing that there are no little hollows left where the limbs join the body. Sew up neatly, commencing at the tail end, always sticking the needle from inside the skin, and keeping the stitches as close to the margin as possible. Place in the eyes in the same manner as in the birds (see previous chapter).

WHAT DISTINGUISHED PEOPLE THINK
Of our Dargai Picture.

——:o:——

We have received letters in appreciation of our Magnificent Photogravure of Mr. Stanley Berkeley's picture representing the Charge of the Gordon Highlanders at Dargai from a large number of Distinguished Personages, including Royal Princes, Cabinet Ministers, well-known members of the House of Lords, and great soldiers. We do not propose to reproduce those letters, but we feel justified in mentioning the names of some of the writers, and in one or two instances briefly indicating the nature of the Compliments they have been kind enough to pay our Picture.

H.R.H. the Prince of Wales, immediately upon seeing a copy of the Photogravure, sent to us an order for four additional copies. Our list of purchasers of the Picture also includes such well-known names as

H.R.H. the Duke of York,
The Duke of Buccleuch,
The Duke of Westminster,
The Marquis of Breadalbane,
Lord Balfour of Burleigh, Secretary of State for Scotland, &c.

Among the distinguished persons who have been good enough to send us appreciative notes may be included—

H.R.H. the Duke of Connaught,
The Duke of Fife, who "considers the Picture is admirably executed ;"
The Marquis of Lorne, who describes it as "a very spirited drawing ;"
The Marquis of Salisbury, the Prime Minister ;
The Right Hon. A. J. Balfour, M.P., the First Lord of the Treasury ;
The Marquis of Lansdowne, Secretary of State for War ;
Lord George Hamilton, Secretary of State for India ;
The Right Hon. J. Chamberlain, M.P., Secretary of State for the Colonies ;
The Marquis of Huntly,
The Right Hon. Sir Wm. Harcourt, M.P., &c., &c.

We have also a very large number of letters from notable soldiers and officers of famous British regiments, all joining in commendation of the Picture.

We are issuing the Picture at the merely nominal price of Half-a-crown, chiefly, we admit, as an Advertisement for HOBBIES, but also in the hope that it may assist in perpetuating the deep thrill of patriotic emotion which the story of the gallantry of our soldiers at Dargai excited throughout the whole country. We are also offering at the same low price, as a Companion Picture, a splendid Photogravure of the memorable scene at the entrance to St. Paul's Cathedral during the special service on Jubilee Day. The two pictures will be sent together, carefully packed and post-free, for 4s. 9d. All Orders must be addressed to

HOBBIES ART SUPPLY DEPARTMENT,
12, PATERNOSTER SQUARE, LONDON, E.C.

"HOBBIES" HANDBOOKS:—"FRETWORKING IN WOOD," POST FREE, 1s.

THE Weasel might be called the Outlaw of the hedgerow, for he is, at least, outlawed by the gamekeeper, and the poultry farmer bears him no great love. Yet this creature, who loves to lurk about the hedgebottoms and the banks where the rabbits dwell, has his good points, and often " pays for his keep," as the saying is, by destroying rats and mice.

The Weasel is a bloodthirsty creature, a regular killer. He can run down a hare easily enough ; he is a hunter of ground-nesting birds ; he preys on rats, bank-voles, mice and other " small deer." And he will kill anything that he can get his teeth into. Yet he is designed chiefly to be a killer of the smaller rodents, as witness his long, narrow body, which enables him to sneak down their narrow holes and tunnels.

It's First Bite

The Weasel is a true child of the wild, born beneath some hedgerow snag or hole in the wall of the barn. The young ones are blind at birth, and helpless. But in a few days they can see the interior of their home. When the days of suckling are over, the mother weasel brings them their first taste of meat, most likely a juicy morsel of rabbit's flesh, red and warm—and from the moment a baby weasel sets its sharp little teeth into the tit-bit, it becomes a fierce little creature, filled with blood lust, the very pattern of a crafty and tireless hunter.

The stoat is also of the weasel tribe, so is the polecat ; but the smaller member of the tribe, the weasel himself, is the most ferocious of the clan, and, indeed, is said to be, for its size, the fiercest creature of the British wilds.

Playful as Kittens

Whilst young weasels are as playful as kittens, and romp together in the long grasses and herbage of the hedgebottom, leaping up at the white-throats' nests in the briers, or snatching playfully at the tall nettle flowers which choke the straggling bushes and nod in the wind.

Although you can hardly say the weasel is likely to appeal as a pet, yet he is a beautiful creature, full of grace in movements, lithe as a snake, with a long slender body, a snakelike neck, a narrow-pointed head set with bright black eyes that almost shoot fire when he catches sight of a field mouse or other prey.

Weasels are full of the joy of living, and even the adults will gambol and play as sportive as kittens.

One peculiarity of the weasel, and a common trait with all the members of the polecat tribe, is the propensity for killing merely from sheer blood lust, and not altogether for food.

A weasel in a chicken-run, for instance, has been known to run amok and kill the lot ; but on his behalf it may be said that he will equally exterminate a hole full of rats. He delights to hunt underground, searching the tunnels of the voles and other rodents.

Fierce and Daring

No creature of the fields is so utterly fierce and daring, size for size. He will attack creatures much larger than himself ; he will face a dog or cat when cornered, and is said to be audacious enough to attack a man, especially if accompanied by others of his clan ; an army of migrating weasels are not readily turned aside from their route.

Weasels migrate from covert to covert, shifting quarters pretty regularly, especially in autumn, often for no particular reason discernible.

There was never a more persistent hunter than the weasel. He will mark down a rabbit, and no matter how many other bunnies are in a burrow he will not turn aside, even though he brushes past terrified rabbits crouching spell-bound with fear.

He will stick to the trail no matter how much the frightened victim twists and turns or leaps aside.

A Climber

Weasels also attack birds, and will actually climb trees and bushes to reach their nests. When birds are sheltering in ivy—such as clings to tree trunks or old walls—the weasel will readily follow them, and seems to find no difficulty in climbing among the ivy stems and tendrils.

The propensity to store up food, common in so many wild creatures and to be noted in your pet dog when he hides his bones in the garden, is prominent in the weasel. He often hides up food that he cannot eat then and there. But whether he ever troubles to seek it again is hard to say.

Something Fresh Preferred

The fact that the weasel is renowned for his blood-lust, killing right and left when he has the chance, suggests this desire to store his kill.

(Continued on facing page)

Yet if truth be known, the little demon seldom returns to his cache, for the simple reason that he invariably prefers something hot and fresh in the blood line, and only when desperately hungry will a weasel condescend to indulge in a cold meal.

Weasels frequently kill each other. Indeed, were this not the case, the weasel population in the hedgerows would be much greater. If a weasel finds a rival on his selected bit of territory, the intruder may have to either run for it or fight, and it is his nature to do a bit of " scrapping "— and then one of the combatants die ; for there is no deciding the battle " on points" in Weaseldom.

Weasels make their homes in holes, in woodstacks, hayricks, and corn stacks where rats also dwell, under hedgrow snags, and similar places. Weasels do not hibernate like the squirrel and dormouse, but are active all the winter through, and and you may often see the marks of their feet following the blurred imprints of a scuffling rabbit in the snow.

Life in Weaseldom is very uncertain, and a family soon becomes depleted. Father Weasel, visiting the farmer's chicken coops once too often, may spring a well-concealed trap ; Mother Weasel, hearing a squeaking as she lies beneath a bush in the covert, pops out in order to satisfy her curiosity—and is promptly shot, for it is the gamekeeper who has made the noise with his lips, having seen the weasel go under the bush.

LET'S RAISE SILKWORMS

SILKWORMS' eggs should be procured in early summer. Put the eggs in a shallow tray and cover them with a piece of gauze. Then place the tray in a window that faces due south in such a way that the eggs catch the full benefit of the sun's rays.

By

R. L. Cantwell

An old cardboard box lid makes a good tray. Leave the eggs undisturbed till they begin to hatch. But directly the first little worm appears, remove them to other trays filled with lettuce leaves.

You'll find the worms are funny little things, black in colour, about $\frac{1}{4}$ in. long, and very hungry. Your spare time, for the next few days, will be spent keeping them clean and supplied with fresh food.

About five days after hatching, the caterpillars will shed their first skins. The second moulting takes place about five days later; the third in about another five days; and the fourth in about eight days. At the end of thirty-two days from hatching they will be full grown — about three inches long.

Your silkworms will soon need nests to spin their cocoons in. So get some pieces of note paper, twist them into cones, and fasten them in rows to a piece of tape with the pointed ends hanging downwards.

When the caterpillars leave off feeding, put them into these cones — one in each cone.

Your paper cones will soon contain fluffy little cocoons. Now the silkworm decreases until it is barely half its original size and casts its skin for the last time, together with its head and jaws, before becoming a chrysalis.

Normally, the moth will emerge from the chrysalis, and eat its way out of the cocoon, thus ruining the silk. But we want to avoid this. So as soon as the silkworm has passed into the chrysalis stage (shake the cocoon and note if the chrysalis rattles inside) we must wind off the silk.

To do this drop the cocoon into a cup of warm water, and, after you have taken off the loose outer silk, which is of no value, get an end, and wind off the silk in one continuous thread on to a piece of card.

Put the chrysalides into a separate box. They will remain unchanged for about three weeks. Then they will suddenly turn into creamy coloured moths with dusky transverse bars on their wings.

THE ROOK SEASON.

BEFORE the war the rook had begun to decrease generally. This was in no small measure due to mistaken ideas of the farmer and the gamekeeper as to the harm it is supposed to do, and an omission to recognise the great benefit it renders to agriculture. It is, however, satisfactory to note that owing to the absence of rook shooting during the war, the rook has now become more or less restored to its former status. And those who look forward annually to the commencement of rook shooting will not be disappointed with the sport that they promise to afford.

Shooting Rooks.

Rook shooting, indeed, is an excellent sport, and commencing as it did in mid-May, when there is no other shooting, save that of young rabbits, to be had until August, and in most districts till September, it forms a welcome interlude for the sportsman during the long close season, which is so tedious a time for the keen sportsman. As a rule, rook-shooting is a farmer's sport, for on big estates tenants are usually invited to shoot. This is as it should be. And for success one needs plenty of guns. It is a mistake to shoot all the young birds, excellent as these are in a pie. For a fair proportion should be left to breed, and to improve the stock. Nor should all the old birds be killed off for a similar reason, as if they are the young ones may forsake their ancestral homes. It is necessary to display some skill in posting the guns at strategic points. After the birds have been well peppered, they will leave the nesting trees and settle at some distance in other clumps of trees. But the young ones will not go far, nor the old ones, as the latter will not leave their young to their fate. Posting one's guns suitably makes all the difference between a big and a small bag.

Guns, Decoys, Etc.

Rook-shooting is not so easy a matter as may be thought, for a soaring rook affords quite as difficult a shot as a rocketer at the lowest side. One gets both long and short shots, on plenty of occasions when one can pull off a left and a right, with skill. This type of shooting indeed requires good marksmanship. As an all-round useful gun the 12-bore may be recommended for rook-shooting, and the most suitable pattern of shot is No. 5 or No. 6. Excellent sport may also be had with the rifle, and a ·22 rifle will carry quite 200 yards effectively. If rooks become wary, decoys may be used, as for wood pigeons, but wooden decoys must be used, as stuffed birds will be torn to pieces.

The Rook's Usefulness.

Much rubbish is both talked and written as to the harm rooks do. But their usefulness is usually entirely ignored. Admittedly they eat corn during the Autumn and Spring, but the amount they eat is much exaggerated, and they do not eat corn only when on arable. When following the plough in Spring rooks devour large numbers of worms. And they do the same in pastures and meadows, where also then and at other times they destroy vast quantities of wire worms, daddy-long-legs, and chafer grubs, which do incalculable damage to grass roots if left to increase. In Autumn, too, like the partridge and pheasant, the rook frequents root crops and destroys large numbers of the pests that infest the turnip and mangold. It is thus clear that the rook is the farmer's friend.

How the Rook Does Harm.

Apart from its corn-eating propensities the rook is also fond of fruit, and will not hesitate to pilfer walnuts. On occasion where a rookery adjoins a poultry yard a few chickens may disappear. But perhaps the gamekeeper has most to grumble at. For no doubt rooks are fond of eggs, and a flock quartering the field and hedgerows may destroy several partridges' and pheasants' nests. Later on a few chicks may be taken. And in autumn the stores of acorns reserved for pheasant food are depleted by them.

Rook and Crow.

Probably a good deal of the harm the rook is supposed to do is really wrongly laid to its charge. For farmers are very ill-informed and unable to distinguish between rook and crow. The former has a bare patch at the base of the bill, and is also a bigger bird, having a more blackish-blue lustre. A rook's caw is very different to the note of the carrion crow. There is a vast difference between the crow and the rook in other ways, the former being paired for life, the latter being a gregarious bird. Carrion crows are, as their name implies, fond of flesh and are great egg thieves. To the keeper they are as great a pest as any type of vermin.

Rook Habits.

Gregarious and social in their habits, rooks form rookeries in which to nest, and roost in other clumps of trees. They perform all their actions in concert. They fly to and from their feeding grounds at regular times in flocks. They have a commonwealth of their own, and hold conferences, hold trials for the judgment of offenders. Their affection for their homes is extraordinary, and they will not brook the intrusion of an interloper. If one of their number is wounded or hurt the rest do their best to rescue or to succour it. The cawing of the rooks in the high elms is one of the most pleasant features of English country life.

Rook Pie.

Some people do not relish rook pie. The flavour of the rook is strong. But properly treated one cannot distinguish between rook and pigeon pie. The secret of success lies in soaking the birds in water for an hour or so before they are cut up.

Another plan is to soak them in milk. This done, one can do with rooks all that can be done with pigeons, and little or no difference then can be detected between the two birds, whether used in a pie or in the many other ways in which rooks can be served, as when roasted, broiled or made into pasties and the like.—H.

WHEN suitable weather calls, the fisherman will always be found at "the ready," and his naturalistic ideas join in the picture which completes the whole, for his hobby is one (to him) that forms a peculiar, yet enjoyable,

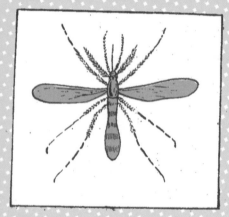

THE GNAT.

asset in the following of his favourite quest. It is a happy idea, and he is content with it. In these queer times of ours, it is, as Shakespeare puts it, "A desire devoutly to be wished."

The Gnat.

There are not many of my readers who are not familiar with the gnat. Most of us have a cause to remember this fly, when sitting on a summer's evening by lake, river, or pond. Singularly enough, it is the female gnat which does the "biting" part of the business, and honours us with her intentions when they are not wanted. She is provided with an upper lip which is prolonged into a tube and five lancets. She thrusts the lancets into the skin of her victim and sucks the blood through the tube from the wound made by the lancets.

The female gnat lays her eggs on the water, arranges them carefully, side by side, two or three hundred of them; being covered with a sticky substance, which dries in the air, the whole number hang together in the form of a circular raft.

When the larvæ emerge from the egg they are without limbs, and move about by wriggling their bodies. The larvæ becomes in time the pupa, in which stage it takes no food. When the pupa skin splits, the perfect insect emerges, using the pupa skin as a raft until its wings are dry and it can take the air.

The body of the gnat is shaped like a club, with long and slender legs, and the wings long and narrow.

The Tench.

This fish is found in the ponds and slow-moving streams, and it likes a muddy bottom. It is a lazy, indolent kind of fish, and passes most of its life on the bottom resting on its fins.

It burrows in the mud in the winter as a sure protection against the cold. It is very tenacious of life, and in the eastern counties the fish is brought to market in the morning, offered for sale, and if not sold taken back again and put into the water. It has been proved this fish can live a day out of water.

The Tench is covered with slime, making it very difficult to hold, and is as slippery as an eel. It is about four times as long as it is high, has a small mouth, with two small barbels at the angle of the jaws. All the fins of the Tench are rounded in form. The colour varies—in muddy water it is dull, and changes from a warm green to a black, with a peculiar golden shimmer. The body is a greyish white. The usual full length of a Tench is about 18ins.

What has always interested me about this fish is its wonderful colour—it has always held a fascination for me—and I always like to hook a decent Tench, if for this purpose alone. It is so much out of the ordinary run of fish.—SALOPIA.

THE TENCH.

Always Read our Advertisements; you may find something which will specially interest you.

WASP SCISSORS!

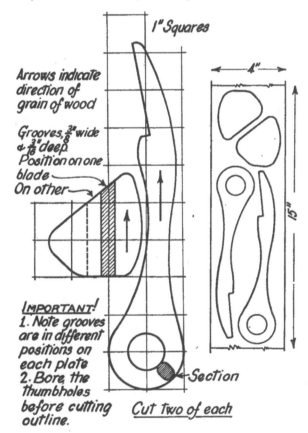

DURING these summer days, the following comedy, or something like it, will be frequently performed at picnics, camps, and other alfresco meals. A fat wasp will land on the jam pot and everyone (especially the ladies) get excited. Father, attempting to swipe the wasp with a rolled up newspaper, knocks the milk over into the sugar. The wasp, now thoroughly alarmed, stings someone, and whilst the sting is being attended to, about a dozen other wasps get stuck in the jam. Mother thereupon scoops out the contaminated jam, and so wastes a lot.

Safe and Simple

Now, if you only had the pair of wasp scissors shown in the drawing, you would not have all this bother. One little nip, and the wasp is quickly, cleanly, and humanely extinguished. You can

1" Squares

Arrows indicate direction of grain of wood

Grooves, 3/8" wide & 3/16" deep. Position on one blade — On other —

IMPORTANT!
1. Note grooves are in different positions on each plate
2. Bore the thumbholes before cutting outline.

4"

5"

←Section

Cut Two of each

make a pair in one evening, at very little cost. They sell very well, too, among friends and neighbours, or at sales, etc.

The first thing to do is to draw the shapes of the sides and plates full size. This is easily done by making a framework of 1in. squares. Draw these on a piece of thin plywood or thick smooth cardboard, so as to make templates. (It is not necessary to cut out the thumbhole in the template : just punch a little hole through the centre).

The wood used is White Chestnut, 3/8in. thick. From the smaller diagram, it will be seen that the whole of the parts required can be got on a strip 4ins. wide and 15ins. long. Before cutting out the outline cut the thumb holes, preferably by boring with a 1in. centre-bit. If this is done after the cutting, you are practically sure to split the wood.

The Important Groove

Here is another very important point. On each plate, there is a groove 3/8ins. wide and 3/16in. deep. Owing to the fact that one arm of the scissors is on top of the other (i.e. 3/8in. higher) the grooves on the plates are *not* in the same position on each part.

Cut the outlines, using a thick " toymakers " sawblade in the ordinary fretsaw frame, or coping saw, and placing the two corresponding parts together in a vice, go round their edges with a file to smooth them. The grooves are cut in the plates, and the arms glued in. A couple of tiny screws might be useful if your joint is not tight.

The Flat Plates

When the glue has set, go over the parts, rounding off all square edges (especially round the thumbholes), with glasspaper. Place the two top plates together. The position of the screw pivot will then automatically be found. The whole should be such that when shut, the plates are quite flat, and the thumbholes close together.

The pivot is a round-headed brass screw. It should be tightly driven in the lower arm, but the upper arm should be an easy fit on it. It may be necessary to file off the tip.

Take the screw out again, and then paint the parts well with art enamel or cellulose lacquer. Upon reassembling, the scissors are now done and ready for the instant slaughter of any wasps venturing within reach.

Enter our Photographic Competition and win a prize

THE GENTLE ARTS

HOW TO READ CHARACTER IN THE FACE

Sweets for special occasions

MAKE TREE WINE!

Perfume Making

Fred is the life of the party

OUR JUNE PHOTOGRAPHIC COMPETITION.

OCTOBER EVENING.
(By W. Whitlam, Goole.)
First Prize.

Waterscapes Take First.

Mr. W. Whitlam took the first prize for two "waterscapes," the better of which is "October Evening," a very beautiful rendering of a sunset, with sun, boat, and foreground all nicely "placed." No process of reproduction can reproduce the delicate tones of this beautiful print; it is like an old engraving in quality, and one of the best things this well-known Goole worker has produced. If the picture is fairly well reproduced in our pages, readers will note the pleasing composition—the high horizon-line, the place of the boat, and the inclusion of a foreground of reeds, etc., all of which combine to make the picture a work of art.

A Fine Mist Picture.

Mr. A. W. Breed, who took the second prize, is to be congratulated on the production of "Mists," a photograph of the decorative design type in which a good foreground of bulrushes is made to stand out well against the water and mist. The picture composes well and is technically perfect; a very fine rendering of high artistic merit.

AGAIN we have to chronicle a most successful photographic contest, for although the number of entries was a little below those for the previous contest, the work was of a very high quality, and the number of new competitors larger than usual. There is one fact worthy of mention, namely, no lady's name appears in the prize list. Ladies have been particularly prominent in our contests for many years past, and we always welcome them, knowing well the perfect photographic work they do, but in this contest we do not find them winning any of the cash prizes.

MISTS.
(By A. W. Breed, Bedford.)
Second Prize.

A Unique Subject.

Mr. J. W. Gannan, who for many moons has sent us the most perfect prints on self-toning paper, now sends us gaslight prints, but we hope Mr. Gannan has not given up self-toning paper, because few people can manipulate the daylight paper so well as he

THE PET JACKDAW.
(By W. H. Evernden, Faversham.)
Fourth Prize

common subjects in the summer—it is above the average of such pictures.

Where Real Picture Making is Difficult.

Many thousands of snapshots have been taken at Wembley, and our own and other contests get shoals of them, but few of the snapshots taken at the exhibition have any real pictorial merit. One of the best we have seen is by Mr. F. G. Clements, who took the fifth prize. This picture is technically better than most of the Wembley prints, the lights and shades being beautifully rendered, particularly on the Canadian building and on the water.

DEATH BY MISADVENTURE.
(J. W. Gannan, Darlington)
Third Prize.

does. However, this competitor has photographed a novel and interesting subject, and has done it splendidly. The title of the picture is "Death by Misadventure"—a mouse and a coconut. The mouse having eaten his way through the soft core of the nut, partook too freely of the milk found inside, and then found he could not return to his family, hence the verdict "Death by Misadventure." The nut is beautifully pictured and the whole forms a most unique subject to which the third prize was awarded.

A Pleasing Competition.

Mr. W. H. Evernden took the fourth prize for "The Pet Jackdaw" and "The Spirit of Holiday," the former a picture of two children with a jackdaw. The children are caught in very pleasing poses, most natural and effective, the whole forming a very pleasing composition. Mr. Evernden has a keen eye for uncommon subjects, and although his second picture is a snapshot of some bathers—

DANCING AS A HOBBY.

THE writer does not propose to allude to present-day "freak" dancing, which is nothing more or less than an *insult* to the Terpsichorean art, but merely to dancing as conducted by all those who really hold such art in respect.

Dancing has always been popular. If we peep into the history of dancing we shall find it a most interesting and instructive study. This recreation (dancing) which, in modern times, is the delight of the youthful, was deemed worthy of notice, as an amusing and beneficial exercise, by many of the sages of old times, several of whom were at once fine philosophers and good dancers, and a few of them, even when far advanced in life became pupils in the art. Thus Timocrates, we are told, first beheld an entertainment of dancing in his old age, and was so pleased with what he saw that he is said to have exclaimed against himself for having so long sacrificed such an exquisite enjoyment to the vain pride of philosophy.

An Erroneous Impression.

It has been erroneously stated that the Egyptians were the discoverers of music and dancing. History records that the Egyptians were averse to music, while dancing, or rather, that species of the practice which in after-times arose into the dignity of a liberal art, was unknown to them.

The Jews indulged in dancing during their passage through the wilderness, shortly after their departure from the land of Pharaoh. David danced before the ark; Jeptha's daughter is described as meeting her father with a dance; and one of the joys enumerated by the prophet, when foretelling the return of the Jews from captivity, is that of the virgins rejoicing in the dance.

For the advancement of the art towards some degree of perfection we must look to Greece, where we find, according to Greek history, that music and dancing were culti-vated in the earliest ages. The Greeks carried the sacred, as well as the social dance, to the highest point of attainable perfection.

According to the history of Rome, the ancient Romans undoubtedly performed dances at their religious ceremonies in the earliest ages.

In France, at so early a period as the year 1581, during the reign of Henri III., a splendid *ballet* was produced under the auspices of the Court. The Queen also produced a superb féte at the Louvre, in honour of her sister's nuptials, in which a *ballet* was exhibited, called "Céres and her Nymphs." From that time, which may be considered the age of its revival in Europe, dancing made gradual progress towards its present state of refinement in France and the neighbouring nations.

An Ingenious Invention.

To the French we are indebted for rather an ingenious, but, in the opinion of many pro-fessional dancers, a useless invention, by which it was proposed, that as the steps in dancing are not very numerous, although they may be infinitely combined, *characters* might be made use of to express the various steps and figures of a dance, in the same manner as words and sentences are expressed by letters; or what is more closely analogous, as the musical characters are employed, to represent to the eye the sounds of an air. The well-known Monsieur Beauchamp, and a French dancing master, each laid claim to be the original inventor of this art; and the conse-quence was a law-suit, in which, however, judgment was pronounced in favour of the former.

There are a variety of dances to which the term "National" may, with some propriety, be applied. Among the most celebrated of these are—the "Italian Tarantula," the "German Waltz," and the "Spanish Bolero" —of which so little is heard in these days.

An Agreeable Pastime.

Dancing has ceased to be a difficult and toilsome exercise, and is now softened down, as it certainly should be in society, to a most agreeable pastime. It must not, however, be forgotten, that the ease, grace, and neat execution, which are confidently looked for in ballroom dancing, must needs to be the result of diligent practice; without it, the pupil—irrespective of sex—cannot expect to go through a quadrille with credit to himself or herself, or comfort to those with whom they happen to be associated. The facility displayed by the accomplished should lead a man or a woman to imagine that dancing, as they see it practised, is *easy* of acquirement; they must have previously devoted that attention to the preliminaries of the art, which is required by all those who desire to see themselves capable of displaying an equal degree of ease and elegance.—E.C.

with Black & Decker
it costs so little to do so much

It costs us so little to make our home attractive. Whatever we want — from the bench John's working on, or the little table he's just finished, to extra cupboards in the kitchen — we just make them all with our Black & Decker   Furthermore we made an early start on the Spring-cleaning this year and our Black & Decker was an enormous help de-rusting and preparing doors for repainting — now the old home simply sparkles with spring-newness.   And I'd hate to be without Black & Decker for the daily housework.   I can whizz through polishing, scouring, oven cleaning — everything.   We save so much time and money — it's wonderful.

What a wide choice!

You get value for money and the advantage of free choice when you buy Black & Decker.   You can buy the popular ¼″ Drill or the more powerful Sander-Polisher-Drill which will give you an indispensable household and workshop unit in itself Add low price attachments to it as and when you wish, or select your own choice of tools for a complete electric home workshop to your own particular requirements for only 30/- down

Black & Decker

ELECTRIC HOME WORKSHOPS

Write TODAY for full details and Sawing and Woodturning Hints Booklet

BLACK & DECKER LIMITED · DEPT. 57E. · HARMONDSWORTH · MIDDX

CLASSICAL DANCING.

THE value of dancing in the physical training of girls is becoming more fully recognised every day. To acquire that ease and dignity of bearing, grace of movement and something of that perfect self-control, associated always with the wonderful Pavlova, should be the ambition of every healthy girl.

Everybody knows the awkward woman who blunders into a room, brushes against a table, knocks into a chair as she hastens to greet her hostess. Watch her as she stands with rounded shoulders, head hanging forwards, nervously fidgeting from one foot to the other as she talks. Could anything be less beautiful ?

Graceful Carriage.

Where is the graceful carriage or repose of manner which is the *sine qua non* of good breeding and culture ? In classical dancing the remedy for this awkwardness is to be found, and girls of all ages should be trained to make their way through life graciously and gracefully.

In ancient Greece, when the worship of strength and beauty was almost a religion, the human body reached the highest pitch of physical perfection the world has ever known.

In those far-off days natural dancing was one of the chief recreations of the people and to-day a conscious effort is being made to return to the methods, which produced such beauty of form and harmony of movement enjoyed by those people of by-gone age.

Stimulate the Body.

Classical dancing stimulates every portion of the body. All the muscles are used, the lungs exercised, and the circulation quickened, so that dancing becomes a sheer joy and delight.

When watching a class the onlooker is struck first of all by the well-balanced, easy carriage of the girls, even in those who have had but few lessons in this beautiful art. Their minds seem to exercise an almost unconscious control over every movement. With practice this control becomes permanent, resulting in a temperamental, as well as a physical, grace. For the nervous or delicate child, dancing in the open air is, perhaps, the most perfect form of exercise known, and every mother should do her utmost to procure such lessons for her child.

CLASSICAL DANCING BY GIRLS AT THE BINGLEY GRAMMAR SCHOOL, YORKS.

It is surprising how soon even the youngest learns to express music by movement in her own particular little way. The pleasant control of body needed for rhythmical movements has naturally a most beneficial effect upon a nervous child, gradually eliminating all consciousness of self, as the pupil progresses.

A girl should take a course of classical dancing and in between her lessons practise the movements at home. Wearing a loose silk tunic, and with bare feet, she should spend a short time perfecting arm, leg and body movements, learnt at class. When warm, practise outside on the grass, humming or singing to get the correct rhythm.

If possible, put a Chopin waltz, or something of Mendelssohn on the gramophone, and try to express by movement the meaning of the music.

Quite apart from the physical and mental value of such exercise, dancing teaches a girl how to wear her clothes to the best advantage. The best cut costume, the most dainty of little French frocks, have an increased value when worn by a girl who has learnt the true art of movement and grace of carriage.

ANOTHER EFFECTIVE PICTURE.

How to Read Character from the Face.

BY WILL OAKDEN.

CHAPTER V.—THE CHIN.—CONCLUDING HINTS.

IN no other feature of the face is the extent of a person's will-power so unmistakeably portrayed as in his chin. Glance for a moment at our first two diagrams—can there be any doubt as to which of these two chins shows the most powerful character? We think not. The chin illustrated in Fig. 36 could scarcely be associated with a determined nature, whilst the one in Fig. 37 could never belong to a really weak-willed person.

The faculty of will is (we need hardly remark) capable of considerable variation, for we see it demonstrated in a great many different ways. A person may, for example, be unreasonably obstinate at times, yet not sufficiently firm at

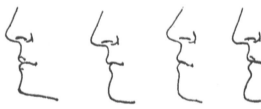

FIG. 36.   FIG. 37.   FIG. 38.   FIG. 39.

others. Such a man (or woman, for our remarks are of course equally applicable to the fair sex) will probably possess a long, slightly receding chin, something like that shown in Fig. 38. In contrast to this is the one next illustrated (Fig. 39); here the chin is about the same length as the one in the preceding sketch, but it projects forward instead of receding. A chin like this shows its possessor to be a person who has the gift of mental concentration—whatever work he may be engaged in, he can always keep his mind fixed upon it as long as it is necessary. Inventors, and people engaged in scientific research, frequently have chins of this conformation.

Differing from concentration, yet none the less a faculty of will, is resolution, which is shown by a chin that almost forms an angle at the point indicated by an arrow in Fig. 40. An individual with such a chin will be extremely tenacious, and—given anything like favourable opportunities—he will be certain to force himself to the front in whatever profession he follows. This type of chin is generally found in the faces of successful detectives, explorers, and army officers.

Besides showing his will-power, a person's

chin is also a key to his affections and social instincts. A chin which is plump in the centre, like the one in Fig. 41, denotes ardent and often passionate love. The owner will pay a great deal of attention to members of the opposite sex, but being rather changeable in affairs of the heart he will not confine his attentions to any particular one for long, preferring to make himself agreeable to all.

A person who is constant in his affections invariably has a chin which, viewed from the front, is fairly broad and round in outline (Fig. 41). Whilst treating all members of the other sex with the utmost consideration, he will be likely to select a certain one of them as the sole object of his esteem.

Having dealt fully with the chief signs of character in the face, we now propose to show our readers exactly how they should proceed in delineating a person's character and temperament.

In the first place it is highly important that every feature of the face shall receive an equal amount of attention and consideration; it is a great mistake to base one's opinion solely upon the indications given by one or two features, for it sometimes happens that one feature will counteract another.

A person may, for instance, have a long chin, and a very small, insignificant nose, as in Fig. 42. Now it will be remembered that such a chin—judged entirely upon its own merits— denotes force of character and will power,

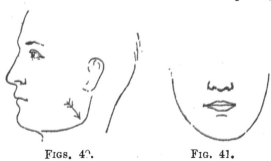

FIGS. 42.   FIG. 41.

whilst the nose which is depicted in the diagram clearly indicates a weak and puny nature. Were either of the two features in question to be judged independently of the other, the delineation would be incorrect. What should really be done is to consider the indications given by *both* organs, and then to strike a balance between them.

Again, just study for a moment the face shown in Fig. 43. The owner has a splendidly shaped forehead, but glancing lower down we find he has a very badly shaped chin. This is an unfortunate combination, for whilst the possessor is endowed with capacity for intellectual growth, yet, on account of his unstable will power, he will be unable to properly control his mental faculties, and sooner or later he will break down through the consequent strain. For the persistent and vigorous exercise of the brain, there must also be strength of will.

When a prominent nose is observed in the same countenance as a very low forehead, the possessor will have plenty of energy and executive ability, but he will be unable to devise any system of working—hence he will only be able to do work which has been planned by someone else. Nevertheless, he will most likely be

a domineering individual, whose desire for power and control will often get him into trouble.

In delineating, it is always advisable to form just a broad outline of your "subject's" nature, before proceeding to more minute details. To do this, mentally divide the face into three distinct parts—marked respectively A, B, and C, in Fig. 44. If you find that these sections are all about the same length, you may take it for granted that your subject is the fortunate possessor of an evenly-balanced, harmonious temperament. He will be eminently practical and persevering, possessing plenty of intellect, and a good support of prudence and energy.

Should the upper section (A) predominate,

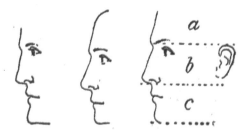

FIG. 42.   FIG. 43.   FIG. 44.

the owner will be a deep thinker, and will exhibit much delicacy of feeling and refinement of manner. If his face is longer between the eyebrows and the base of the nose (section B), the owner will be intensely ambitious, forceful, and active. When the lower part of the face (C) is the longest, the will power will dominate, often to the detriment of the moral and intellectual faculties.

(THE END.)

The Story of a Caxton.

AMONG the "Enemies of Books" mentioned by Mr. William Blades, in his volume bearing that title, is ignorance, of which he gives the following example:— "Many years ago I discovered in a dirty pigeon-hole, close to the grate in the vestry of the French Protestant Church, St. Martin's-le-Grand, a fearfully mutilated copy of Caxton's edition of the "Canterbury Tales," with wood-cuts. It had long been used, leaf by leaf, in utter ignorance of its value, to light the vestry fire. Originally worth at least £800, it was then worth half, and, of course, I energetically drew the attention of the minister in charge to it, as well as to another grand folio by Rood and Hunte, 1480. Some years elapsed, and then the Ecclesiastical Commissioners took the foundation in hand, but when at last trustees were appointed, and the valuable library was rearranged and catalogued, this 'Caxton,' together with the fine copy of 'Latterbury,' from the first Oxford press, had disappeared entirely."

A SIMPLY MADE FLUTE PIPE

How to make a real playing instrument almost for nothing

THE instrument whose construction is now to be described, was evolved with a view to cheapness and efficiency after considerable experiment with pipes of the Recorder type made of bamboo and cane. It is a reversion to the idea of "across the end" blowing, combined with a wide bore, which makes for ease in blowing the low notes and greater power than in the Recorder; while the loudness is increased to that of a side blown flute and it has an effective compass of over two octaves, obtainable with ease after a little practice in the regulation of the breath.

An Alto Instrument

Its fundamental is the usual low "D" of the orchestral flute, an octave below that usual in the pipe type of instrument. For solo playing, however, the writer himself prefers an alto instrument, pitched in "G," and dimensions of this are given in Fig. 4. The cost is negligible.

To begin with obtain a piece of bamboo, 19½ins.

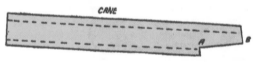

CANE

Fig. 1—Section of cane cut for mouthpiece

long by about 1⅜ins. internal diameter. The writer used a piece of old curtain rod. The length is not absolutely vital, provided it is a little over 18ins., but the surplus gives the possibility of an extra low note as obtainable on some flutes. Select, if possible, a piece with a joint as near as possible 9½ins. from one end.

Alternatively two joints equidistant from the ends. The idea is that the irregularity of the tube, practically unavoidable at the joints, however carefully cleared out, shall come at a point symmetrically placed with respect to the whole length, so helping the production of "harmonics," on which the change of octave depends.

Cleaning Inside

Clear out the thin diaphragm at the joint with a long boring tool. Ideally, the natural smooth inner coat of the bamboo should remain, but this is not usually practicable when joints have to be cut out. So if you have jagged and torn this coat in clearing out the joints, smooth the whole internal bore, beginning with a long rasp and finishing with a file and glasspaper,

the latter glued onto a half round length of wood of a diameter slightly less than the bore.

The performance of the instrument will be greatly improved by an absolutely smooth and regular bore, so time and trouble here will be amply repaid.

Now take a piece of cigar-box wood and, with a fretsaw, cut from it a disc to cover one end of the bamboo tube. If there is any taper choose the larger end. Through the centre of the disc drill a hole about ⅛in. diameter and countersink and enlarge it with an ordinary carpenter's rose-bit held in the hand to a finished diameter of 3/16in. on the smaller side. This hole must have a good sharp edge, for on its regular splitting, of the air current the whole performance of the pipe depends. The writer has used metal here, but prefers wood as improving the tone. It is an advantage to waterproof the disc when finished, by varnishing with cellulose or similar varnish, but care must be taken not to dull the edge.

The Mouthpiece

Next take a piece of cane, of the sort used to support plants and having an internal diameter slightly over 3/16in. Cut a section free from joints and about 4ins. long and clear the bore. Cut the end to the shape shown in Fig. 1, the distance 'a b' being such that the point 'a' is directly above the nearer edge of the hole when fitted over the disc as in Fig. 2.

Now hold the disc and cane tightly over the end of the bamboo tube (Fig. 2), taking care that the fingers are not directly in line with the outlet from the cane, and blow gently into the latter. You should get a deep musical note.

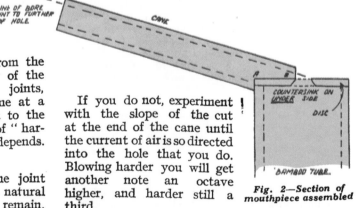

TOP LINE OF BORE TO POINT TO FURTHER EDGE OF HOLE

CANE

COUNTERSINK ON UNDER SIDE

DISC

BAMBOO TUBE.

Fig. 2—Section of mouthpiece assembled

If you do not, experiment with the slope of the cut at the end of the cane until the current of air is so directed into the hole that you do. Blowing harder you will get another note an octave higher, and harder still a third.

Now assemble the instrument. Use a good waterproof glue or a hard wax for this. Ordinary glue is useless, giving way at once from the warm condensation of the breath. For extra security you can fit a small wooden bridge rasped out to fit the cane as shown in Fig. 3.

The pipe is now ready for tuning. Try its fundamental note against a piano or pitch-pipe. For a 19½ins. tube this will be round about " C." If deeper, cut very small pieces off the end till it is exactly " C." If already above " C," make it either " D flat " or " D sharp."

In either of the former cases drill a small (¼in.) hole, 1½ins. up the tube and on the side opposite to the mouthpiece and, in the case of a flute

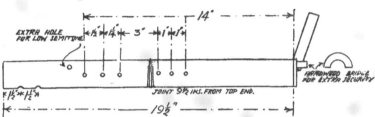

Fig. 3—The instrument complete showing position of holes

giving a bottom " C," another one 1½ins. above this. Tune these two holes by gradually enlarging them till the note with the lower one open is a semitone and with both open a full tone above " C," i.e. until you have the " D " in the key of which the flute is to be tuned.

Leaving on the end and tuning by these holes will enable you at any future time to fit keys to give you the extra low note obtainable on many modern flutes. For a start however be content to finish your instrument simply as a keyless " D " one.

The Finger Holes

Now drill the fingerholes, as shown in Fig. 3. These are on a line at right angles to the mouthpiece, the flute being held in playing obliquely across the body—like a saxophone. Drill the holes small at first—not over ¼in.—and be careful to get the edges sharp, especially on the inside. Use your half-round piece of wood with glass-paper for this.

Hold the flute as in playing, carefully cover all these six holes and tune to the scale by enlarging each in turn, beginning at the bottom.

You will find that the first two holes want a lot more enlarging than the third, but be careful

to keep a little on the " flat " side until you have got the scale exactly, for a " sharp " can only be correct by lugging and reboring, a difficult and not usually satisfactory process. When you come to the top complete the scale by closing all the holes and blowing a very little harder. You should get the second " DO " exactly an octave above the fundamental.

If the octave is not perfectly true in this way—due to irregularities of the tube, etc.,—you can get it by cutting another small hole in the back, where your left thumb comes. This hole is usual on the old recorders and may be found an advantage in any case. But try to keep down the number of holes, even if you have to practise a bit to blow your scale accurately and quickly.

Flutes generally have a seventh hole at " x " (Fig. 3), tuned a semitone between the two lowest notes. This is ordinarily covered by a key, but in a flute held as this one and in Recorders, which normally have this hole left open, it will be found that it is easy to accustom oneself to keep it closed with the little finger.

It is chiefly of use in playing in keys other than the normal scale of the flute and

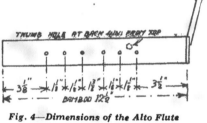

Fig. 4—Dimensions of the Alto Flute

the novice may very well do without it until he has attained some skill. If the extra low note keys are fitted later on it will then be necessary to have a key here too, for those keys also require the use of the little finger.

The golden rule at the outset is undoubtedly simplicity. Nothing could well be more simple or cheaper than the instrument as here described, and with it, without any addition of keys, you can do practically all that can be done with the most expensive and complex of the flute tribe, if you take the trouble to learn to play it properly.

PERFUME MAKING.
SOME USEFUL SUGGESTIONS.

PERFUMES, either in the form of attar or essential oil, may be made from flower petals, scented leaves, roots, and the peel of various fruits, by the process of distillation, enfleurage or maceration, the attar being obtained by the first method. All the processes are suitable for home manufacture, with inexpensive apparatus and very little trouble. Very few perfumes are made from the essential oil or attar alone, the usual practice being to add other perfumes to give greater strength. Suggestions are given below for making up several standard perfumes.

Distillation.

This process is used for obtaining the attar of flowers, etc., and essential oil, but it is only used for the strong perfumes and is not suitable for the more delicate scents. One of the simplest perfumes for the beginner is geranium, which is obtained from the leaves. A narrow mouth glass jam jar, or tin can, should be thoroughly cleaned and filled with a tightly fitting cork. A 3ft. or 4ft. length of piping, either copper, brass or iron, but preferably glass, should be provided. In addition, we shall need two small wide neck jars and an iron pot to place on the fire or gas ring. The tubing should be bent to the shape shown at Fig. 1 and one end tightly fitted through the cork of the large jar or tin. The latter receptacle should be filled with the leaves, and then some commercial alcohol or spirits of wine should be poured in to fill the jar to about one-third the height. The jar

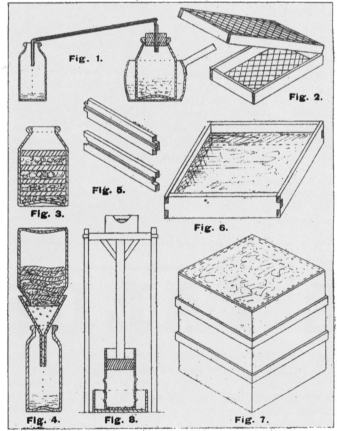

Fig. 1. Fig. 2. Fig. 3. Fig. 4. Fig. 5. Fig. 6. Fig. 7. Fig. 8.

is placed on the iron pot, previously half filled with water, and placed in the fire or gas ring. The small jars should be supported so that the tubing is not strained, and the end can rest inside, as shown in the illustration.

When the water begins to boil in the outer pot, the heat should be reduced to just enough flame to keep the water on the boil. In a few minutes the steam from the inner jar will rise and run along the tubing and condense on the tube, small drops of liquid being formed at the end of the tube, which will fall into the small jar. More perfect condensation can be effected by wrapping the tube in flannel and allowing cold water to drip continually on it. The small jar should be emptied into a glass stoppered bottle as the distillation goes on, in order to retain the full power of the perfume.

The attar so obtained may be made into a perfume by adding a few drops to an ounce of spirits of wine. Various other scented leaves as well as the petals of strongly scented flowers may be distilled in the same way.

The essential oil of flowers and leaves, and also of fruit rinds, may be made in the above manner, but instead of spirits of wine, water should be substituted. The steam will carry the oil along with it, and it will condense in minute globules on the surface of the water in the small jar. The essential oil should be skimmed off and placed in a glass stoppered bottle and used for mixing purposes, or as a perfume, by thoroughly shaking up a few drops in some alcohol or spirits of wine. Fresh orange or lemon peel placed in the large jar with water, and heated, up will give the essential oil of the peel, which will be very useful when used in combination with other oils.

Absorption may be carried out in two ways, one through the medium of pure vegetable oil and the other by means of best melted suet. The former process is quite a convenient one for the amateur, and is carried out as follows. First the flowers are gathered when fully matured and carefully dried inside a double wire covered hinged frame, as shown at Fig. 2. This should be done very quickly, either by holding the frame in front of a fan or by swinging it to and fro in the air. It is necessary to expel all moisture from the petals without them being faded. A wide neck jar should now be provided, together with some cotton wool and a bottle of best Olive or Lucca oil. The cheap oil is useless, as it is either a mineral, or at least an adulterated oil.

Next cut out a piece of cardboard to the inside diameter of the jar, and use it as a template for cutting out a number of circular pieces of cotton wool. Place the wool very carefully in a box or bag quite free from dust and then place them in the oil, which should be poured into a dish or soup plate. Now, having ascertained that the large jar is free from dust, in fact it must be scrupulously clean, sprinkle a little pure table salt on the bottom of the jar, lay a few petals on the salt to form an even layer, and then cover with one of the oil-soaked pieces of cotton wool. Next sprinkle a little more salt, another layer of petals, and cover with another piece of oil soaked wool, and continue this, pressing each layer down a little, until the jar is filled, as shown in section at Fig. 3. A grease-proof paper cover should be tied over the mouth of the jar, taking care that it is air-tight, and then the jar should be placed in a warm room near a window, so that it has sunlight whenever possible. A shelf in a sunny window, or near the top glass of a greenhouse, will be found the best position for the jars, for a warm and sunny position is essential if the full perfume is to be extracted from the petals, etc. If the conditions are quite favourable, a fortnight will be sufficient to draw out the full perfume, and at the end of this time the cover of the jars should be removed, the wool pressed down with a glass rod or pestle, and replaced with fine muslin. The jars should now be inverted, the oil drained off into a funnel leading to a glass stoppered jar, as indicated at Fig. 4. The oil in the bottle will be found to be very highly perfumed and the bottles, as soon as they are filled, should be tightly stoppered. If it is not intended to use the perfume for some time, the neck of the bottle should be coated with wax, paraffin wax is most suitable.

In preparing the perfume for use it should be diluted with pure spirits of wine or absolute alcohol, in the proportion of 3 parts of spirit to one of perfumed oil. The mixture requires to be thoroughly shaken for some time in order to break up the oil into small particles.

Another method

is to use the pure lard instead of oil in the following manner. First prepare a number of strips about 10ins. square and 3ins. deep with a groove in the centre, as shown at Fig. 5. Next fit the pieces together to form frames, with a sheet of glass in the grooves, as indicated at Fig. 6, nailing or screwing the corners. When a few of these frames have been prepared, spread a $\frac{1}{4}$in. thick layer of lard on each side of the glass.

Prepare the petals in the manner advised above, and when quite dry place them on the fat, fit a frame above and continue until the frames have been filled up, the bottom frame need be covered on one side only and the top covered with a sheet of glass. It is important to have the edges to fit neatly and advantageous to nail on fillets each side, as shown at Fig. 7. The petals should be left for a few days and then changed, the same kind of petal or leaf being replaced; the surface of the lard should be disturbed with a fork before each lot is renewed. The process may be continued for a month or so, and then the fat should be scraped off and kept in wide-necked jars, if not immediately proceeded with. The next operation is to make a press or to use some available form of exerting pressure to press out the oil. One method is to pierce the sides of a stout round tin from the inside and fit in a round piston or ram, support the ram in some suitable method, place the tin, which should of course be perfectly clean, in a large saucer or dish, and then place weights on the top of the ram. The method is illustrated at Fig. 8.

The fourth method, known as maceration, is to place the petals or leaves, as the case may be, in a double saucepan, together with a quantity of lard or pure fat. The pot should be kept boiling for some time, and the boiling point raised by adding salt to the water in the outer pot. Six hours or so after the boiling point is reached will generally be sufficient, and the resulting mixture of fat and leaves should be strained off, and when cool the fat may be placed under pressure, or it may be treated direct with alcohol. The latter method consists in cutting the fat in small pieces and leaving it in the spirit for some time, at least a few weeks. The liquid should be strained off into bottles, and will provide a strong perfume.

It will be seen that there are really three methods of obtaining perfumes, one by the use of distilling apparatus, another by means of oil, and the third by the use of pure fat. In the case of oil-produced perfumes, the scent is prepared by diluting with alcohol, and in the case of perfumed fat the perfumed oil may be extracted by pressure, or it may be placed in alcohol for infusion.

The maceration method is quite a usual one. The blending of perfumes is quite a fine art, and often by accident a maker will discover he has produced a new perfume. The usual method is to mix several essences together, but much may be done by mixing petals and aromatic leaves together.

A Gauze Hand-Screen.

ERY lovely and most varied effects are to be obtained by the mixture of gauze of two colours, whether for dress or for fancy knick-knacks. Pale pink and pale blue, pale green and pale blue, heliotrope and green, pale yellow and rose-colour, are but a very small number of the changes that may be rung when once the experiment is made. So fascinating is it to use

silks and gold thread. Very frequently some handsome scroll work having a lattice of gold and sprinklings of small gilt beads or spangles is twined in and out among the flowers. Amateur workers who are ambitious enough to try this elaborate embroidery will find that money is well spent in having it professionally traced, for as a rule, the best of home efforts do not produce designs that are bold enough to be effective. Upon some future occasion we shall hope to give a few details concerning the making of gauze flowers, but just now our attention must be directed to the making of a hand-screen. This is a pretty toy that is returning to popularity again, and the more daintily and gracefully it is made, the better. If gauze is employed, a spade-shaped foundation should be made of fairly stout wire, the centre being filled in rather tightly with stiff muslin, or net. Upon this foundation the gauze petals have to be sewn, in such a way that one round overlaps the next, beginning with the outside and finishing either in the centre, or at

HAND SCREEN.

two layers of chiffon, or gauze, that every worker who is able to manipulate these delicate materials can produce many lovely fancy knick-knacks.

For the trimming of evening dress skirts gauze work is in great favour. The flowers—and these lend themselves best to the purpose—are all made and, as it were, moulded in gauze. They are interspersed with delicately coloured leaves, such as are mounted with artificial flowers, the stems are embroidered in the ordinary way with

the base where the handle is attached. The handle itself may be bought from any kinder-garten depot—two are usually sold together—and it may be enamelled, or gilded, according to taste.

The flower-like covering of the screen itself is made up of a number of petal-shaped sections. Each of these should be cut square in shape, the two upper corners being rounded off and a slight dip made in the centre of the upper edge. Two.

pieces of gauze should be used together, say pale pink and dark red, the latter being put at the back. They must be lightly run together round the edges ; then turned inside out. Each petal, as it is made, should have the creases smoothed out with a moderately warm iron. Some pleats, or a row of gathering stitches, must be made at the base to draw the petal into shape. The whole of the stitchery must be executed as neatly as possible. A tuft of rather large artificial stamens makes a suitable finish for the centre, and they must be bent and coaxed about so as to completely conceal the centre of the screen where, naturally enough, there must be a few imperfections.

Another way of making such a screen is simpler, and does not involve nearly so much work. For this the gauze must be cut into a long strip about six inches wide. It should be folded in half, lengthwise and within the double layer of material should be laid another and a single strip of gauze of some other colour. A line of gathering is then made along the lower edge of the gauze strip, the stitches being taken through all three layers. After every four inches or so, a single overcast stitch is made completely over the whole width of the gauze. This draws up the strip to form a single petal. The material must be arranged a little, or it will set all in a heap instead of in the folds necessary to suggest, if not exactly to imitate, the petals of a flower.

After the gathering has thus been done, the strip must be sewn upon the stiff muslin foundation of the screen, beginning at the outer edge, beyond which the gauze must project about an inch or an inch and a half. Instead of carrying the strips round and round they may be sewn three parts of the way round, then turned and sewn to the opposite side, turned again, and so on until the whole blade has been covered. Some ribbon will be needed to complete the handle and to hide imperfections.

The back of the screen should be covered with a scrap of China silk, or with gauze, sewn on with very tiny and neat stitches. If a full and fluffy screen is desired, it is a good plan to trim the back in the same way as the front sewing both back and front petals on with the same set of stitches, which will make it all quite neat on both sides.

Persian Painting.

SOME very charming and distinct-looking boxes and chests have made their appearance of late in the shops of London and Paris. No artist, seeing them for the first time, would fail to be pleased with their gay effect or feel in wishing to emulate their foreign and bold designs. That the same idea has occurred to artists already is evident, and in the current number of *Home Art Work* we find a welcome description of these chests and some hints on the best method of imitating the manner in which they are decorated. From this we take the following extract, and we feel sure that those of our readers to whom this quarterly journal is no novelty, will with delight ransack their treasured copies for suitable designs : " Possibly to the oriental love of display, or to a survival of some old traditional method of painting, must be attributed the decoration of a delightfully quaint box, which, filled with dates, found its way from far Teheran to gay Lutetia. A rough box, just such a box as candles, soap, starch, and chocolate are packed in for grocers, but decorated, roughly, it is true, but with so free-handed a touch, and so liberally filled a brush, as to convert it into an object of considerable fascination for all, and they are many, who have a hankering for barbaric-looking odds and ends. Imagine, then, this box, with the historic Sassanian lion in company with a very diminutive camel, both in gold, disporting themselves amidst a pasture of red and orange coloured flowers with golden foliage upon a dark green ground, the design confined within a sharp oval, outlined with a broad band of vermilion, the corners filled in with gold upon which a few sweeping strokes of orange are grouped, and another broad band of vermilion round the edge of the box. The sides are decorated by borderings of gold and vermilion carried round each one, thus leaving in the centre a panel painted green, upon which a very rough design formed by five sweeps of the brush, laid on with gold, forms a conventional fleur-de-lys or honeysuckle pattern, this again, swept partly over with orange, and the base of each finished off by a blob of red. Now, the gold on the Persian box is leaf gold, too expensive a commodity for amateurs to dabble in with a lavish hand, so when, by kind permission of the owner, we made a reproduction of it, gold paint was substituted.

A few hints anent the painting may not be unwelcome to some of our readers who may be wishful to have useful boxes that they can keep tools, painting materials, and other odds and ends in, the boxes, of course, being obtainable, with a little mild persuasion, from any local grocer. In the first place, the surface of the wood must be rubbed down as smoothly as possible with sand and glass paper, and it should then, to prevent suction have one, or if very porous, two, coatings of Messrs. Tillyer's transparent Japanese lacquer. The design must then be sketched or traced on the top. If our readers happen to own some of Liberty's quaint Indian printed curtains or table covers, they will probably find there some excellent subjects ; if not, some of Mr. Vallance's quaint birds and beasts will come in very handy—admirable designs for this style of work will be found in Parts 59 and 82 of *Home Art Work.*—The next process is to fill in the green background ; after that to paint the vermilion and gold borders, then to paint the animals in gold and the coloured flowers. When all these are perfectly dry, the golden foliage can be painted on the green background, and sharp touches of crimson laid over the petals of the flowers, then the animals must be outlined, and have spots, or stripes; or other markings laid on the bodies with dark brown : finally, a few blobs of white and very pale blue must be added, these latter being introduced in and about the flowers and the foliage. The interior of the box may be lined with paper, or preferably coloured with red or yellow enamel thinned with turpentine, a little of which latter should be at hand whilst the painting is in progress. The outfit required merely consists of a small pot of Messrs Tillyer's bright gold, and one tinlet each of vermilion, dark green, blue, crimson, white, and dark brown, or, if the worker owns oil colours, these can be dispensed with, and in this case vermilion, green enamel, and the gold will be the only requisites, with, in addition, a bottle of Japanese lacquer, a most useful stopper for using when painting white wood.

THE LADIES' SPHERE

I CALL this article " A Cosey Cover," and not " A Cosey," because I propose to describe how an old cosey may be very satisfactorily restored with but a little patience and a piece of linen. My experience is, that one's cosey wears out on the *outside* long before the inside and I propose to describe how a simple cover can be made for it, and just tacked in place. Of course you can make it of anything you may have to hand, such as a piece of dark dress material, a piece of serge or cloth, satin, silk, sateen or even muslin, but I like a piece of coloured linen or canvas or crash. I have now tried HOBBIES colours on every kind of material, and find they are equally good on all—the only thing one must remember is, that if you are stencilling on a dark material you must use a little flake white if you wish the colours to show light against the material. There is another thing I will mention while writing of colours. When stencilling on coloured back grounds try all your colours first *on a piece of the material*, because you will often have alarming surprises if you do not ! Here is an instance, if you mix a pretty sage green (that is a yellow green), and you use it on a yellowish ground, you will find your green is nearly yellow because some of the yellow of the ground will show through your colour which is somewhat transparent and also the colour of the ground is sure to use its influence on the painted colour. So it follows that you must make a green which you wish to use on a yellowish ground much bluer than seems necessary in order to balance things. This rule applies equally to all colours, the ground is sure to show through (or mix itself with your colour), and to generally influence it. For an instance put

a pale heliotrope on pink and you will find you have pink instead of heliotrope. In this case more blue was required. Now to return to the cosey cover. Obtain half a yard of linen, I should choose a fairly dark green (I say dark because more serviceable), cut out the shape of your cosey in paper, pinning the paper to your cosey to make it quite correct, then cut out two pieces, leaving turnings beyond your pattern. I have measured two cosies I have, and find them both 15 in. wide, and 10 in. high. These two pieces you will stencil in the design I supply or any little sprays you may have by you. You might even use a border pattern like I gave some months ago for casement curtains ; just put it along the base of the cosey : I think this would be rather novel. Anyway I give a design which is made, as you see, to fit the shape. I have founded my design on the common dandelion, and I think it would work out very well indeed. If you copy it you can either square it up, covering it with squares to represent inches, that is, divide the base into 15 equal divisions and draw perpendicular lines through each division, then to complete, divide one of the perpendiculars in the same sized divisions as your base, and draw horizontals through them, then your design will be covered with squares, and all that remains is to draw inch squares on a sheet of paper, and copy the design in to it. I know all this is a bother and, of course, there is an easier way, viz., to use HOBBIES Pantograph, which saves heaps of work, and with it you can make your design any size, with only one drawing.

This is an easy design to cut, especially the leaves and you can obtain beautiful effects in shading, as all the leaves turn over.

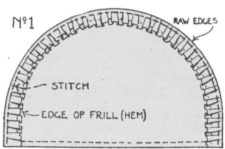

A STENCILLED TEA COSEY COVER.

By E. M. Barlow.   COST 1/-.

AS most smokers seem to appreciate a dainty smoking cap as a present, I am giving a design that will be found to have a very rich effect if the colours are carefully selected. Since tobacco and Turkey are so intimately connected, the design is appropriately adapted from a sixteenth century Turkish arabesque which at Constantinople honoured Mahommed, son of Solyman the Magnificent.

Use brown velvet for the cap, choosing a shade of warm grey brown corresponding with what would be obtained in pigments by mixing crimson lake, cobalt blue, and burnt umber—a pretty and a most becoming tint. As it is not advisable to trace much on velvet, I would suggest that the main lines only should be transferred, and that the correctness of the eye of the worker should be trusted to fill in the details in their proper relative positions. Of course, the border design for the upright portion of the cap must be repeated to stretch the required length, care being taken to

CROWN OF SMOKING CAP.

slate grey; all the parts shaded by cross hatching (crossed lines) are to be old gold; all the parts marked by dots are to be soft rose red. Use filosel or similar silk for working all the parts excepting the chocolate brown which should be twist silk.

Notice that the ground colour is left to blend with the grey in parts, and that the rose red is worked over the grey. It is this blending of the colours that gives half the charm to the finished design by the mingling of the threads preventing harshness. Rose-red piece silk or sarcenet would make a complimentary lining to the cap. There is a kind of traditional idea that a tassel should be used. This may be made by combining all the colours used in the embroidery. It can easily be home-made, the little wooden knob for the head of the tassel being procurable at any fancy-work shop. But if preferred, a ready-made tassel of old gold will serve. Of course, it should be attached to the centre of the crown.

UPRIGHT BAND OF EMBROIDERED SMOKING CAP.

make the joining fit the continuity of the curves.

I have indicated in the sketches the different colours to be used by differing lines. All the outlines and solid black patches are to be worked in chocolate brown; all the parts shaded by horizontal lines are to be light

This design may also be used on an ordinary Turkish fez; but as the ground colour then would be red, I would suggest that bright eastern green should be used as a substitute for the rose red that otherwise gives the pleasing touch of warmth to our pattern when used on the smoking cap.

Have you commenced work for the Stencilling Contest yet?   See Competition Page.

INTERESTING EXPERIMENTS WITH THE
MAGIC LANTERN.

THE use of a magic lantern is not confined to the exhibition of slides, and for many years the instrument has been used in colleges and schools for the purpose of showing certain electrical and chemical experiments upon a screen. The lantern is used more to-day for education purposes than it ever has been, and now that the cinematograph has come along it may in time find a place in all schools. Many interesting experiments, chiefly chemical, may be carried out with a standard lantern, but for the best work a proper demonstrating lantern as used in colleges is necessary. Such a lantern is in principle like ordinary magic lanterns, but it usually has an open stage—open between slide carrier and front lens—in which

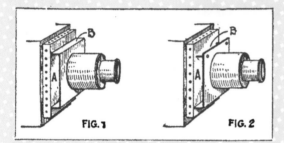

FIG. 1   FIG. 2

space objects more or less bulky can be placed and projected upon the screen. In ordinary lanterns the opening where the carrier or slides go in is, in most cases, barely an inch in width, so that the insertion of bulky objects in place of a slide is not possible. Demonstrating lanterns are very expensive, and as they are rarely used at home they need not be further discussed here. Lanterns of a type known as students' lanterns are a happy medium, and are specially made for taking a tank, an accessory described below. The feature of these lanterns is the open stage or place where the slide is put in. In the cheaper form of lanterns the place for the slide, against the condenser, shown at a, Fig 1, is covered with metal b, but in the better lanterns the top is open as at b, Fig. 2, the slides going in at a in the usual way. Obviously the latter pattern of front must be very strong and well supported, as it has to hold the heavy front lens and tube, and as there is no "brace" at the top two large screws are often employed, one at each top corner. The object of the open top is to allow one to drop or hang things before the condenser when it is not possible to push them through in the usual way. It is quite a simple matter for a handy man to make a new front and convert a lantern of Fig. 1 pattern into one of the Fig. 2 type, but there is no need whatever to do so if ordinary slides are always used.

The Tank.

Proper tanks for lantern experiments may be bought for about half-a-crown, but very good make-shift troughs may be made at home. The idea is to have a narrow tank of water or other liquid in place of the slide, and whatever happens in the tank will of course be projected upon the screen, but upside down. Precipitates and objects falling to the bottom of the tank will go upwards on the screen, while bubbles going upwards in the tank will travel from top to bottom of the screen. Water beetles, fleas, and other insects may also be put in the tank and their movements watched upon the screen.

As many workers will prefer to make their own tanks, we give three patterns of useful home-made accessories. Fig. 3 consists of two pieces of plain glass, a and b, cut to fit the slide stage, no carrier being required. Between the glasses is placed a piece of rubber pipe about ½in. in diameter, c, and bent as shown. The glasses are held together, pressing the pipe between, by means of strong elastic bands, d d, at the ends; if the bands are strong the U-shaped part will hold water. The advantage of this pattern is that the tank may be made to come outside the carrier stage by lengthening the glasses and broadening the curve of the rubber pipe, it is therefore suitable for lanterns with closed-in stages. A more permanent form is shown in Fig. 4; it is made by cementing three narrow strips of glass, c, c and d, between two plain glasses, a and b, of the required size. Fig. 5 is a pattern of the size and shape of an ordinary slide, and made to

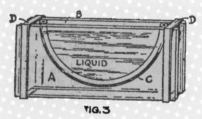

FIG. 3

go in the usual slide carrier. It is made by taking a piece of glass 3¼in. square, a, and cementing thereon a piece of very thin glass, d, at the base, 3¼ by ¼in., and two pieces, b and c, at the sides, 3 by ¼in., another piece of glass exactly like a is then cemented over the pieces, when the part e will form a tank. Canada balsam or marine glue is used as a cement, the former preferred. The balsam and the glasses are warmed and the cement applied by means of a stick, the glasses are then put under pressure to dry. The type of tank selected will depend upon the work to be done, we are rather in favour of Fig. 3 as it has no troublesome inside corners, and is easy to clean.

Most of the bought tanks are U-shaped inside in order to facilitate cleaning.

Chemical Changes.

All students of chemistry will know of many solutions which will give pretty and changing colours, as school chemistry books contain many. We, however, will give a few. In cases where one chemical is to be added to another it is advisable to use a pipette or a clean fountain pen filler, and to add the solution to the centre of the surface of the solution.

(1) Fill the tank with a solution of sulphate of iron and add a solution of gallic acid. Black clouds will be formed, such clouds being ink, as this experiment shows how ink is made.

FIG. 5

(2) A solution of ferricyanide of potash added to a solution of ferric chloride produces a blue and shows how Prussian blue is made.

(3) The production of carbonic acid gas can be shown by filling the tank with a very weak solution of hydrochloric acid and dropping in a small piece of chalk, which causes bubbles of gas to appear.

FIG. 4

(4) To show how carbonic acid is given off from the lungs in the act of breathing, fill the tank with lime water, and by means of a glass tube blow into it with the mouth, when the solution will become cloudy, in consequence of the formation of carbonate of lime.

(5) The formation of bubbles of hydrogen gas may be shown by filling the tank with a solution of very weak sulphuric acid, and then dropping into the tank a small piece of zinc. The metal will begin to dissolve, with evolution of gas.

(6) Fill the tank with a solution of litmus, which will show blue on the screen, add a weak solution of any acid, when the solution will turn red. Then add to the red solution some weak ammonia or soda, when it will turn blue again. A solution made from purple cabbage leaves will act in the same way. The cabbage solution is made by slicing a little of the vegetable and pouring boiling water upon it and allowing to stand.

(7) Another experiment with the cabbage water is to fill the tank with the same, and to add a few drops of a solution of alum which will turn it a pretty purple, while a drop or two of potash solution will turn it green, and weak hydrochloric acid, crimson.

(8) To show the presence of certain salts in hard water fill the tank with the latter and suspend in it a crystal of oxalic acid. Long opaque threads of oxalate of lime will be given off until the water becomes quite opaque.

(9) Fill the trough with a solution of copper sulphate and add a little of a solution of potassium ferrocyanide, the blue solution will change to a reddish brown.

(10) Fill the trough with the same copper solution as used for the above experiment and add weak ammonia, the solution will change from blue to green, precipitating a cloudy grey, if more ammonia is added the precipitate will dissolve and the water will become a sky blue.

Other experiments consist of adding ice, wine and ink to the tank of water, when curious effects of mixing will be seen. The tank may also be put in the lantern empty and dry, and strong solutions of sodas and other chemicals dropped or squirted in very small quantities upon the side of the tank, as the glass becomes heated the water will evaporate and leave pretty crystal-like formations upon the glass. A solution of sal-ammoniac as used for electric bell batteries gives excellent crystals, as also does sulphate of soda (Glauber's salt) and oxalic acid. Bubbles can also be blown into the tank, and when a mixture of equal parts of glycerine and a solution of common soap in water (½oz. of soap to one pint of water) is used the shapes are very interesting, and prismatic colours may be seen. Space does not permit us to describe any more experiments in detail, but many other solutions and uses for the tank will occur to the reader.

The solutions named above must not be too strong. About one ounce of the solid chemical or liquid acid named mixed with eight to sixteen ounces of water will serve in most cases. All the chemicals are cheap, and should the chemist be told what they are wanted for, he will mix up the right quantities for a few pence, and perhaps suggest other chemical experiments.

SOME WINES WITH A SPARKLE

CHAMPAGNE was originally made in the French province bearing that name, but now many other countries produce an excellent type of the wine. It is one of the best known of all wines and is highly prized by the connoisseur.

Genuine champagne is made by a process of double fermentation. First a dry wine is made from red grapes, then sugar is added and the mixture put into strong bottles, the corks wired in and the wine allowed to ferment in the bottle.

The home wine maker need not go to all this trouble, and it is possible to make excellent kinds of champagne quite easily. In many cases the wine is bottled before fermentation is complete, or in other words the fermentation has been arrested.

Most of the flower wine recipes will produce quite good 'champagne', but almost any kind of wine, especially the fruit types, can be used for this purpose. The most important thing to remember is to have good strong bottles, and the best kind are those having hollow bottoms. Never use square bottles as these will soon be blown to pieces by the great pressure exerted by the fermenting process.

Good sound corks are also essential and these must be wired to the bottle neck. String in most cases will snap under the great strain and it needs a well-wired-on cork to keep the contents secure. The illustrations below show the best way to attach the wire to the bottle neck.

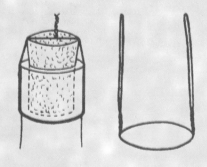

Elderflower champagne is one of the easiest wines of its kind to make and will be a good one to start off with.

Elderflower champagne
4 large heads of elderflower
1 gal. water
2 tablespoons white-wine vinegar
1 lemon
1½ lb. sugar

Best results are obtained if the elderflowers are picked on a sunny day when they are in full bloom. Cut off the small flowers with their tiny stems and put them in a bowl together with the juice and thinly peeled rind of the lemon. Add the white-wine vinegar and the sugar and pour on a gallon of cold water.

Allow this to steep for 24 hours, stirring it as much as you can during that time. Then strain and put into strong bottles, filling them as full as possible and wire down the corks. Lay the bottles on their sides. This keeps the corks wet and prevents the escape of any gas.

It should be ready to drink in about two weeks and when the bottles are opened it should be very effervescent. Like all champagnes once the bottle has been opened it should be drunk as soon as possible. Any left over can be put into a smaller bottle so that the smallest amount of air comes into contact with the liquid.

Apple champagne
7 lb. apples
½ lb. sultanas
¼ lb. barley
3½ lb. brown sugar
1 gal. water

Remove the cores but do not peel the apples, and cut into small pieces. Put into a bowl together with the sultanas and barley and pour on a gallon of cold water. Squeeze the apples each day for about 14 days and stir whenever possible. After this, strain, add the sugar and see that it is thoroughly dissolved before putting into bottles and allowing to ferment for 14 days. This wine does not mature so quickly as the last recipe, but should be ready to drink in about 6 months.

Most recipes for apple wine can be made sparkling by bottling before fermentation has ceased, and this applies also to many other fruit wines of a similar character. The time to bottle up will of course vary with each particular kind and in most cases will be found by experiment. If you can arrange to have several bottles of a particular wine it is a good idea to cork them up at different times and note exactly the results. You can cork them up at intervals of, say, 2 days.

Greengage champagne
3½ lb. greengages
1 gal. water
3½ lb. sugar
16 vine leaves
1 oz. yeast

Cut the greengages in half, place them with the vine leaves in a bowl and pour on a gallon of cold water. After 3 days remove the vine leaves and let the greengages remain for another 7 days with periodical stirring.

Now strain through butter muslin, add the sugar and yeast and allow to ferment for 12 days. The yeast should be mixed with a little of the liquid warmed to a temperature of 98°F. before adding it to the wine. Bottle up and wire the corks as mentioned previously.

Cottage cider champagne
3 lb. apples
1 gal. water
2 lb. sugar
1 oz. root ginger
12 cloves

½ teaspoonful cinnamon
½ oz. yeast

This recipe is a great favourite with many country wine makers and is sometimes called Cottage Cider. In fact many kinds of cider are very similar to champagne.

After well washing the apples grate them into a bowl, add the yeast and cold water and allow them to steep in a warm temperature for 7 days. Keep the bowl covered with a thick cloth and stir the contents several times each day.

Strain through muslin, add the ginger which has been well bruised with a hammer, the cloves, cinnamon and sugar. Stir until thoroughly dissolved and leave for 24 hours. Then strain again, put into bottles and wire the corks.

As for all the other kinds of champagne the bottles should be filled as full as possible. This wine will be fit to drink in about 2 weeks.

The same recipe can be used with pears instead of apples, and in some cases this will turn out to be more sparkling and effervescent. Some of the spices may be left out altogether or their quantity reduced.

Gooseberry champagne
3½ lb. gooseberries
1 gal. water
3½ lb. sugar
1 lb. sultanas
½ lb. barley
½ oz. yeast

Many country wine makers consider that gooseberries will make the finest 'mock champagne'. The best is made with green gooseberries and these should be gently boiled with the sultanas and barley in all the water for about 30 minutes. Strain through muslin and add the sugar. See that the sugar is thoroughly dissolved and while still warm (about 98°F.) add the yeast.

Let this ferment for 7 days, then bottle up and well cork. It matures fairly quickly and can be drunk in a month. It does however improve greatly with keeping and like many genuine champagnes is excellent after from 12 to 15 years. Some, indeed, may be kept and drunk with relish after even much longer periods.

Prune champagne
3½ lb. rhubarb
2 lb. prunes
4 lb. sugar
1 gal. water
½ oz. yeast

Rhubarb, like gooseberries can make a good champagne and when allied with prunes produces a stronger and more agreeable wine. Cut up both rhubarb and the prunes into small pieces and put them into a bowl and fill up with cold water. Well stir each day for 10 days, keeping it covered with a thick cloth. After straining add the sugar and yeast and allow to ferment for 10 days. Bottle and cork up as for the previous recipes.

TREE WINES

TREES can play an important part in the manufacture of home-made wines. To many of us, it is not looked upon as a suitable subject for our experiments in wine making but there are a large number of splendid drinks that can be produced from the various parts of trees, including the leaves, buds, flowers and even the sap.

Oak leaf wine is probably the best known, and there are two distinct types. One is made in the spring from young leaves while the other makes use of the old leaves just before they fall in the autumn.

By A. F. Taylor

The young leaves picked in the spring when the tree is bursting with activity is considered to produce a better brew than the more mature crop that is ready in the autumn, but that is a matter of personal opinion. Try both recipes and see which you like best.

Oak Leaf Wine (Spring)

Some people recommend picking the leaves just as they have opened in the spring while others name the last week in June or the first week in July as being the best time.

1 gal. Oak Leaves
4 lb. Sugar
2 Oranges
2 Lemons
1 gal. Water
½ oz. Yeast

Remove the dust from the leaves by washing well in cold water. Cut the peel from the lemons and oranges so as not to include any of the white pith, which will make it bitter, and add to the leaves. Pour over this a gallon of boiling water and allow to steep for a day. Then bring to the boil and simmer for about a quarter of an hour. Strain through butter muslin, stir in the sugar until dissolved and add the juice of the lemons and oranges.

When the temperature has fallen to blood heat (98°F) add the yeast, which has previously been dissolved in a little of the liquid. Let this ferment until the gas bubbles have practically ceased, then strain without disturbing the sediment and put into bottles, corking lightly at first.

Young oak buds may be mixed with the young leaves as a slight variation of the above recipe.

Oak Leaf Wine (Autumn)

1 gal. Oak Leaves
3 Oranges
¼ oz. whole Ginger
4 lb. Sugar
1 gal. Water
½ oz. Yeast

Pick the leaves in late September or early October when they are beginning to turn yellow. They will need washing well in cold water. Put the leaves in an earthenware jar, pour over them the boiling water and allow to stand for three days before straining through butter muslin. Well bruise the whole ginger by hammering it and put this with the grated rind of the oranges, their juice and the sugar and boil gently for half an hour. Add the yeast when the liquid has cooled to blood heat, ferment for fourteen days and bottle as in the previous recipe.

Walnut Leaf Wine

Perhaps not so well known, this is quite good and easy to make.

1 large handful Walnut
    Leaves
1 lb. Raisins
3 lb. Sugar
1 gal. Water
½ oz. Yeast

After rinsing the leaves in cold water put them in a bowl or earthenware jar, pour on the boiling water and leave to soak for twenty-four hours. Then strain, add the sugar and stir until dissolved. Chop up the raisins and add these to the mixture, then add the yeast and leave to ferment for 21 days. Bottle up as usual and store in a cool place.

Lime Wine

One of the joys of a walk through the countryside in early summer is the scent of lime trees in full flower, and the wine made from them is equally delightful. The flowers are pulled from the tree when they are fully open and preferably on a sunny day. They are then dried in the sun for a few days, which is supposed to bring out the flavour to the full.

1 pint Lime Flowers
¾ lb. Raisins
3½ lb. Sugar
1 gal. Water
½ oz. Yeast

The flowers are first put into a saucepan with the water, brought to the boil and then allowed to simmer for thirty minutes. Strain, add the raisins chopped up into small pieces together with the sugar, and when the temperature has fallen to blood heat (98°F) mix in the yeast.

Let this ferment for fourteen days, then bottle up in the usual manner.

Birch Sap Wine

This is a wine that has been made for centuries in the Scandinavian countries.

1 gal. Birch Sap
1 Orange
1 Lemon
3 lb. Sugar
½ oz. Ginger
½ oz. Yeast

A little care is needed when gathering the sap so as not to damage the tree in any way. A gallon is a good allowance to expect from one tree, and it may take a week or two to gather this amount. March is the correct time to gather the sap and it is best done when the weather is cold.

First drill a small hole (about ¼ in. diameter) in the trunk of the tree about 15 in. from ground level. The depth of the hole should be from 1 in. to 1½ in. according to the size of the tree trunk. A tube is then inserted in the hole and this can be glass or a hollow wood stick such as a piece of elder stem with the pith extracted. Do not use a metal tube because it is liable to affect the flavour of the resulting wine.

The sap is allowed to drip into a glass or earthenware bowl (not metal) and boiled each day until you have collected enough for your requirements. Put this into a bottle and cork up tightly.

The wine is made by first thinly cutting off the peel from the orange and lemon, then boiling it gently in the sap and the crushed ginger for about half an hour. Any liquid lost by evaporation is made good by adding water. While still hot dissolve the sugar and then add the yeast when it has cooled to 98°F. Allow to ferment in a warm temperature until most of the gas bubbles have ceased to rise to the surface. Strain through muslin, put into bottles and cork up.

Carefully decant after three months without disturbing the sediment, and cork tightly. Sometimes the corks are wired down and the bottles stored on their sides until ready to sample after at least six months.

This last recipe can be varied by adding ½ lb. raisins and leaving out the ginger, or you can use two lemons instead of the orange and lemon. Using the same recipe, you can substitute either walnut or sycamore for the birch sap.

You may also like to try peach leaf wine. Although not classed as a tree, a very good wine is made from grape vine leaves.

Sweets for Special Occasions

NO party would be complete without a dish of sweets and when these are home-made the pleasure is even greater.

Let's start off with sweets that can be made without cooking any of the ingredients.

Orange dreams

> 1 lb. icing sugar
> 2 teaspoonfuls lemon juice
> 2 tablespoonfuls orange juice
> 1 egg white
> grated rind of 1 orange
> angelica and orange colour

Thinly grate the rind of the orange and mix it with the orange and lemon juices. Pass the icing sugar through a fine sieve and add the juice and rind together with just enough of the egg white to form a firm mixture. Add the liquid gradually to the sugar and thoroughly mix, but be careful not to add too much and make it sticky.

While mixing the ingredients add a few drops of orange colouring and see that it is evenly distributed throughout the whole mass. Mould into small balls and put a small piece of angelica in each to represent a stalk. Allow at least 24 hours for the sweets to set.

Chocolate crispies

> 2 oz. bar plain chocolate
> 1 tablespoonful (heaped) cereal

Break up the chocolate into small pieces and put them in a small basin. Stand this in a saucepan of hot water and stir until the chocolate is melted. The water should not boil and a temperature of about 100° is usually sufficient.

Take the basin out of the saucepan and stir in the cereal. Before it cools too much spoon out on to a sheet of waxed paper in small rounds and allow to set till next day. There are many varieties of cereal which are suitable. Desiccated cocoanut and chopped up nuts can also be tried.

Chocolate truffles

> 2 oz. butter
> 2 oz. icing sugar
> 2 egg yolks
> 3 teaspoonfuls milk
> 4 oz. powdered chocolate or cocoa
> coffee essence

Well beat the egg yolks, then cream the butter and mix these with the other ingredients. It is necessary to stir thoroughly until it forms a thick creamy texture. The coffee essence is added according to taste but the flavouring should not be overdone.

Shape the mixture into balls or small pyramids and roll in some of the chocolate powder. Lay aside until next day to set in a cool room.

Now let us have a look at some recipes which need cooking. Fondant forms the basis of so many sweets, and when you can make a good batch of fondant you have solved a lot of sweet problems.

De luxe satin fondant

> 1¼ lb. granulated sugar
> ½ pint cream
> 1½ teaspoonfuls glycerine
> ½ teaspoonful vanilla essence
> pinch salt

It is very important that a large saucepan is used for this fondant, and one that is three times the size of the batch will not be too large. With the exception of the vanilla all the ingredients are placed in the saucepan and boiled over a medium heat.

Unlike the usual method of making fondant this mixture must be stirred all the time, but it should be done gently. When the temperature of 238° is reached remove the saucepan from the stove and leave it undisturbed for a few minutes. Pour out on to a large meat dish which has been damped with cold water and allow to become lukewarm, then cream in the following way.

With the aid of a spatula keep turning the edges of the batch into the centre until it appears cloudy and then finally sets in a lump of firm white cream. The vanilla essence is gradually added to the batch as the creaming process is carried out. Cover with a damp cloth and leave for an hour or so to mellow, after which it should be kneaded with the hands until it becomes soft and creamy. Store in a stone jar covered with a damp cloth or piece of waxed paper until needed.

Bonbons

A bonbon is a confection that has a fondant centre and an outside coating of a slightly harder fondant. The centre can be plain fondant flavoured and coloured in various ways or it may contain nuts and fruit. Here are a few suggestions you may like to try.

The nuts or fruit are usually cut into small pieces and well mixed into the fondant. Most kinds of nuts can be used, such as almonds, brazils, walnuts and desiccated cocoanut, or you may like to try whole pea nuts, either plain or salted.

The fruits may be dates, cherries, figs, raisins, pineapple and crystallized ginger all chopped up into small pieces. It is a good idea to use both fruit and nuts in the same bonbon, and there are endless varieties for you to experiment with.

The nuts and fruit can be mixed in the fondant in bulk or it may be moulded into small balls or pyramids and then added as the shaping proceeds. Place the bonbons on waxed paper and leave until next day to set firm.

If they are not needed at once it is advisable to dip the bonbons in a fondant that has been boiled to 245°. After it has been creamed and allowed to mellow place in a basin and stand in hot water to melt it. Then dip each bonbon and place on waxed paper to set.

The tops of the bonbons may be decorated with pieces of nut or fruit and these have to be put on before the dipped bonbon has had time to set.

Chocolates

The production of chocolates is a most fascinating part of sweet making. Some amount of care is needed however in their preparation.

Firstly the room should have a temperature of 65° and they should be hardened off in slightly lower conditions. The chocolate used for coating must never be melted over direct heat, but should be put into a large basin; this is stood in water having a temperature of about 110°. The temperature of the actual chocolate during the dipping process should be between 86° and 88°, according to the type of covering used.

Either chocolate couverture or plain bar chocolate is grated into a basin placed over hot water to speed up the melting and when the correct temperature is reached the sweets can be dipped into the mixture. Each sweet in turn is dropped into the basin and immediately removed with a two prong wire fork. Scrape off the superfluous chocolate on the edge of the basin and place on waxed paper to harden.

Almost any type of centre is suitable for covering with chocolate and can include plain and nut fondant, fudge, nougat, caramel, marzipan, turkish delight and many others.

Decorating the top of the chocolate after it has been dipped can take many forms. Whirls made with the dipping fork or pieces of nuts and crystallized cherries and ginger are some of the many types available.

Chocolates that are dipped at too high a temperature will be dull and not glossy. Too much heat also produces a spotted or grey coating. Damp or foggy weather are not good conditions for chocolate making and the centres should be perfectly dry before dipping.

(A.F.T.)

USEFUL DOMESTIC RECIPES

WHILE the initial outlay on materials to make a particular household product is often more than is needed to buy one lot of the ready-made product, the eventual saving of money is usually so great as to make the first expenditure well worth while. Once you have the materials you can make several lots without further outlay. In addition, you will have had all the pleasure of making them.

In the following formulas all ingredients which will be used on the skin should be pure. To ensure this, ask your chemist for B.P. or B.P.C. grade; where these are not available buy 'pure laboratory grade'.

Vapour Rub

When colds are about, the use of an aromatic antiseptic salve is much to be recommended. Normally, these are used solely for relieving chesty symptoms. Far more important is to use them as a preventive. Quite a lot of colds can be dodged by the simple method of pushing a little of the salve up each nostril two or three times a day, but especially at night.

An excellent salve can be made by first melting in a water-bath 128 grams of petroleum jelly and 8 grams of paraffin wax. When the liquid is clear, add 4 grams of menthol crystals and stir until dissolved. Remove the vessel from the bath. When it has cooled somewhat, add 16 c.c. of oil of eucalyptus, 1 c.c. oil of cassia, 4 c.c. oil of turpentine (NOT turpentine substitute) and 1 gram of phenol. Stir well to incorporate the whole. Pour into tins or warmed jars when the mixture begins to grow slightly thick.

Smelling Salts

These are always a useful item to have at hand. Recipes vary. The simplest and cheapest consist of ammonium carbonate, 3¾ ounces, and ammonium hydroxide (specific gravity 0·88), 1 fluid drachm (roughly 1 teaspoonful). Simply pour the ammonium hydroxide on to the carbonate.

A more elegant preparation is made by pouring 3 c.c. of ammonium hydroxide over 90 grams of ammonium carbonate. Next mix by grinding in a small evaporating basin 1 gram each of phenol and menthol, 2 grams of camphor, and 1 c.c. each of oil of eucalyptus, oil of pumilio pine and isopropyl alcohol. Add this to the first mixture.

Smelling salts should not be kept in corked jars, since the ammonia fumes affect the cork. Glass or rubber stoppered jars should be used.

Menthol Sticks

Headaches arising from eyestrain or other simple causes can often be relieved with a simply made menthol stick. Enough for several will result from melting together in a small evaporating basin on a water-bath, 7 grams of stearic acid and 3 grams of menthol The liquid must then be poured into moulds to set.

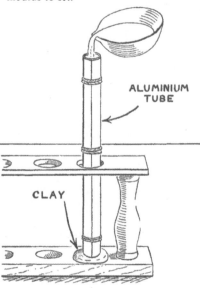

Moulding menthol sticks

A simple mould is shown in the diagram. It consists of a length of aluminium tubing of about ⅜in. internal bore. This has been cut in half down its length and the edges ground so that they meet flush when put together. Rubber bands doubled tightly round the halves hold it together. To stop the liquid running out at the bottom, the end of the mould is pressed into a disc of modelling clay.

When the mould has grown cold, open the halves and carefully remove the stick. Any difficulty experienced while doing this can be remedied by running a gas flame along the mould — just long enough to cause the surface of the stick to soften. Cut up the stick into the usual sized lengths, half wrap them in silver paper and then wholly in Cellophane.

Drain Disinfectant

Mix together 1¼ pounds of quicklime (not slacked lime), ½ pound of bleaching powder (chloride of lime) and ¼ pound of technical grade potassium carbonate. This should be kept in a well closed jar. When required for use, sprinkle it liberally over the drain grid, allowing some to fall into the water below. Any 'drainy' smell formerly present will vanish.

This preparation is also excellent for cesspools. Sprinkle liberally. The sewage will gradually liquify and be deodorised.

Metal Polish

A polish for brass and similar metals which is quick and easy to make contains 1¼ pints of turpentine substitute, 1 teaspoon of oleic acid and ½ pound of whiting. Run the whiting into a large bottle, add the turpentine substitute and the oleic acid and shake well. This product is inflammable, as are most common metal polishes. Shake before use and allow the film to dry out on the metal before buffing up.

Silvering Brassware

If you wish to plate a piece of brassware or touch up a silver-plated cruet on which the brass is showing through, there is an easy way to do this. No electricity is needed. Grind separately to fine powder, 15 parts of table salt, 7 parts of silver nitrate and 6 parts of cream of tartar. Add these ingredients to 50 parts of whiting. All parts are by weight. Grind the whole thoroughly, pour out on to paper and roll it backward and forward to form an intimate mixture.

To use this preparation, first degrease the metal by brushing with a warm solution of a household detergent. Rinse well and allow to dry. Mix some of the silvering powder to a sludge with water and brush on to the metal. After a few moments, rub up with a rag moistened with the sludge, then with clean rag. The deposit is not so thick as one obtained by electroplating, but is pretty durable.

Furniture Brightener

Wood furniture which has acquired a dull look over the years can be effectively brightened by an occasional rub over with a simply made and cheap preparation. It consists of equal volumes of salad oil, vinegar and kerosene (burning paraffin). Shake the bottle vigorously immediately before use, so as to disperse the contents through each other. Take up a little on a rag and rub lightly over the furniture, replenishing as you go along. Then polish with a soft cloth.

Carved, turned or other intricately worked wood furniture which has grown dull cannot easily be toned up with the former preparation. A brushing polish is needed. To make one, pour ½ pint of methylated spirit into a dry bottle. Add 3 ounces of shellac and 1 ounce of rosin. A screw-top bottle is advised, since a cork may set fast. Let the mixture stand, with occasional shaking, until the solids have dissolved.

Brush out the crevices of the wood and then apply a thin coat of the reviver with a fine hair brush. Other coats may be given, but let each harden thoroughly before applying another. Wash the brush, after use, with methylated spirit.

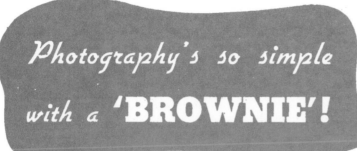

CARNIVALS.

URING the summer months the spirit of carnival is with us, and thousands in the country make it a delightful hobby in regard to get up and fancy dress. Whilst the many displays of characters,

BINGLEY CARNIVAL.
THE DEVIL STOPS TO HAVE A COOLER.

etc., representing the seasons of the year, League of Nations, industrial subjects, etc., are quite of an educational nature, the spirit of carnival seems to be most amused with the various comic characters which are about.

Development.

These modern carnivals, at any rate in England, have now developed from the villages to the towns and cities, and have become quite business propositions; those at Blackpool and Morecambe, in Lancashire, can be cited as examples. Not only that, from the carnival we have got shopping weeks and special displays, where the policy is to sound the business drum for publicity.
Continental carnivals, such as the one at Nice, are world known, and years are spent in getting special displays of an original nature. The Lord Mayor's Show, in London, can truly be said to be a carnival of its type, and of a fascinating educational nature, and it is questionable if the average Londoner sees in it the great value it is to their children, and also providing a big revenue of business in the preparation.

Aim at Originality.

If is often said there is nothing original, but if not exactly so, there is always something in the "get-a-way" which is not exactly a copy, but a something which appeals to the public taste of sense and humour.

The things which appeal most are the contrasty ones, like the young policeman in the illustration. The thing is so striking from the fact that the policeman is in proportion in every way like a real one.

Tom Thumb, the one-time American midget, was made to appear a lot smaller than he really was, from the fact that the showmen used to place him next to a giant, the result being very convincing that one was exceedingly tall, whilst the other was very small. Now in regard to dresses for comics or otherwise, it is not sufficient just to dress. Thought must be given to it. As a case in point, a person carrying an umbrella representing "It's not going to rain any more" would hardly be effective with the cover intact, but let it be torn with the wires broke, and you begin to attract attention.

There is a lot of truth in the fact that it takes a wise man to be a fool, and it especially applies to the "comic get-ups" at the carnivals.

Finally, there is a great humanitarian feeling in most of these carnivals, and that is, they are held usually for some charitable object to help those who cannot help themselves. What could be greater?

THE TALLEST AND SMALLEST IN THE CARNIVAL—
6FT. 7IN. MEETS 2FT. 6INS.

Fred is the Life of the Party . . . !

Folk gather round you when you can play a Uke or Mandolin. You are the life of the party. If you take your Tube-o-Phone along as well, you are certain to be the 'star-turn' of the evening ! No need to worry about expense—any fellow handy with tools can make his own instruments. Hobbies show you how to make them and how to play them ! Get started NOW.

Hobbies Designs tell you all you want to know about the construction.

We also supply a One-String Fiddle design. Write for details.

UKULELE

The design (No. 1825) costs only **4d**. The wood for all parts is **2/9**; postage **6d.**, whilst the set of strings and pegs costs a further **1/6**; postage **2d**. A complete parcel **5/-**, post free.

MANDOLIN

This beautiful instrument is worth anything from **25/-** to **30/-** when completed. The design is No. 1883 and costs **4d**. The wood, including a specially shaped neck is **4/-**, postage **6d**. The complete set of strings, keys, plectrum, etc., costs a further **3/6**, postage **3d**. A complete parcel, **8/4**, post free.

UKULELE

Design 156 special, **6d**. Wood for all parts, **2/-**, postage **6d**. Strings and pegs, **1/6**, postage **2d**. A complete parcel, **4/6**, post free.

TUBE-O-PHONE

Hundreds of home woodworkers have made this delightful instrument. It is a sure winner at any party. Not so easy to make as a Uke, but not at all difficult if you follow the simple instructions. The design (No. 183 special) costs **6d**. Selected oak for all parts, including turned legs, **11/6**; postage **1/-**. The special tubes, transfers for marking the various note positions, two beaters and a pair of hinges, **18/6** postage **6d**.

HOBBIES LIMITED, DEREHAM, NORFOLK.

There's a Hobbies Branch or Agent in most Cities and Towns.

Printed by BALDING & MANSELL, London and Wisbech, and Published for the Proprietors, HOBBIES LTD. by HORACE MARSHALL & SON LTD., Temple House, Tallis Street, E.C.4. Sole Agents for Australia and New Zealand : Gordon & Gotch (A'sia) Ltd. For South Africa : Central News Agency Ltd. Registered for Transmission by Canadian Magazine Post.

54 Miles an hour
for 24 hours *(consecutive)*

At the Montlhery Track, near Paris, last month, a Rudge-Whitworth Motor Cycle ridden alternately by Lieut.-Colonel R. N. Stewart and Mrs. G. M. Stewart, created a 24 hours world's Motor Cycle Record.

A WORLD'S RECORD.

1,300 miles covered in 24 consecutive hours.

Average speed 54 m.p.h.

21 World's Records captured.
(Subject to Official Confirmation.)

That this record has been established with a machine of only 3.46 h.p. will be sufficient indication of the value of four valves—and the built-for-long-service design of the Rudge-Whitworth Machine.

Rudge-Whitworth
FOUR VALVE *FOUR* SPEED

Rudge-Whitworth Ltd., Coventry.
LONDON - - - 230, Tottenham Court Rd., W.1.
MANCHESTER - - - - - 192, Deansgate.

EXPLOSION & DISASTER AS AN ADVERTISEMENT

The recent volcanic disasters have caused an enormous demand for St. Pierre stamps. We now offer as an advertisement a set of two St. Pierre stamps, free of charge to anybody sending 1d. for postage and promising to distribute three of our lists. Only one set given to each person. Don't miss this opportunity, these stamps will become scarce. Ask to see our noted approval sheets.

Illustrated Lists Free.   Best Value.   We invite comparison.

ERNEST WOOD & CO.
CHORLTON-CUM-HARDY, MANCHESTER.

HYPODERMIC SYRINGES

Are ideal for oiling that inaccessible spot. Treatment of Woodworm. And a variety of uses where you want to inject a liquid into a confined space.

Size 5cc Glass syringe, Metal nozzle, only 5/6d. each post free. Size 2cc ditto, 4/- each.

STAINLESS STEEL NEEDLES to fit above, 4d. each.

Solid metal surgeon's scalpel is ideal for dissecting, Woodwork etc., 4/- each post 3d.

H. BLOOM, Dept. H, Upper Street
London, N.1

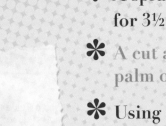
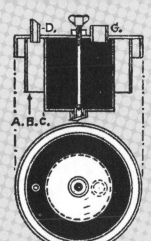

DANGEROUS PURSUITS

Home-made Fireworks

* A sprained knee for 3½ years!

* A cut artery in the palm of the hand

* Using an underwater spear

Build and Fly "Hobbies" Model Airship!

By Fredk. Jace

THE making and flying of model aeroplanes is an established hobby, with thousands of enthusiastic supporters. It is now possible in our fields and meadows to reproduce in miniature (even including crashes!) the performances of full-size machines. It is an odd fact that very few have tackled the construction of a model airship.

The building and flying of model airships is every bit as fascinating as model aeroplaning. Model airships are not difficult to make, they are not expensive, and one can carry out quite a number of interesting little experiments, such as bomb-dropping—the bombs being small and light devices sold by most shops who retail fireworks. A model airship, too, does not descend when the propeller has run out, as a model aeroplane does. It will remain floating about, and if not held captive by means of a light string, might remain aloft for days !

Coal-Gas and Hydrogen.

There is no need to inform the readers of HOBBIES that an airship must be lighter than air, and the lifting

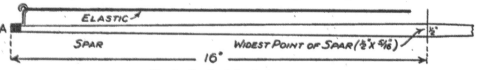

Fig. 1.—Details of the elastic-motor spar.

power of the airship depends absolutely upon its size—the larger the model the more weight will it lift. Two readily-obtainable gases are available for inflation purposes—coal-gas, which lifts about 40lb. per 1,000 cubic ft. and pure hydrogen, which lifts about 70lb. per 1,000 cubic ft. The former is obtainable from the gas-jet at home, and the latter is obtainable in small cylinders containing about 100 cubic ft. for a few shillings. Owing to its greater lifting power, it is recommended that, where possible, hydrogen should be used. It is necessary to point out here that both coal-gas and hydrogen are highly inflammable, and, because of this, extreme caution is necessary.

"Hobbies" Model Airship.

The HOBBIES model airship now to be described is not a suggested design ; it is one which has been the subject of special experiment by the Editor of HOBBIES, acting in conjunction with Messrs. Spencer Bros., 22, Bouverie Road, London, N.16, the well-known balloon and airship manufacturers. Carrying a dead weight of 1lb., the envelope easily ascended to a height of 200ft., and

as the weight of the elastic motor, propeller, and rudder, does not exceed 8oz., the model will readily ascend to a higher altitude than this.

The Envelope.

Two materials are available for the construction of the envelope—rubber and gold-beater's skin. Gold-beater's skin is a fine membrane prepared from the intestine of the ox, and it is used by the manufacturers of gold-leaf to lay between the leaves of gold whilst they are beaten out. It is lighter than rubber and much stronger. The construction of the envelope, however, will be fully dealt with next week, but it may here be mentioned that those who do not wish to go to the trouble of making this part of the model may obtain the envelope ready made from Messrs. Spencer Bros.

The Elastic Motor.

It will be seen that the elastic motor consists of a spar 4ft. long and tapered off to the dimensions shown in Fig. 1. A hook made from 18-gauge piano wire is bound on at the front end of the spar and an 18-gauge brass bearing for the propeller at the other end. Beneath the rear end of the spar a wire frame covered with fabric to act as a rudder is fixed ; its size is unimportant. It is fixed to the spar by means of a projection bent down in the manner shown in Fig. 2. The spar should be made of light, straight-grained pine or silver spruce, and the elastic motor consists of eight strands of $\frac{3}{16}$in. by $\frac{1}{32}$in. strip elastic. The propeller is 12in. in diameter, carved from a solid block of mahogany 1$\frac{1}{2}$in. wide and

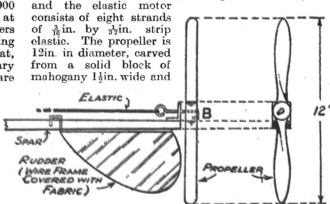

Fig. 2.—Details of the bearing, propeller, and rudder.

½in. thick. (See HOBBIES, October 18th issue, for details of propeller construction.)

Adjusting the Balance of the Model.

To adjust the trim of the airship, so that it floats on an even keel, a small piece of sheet lead is wrapped round the spar in the position shown in Fig. 3, and by sliding this along the spar adjustment may be made to the balance of the model. In next week's issue we shall explain how to make the envelope and complete the model.

Fig. 3.—General arrangement of the "Hobbies" model airship.

A New Tale by

W. E. CULE.

"Mr. Herne's Hallucination."

BEGINS IN THE

Boy's Own

FOR JUNE,

Now Ready. Sixpence.

A BEAUTIFUL COLOURED PLATE,

H.M. KING EDWARD VII.

is given with the JUNE Part.

HOW TO CONSTRUCT AN
EFFICIENT ACETYLENE TABLE LAMP.

THE portable gas-lamp to be described is not only something of a novelty, but it will be found extremely useful to those who require a small, but steady and very brilliant white light which may be shaded as required and concentrated on any work in hand. Fretworkers, amateur jewellers, and others engaged in minute operations will find it of much service.

Simplified to the utmost the device need not cost more than a few pence to make, but better materials than those suggested below are desirable with a view to greater durability and a better appearance. The tin canisters and other scraps were, however, purposely employed to make the trial lamp on which this article was written, and the results satisfactory in every way (copper must not be used in construction.)

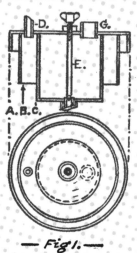

— Fig 1. —

Take a strong tin canister, having clamped seams and a spun lid that fits closely; wash it in strong soda and water to remove the paper or laquer labelling and after rinsing thoroughly, solder the side and bottom seams both inside and out. This canister may be say 6in. by 3½in. Now procure a smaller tin about 2in by 2½in. (the lower end of a one-pound carbide of calcium canister is suitable). Wash and solder as was done with the larger one and bore a ⅛-in. or 3-16in. hole exactly in the centre of the bottom. Into this hole fit and solder a 1½in. length of small-bore brass tube (1-32in.) let the end be nearly flush with the tin inside. When fixed reamer out the mouth of the tube slightly conical with a pointed tool.

Roll up and solder a small tinplate tube ½in. diameter and 2in. long trim one end of this square and level, and the other at a angle. Solder the squared end to the bottom of the small tin centrally outside the short brass pipe already in place.

Next cut a strip of tinplate 10in. long and 1½in. wide bend it into a ring lap the ends ¼in. and solder; afterwards true-up to a perfect circle on a wooden mandrel.

Now take the lid of the large canister and strike its centre with compasses; draw two circles on its inner side one the size of the mouth of the small canister and a larger one of the diameter of the tinplate ring. Afterwards bore through the centre point about 3-16in. in diameter. Besides the central hole, two others are required in the lid, one of ½in. diameter, within the smaller circle and another say ¼in. diameter between the two circles.

Now securely solder the small canister and the larger ring inside the lid exactly on the circles drawn within it. Fig. 1 shows this part. A is the lid, B the ring, and C the small canister, or water tank, with its two tubes. The space between B and C is to contain cotton-wool or other filtering material to dry the gas before it passes to the burner by way of the gas-tube D, which is soldered into the hole bored between the two circles. The tank C is filled through the ½in. aperture bored in the lid above which is soldered a short piece of tube G to take a tightly-fitting cork in which one minute hole is bored with a hot needle to admit air. (Note that Figs. 1 and 3 show the tank as 2in. by 2in. but its depth should be 2½in.; also for clearness sake, the water tube is drawn larger than its actual size 1-32in. bore).

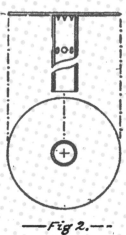

— Fig 2. —

The water reaches the carbide through the fine-bore pipe at the bottom of the tank and is led downward by the larger tube with the spouted end. But the flow can be cut off or regulated by screwing down the valve-stem E, which is screwed to stiffly fit a nut soldered above the central hole in the lid and provided with a winged nut to operate it. The lower end is filed to a cone to enter the conical mouth of the brass pipe.

The valve stem is tipped with a length of fine wire, soldered on, to encourage the regular fall of water drops into the larger tube when the valve is open (Fig. 3).

Cut out the two circular discs of tinplate of a size to slip easily into the large canister. In the centre of one of these, solder an upright tube ¾in. in diameter and 3in. high; the bottom of the tube must be nicked in half-a-dozen places, where it is joined to the disc, to permit the water to escape; and a ring of small holes may be bored about 1in. from the bottom for the same purpose. This false-bottom, with its tube, is shown at Fig. 2 in plan and elevation. The other disc is perforated by a central aperture of about ¾in. diameter to fit over the upright tube of the false-bottom and it is punctured all over with small holes. A wide spiral spring of thin wire is soldered to it. This perforated disc rests on the surface of the granular carbide and the helical spring, bearing against the tank bottom, maintains a slight pressure on the material, keeping it in position.

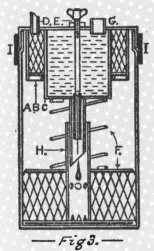

— Fig 3. —

Fig. 3 shows this disc and spring in section in its place in the complete generator at F. The other parts are lettered as follows :— A is the large canister and lid, B is the packing ring, C the water tank (2½in. deep), D the gas pipe, E the valve-rod, G the filler-tube, H the false-bottom, and its tube, and I is the rubber ring and binder (to be described). The gas-filtering material at the top, and the carbide granules at the bottom, are indicated by hatched lines. Although not strictly necessary, the lid and canister may be rigidly connected by a lashing of wire or whipcord passing over three wire hooks soldered to the generator and its cover respectively, as indicated in Fig. 4, which is a line-sketch of the finished lamp.

The gas-filter in the annular space between B and C, may be of plain cotton wool pressed in and held in place by a perforated ring of sheet metal and a split-ring of wire, but a better purification results from passing the gas through a layer of granular coke or carbon. Make a small tube of canvas or strong muslin, ½in. in diameter and about a foot long ; fill this with pounded coke, free from dust, but passing a mesh of say 32 to the inch, sew up the ends to a length just sufficient to coil round in the filter space. Pack in ½in. of cotton wool for the coke bag to rest on, press this down lightly and back up with another layer of wool, securing all with the perforated ring, and the split wire ring, mentioned above. After a month's use the filter may be renewed if necessary.

The familiar design of external detail sketched at Fig. 4, need not be followed, but it is convenient for several purposes, and it utilises the shade and supports of a disused oil lamp in a way requiring no explanation ; the wires are rebent suitably and soldered to the cover of the generator. But, if preferred, the flame may be enclosed in a ventilated conical or parabolic reflector, slanted to project the light downwards (such reflector are sold cheaply for use with paraffin lamps), or a small globe, coloured or otherwise, may be fitted if the light is used to illuminate an entrance, lobby, or staircase.

In the case illustrated, the gas pipe D, is about 6in. long and bent to a central position ;

a 1in. length of larger tube is soldered to its top to take a cycle lamp burner having a push-in socket (red lead and paper will secure the nipple).

To charge the lamp, place the false-bottom H, within the generator and cover it with carbide to about 1in. in depth ; level the granules and cover them with the perforated disc and spring F. Now slip the tank-tube within the false-bottom tube and force on the cover tightly. This joint must be made perfectly gas-tight with a broad rubber band. If not procurable, use a 1in. wide cutting from a cycle inner tube ; spring the band into space and bind firmly over it about 1 yard of broad tape, or garter elastic, secured by a hook and eye, or a couple of spring fasteners from an old glove.

Next screw down the valve stem E ; fill the tank with cold water through the tube G, and close with the perforated cork. Unscrew the water valve half a turn and the jet may be lit as soon as sufficient gas has been generated to expel the air. Never unscrew the valve too much at first or overgeneration may occur, making the flame hiss and possibly causing the gas to bubble back into the tank (in which case the valve must be turned off until the excess pressure has passed by the burner). When the light has fairly started the correct height of flame is readily adjusted by the thumbscrew, which may be marked with a file-nick to correspond with one upon the lid, for future guidance. The lamp will burn steadily for from two to six hours according to the capacity of the burner. When exhausted, the false bottom much facilitates cleaning, its removal withdraws nearly all the sludge. The parts are then rinsed, *thoroughly* dried, charged and re-assembled as before.

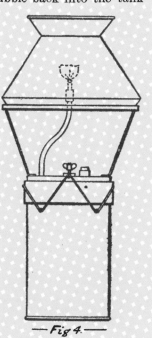
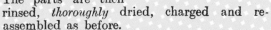
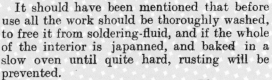

— Fig 4. —

It should have been mentioned that before use all the work should be thoroughly washed, to free it from soldering-fluid, and if the whole of the interior is japanned, and baked in a slow oven until quite hard, rusting will be prevented.

A few hints in conclusion. This water-to-carbide generator acts automatically on the displacement principle. If well made, the flame will neither sink nor roar from the beginning to the end of the charge, once the thumbscrew is correctly adjusted. But the slightest leakage anywhere upsets the whole action; therefore be sure to make every joint secure. So long as the only inlet to the carbide chamber is through the water-valve and the only outlet therefrom is by way of the burner, the success of the lamp is assured and neither too much nor too little gas, will at any time be generated.

Owing to the proved efficiency of the gas filter contained in the annular space, the impurities of the acetylene formed by this method of generation are considerably absorbed before reaching the burner which therefore does not so soon foul as commonly occurs in cycle lamps. When, however, after long use the batswing flame loses its symmetry the burner should be replaced. A new burner (costing 1d. to 4½d.) will last many weeks.

The lamp is at its best when allowed to burn completely out; its construction does not permit of its being readily re-lit upon a half-exhausted charge (although this may be done). When it is desired to extinguish the lamp, the water is turned off, and if left to itself the flame slowly expires. This gradual sinking tends to foul the nipple, so it is best to blow out the flame when the water is cut off. But in this case the extinguished lamp must be placed out of doors as the escaping fumes are unpleasant if not dangerous. When permitted to burn right out, the flame quickly sinks, at the last, and no harm results, either by carbonising the burner or polluting the air of an apartment.

The reservoir being rather small, a little water may be added in the course of a long evening, if the light shows diminution.

A disc of thick blotting-paper may be placed beneath the false bottom if it is found that water collects there (causing the flame to rise when the lamp is suddenly moved); but if the cannister bottom is quite flat this is seldom necessary.

This simple device cannot fail to give satisfaction to its constructor if the above instructions are faithfully carried out.

BENDING WOOD.—The bending of wood requires a steaming apparatus that would take considerable time to make and involve some cost for material. Where a few bent boards are wanted a costly apparatus is not necessary, as the boards can be bent equally as well by soaking the wood in water for several days to make it thoroughly waterlogged and then passing it over a gas flame several times. The wood, being soaked through, cannot burn, and the steam from the water softens the wood as well as if it were steamed in the regular way.—"Popular Mechanics."

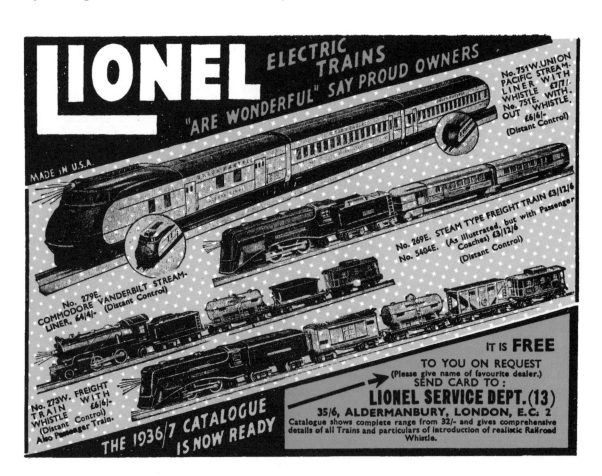

Full-size Patterns and complete instructions for making
A PETROL LIGHTER

WHILE it is almost impossible to buy matches the question of a petrol lighter arises. You can buy them of course at dandy prices, so how about trying to make a lighter, using thin wood and odds and ends

Impossible? No fear. You can do it and we show the result herewith. It is a fairly large, sturdy affair, as you can judge from the full-size patterns provided on Cover iii, but it does, at least, get you out of a difficulty in these times.

It is meant more for house use, although it can be carried in the pocket. The finish is ebony black polished, with brass-headed screws, or nickled-plated ones. It is imperative that you should use pieces of ⅛in. birch plywood. You should have some small pieces about the house that would be suitable.

The Flint Wheel

Quite a lot of you will have, in your boxes of nails, screws and odds and ends, parts of old cigarette petrol lighters. The main part you need is the flint wheel. This should be ½in. diameter.

Now, do not get discouraged. If the wheel you have is only ⅜in. in diameter, keep it and try your luck at a junk shop or repair specialist. Perhaps a friend can help you. Search around and see what you can do, meanwhile. Nurse the idea and gradually gather together the small parts required.

Construction of Lighter

Assuming you have the necessary materials to proceed with the work, paste or trace the patterns on the

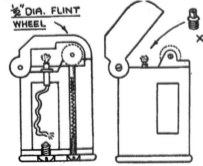

Fig. 2—Side view showing parts   Fig. 3—Elevation and wick detail

plywood and carefully cut out the parts, using a fine fretsaw blade for the job. All the case parts are shown, so it is only a matter of cutting and separating the pieces according to the lines.

The parts are glued on top of each other to build up the casing in a complete form. So do the cutting extra carefully and keep the saw upright as much as possible if the case is to be built in true shape.

Assembly

To assemble the casing, select the four central parts and glue them neatly, in true formation, on one of the cover pieces. On top of the cover pieces, glue the lid and overlay pieces. Take care not to coat the "lugs" of the lid piece with glue, however.

These "lugs" are part of the hinge. They must turn freely when screwed to the "knuckle" of the hinge (combined in the shape of the lighter case) with tiny screws, or a single screw running right through as a pivot.

Having built up one half of the casing, turn it over and add the other cover pieces, plus the overlay parts, to complete the assembly. When dry, level off the bottom and glue the bottom piece (A) in position, right way about. The smaller hole goes over the ⅛in. square hole in the work, this hole being for the flint-spring and spring screw.

Levelling Off

When the glue has set, screw the lid part (now a complete shape) in position, using ⅜in. by 3 roundhead or flathead screws. Level off the work all over with glasspaper. A flat file will be found extremely useful in this connection, too.

When glasspapered smooth and level, attach the other bottom piece (B) truly in place and round the edges, as shown in the diagrams. Now, here, at this stage, you must coat the inside of the wick aperture with polish —ebony black stuff, will do.

You see, if you fail to coat the aperture, the big chances are that the petrol will soak through the "pores" of the wood and evaporate much too quickly. To apply the polish inside, simply plug the wick hole with a match and pour a supply of polish in through the base screw hole.

Shake the polish about inside for a while, then pour the remaining surplus out. Remove the plug and allow the polish to dry. This process could be repeated several times to make sure of a proper job.

Fitting Up

To fit up the lighter, you need a wick spout, a spring and two bolts. The wick spout (see X at Fig. 3) can be made from the arm of a scent spray—the part over which the rubber bulb fits. Alternatively, a piece of ⅛in. brass tubing could be used.

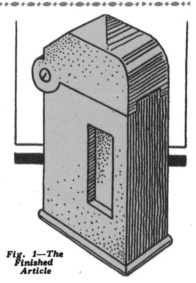

Fig. 1—The Finished Article

You need a piece about ½in. long. There are many things from which the spout can be made, such as a small cupboard lock key. Make sure the hole is deep enough prior to cutting off the length required.

Fitting the Tubing

Force the tubing into the hole and base the top end with a tight-fitting washer. Note, from Fig. 2, how much the spout sits up. Countersink the top end of the spout with a drill to facilitate the entry of the wick which is threaded through by pushing a threaded needle through first and tying the wick to the end of the thread.

The base screw for the wick aperture is ⅜in. long and fairly thick. Screw it in a suitable-sized hole made in the base piece. It should cut a thread in the wood for itself. This also applies to the flint-spring screw.

Spring and Flint

This screw is ¾in. long and ⅛in. thick. You could buy a spring or make one from piano wire. Ideal small springs are to be found in the contacts in old standard electric light fittings. They are about ½in. long and two will thus be required.

The flint wheel is fixed in place with a single screw or piece of wire nail. Be sure to have the "teeth" of the wheel turned the right way about, i.e., so the sparks are flung against the wick properly.

Complete the lighter by staining it black and then polishing it with ebony polish. Give the wood three separate applications and rub with knife powder to produce a dull gloss.

When dry, stuff the wick aperture with cotton wool and saturate it with the petrol or substitute.

FIREWORKS TO MAKE FOR "THE FIFTH"

WITH some sheets of paper, a pound or so of "meal" gunpowder, a few ounces of steel and iron filings and a little patience, you should be able to arrange quite a spectacular display of home-made fireworks for "The Fifth."

The first part to take in hand is the making of the paper cases, and it is as well to make up a good number before the filling process is commenced. The cases are rolled around a wooden former made in the following manner.

The Container

Get a 12-inch length of ⅜ dowel rod and make sure that it is perfectly straight and smooth. From one end saw off a length of 3 inches, centre it, and the end from which it was sawn, very accurately and drill a small hole in the centre of both pieces. Into the hole in the longer piece of rod drive a 1½in. wire nail, cut off the head and file it to a point, leaving about ¾in. projecting from the rod.

Now push the short piece on to the nail so that only about ⅛in. of it is seen and shape away both ends of the rod, rounding them neatly and smoothly The sketch at Fig. 1 should make all this quite clear.

First Casing

Cut a number of strips of paper—old newspaper is quite good—a little over 10 inches in width and as long as you like and taking one strip, commence to roll the first case. Lay the roller at one end and revolve it so that the paper is rolled rightly around as the roller is pushed forward.

Have a length of strong, fine string fixed to a stout nail in the wall and take a turn of it around the the case just at the point where the space exists between the two pieces of dowel-rod. Gripping the case tightly in the left hand, move it up and down the tightly held string, so that the paper case is drawn in tightly around the nail.

The Cover

Roll on another length of paper and repeat the operation; continuing to roll on and pull in until the wall of the case is about 3/16in. in thickness. Cut a short strip of brown paper with an angle at one end (Fig. 2) and place the case on it so the point comes just above the groove. Roll it on and secure the pointed part into the groove with a piece of thin thread, so forming a neat outer covering.

Now pull out the short piece of rod and by gently pulling and revolving, remove the long rod from the interior of the case. You now have a stout tube of paper with a small touch-hole at one end—the completed case ready to be filled with powder.

Silver Rain

To make a "Silver rain," mix steel filings with the fine "meal" powder in the proportion of three teaspoonsful of filings to one pound of powder. Mixing thoroughly with the fingers and taking great care to work well away from any danger of fire and also, never to use any metal tools which are likely to cause the least spark.

Push a tiny "screw" of paper into the touch-hole and hold that end of the case down on to a smooth, level surface. Pour a teaspoonful of the powder mixture into the open end, insert a length of smooth rod—a piece of the ⅜ rod will do well, if it is reduced so that it slips easily into the case—and give the end two or three light taps with a wooden mallet.

The "Touch"

Pour in some more powder and ram again; working in this way until less than an inch of the case remains unfilled. Close the end of the case by tucking in the layers of paper until it is securely closed and laying the whole thing to one side, continue filling until you have made enough "Silver Rain" for your display.

Each firework must now be fitted with a

(*Continued on facing page*)

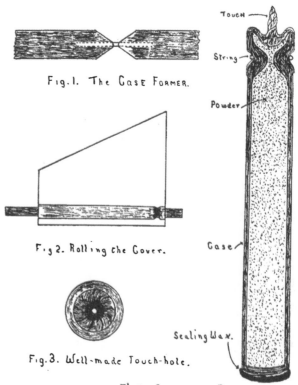

Fig. 1. The Case Former.

Fig. 2. Rolling the Cover.

Fig. 3. Well-made Touch-hole.

Fig. 4. Section of Firework.

Fireworks—(*Continued from opposite page*)

" touch " made by soaking narrow strips of thin paper in a solution of saltpetre and then hanging them up until they are quite dry. Cut off a length of the paper, wrap it around the end of the case so that it projects about an inch and tie a piece of thread around the groove to keep it in place.

Pull the " screw " of paper from the touch-hole and dust in a little powder, then twist the touch-paper lightly together and push it down so that it comes into contact with the loose powder.

Sealing Up

Melt some sealing wax in a tin by immersing it into boiling water and when it is quite soft, dip the lower ends of the fireworks into it to seal them.

A firework made in this manner is quite safe to hold in the hand when letting it off and if made as directed, will throw out a brilliant display of silver sparks ; shooting them to a good distance and burning for some considerable time.

Golden Rain

" Golden Rain " may be made in exactly the same way if iron filings are substituted for steel, while if the two types of filings are mixed and added to the powder in the proportions already given, a rather pleasing, mixed effect will be obtained.

Coloured Fire

Various shades of coloured fire mixed with the powder and filings will add some variety to your display. You can make these in self colours by filling the case entirely with one colour of mixture, or vary them still more by filling one third with a red, the next third blue and the final portion green ; the colours changing as the firework is consumed.

Rockets

If you wish to make some rockets you can do so easily by reducing the amount of filings added to the powder, as these reduce the lifting power. Allow one teaspoonful of filings to each pound of powder and fill and ram in exactly the same manner, fitting a light, well-balanced stick in order to give them a lift.

By allowing a space at the finishing end and into this pouring one teaspoonful of " F " gunpowder, you will get a terrific " bang " as the rocket explodes at the end of its flight. Coloured fire mixed with the " F " will send out a star of the same colour.

" I hear they want more **BOVRIL** "

WE must break off from our study of work this week, as, with the approach of Guy Fawkes Day thoughts turn to the fascinating subject of fireworks. And what better excuse can the readers of these articles have for experimenting with the various ingredients and, in fact, making their own supplies of fireworks?

It is quite easy to produce a variety of impressive effects. Of course, some of the more elaborate types of fireworks on the market are too complicated to make, but the amateur chemist will soon find that he can produce quite enough results to give himself and his friends a pleasant hour or so.

Bombs

Small explosive pellets or "bombs" are extremely easy to make and are very effective. You need only two ingredients, potassium chlorate and sulphur, a good supply of the latter being found in "Hobbies" outfits.

Shake some of each of these powders on to a sheet of clean paper and mix thoroughly together. Cut a number of small squares of thin paper and put enough of the mixture into each of these squares to make a firm pellet when the four corners are screwed together.

Explosive Caps

You can have a lot of fun with these, for if struck smartly with a heavy stone or a hammer they will detonate loudly. If made properly, they will even explode when thrown sharply against a wall.

MORE HOME-MADE
FIREWORKS

And this directs one's thoughts to that most elementary form of firework, the paper cap.

These, as you know, are usually bought in strips, which you cut up yourself, though sometimes they can be obtained in their form of little pink squares with the circular brown centres. In this case it is necessary to mix the ingredients, which are potassium chlorate and sulphuret of antimony, into a paste of the consistency of cream.

Take a pointed stick and place drops of the paste at regular intervals along a strip of paper. Allow the drops to dry, then paste a similar strip of paper over the top and cut out the little squares.

Coloured Fire

Naturally, you would like to know as much as possible about coloured fires. This particular subject is inseparable from the science of chemistry and has a fascination all its own. It is rather queer that various chemical substances should produce different coloured flames, nevertheless it is a fact, and one which gives the amateur considerable scope for experimenting.

The simplest example of this is the action of iron filings or aluminium filings upon a flame. Just sprinkle some into the flame of your Bunsen or a candle, and showers of sparks or stars will fly out.

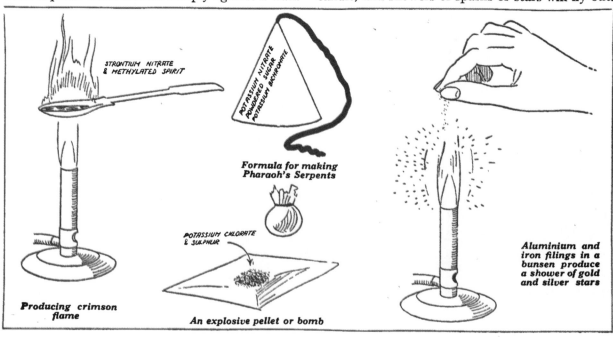

STRONTIUM NITRATE & METHYLATED SPIRIT

POTASSIUM NITRATE POWDERED SUGAR POTASSIUM BICHROMATE

Formula for making Pharaoh's Serpents

POTASSIUM CHLORATE & SULPHUR

Producing crimson flame

An explosive pellet or bomb

Aluminium and iron filings in a bunsen produce a shower of gold and silver stars

The aluminium produces silver stars, and the iron, sparks of a golden colour.

Here are some recipes for coloured fires :—

Red Fire.

    12 parts of potassium chlorate
    4 parts of strontium nitrate
    4 parts of mercurous chloride
    3 parts of sulphur
    1 part of charcoal
    1 part of powdered shellac

Yellow Fire

    6 parts of potassium chlorate
    2 parts of sulphur
    2 parts of sodium oxalate
    1 part of powdered shellac

Green Fire

    6 parts of potassium chlorate
    12 parts of barium nitrate
    3 parts of sulphur
    2 parts of mercurous chloride
    1 part of charcoal
    1 part of powdered shellac

It is usual to ignite the mixture you have prepared and so obtain the coloured effect you are seeking, but you can produce flames of various colours by sprinkling on to an open fire certain mixtures.

If, for instance, you sprinkle a mixture of potassium nitrate, calcium chloride, strontium nitrate and barium chloride upon the fire, you will produce a very spectacular result.

Bengal Lights

The brilliant white flame known as Bengal Lights can be produced by mixing together 2½ ozs. of antimony sulphide with a pound of saltpetre and 5 ounces of sulphur. This can be mixed on an old dish with a knife, and if a small quantity at a time is lighted it will burn brilliantly. As you know from photography, magnesium powder produces a brilliant white light, and if you add some of this to the above mixture the intensity of the light will be increased even more greatly.

An old iron spoon comes in handy, too, for if you fill it with boric acid and pour in a few drops of methylated spirit, then light the spirit, you will get a bright blue flame.

Crimson Flame

Crimson flame may be produced by heating a small amount of strontium nitrate in the spoon until it is quite dry. Take the spoon away from the flame and after it has cooled, add a little methylated spirit, hold the spoon over the flame again and apply a match to the spirit.

From the above hints and information you will find plenty to interest you and many are the experiments you can carry out in endeavouring to produce original effects.

Pharaoh's Serpents

To close with, we will describe how one of the most fascinating and remarkable types of firework curiosities are made—Pharaoh's Serpents. These little things are usually purchased in the form of a rather heavy cone of yellow paper, and when you apply a match to the apex a snake-like coil issues forth, slowly and very strangely. The effect never fails to amaze onlookers, for the " serpent " keeps coming for a most surprising length of time, and one wonders where on earth it is all coming from.

Well, the secret lies in the chemical compound known as sulphocyanide of mercury. This is simply mixed with a little gum water and packed into the stiff paper cone.

It is advisable to stand the finished article on the hearth if you light it indoors, so that the fumes may escape up the chimney. Pharaoh's Serpents are so astonishing that this method, which is the basis of their commercial manufacture, is given here as a matter of interest, but readers are not advised to make them by this process as the mercuric sulphocyanide is poisonous.

In fact, it is safe to say that you could not do so anyway, as no chemist would serve you with the compound. But you can make them by another method, and although the effect is not so astonishing, it is quite effective enough to give you a good

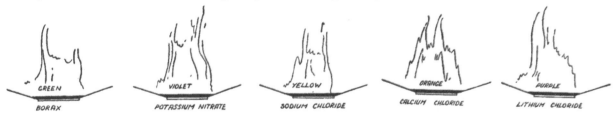

Salts which, mixed with spirits of wine produce coloured flames

Spirits of wine is useful for producing coloured flames, for if you mix the following salts, finely powdered, with the spirits, the salts will give to the spirit their distinctive colouring when lighted :— Calcium chloride will produce orange ; lithium chloride will produce purple ; borax will produce green ; potassium nitrate will produce pale violet ; and common salt will produce yellow.

deal of interest in trying it out, and the ingredients are quite harmless.

Take one part of potassium nitrate, one part of powdered sugar, and two parts of potassium bichromate, powder them separately very thoroughly, then mix them together. Press the mixture into small paper cones, and remember always to light them at the apex.

Look out for more Home Chemistry articles

DIVING LESSONS.

III.—JACK-KNIFE, DEAD DROP, SOMERSAULTS, HANDSPRING, CUT-OUT HANDSPRING.

IF I had my way I would make it illegal for any high diving to be attempted into water shallower than 9 feet. I know that 7 feet is often considered sufficient for experts, and it usually is. But it is not the expert who runs the risk of striking the bottom, it is the learner—and all baths should be constructed with the learner's welfare in view, especially when, as in this instance the expert, too, would reap an advantage.

In all high diving great care needs to be exercised. But, if only you graduate your exercises properly, in the manner described last week, you will have no cause to be nervous when attempting new feats.

Just one last hint applies to all fancy diving–really master one feat before going on to another.

The Jack-Knife Dive.

This begins like an ordinary plain header, with an upward and outward spring, but the hands, instead of swinging beyond the head, reach forward until they touch the ankles —the body bending sharply at the hips. In this triangular position you will fall towards the water, with the head about the level of the feet. Then, when you are near the surface straighten the body,

JACK KNIFE DIVE.

by raising the legs and dropping the arms so that you enter the water as from a header.

Take care during the fall that the knees do not bend. It is a good plan to test the jack-knife position first on land—bending forward sharply to reach your feet, and then straightening up.

By standing with one's face to the bank a back jack-knife can be performed. This is rather less easy, for it is necessary to spring well out so that the head clears the board, and so that there is room enough to rise easily to the surface after the entry. Remember that all jack-knives finish head first.

The Dead Drop.

There is no spring made in this dive, and, although not difficult, it requires a fair amount of nerve. Begin by standing on the take-off, with arms down by the sides, and toes over the front edge of the board. Hold the body stiffly, and allow yourself to topple forward, until you lose your balance and fall towards the water. All the time you must be absolutely rigid. In your early attempts it is wise to recover the hands below the head in time for the entry ; later, providing the water is deep enough, you may keep the arms at the sides until you are immersed. In some countries this feat is called "the wooden soldier dive"—a usefully descriptive name.

The Backwards Header.

Stand on the take-off, facing towards the shore. This time the heels will be just over the end of the board. Raise the hands above the head, with the palms in flat diving position. Then lean slowly over backwards. At the instant when you pass the balancing point give a slight push from the feet, and this will cause you to turn over backwards so that you enter the water vertically, your back towards the bank.

Because of this vertical descent deep water is obviously necessary.

The most common fault in back dives is that of allowing the legs to sag at the knees, and to drop apart. This is often the result of faulty balance, so be particularly careful to get a square spring, and to keep your head steady.

Somersaults.

Somersaults can be performed in great variety from the springboard.

For instance—take a short run and hurl yourself forward and upward as for a swallow or a plain header. Then, at the highest point, drop the head sharply; draw the knees up, and make a swing of the arms in the direction you wish to turn, and this will result in a sharp somersault in mid-air. Immediately you are over the arms will be dropped and the body straightened — in rather the same manner as from a jack-knife—and you will fall cleanly into the water.

Backward somersaults, double somersaults, one and a half somersaults either backwards or forwards, all these things do not need much explanation. Some finish head first, some feet first; and when they are taken from a standing position the body is generally kept fairly straight throughout, instead of being drawn up as already described. In such somersaults the arms should be spread in a swallow position and you should try to imagine your whole body revolving round a pivot passing through the shoulders. The spreading of the arms is very helpful in preserving balance.

When somersault entries are made feet first the arms are brought down to the sides of the body— otherwise they drop beyond the head.

The Handspring.

This is a moderately easy, but very graceful dive.

Kneel on the end of the board, gripping its sides with your hands, and slowly leaning forward until you can take a hand balance—your body and legs will be vertically in the air. It does not matter whether your elbows are bent or straight, though the latter is preferable.

When you are quite steady let yourself slightly overbalance outwards, and at the same instant push yourself right out clear of the end of the board, and release your grip. Instantly re-adjust your hands below your head, and so drop in a plain header.

It is important that before pushing off you let yourself topple outwards, so that your legs do not graze the board as they descend. Be careful also that the legs do not lapse from their proper straightness.

Cut-Out Handspring.

Again begin with a handspring balance. But this time allow yourself to drop down towards the board, as if you were going to stand up again. As you fall, spread the legs widely apart so that they clear the board and come into contact with the wrists. At this precise instant the hands give an outward push and loose their hold—so that the legs " cut them out."

The impetus of the leg swing and the push should have carried you well clear of the board, and now you will straighten into an upright position and descend vertically into the water, feet first, and with hands at the sides.

Try not to get any bending at the hips in this dive, it looks best when the body is straight all through. But certainly there should be no bending at the knees.

Naturally this dive will be most easily performed on a fairly narrow board.—S.G.H.

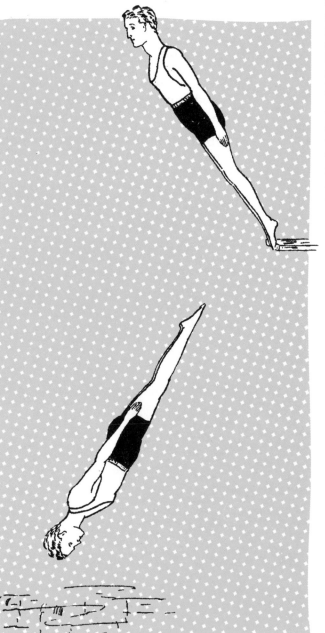

A DEAD DROP DIVE.

Be Constructive...

Make and Do with Handframe or Machine!

NOW—you can make the things you have always wanted to make.... easily and quickly. Modern Fretwork, with a HOBBIES outfit or machine, is a fascinating pastime which allows anyone with two hands to make models in wood, toys, furniture and hundreds of other things.

HOBBIES provide an outfit of all tools you need—or a treadle fretmachine at amazingly low prices. Design charts are obtainable which tell you step-by-step how to build. You can make toys, models, furniture, etc. at a fraction of shop-prices. The Hobbies Handbook (6d. everywhere) shows you over 500 things to make and do.

THE CROWN OUTFIT

A practical set at a low price. Gives you all you need to make a start, with design on wood and instruction book. In attractive box. **5/-**
Post 7d.

10/6
Post 9d.

THE AI OUTFIT

The most popular set. The choice of craftsmen everywhere. Contains a wide range of the better-grade tools with six designs and planed wood, and a new 64-page book of instructions. Worth every penny its cost.

MACHINES

A machine doubles your output in half the time. You can buy one from Hobbies for as low as 30/-. We have machines, too, for driving by electricity, off the mains.

The mark of good value and a square deal

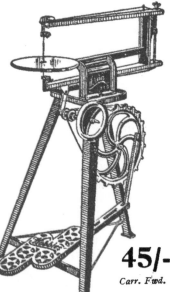

45/-
Carr. Fwd.

FREE

Let us send you interesting literature about HOBBIES outfits and machines. Write to Hobbies Limited, Dereham, Norfolk, or call at any Hobbies branch.

THE POPULAR AI MACHINE

Printed by BALDING & MANSELL, London and Wisbech, and Published for the Proprietors, HOBBIES LTD. by HORACE MARSHALL & SON, LTD., Temple House, Tallis Street, E.C.4. Sole Agents for Australia and New Zealand : Gordon & Gotch (A'sia) Ltd. For South Africa : Central News Agency Ltd. Registered for Transmission by Canadian Magazine Post.

OPEN-CASTING AT HOME

IN this article the emphasis will be on simplicity and cheapness, especially the latter, so none of the equipment described is very elaborate and can mostly be obtained or made without cost. Even so, quite a high quality finished article will be the result if a certain amount of care is taken.

The requirements for home-casting are: a flat baseboard known as the 'ramming-board'; a wooden box up to

removal from the moulding-sand. This applies equally to home-made wooden patterns.

In foundries it is usual for a mould to be made of two parts, the upper part known as a 'cope' and the lower or 'drag'. In simple home casting, however, only one box, the latter, is used, which gives us the term 'open casting'.

To make the mould the box framework is placed on the ramming board to

over, so that the pattern may be gently removed, after this thoroughly dry the mould by playing the flame from a bunsen-burner on to the sand for about ten minutes.

As the melting point of lead is only 327°C., it can be easily melted on an ordinary gas ring. The same method can also be used for melting most alloys. When alloy or lead is quite liquid, i.e., easy to stir, hold the tin firmly with the

Fig. 1—Ramming down the moulding sand around the pattern which has been previously dusted with 'parting-powder'. The easily-made sprinkler in the foreground is for moistening the sand. Note strips of wood inside box

J. C. M. here describes how perfect castings can be made in your own kitchen by a very simple method.

grippers and pour it into the mould. It is essential that the mould be on a level surface and if possible, the molten lead or alloy should be poured on to a flat surface in the mould itself. Do not overfill the mould.

12ins. square and 4ins. deep, without a bottom (small strips of wood should be fixed on the inside to prevent the moulding sand from falling out when the mould is inverted); moulding sand, which is easily obtained from any foundry, together with the special 'parting-powder'. Before using to make a mould, the sand should be moistened, so that if a quantity is compressed in the fist it may be broken cleanly. This last point is extremely important, as it is virtually impossible to obtain a good mould with sand that is either too dry or too wet.

The only other items needed are the lead or alloy, which latter can usually be obtained from a garage in the form of scrap pistons, etc. The melting tin may be a large cocoa-tin or something similar. Grippers are used to hold the tin while pouring the molten lead or alloy into the mould. Lastly, a steel rod for stirring the melting alloy and some blocks of hardwood with which to ram down the sand round the pattern.

The pattern may be any small household article such as a tea-strainer rest or ashtray, or it may be made from a block of wood to your own design and painted with a high-gloss paint for a surface equal to that of a metal object. To be suitable for moulding, a pattern must have its sides sloping inwards for easy

Fig. 2—Turning over the 'drag' so that pattern is uppermost

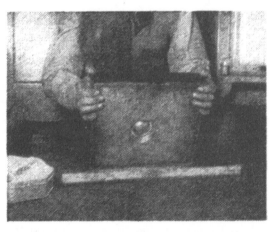

form the 'drag'. The pattern is then placed on the ramming board and lightly dusted with the parting-powder to form a thin dry layer between the previously dampened sand and the pattern, so that they will not stick together. The moulding sand is placed around the pattern beginning at the edges of the box and working inwards, firmly ramming it down with the hardwood blocks until the box is completely filled. Level off the sand to the top of the box with a straight edge.

The 'drag' is now carefully turned

When the mould is completely filled, allow it to stand for 10 minutes without disturbing, after this, holes should be pierced around the casting to assist its cooling. A short while later the casting may be removed from the mould and put on one side to cool, but do not stand it on a cold surface, as there is still some danger of it cracking.

The casting, when quite cold, may be cleaned up with a small file, emery-cloth and metal polish. If a reasonable amount of care is taken with the process, perfect articles will result.

How to Treat a Case of Poisoning

IF you know that a person has taken poison send for a doctor at once, and if you know what the poison is mention it in your message.

Use your eyes and note if there is a bottle near-by which might have contained poison. If you know what the poison is you have a clue to the proper treatment.

If a perfectly healthy person is taken violently ill after a meal you may suspect food poisoning; if you find someone with burns about the mouth or lips you may conclude they have taken a strong acid or alkali.

There are four main classes of poisons as follows :—

1. Corrosives (causing burning). These are strong acids such as sulphuric, hydrochloric or nitric acid; salt of lemon; or strong alkalis such as ammonia caustic soda or potash.
2. Irritants. These are chiefly bad foods, arsenic, phosphorus and poisonous fungi.
3. Narcotics (which send one to sleep). The chief is opium, forms of which are laudanum, morphia and chlorodyne); alcohol; carbon monoxide (which is the gas given off from a car exhaust).
4. Deliriants. Strychnine; belladonna (the seeds of deadly nightshade are often eaten by children); laburnum seeds.

The corrosives, both the Acids and Alkalis, burn or stain the mouth and lips. If these signs are present you must on no account give an emetic.

If you know that the poison is an alkali you can give an antidote to it in the form of a weak acid such as one or two table-spoonfuls of lemon juice with plenty of water, or vinegar and water.

If you know the poison is an acid give the antidote which in this case will be an alkali such as chalk, plaster, whitening or white-wash, or some bicarbonate of soda (not washing soda), in plenty of water.

If you know that a corrosive has been taken, but do not know if it is acid or alkaline, dilute it as much as possible. That is, make the patient drink plenty of water, milk, barley water, or raw eggs beaten up in milk; strong tea or coffee.

If there are no stains about the mouth in all cases give an emetic to make the patient sick, in one of the following methods.

1. Tickle the back of the patient's throat with your finger, or a stiff piece of paper rolled up tightly.
2. Put a dessert spoonful of mustard in half a tumbler of warm water and make him drink it.
3. Put two tablespoonfuls of salt in a quarter of a tumbler of warm water and make him drink it.

In the case of food poisoning the patient will suffer severe pain, possible sickness and diarrhoea. Give an emetic as above (unless he is already sick), and after the vomiting has ceased give two tablespoonfuls of castor oil.

The patient will probably be very exhausted and suffer from shock, so keep him warm in bed with hot bottles and give him plenty of strong tea or coffee with lots of sugar.

Narcotic poisons send the patient to sleep; when the pupils of his eyes are reduced to pinpoints. You must do all you can to keep him awake. Give him an emetic if he is sufficiently conscious to swallow.

Walk him up and down, and give him strong tea or coffee to drink. If he becomes completely unconscious and ceases to breathe perform artificial respiration.

If the poisoning is caused by breathing carbon monoxide from a car exhaust drag him from the garage into fresh air and if he is completely unconscious perform artificial respiration.

The Dilirants cause the patient to become very excited and he may even have convulsions. His face will be flushed and the pupils of his eye very large (the opposite symptoms to the Narcotics). Give an emetic and try to keep him quiet.

To sum up. Give the antidote when you know for certain that an acid or alkali has been taken but do *not* give an emetic.

In all other cases if there are no signs of burning or staining of the mouth give an emetic.

Dilute the poison with water or other liquid, but never give food or drink to an unconscious person. Treat shock in all cases of poisoning—chiefly by warmth.

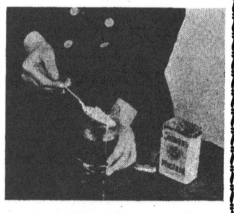

A dessertspoonful of mustard in half a tumbler of warm water

A Cut Artery in the Palm of the Hand

A CUT artery is a much more serious matter than a cut vein. Blood is being pumped out directly from the heart and a person may bleed to death in a few minutes if prompt steps are not taken to stop the bleeding.

There is no mistaking when an artery is cut for the blood spurts out and is bright scarlet in colour.

In the case of a cut in the palm of the hand—such as might result from cutting bread—raise the patient's arm as high as possible. Make a really hard pad of a clean handkerchief, place a clean piece of lint or gauge on the cut and then the pad.

Tell the patient to grip it tightly. Fold a large handkerchief narrowly and bandage across and across the knuckles, bringing all the pressure you can to bear on the pad. Lay the patient down and keep the arm raised. If this does not stop the bleed-

ing you must try to stop it at a point nearer the heart. Roll up his sleeve and then make a pad about the size of a golf ball from a handkerchief. This pad must be as hard as you can make it.

Place it in the elbow joint and tell the patient to bend his arm and press on the pad. Now tie a handkerchief in a figure of eight round the wrist and upper arm, so squeezing them together and pressing the pad into the joint. Tie the handkerchief tightly.

This compresses the artery in the elbow joint and prevents blood from flowing down into the hand.

In all cases of arterial bleeding *send for a doctor*, and in the meantime try by pressure on

the bleeding place, or above it to stop the flow of blood. Your prompt action in such a case may easily be the means of saving a person's life.

The question of dressing the wound does not arise as you will leave that till the doctor comes.

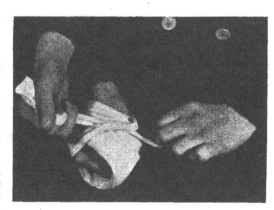

Underwater Spear

UNDERWATER fishing is becoming an increasingly popular pastime and there are many places around the coasts of Britain where people may try this sport.

The fishing spear described here will make a useful addition to the enthusiast's kit, and it can be quickly made.

Purchase a suitable spike for the end. These are readily obtainable in a variety of shapes and sizes from any shop that sells fishing equipment. Possibly, such a spike could be made. A piece of tubing 3½ins. long is also required and a 1in. length of rod (brass, copper or steel).

Firstly shape the smaller length of metal as shown. The ideal would be to turn this on a metalwork lathe, but alternatively it can be filed. Hold securely in the vice and drill a hole down

the middle to the size of the diameter of the spike and then solder the spike into the hole.

Cut the piece of tubing to the required length, making sure that the ends are

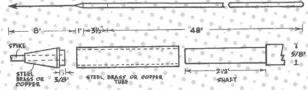

perfectly square. Fit the solid piece of metal into the tubing. Drill a small hole through both and secure with a brass pin, riveting over the ends.

A piece of ⅝in. dowel rod is required for the shaft. This should preferably be

of a hardwood and must be straight grained to prevent bending after immersion in sea water. Round one end and then carefully shape the other end so that it is a good tight fit into the metal tube. Knock into the tube with a mallet.

Glasspaper the shaft smooth and give it several coats of yacht varnish, glass-

papering down between each coat. Paint the metal parts to prevent rusting or tarnishing.

Always remember for safety reasons to keep an old cork over the spike when not in use.

(A.E.H.)

" WHERE DID YOU BUY THIS PAINT, MA? "

Sprained Knee for 3½ Years.

From among the numerous unsolicited testimonials which have been received by The Charles A. Vogeler Company in praise of their grand preparation St. Jacobs Oil, we select that of Mr. Arthur Harrison, Wilford Crescent East, Nottingham, who suffered from a sprained knee for 3½ years, and being devoted to the manly sport of football, he felt it a great deprivation that he was unable to join in a game for that period. He tried many remedies without success, until one day a friend persuaded him to try St. Jacobs Oil—The Wonderful Oil, he calls it—when he experienced immediate relief from pain, followed by a permanent cure. He says : " I had been suffering from a very bad sprained knee for 3½ years through playing football. I had been under the Doctor's care twice, and had used all kinds of Oils, Embrocations, and cold water bandages, etc., etc., when I was recommended to try your valuable Oil. I had been suffering so much that it was impossible for me to kick a ball, but after trying two small bottles I am pleased to say my knee is now as perfect and strong as ever. I should have written you before, but wanted to give it a thorough trial, and am glad to inform you that since using St. Jacobs Oil I have never felt another twinge of pain. You can make use of this if you think fit, as I am delighted to acquaint the football public with what St. Jacobs Oil has done for me." Had it not been for this truly grand remedy, Mr. Harrison would still have been deprived of the enjoyment of his favourite pastime, and all Englishmen who delight in athletic exercises will rejoice to read of this reliable preparation which does away with the ill effects of accidents which cannot always be prevented.

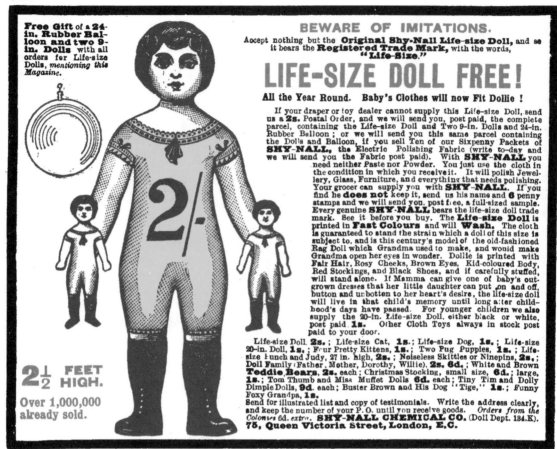
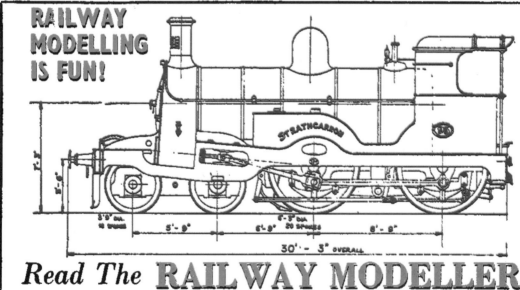

SNAP

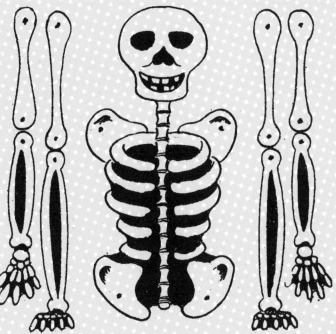

"Build it yourself"

SEEN BUT NOT HEARD

SPLICING ROPE ENDS
PLASTIC PICTURES

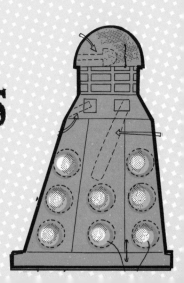

THE HOME MUSEUM.

A VERY interesting museum can be got together at small cost by any boy who has a taste for collecting interesting objects. Such a museum could, of course, specialise in objects connected with the collector's favourite hobby, and could easily be arranged in a small spare room, or bedroom. The most fascinating branch, and one that gives the greatest scope for getting together a wide range of subjects is the collection of Nature objects: shells, birds' eggs, butterflies and moths, beetles, pressed plants, bones, skins, stuffed specimens, etc., etc., the chief advantage of taking up such a line being the fact that the specimens may be obtained for nothing in pleasant country rambles and walks on the sea-shore. A boy's museum, however, is not by any means limited to Nature objects, for many are enthusiastic over coins, stamps, old relics of every description ; the collection of objects in a home museum being all the more interesting if varied, providing the subjects are properly classified and labelled.

A CORNER of the "NATURE" SECTION.

Having observed that natural objects give the greatest scope for forming an interesting collection, we propose in this article, to give a few suggestions for their collection and arrangement. Butterflies and moths are no doubt the most popular branch of outdoor Nature collecting, there being an immense variety in this country to be sought for, and they look very beautiful when properly mounted and set. The usual method of storing is, of course, in cabinets with drawers, or in boxes, the only disadvantage to these methods being that they are not always on view, and a system of storage that allows them to be exhibited on the walls has much to recommend it. The writer has found that a simple oak framing applied round a box, is in every way satisfactory, providing due care is taken that the frame is well fitted, so that no dust can get inside. Fig. 2 makes the idea clear,

A. being a box about 2in. deep, that exactly fits the picture frame B. It is rather a good plan to glue a piece of cloth round the rebate of this, to make it quite dust-proof, the frame with glass being held in position over the box by means of six catches, one of which is shown in Fig. 2. Fig. 2, C., shows one of the little brass pieces that is screwed to the back of the box for hanging it up by. Fig. 1 shows the effect of these cases hanging on the wall, which will do much to help the appearance of the museum. In this sketch, is shown also two sets of shelves, one over the mantelshelf and one beside it. These are of such a simple make that any boy could easily construct a number, according to his requirements, and they will be found invaluable for arranging many objects upon. They need be only very narrow, about 3 to 4 in. being ample for most purposes, such as for exhibiting shells, minerals and the like. An egg-box, procurable from any grocer's, would supply excellent material for the making, which will be made quite clear by glancing at Fig. 3. Be sure and plane or sandpaper each board before nailing together, and then when completed, stain a nice brown colour by brushing over with a weak solution of permanganate of potash, when they are ready for use.

Birds' eggs, because of their very fragile nature, are best kept in a closed cabinet, as if exhibited openly, they are extremely liable to damage. A simple home made drawer cabinet is shown by Fig. 4, which can be made out of cigar or sweet boxes, and fretwood ; the boxes, of course, require to have all the paper cleaned off, and must necessarily be all the same size. Carefully sandpaper inside and out, and then place one upon the other, with a piece of $\frac{1}{4}$ in. fretwood between each, the outside measurements being then taken, and the framework of the cabinet put in hand, the pieces of wood between the drawers being afterwards glued

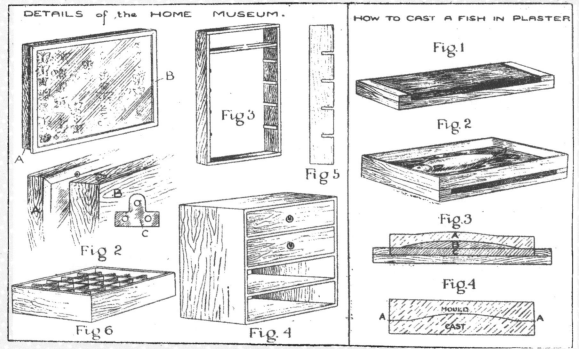

DETAILS of the HOME MUSEUM.

Fig 3

Fig 5

Fig 2

Fig 6

Fig. 4

HOW TO CAST A FISH IN PLASTER

Fig.1

Fig.2

Fig.3

Fig.4

in to serve as shelves for supporting them. Fix a screw with a ring attached to the front of each drawer, for drawing them in and out. The drawers are divided up into compartments, in accordance with the size of eggs they are intended to hold by means of strips of wood or card, that are cut as shown by Fig. 5, for slotting into one another where they cross, being finally glued in place. Birds' eggs are, of course, always " blown "; this simple operation being done, as most collectors will probably know, by making a pin prick at the top and bottom, and then vigorously blowing through one of the holes to remove all the interior matter, taking great care not to fracture the delicate shell that remains.

Skinning and stuffing small birds and animals in a simple manner is a subject which we hope to deal with later in this series. Some collectors prefer to keep their skins flat, rather than stuff them, as they are more convenient to store when one has a goodly number. Skinning is quite a simple operation, the method, after having obtained a good specimen, say a squirrel or rat, being to open the skin from the tail right up to the end of breast, with a sharp pen-knife; you can then beign to skin, and proceed to cut the legs off *from the inside*, when the skin can be turned right over until you come to the end of the head, the ears being disunited like the legs, when the body can be cut off close to the back of the skull. The greater part of the skull can now be cut away, and the eyes removed, and every scrap of flesh taken away from the interior. The legs are then skinned as far down as possible, if there is any flesh upon them. Next stretch it flat upon a board, with the inside of the skin exposed, and sprinkle with powdered alum to preserve it.

There are a large variety of skins of the smaller animals that may be preserved in this way, not mentioning the birds, which are done similarly, but are more difficult to manage on account of the feathers. So the country collector should not fail to obtain the body of any dead specimen, especially if it happened to be somewhat rare, for adding to his collection.

Snakes, newts, fish and such like, are frequently kept in tightly corked bottles filled with spirits of wine; or methylated spirit serves almost as well. The great thing is to see that the specimens are wholly covered with the spirit, and that the jar is made perfectly airtight, when it may be preserved indefinitely.

Drying and pressing plants is a subject that will appeal especially, of course, to our readers with a taste for botany, but the subject is one that it well worth the attention of the general collector on account of the beauty of the specimens, if nicely pressed and framed. Although the greater part of the vivid colouring of the specimens if, of course, lost in the pressing, there are many plants that still preserve their dainty hue, even after years of keeping. An ordinary picture frame, with a wooden back is an excellent manner of preserving and keeping such specimens.

A very good method of exhibiting the different varieties of fish is a home museum, is to make plaster casts of the natural specimens, and then to paint them in their correct colours. This will be found much easier than stuffing; the manner in which it is done we will describe in a separate paragraph.

How to Cast a Fish in Plaster.

With a little patience, anyone may easily produce perfect facsimiles in plaster of fish, and similar natural objects, provided he carried out the following directions.

First make a board, and nail on a ledge at each end about 1½in. thick, the space between being filled in with clay that is scraped quite level. Now lay the fish that it is required to cast on the clay slab, and mark round it, the part underneath being sunk a little so that the fish may be embedded to about half its depth. Now put four strips of thin wood which are nailed together and fixed to the board, to form a wall that will prevent the plaster from running off.

Obtain two-pennyworth of plaster of Paris from an oilshop, also a clean basin, a little powdered yellow ochre, and some soap. Then mix up some of the plaster of Paris with water and a pinch of yellow ochre, to make a thin cream, and having damped the model quickly, pour over the model and background. Leave for at least half an hour to harden, and then take off the wooden strips round the sides. Fig. 3 gives a diagram showing A., the plaster shell, B. the fish, and C. the clay background. You will find it quite an easy operation to lift the mould off when it has set.

Thoroughly brush the mould with soapy water or oil until it shines everywhere; then mix up some plaster as before, but somewhat thicker, and without the yellow colouring matter, and pour it into the mould, building it up at the sides to make a thickness from ¾ in. to 1in.

When the plaster has become hard, the model can easily be separated from the mould, by inserting a knife or chisel where the white joins the yellow at the sides shown by AA in Fig. 4.

* * *

W. J. HORNSBY of 149 High Street, Burton Latimer, Nr. Kettering, Northants, is fond of animals, collects stamps and labels, and would like pen friends throughout the world.

"ALRIGHT! ALRIGHT! I'M GOING TO TURN THE BABY ROUND."

THE BOY'S MVSEVM

Flint Implements.

MANY flint implements have been found in the old barrows and graves of pre-historic man, some beautifully chipped and fashioned with care; indeed, it would seem as if those buried were the favourite implements of the departed, upon which they had expended a special care. These are often accompanied by a few beads and an earthenware jar or cup intended as a receptacle in which to place food. Flints at first look very crude and uninviting, but when classified and arranged in a cabinet, they show the true purpose for which they were fashioned, and in them can often be traced the germ of later inventions. Many of the tools we are using to-day are but little improved, or at any rate the original principle is the same. Thus the hammer head of flint and stone, with its round hole or socket for a shaft, differs little in shape to the steel head of the hammer we use now. The finely pointed borer of flint gave the inventor of the awl his cue, and the germ of the toothed saw may be seen in that little piece of flint in which a jagged edge has been laboriously fashioned by another flint, so that by holding tight between finger and thumb and rubbing backwards and forwards, soft stone and wood could be sawn asunder. Those were days when time was no object, and when the primitive savage could hold in his hand the little piece of flint with a firm grip. He could chip and chip away until quite a keen cutting edge was formed and a knife or saw was evolved out of a flake of flint. The beautifully formed barbed arrows used in the later periods of neolithic man are exquisitely shaped and have never been improved upon as an arrow point. Some show by their chipping that early man could use his left hand just as well as his right.

The Older Implements.

The flint implements found in this country are divided into two distinct groups—the paleolithic and the neolithic. The former are chiefly found underground in gravel beds and in caverns. They are, of course, very crude in form and comparatively uninteresting, but the collector will gloat over a piece of flint which has assumed a hammer or celt-like form, evidently not by its rough usage in pre-historic seas, but by the aid of man. It may have been polished by friction with other flints in the gravels in which it was flung or lost thousands of years ago, but there it remains to the careful observer a tribute to the ingenuity of our early ancestors, and to their knowledge of the greater possibilities of work accomplished with tools. Most of these celts were used in the defensive against animals, but probably a few of the flints of these early days were used as knives or scrapers for cleaning the skins of animals. Sir John Evans, a great authority, divides paleolithic implements into three kinds: (1) flakes for arrow heads or knives; (2) pointed weapons like lance and spear heads; (3) tongue-shaped implements, cutting all round. When such implements were used, the woolly rhinoceros and bison roamed in the forests of Britain.

The Newer Flints.

There was a long interval apparently between those days and the time when man again seems to have been active in this country. Among the remains of this neolithic or newer age, flint implements of better forms and more advanced types are found. They represent the tools used for very many years, for side by side with those which have remained in the fields along the Thames valley since quite savage races paddled across the river to their huts of wattle on its mud banks, lie flint arrows and implements which were used down to Saxon days.

We wonder whether any of our readers have been fortunate enough to come across one of the fields where flint implements have been turned up by the plough? If so they will have been surprised how many implements of well-defined shapes are sometimes to be found. Specimens of these may be supplemented by a few purchases, so that different groups, showing the implements used by primeval man in many countries, may be formed. They may be purchased for quite trifling sums, for the prices remain low. Of course, those chipped with care command fancy prices, and some of the rarer types sell for several shillings each. Perhaps the scarcest are those relics of the war which was perpetually going on between tribes and between man and beast, especially the arrow heads, which, when bound on withy stems, formed such deadly weapons in the hands of the savage, who, if he knew little about handling tools, knew how to wing an arrow with deadly aim. All such should be collected where possible.

DALEK

"TREASURE [

CUT IT OUT
WITH YOUR
FRETSAW

CUT ANTENNAE
FROM 1/8IN.
WOOD

DALEK

CUT "DALEK" TO OUTLIN
FROM 1/4IN. MATERIAL

CUT TO
OUTLINE 1/4 IN.

GLUE DOWN

DALEK

CUP HOOKS

BBIES NO.19
OD KNOBS

OO GAUGE RAILWAY GOODS TRAFFIC

THE item of timber traffic in relation to railways and railway modelling may, of course, be divided into a large number of different branches. Trees are felled at some forest site which may be situated some distance from a railway line. In this case, they are conveyed to the nearest goods siding, probably at a country station, on horse-drawn or motor lorries, where they are loaded on to the special type of wagon most convenient for their particular variety.

Varied Loads

Long trees are often carried on flat bogey wagons having three, four or more pairs of bolsters—that is, swivelling bearers having heavy iron pins at each end to retain the load in position. The load is chained down to these bolsters, which are so arranged as to permit the wagon beneath to swing over points and curves. We shall later discuss some of these vehicles and their arrangement on trains.

The Locomotive

Meanwhile, Fig. 1 shows a familiar type of road vehicle, used in conveying heavy logs over rods, which can be very easily modelled. The vehicle itself has four wheels of the same size, which consist of spoked brass wagon wheels from which the flanges have been turned off, and these wheels may be ordered in this form at the cost of a very little extra.

The wagon is best made up of various grades of wire, the heaviest being a length of $\frac{1}{8}$-in. copper telegraph wire for the main member. For the fifth wheel, a large sized press-stud is recommended,

as this allows the necessary swivelling movement, and is convenient in that it may be detached into two pieces while the model is being made.

The dummy springs are of bent wire, the axles of a slightly thicker gauge. The bolsters are of $\frac{1}{8}$-in. square brass strip. The shafts are of wire bent to correct shape. The animal figures can be made up from a small toy horse sold by a famous department store, which requires a little length filing from the legs, and from the tails, the defects being made up in plastic wood.

The heads may be removed and carefully set in varied positions with the help of the same material, the finished models being painted with flat paints and correct harness being worked up from passe partout tape and fine wire. Ship's chain (model) may be used for the traces and collars.

In Fig. 2 we have a typical goods yard crane such as would be used for the work of transferring these timbers. The base is a block of wood, with steps of stripwood. The jib is formed of a length of brass strip filed to a suitable taper.

Crane Parts

The pulley is an O-Gauge signal pulley set between two spare clippings from a OO Gauge coupling, which are ready drilled, and are sweated on to the jib, a piece of wire serving as axle for the pulley and as the struts extending to the main member of the crane.

The mechanism, which does not necessarily need to work, is made up of watch-cogs, a watch pinion and wire, the main bearers being filed up from

An idea of what a timber yard is like, with gantry, rails, sheds, etc.

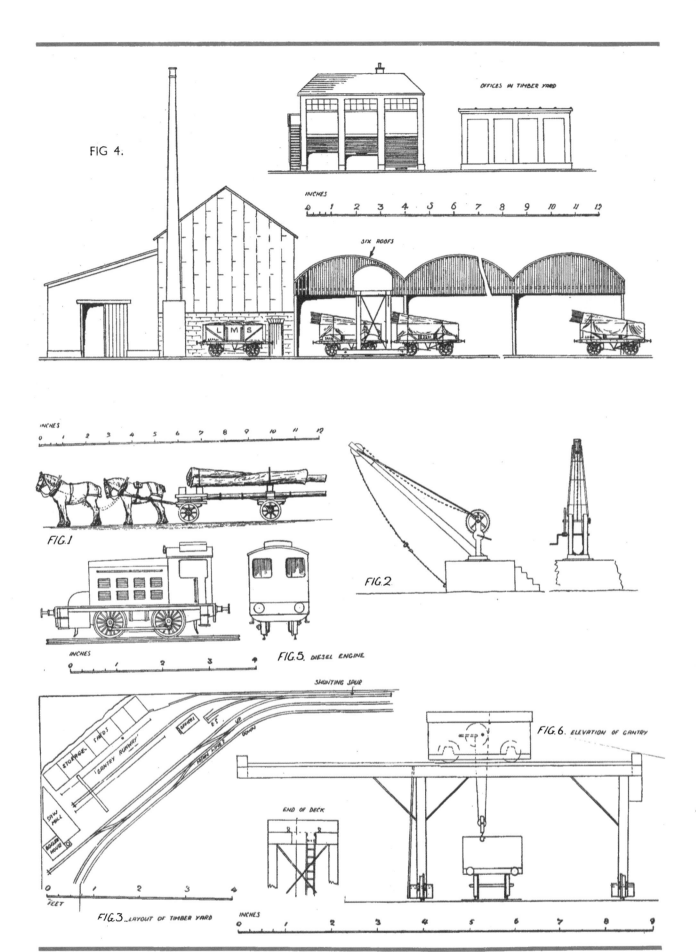

FIG 4.

OFFICES IN TIMBER YARD

INCHES
0 1 2 3 4 5 6 7 8 9 10 11 12

SIX ROOFS

LMS

INCHES
0 1 2 3 4 5 6 7 8 9 10 12

FIG.1

FIG.2

FIG.5. DIESEL ENGINE

INCHES
0 1 2 3 4

SHUNTING SPUR

FIG.6. ELEVATION OF GANTRY

STORAGE YARDS

GANTRY RUNWAY

OFFICES

MAIN LINE UP

DOWN

SAW MILL

BOILER HOUSE

END OF DECK

0 1 2 3 4
FEET

FIG.3. LAYOUT OF TIMBER YARD

INCHES
0 1 2 3 4 5 6 7 8 9

sheet brass, both at one filing. The chain is that sold for model ships, and costs a shilling per yard.

From the country station, the timber is conveyed to sawmills and timber yards located at some distant point on the railway, and a detailed design for such a storage is given.

Shunting Lines

This is shown in the perspective sketch, and in the dimensioned drawing in Fig. 3, which gives the plan of the layout in relation to the main lines. The arrangement of the tracks here is in strict accordance with real practice, provision being allowed for the receiving of trains from both the up and down lines, and for the immediate return of the main line engines when the train has been delivered.

There is also a shunting spur adjoining the yard, with a siding running beneath a travelling gantry crane alongside the storing sheds. Within the yard itself, it is probable that a Deisel locomotive of modern type would be employed exclusively, on account of safety-demands, and there is a small shed for the housing of this engine.

Locomotive and Yard

A design for such a locomotive is given in Fig. 5, while Fig. 4 gives the elevation of the timber yard. The locomotive is designed to take a Reidmere 4-coupled mechanism with 17-millimetre wheels. It should be a very simple model to build, and it would be well to order the mechanism specially geared for slow working.

The site of the yard occupies a mere corner of the layout, and includes a long storage shed built up of cardboard strips to represent lath-construction, a boiler-house and sawmill, an office building with garages underneath, and the engine shed mentioned.

The Gantry

Cardboard may be employed for the semi-circular roofs, and this may be lined out, like the upper portion of the sawmill, and painted aluminium to suggest corrugated iron sheeting. The gantry crane is shown in Fig. 6, and it is made very simply from stripwood or from strip brass, the latter being the easier job. It is provided with a pair of running rails on its main deck, and the travelling portion of the crane consists of a disused coach bogey turned upside down and having the hand crane built into the tinplate hood, which is soldered to the bogey.

Crane Mechanism

For the crane movement, a spoked wagon wheel should be set inside the crane hood on a spindle terminating in a crank outside. This should be so soldered on the spindle as to allow the latter to slide in its holes laterally and to engage when desired a projecting pin passing through the wall, which will retain the hoist in any desired position.

The gantry runs on four wagon wheels of the smallest HO-Gauge size, which are set between washers and between the wheel bearers of brass strip, drilled for the axles. The framework of the gantry should be made in two pieces, these lying flat on a board on which a sketch of the positions of the members has first been made. The chimney stack is made of rolled paper covered with stone paper, which is also used for the walls of the lower part of the sawmill.

(To be Continued)

Making Sand-castle Battlements

A 'SEASIDE' PROJECT

MAKE up this box for the children and take it on holiday to the seaside. Used in conjunction with the bucket and spade, the children will be able to make some wonderful sand-castles.

Cut two of A from ¼ in. wood, one of B, and two of C from ⅜ in. wood, using a fretsaw. Pin and glue them together (using waterproof glue), shaping piece B to fit. The pieces down the centre, forming the battlements, are 1 in. by ¾ in., and the smaller pieces ½ in. by ⅜ in. Give two or three coats of gloss paint to finish.　　　　(M.p.)

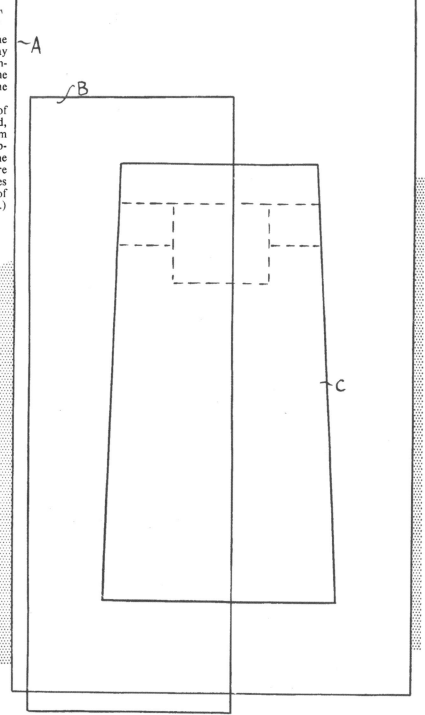

Printed by BALDING & MANSELL, LTD., London and Wisbech, and Published for the Proprietors, HOBBIES LTD., by HORACE MARSHALL & SON, LTD., Temple House, Tallis Street, E.C.4. Sole Agents for Australia and New Zealand: Gordon & Gotch (A'sia.) Ltd. For South Africa: Central News Agency Ltd. Registered for transmission by Canadian Magazine Post.

READER'S REPLY
HW JUNE 1961

You do not need a field to be able to use this
PLAYGROUND CRICKET SET

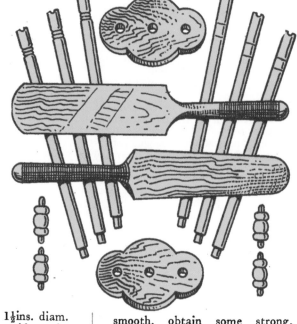

A LOT of school playgrounds and playing fields have this disadvantage—they consist of a concrete surface or a surface too hard to use your cricket stumps, yet they provide an ideal spot for the game on a small scale, and with this thought in view, we have designed the special cricket set shown herewith. With the set, the stumps can be set up in the usual way, on a wooden base. Alternatively, they can also be set up on very soft ground, such as a sandy beach or shore.

A Base Holder

Although mounted on a wooden base, the stumps and bails are just as easy to knock over as if stuck in soft ground. There is the added advantage of being able to extend or curtail the length of the pitch without any trouble, and owing to the fact that the "field" is a concrete one, the pitch lines can be easily marked with white chalk.

Moreover, the same cricket set can be used on a field in the usual way. That is, the stumps can be stuck in the ground minus the supporting base.

Making the Bats

Not only are the wickets dealt with, but also the bats, two designs being provided. The dimensions given are suitable for fellows about 10 or 12 years old. It would, nevertheless, be very easy to make the set to suit your own requirements larger.

The bats should be made from a good hardwood such as beech or oak, but American whitewood and ordinary whitewood like spruce or deal would serve admirably if, particularly, rubber balls or sponge-rubber balls were used.

To mark out the bat shapes, first rule a central line up the wood, same being 4ins. wide by 24ins. long by ⅞in. or 1in. thick. It will be seen that the handle is 10½ins. long, so mark that off with the set-square.

The handle top is 1½ins. diam. It tapers down to 1in. wide at the shoulder to branch out as shown. The bat bottom is shaped with the compasses. The second bat is narrower at the bottom; you have the choice of making identical bats of one design or the other.

When marked out, cut to shape with a panel saw and a padsaw or keyhole, the latter being used in cutting the bottom end and shoulder shapes. When the bats are cut out, spokeshave and glass-paper the handle.

Handle Covering

The handles of the bats must, as you will realize, be rounded. A rasp will enable you to get into the shoulder curves; note that the handle top is rounded sidewise as well as endwise.

When the bats are glasspapered smooth, obtain some strong, black-waxed thread. This is used in covering the handle, but while preferred, fine twine could be used instead, including cobbler's thread.

A Varnish Finish

You can either cover the handle 5ins. long or the full length. Bore a small hole almost through the top and bottom of the handle, then glue the end of the thread in and commence winding it on tightly until you reach the second hole, the thread end being glued and inserted.

Give the bats a single coat of clear varnish. The handle covering can also be coated, but make sure that the varnish is perfectly dry before using the bats. Incidentally, you can round over the back of the bats at the bottom end as shown by the end view at Fig. 1.

Wicket Parts

Now for the wicket parts. The stumps are made from six 20in. lengths of ½in. dowelling. Old broomsticks would do, also mop handles, if you have them handy.

When cut to length, pare a stump tenon on the ends ⅞in. long by ½in. diam. To ensure that the projections will fit tightly into the holes of the base pieces (Fig. 4), these could be cut out first (from ⅞in. thick stuff) and the three holes bored with a ½in. bit.

To make the tenon projections

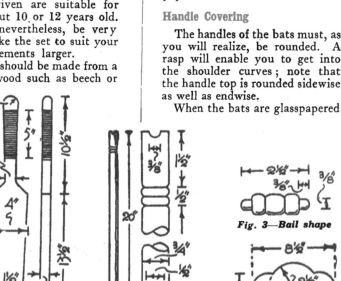

Fig. 1—Front and side view of bat

Fig. 2—Detail of stumps

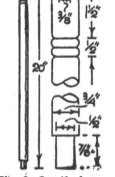

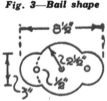

Fig. 3—Bail shape

Fig. 4—The base piece for stumps

first measure the length from the stump ends, then—with a tenon saw—cut the shoulder all round to the depth, being careful not to go beyond the depth ($\frac{1}{8}$in.), otherwise the $\frac{1}{2}$in. diam. tenons will be weakened considerably.

The top ends of the stumps are grooved to suit the bail ends. This is done with a $\frac{3}{8}$in. outside gouge or a V-cut can be made with the tenon saw. You can set off the stumps by filing "beads" around same or simply by cutting "kerfs" around with the tenon saw.

The Bails

Some bails are made separate, others together. For simplicity, however, you can make them separate, one bail piece being detailed at Fig. 3.

Four of these are rasped and filed to shape from 2$\frac{1}{2}$in. length of 1in. or $\frac{3}{4}$in. diam. dowelling or mop and brush poles. Mark off the "beads" as shown, then divide with tenon saw and rasp, finishing off with glasspaper. Varnish all parts when completed.

CHRISTMAS TREE NOVELTY.

PEANUT PARROT.

A VERY attractive Christmas tree novelty is a Peanut Parrot. The requirements for making this pretty little thing is :—1 pint of peanuts, 2 dozen pipe-cleaners, 1 box of matches, 1 roll of fine wire, small rolls of yellow, red, and green crepe paper, tubes of blue, yellow, red, and white paint, a bottle of Indian ink, and some good clean adhesive.

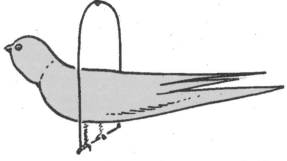

With an old pair of scissors cut each of the pipe cleaners in half. Bend these halves, and stick with the adhesive over the dip A in the peanut. Colour the front portion of the nut in green, yellow, and red, carrying the colour the length of the nut on its under-side. When dry, paint a white ring for the eyes, B, and ink, C, for the beak. Cut out a thin cardboard pattern like Diagram 2, 1$\frac{1}{2}$in. broad at D, and four ins. long from E to F. Lay this pattern on the folded crepe paper, and cut out a dozen or more from each colour.

Arrange these in groups of three, varying the order of the colours, and stick them on to the nut at G, covering the pipe-cleaner. Stick them firmly on the shoulders, and lightly down the sides. The perch is simply a match with the head burnt off. Twist the ends of the pipe-cleaner round the match-stick, to make the claws. Six or eight inches of the fine wire, twisted at each end round the match-stick, makes the loop to hang the completed bird up by.

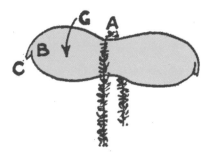

FIG. 1.

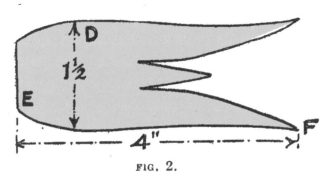

FIG. 2.

KNOTS, AND ALL ABOUT THEM. = I.

THE making of knots is one of the most important branches of seamanship, and from an amateur point of view, perhaps, the least studied. How many minor accidents on small boats are due to the wrong knot having been used! And how often one sees a knot tied which, after a severe strain has been put upon it, refuses to come undone again—a sure sign that the wrong knot has been used! The making of knots, bends, and splices, and all the fancy work attached to ropes and gear, is a most fascinating study to any one who is fond of boats. If much of it is not necessary, it is certain that the more one plays with rope the better one will understand the handling of it and realize why a particular knot is the best for a particular piece of work.

The following knots and bends are all simple ones. Most of them should prove useful at one time or another on small boats. A few, perhaps, are more ornamental than necessary; but every one must admit that, say, a Stopper Knot on the end of a draw-bucket lanyard is more shipshape looking than a figure of eight, and that a certain amount of fancy work improves the appearance of handlines to an accommodation ladder.

All the most useful knots should be so well known that they can be made in the dark and under trying circumstances, and it should never be forgotten that the great recommendation of most of these knots is, not that they hold better than any other, but that they are undone easily; for it is often more important to be able to undo a knot quickly than to make it.

The Reef Knot.

The most common of all is undoubtedly the Reef Knot (Fig. 1). It is unnecessary to describe it or attempt to specify its uses; but a Granny, an absolutely useless knot, is so often made in mistake for a Reef that the two have been illustrated to show the difference.

Hitches.

A Clove Hitch (Fig. 2) is also so well known that description is unnecessary.

A Rolling Hitch (Fig. 2) is used to fasten one rope to another or to a spar when it is necessary that it should not slip. It is made much like a Clove Hitch, but two turns are taken round a standing part and whatever one is tying it to before the final hitch is taken. The two turns are taken on the side to which one does not wish the rope to slip. (In the illustration it will not slip from right to left.) Should it, however, insist on slipping, owing to greasy ropes or any other cause, the end must be bocked (see dotted line) and several turns taken and then seized down.

Figure 3 illustrates the usual and best method of making a rope fast to a bollard. The seizing is not necessary, but it acts as a deterrent on small boys who are fond of undoing ropes.

A Timber Hitch (Fig. 4), as its name implies is used for making a rope fast to a spar or plank, more especially when towing. A half hitch is first taken and the end of the rope used up by twisting it round its own part. This is the Timber Hitch. But it is usual to take another half hitch near the end, as in the illustration, when a spar has to be towed. (A spar, by the way, should always be towed thick end first.)

Figure 5 consists of a Blackwall Hitch, a Blackwall Hitch with two turns, and a Midshipman's Hitch, all used to fasten a rope quickly in a hook. The illustration shows how these knots are made. The only important thing to remember is to get the round turn well up the neck of the hook.

A Marlin-spike Hitch (Fig. 6) explains itself. It is used when an extra pull is wanted in putting on a service or lashing.

Bends.

A Sheet Bend (Fig. 7), or, as it is sometimes called, a Swab Hitch, is handy when two ropes must be fastened together hurriedly, as when sending a hauling-line ashore or running out a kedge. It is far better for this than a Reef Knot, which may capsize and run out if it catches against anything. If two turns are taken, it will hold better and it is not so liable to jamb. To make the knot, form a loop in one rope, and pass the other rope up through this and round the two parts of the first rope and under its own part.

A Carrick Bend (Fig. 8) is the best knot for fastening two ropes together where any long and heavy strain has to be endured, as in a tow-rope.

To make it hold the white rope, as in the illustration, but with the end as shown by the dotted line, pass the other rope up through the loop thus formed over the cross in the white rope and again up through the loop. Both ends are then seized down. This bend will never jamb, and the ropes "take" in so many places that it is not so likely to chafe through or part at the knot as a sheet bend.

A Fisherman's Bend (Fig. 9) is the correct way to fasten a line to an anchor. It is also a first-rate knot for bending a halyard on to a spar. It is made by taking two round turns round whatever one is fastening the rope to, and then taking a half hitch round the standing part and the two round turns, and another half hitch round the standing part alone. For greater security when bending a line to an anchor, the end may be stopped back.

A Bowline (Fig. 10) is used whenever a non-slipping noose is required. It is a knot which never jambs, and therefore can always be undone in a moment. In certain harbours where the rings one has to tie up to are out of reach at certain states of the tide, a long Bowline must be used, or one may find oneself unable to cast the ropes off when necessary. To make a Bowline, take the end and lay it over the standing part, and go through the same action that one would in tying an ordinary knot but let all the turns of the knot be taken

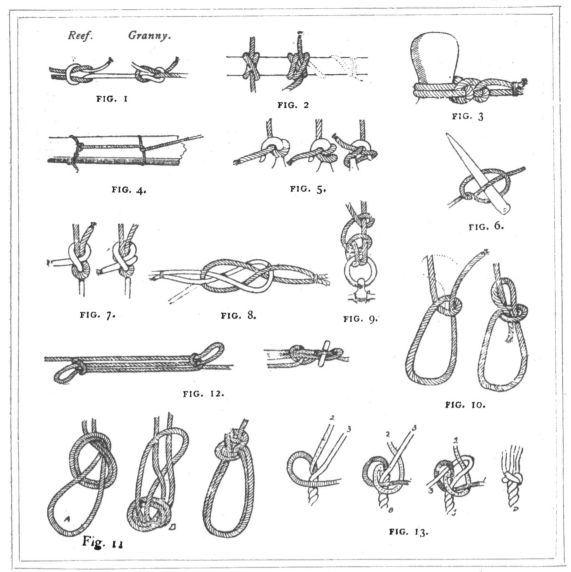

Reef.   Granny.

FIG. I

FIG. 2

FIG. 3

FIG. 4.

FIG. 5.

FIG. 6.

FIG. 7.

FIG. 8.

FIG. 9.

FIG. 12.

FIG. 10.

Fig. 11

FIG. 13.

by the standing part. This will give the first figure. If the end is then made to follow the dotted line, one gets the second figure, which is the complete knot. This knot is usually learned with the noose towards the operator, but when it is necessary to make the knot with the noose the other way as would happen when tying it through a ring, the action is somewhat different; so it is as well to practice both ways.

A Bowline in a Bight (Fig. 11) is by no means as useful a knot as a Bowline. I have, in fact, only found one use for it on a small boat—it makes an excellent bo's'n's chair, one loop forming a seat and the other a back. It is made by forming an ordinary knot, as in the first figure; the loop A capsized over the knot gives the second figure. Now haul on the two parts B until the loop comes down to the knot; this will finish it.

A Sheepshank (Fig. 12) is used to temporarily shorten a rope, such as the topsail sheet when the mainsail is reefed. It is made by forming the rope into an elongated letter S, taking up as much rope as necessary, and then making a half hitch over each end with the standing parts. It may be toggled, as shown, for extra security.

The Wall Knot.

A Wall Knot (Fig. 13) is the commonest of the knots formed on a rope by its own strands. To make it, unlay 6 or 7 inches of the rope, and lay strand No. 1 as in Fig. A. Strand No. 2 is now led over No. 1 and behind No. 3, as in Fig. B. No. 3 is then taken round No. 2 and passed through the loop of No. 1, as in Fig. C. When these strands are worked taut, the finished knot D is the result. The ends may now be laid up again and sewed, or the knot may be crowned.

A USEFUL DISINFECTANT.—A disinfectant that is most effective in moldy cellars, kitchen sinks or bad-smelling places of all kinds, and which will drive away fleas and flies, can be made for about sixpence. All that is needed is to dissolve a pound of copperas in a gallon of water and add 8oz. of carbolic acid.

KNOTS, & ALL ABOUT THEM.

To crown a Wall Knot (Fig. 14) the ends are each passed over their left-hand neighbour and worked taut. The crown may be made first and the Wall Knot worked underneath it, if desired.

A Double Wall Knot (Fig. 15). This figure represents a single Wall Knot seen from on top, and with the marline-spike opening the loop of No. 1 strand. The end of No. 1 now follows the lead of No. 3, its right hand neighbour—that is, it passes under No. 2 and through its own part, which the

COMPLICATED —EXAMPLES.—

through both No. 1 and No. 2 and its own loop. The knot must now be carefully worked tight, and each strand made to lie in its right place. When the knot is finished, and the ends laid up and secured, it will look like Fig. D.

A Diamond Knot (Fig. 18) is useful for ornamenting handlines, &c., and if doubled looks something like a Man Rope Knot. To make it, bring each strand down against the standing part so as to form three loops. The first strand is then taken over the end of the next and led up through the loop of

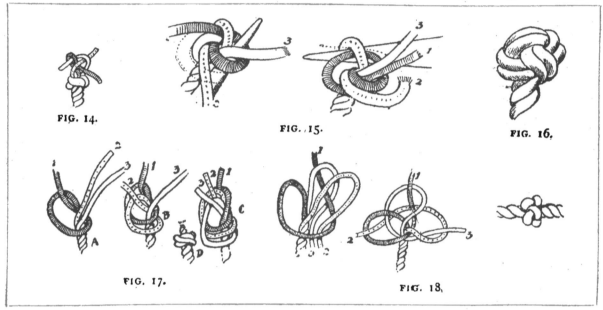

FIG. 14.

FIG. 15.

FIG. 16.

FIG. 17.

FIG. 18.

spike has opened. No. 2 then follows No. 1, as in the second illustration, and is tucked under its own part. Finally, No. 3 follows the lead of No. 2, and is tucked under its own part and No. 1. This finishes the Double Wall or Stopper Knot, as it is sometimes commonly called.

A Man Rope Knot is too complicated to illustrate in construction, but is really quite easy to make. First make a single wall and crown it, not drawing the strands too tight. Then follow round the wall again, and, to finish, follow round the crown. The finished knot will appear as in Fig. 16.

A Matthew Walker (Fig. 17) is another knot for the end of a rope. Start making it as in A—that is, by passing No. 1 strand right round the standing part and through its own loop. No. 2 is treated in the same way, only that it also passes through the loop of No. 1 as well as its own. No. 3 passes

the third. The second strand passes over the third and up through the loop of the first, and the third over the first and up through the second. This gives the middle illustration. When the knot is finished and the ends laid up, it will look like the third illustration. A Double Diamond is made by following the ends round again, as in a Double Wall Knot.

All these roots have been shown in three-strand rope, but they may be made in the same manner in four-strand rope, the fourth strand being treated in the same manner as all the others. The heart of the rope must either be cut out, or, if the rope is to be laid up again when the knot is finished, it may be allowed to come out of the middle of the knot and the strands laid up on it again. When it is desired to lay the rope up again after the knot is made, it is as well to try to keep the natural lay of the strand, as it facilitates the laying up considerably.

SPLICING ROPE ENDS

MOST of us use rope at various times, and a knowledge of the correct way to work it will help to do a craftsmanlike job. In making a swing, for instance, eye splices and whippings are needed to do the job properly. If we are interested in boating, proficient ropework is very important. In practice, eye splices and whippings are the things that matter in most jobs. No rope should be left without a whipping or splice, otherwise it soon frays, and a part of the rope has to be cut off and wasted.

Whipping should be done with quite thin line. For the average rope, the thinnest string is too thick. A stout thread is better. The type used for sewing canvas or carpets is ideal. It is best to draw the thread through a lump of beeswax or a piece of candle before use. This waterproofs the thread and strengthens it by sticking down all the stray fibres.

There are many methods of whipping, but the best one for three-strand rope is the sailmaker's. In this the line goes through the rope as well as around it. The whipping was devised for the ends of reef points on a sail, where the con-

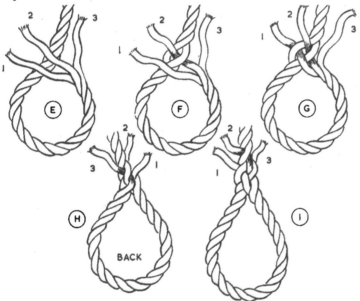

stant flapping would shake loose any inferior whipping.

To make a sailmaker's whipping, open the rope for a short distance (A) and lay in a loop of thread, so that one strand is encircled and the two ends come out of the opposite gap. Have a short and a long end, and do not pull the loop tight. Twist up the strands of the rope again.

Hold the loop and the short end down the rope and put on several turns with the long end (B). Do not make whipping longer than the thickness of the rope.

Lift the loop and put it over the end of the strand it is already encircling and pull

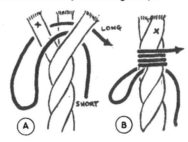 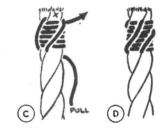

the short end to tighten it (C). The two sides of the loop will follow up the lines of the spaces between the strands, and the short end will be projecting from the only space without one of these outside 'snaking' strands. Take the short end up over the vacant space and into the middle of the rope where the long end is tied to it and the surplus cut off (D).

An eye splice makes a permanent loop in the end of a rope. It may be made around a metal thimble or left loose. With the common three-strand rope the three end strands are woven into the main part of the rope over and under the main strands three or four times. To do this it is necessary to unlay a good length — at least ten times the thickness of the rope.

Bend up the loop and regard the side on which the end strands point across the lay of the main strands as the front (E). Lay the end strands across, so that two convenient ones are at the front and the third held out of the way. Take the front strand furthest from the eye and put it under the nearest main strand (F). With hard rope a spike may be needed to open the rope. Take the other front strand and tuck it under the next main strand, going in the space where the previous one comes out (G).

Turn the splice over and find the remaining main strand which is without an end strand under it. Tuck the third end strand under it, but go in the same direction as the others (H). You should now have an end strand projecting from every space in the main rope. Pull up the strands evenly and arrange them at about the same level around the rope.

The next steps are rather like weaving. Take each strand in turn and work it over the adjoining main strand and under the next one (I). Pull up tight after all three are tucked, then do the same again. This total of three tucks is enough for most purposes. For neatness half of the fibres can be scraped out of each strand, then another tuck made and the surplus cut off. The tucks may be evened up by rolling the splice between two boards. Do not cut off the strands too close, or they may work back under strain. (P.W.)

Attachment for Hedge Trimming

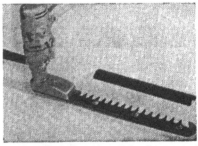

The new Black & Decker Hedge Trimmer and Pruner attachment, shown here powered by the ¼ in. Sander Polisher Drill. The slip-on blade guard converts the attachment for pruning.

THE RIDLEY MONOPLANE.
WINNER OF THREE 1st PRIZES.

THE Ridley Monoplane, No. 34, has shown its good qualities by winning three first prizes during the month of June and July last. It was designed and constructed entirely by Cyril Ridley, one of the leading members of the Arundel House School Aero Club, Surbiton. This school club was first established in October, 1908, and is the oldest School Aero Club, as well as the oldest Aero Model Club, in Great Britain. The club is fortunate in having a most energetic secretary, Mr. Robert P. Grimmer, and it is to his energies that the club owes much of its success.

In the course of the twelve months ending October 1st, 1910, members of the Arundel House School Aero Club, won twelve prizes in public competition. The winner of the youths' competition, held at the Crystal Palace last August, R. F. Mann, whose monoplane has already been described in HOBBIES, is also a prominent member of this club of over twenty-five hard-working members.

The Ridley Monoplane has two outriggers of silver spruce, 33in. by ¼in. square. These are 9in. apart at the rear and 3in. at the prow. At the rear the outriggers are joined by a piece of the same wood, 9in. by ¼in. square, and at the front by a semi-circular piece of ⅛in. cane, this being lashed to the wood, and forms an efficient landing skid.

The main plane has a span of 24in., tapering from 4½in. wide in the centre to 2in. at the tips, the camber being ⅛in. The framework of the plane is ⅛in. square hickory, and the five ribs are of whitewood. The aero curve is obtained by judicious heating over a gas jet. The approximate area of the main plane is 72 square in., and the sides are set at a dihedral angle, as shown in the sectional view; but there is no angle of incidence.

The fabric used is "Pegamoid." This is cut to size, and then sewn to the main plane, so that it is stretched as tightly as possible.

The *elevating plane* is 10in. by 2in., and like the main plane has no angle of incidence. It is made from a piece of 1-32in. spruce, the ailerons, each 2in. square, being made as a part of the elevating plane. The area of the front plane, including ailerons, is 28 square inches, giving, with the 72 square inch of the main plane, a total surface of 100 square inches. Both planes are attached to the frame with bands of rubber.

The propellors are 9in. diameter, and 18in. pitch, and are constructed from 1-16in. whitewood; they are cut to exact shape, sandpapered quite smooth, and then steamed thoroughly, and bent to correct pitch. The Ridley screws have a remarkable efficiency; the slip loss being extremely small. The pitch is that usually described as compound, that is the angle varies from base to tip, so that the maximum thrust may be obtained; an aero curve is also given to the blades.

Bearings.—The shafts are made of hairpin wire, carefully bent over and twisted round the bosses, two small steel collets are placed between the bearing and the propellor boss. The bearings on the end of outriggers are cut from sheet brass, bent, drilled, and then tacked and lashed on with fine wire. The rubber hooks being provided at the end of a length of wire passing through the front framing.

The Rubber Motor.—Each propellor is driven by twelve strands of 1-16in. rubber. Cycle valving is placed over the rubber hooks, and the hook of the propellor shafts and a rubber lubricant is used to improve the elastic. Average number of turns: 500.

Over a measured course in a calm the machine has attained an average speed of 15 miles an hour, and it has flown in a straight line for a distance of just under 900 ft., when aided by a gentle breeze. The machine shows good stability, and possesses excellent powers of straight flight; the maker attributes this to his use of ailerons on the front plane.

It is interesting to note that the maker of this model is also the designer and pilot of several gliders, two of which have been very successfully flown. He has also designed and manufactured a team of man-lifting kites, each of which is 80 sq. ft. in area. He is a youth of remarkable promise, and even at the age of 16, has already a record of which many model makers would be proud. Needless to say, he is taking up the profession of aviation.

DIMENSIONS OF MACHINE.

Length of framework, 33 ins.
Width of framework at propellors, 9 ins.
Width of framework in front, 3 ins.
Length of main plane, 24 ins.
Width of main plane, 4½ ins. tapering to 2 ins.
Size of front plane, 10 ins. by 2 ins.
Ailerons, 2 ins. by 2 ins.
Camber, ¼ in.
Propellor, 9 ins. diameter, 18 ins. pitch.
Rubber, twelve strands, 1-16 in. square.
Weight of model, 4 ozs.

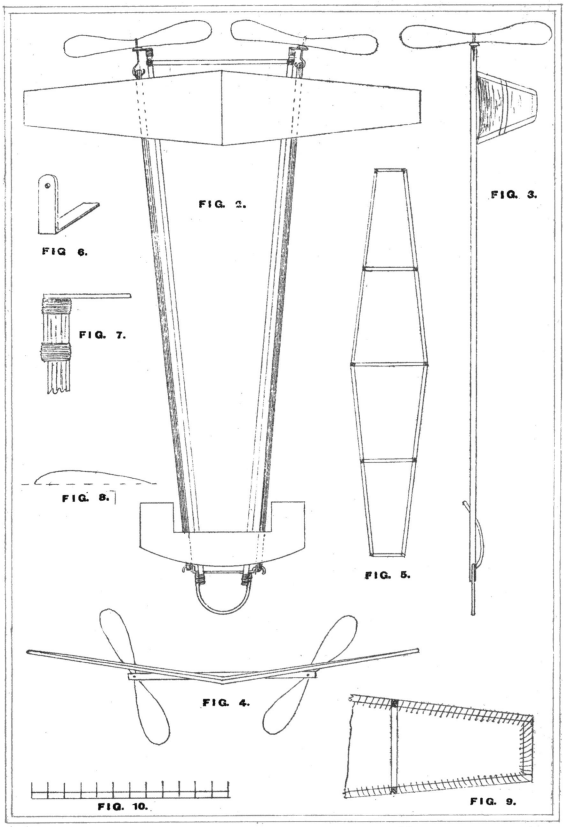

FIG. 2.

FIG. 3.

FIG. 6.

FIG. 7.

FIG. 8.

FIG. 5.

FIG. 4.

FIG. 9.

FIG. 10.

2. Plan of machine with position of planes and propellors.
3. Side elevation, showing the cambered front plane.
4. Section showing the dihedral angle of the main
   plane.
5. The under-surface of main plane, showing ribs.

6. The brass-bearing for propellor shaft.
7. Method of fixing the bearing to the frame.
8. Diagram showing aero-curve in the main plane.
9. Enlarged detail, showing method of lacing the
   fabric to the frame.
10. Scale of inches.

Instructions. ~~Cut~~ the base, No. 1, in wood ½in. thick. The remaining parts in Ivorine. The positions of the various parts are indicated on the key illustration in Hobbies of Sept. 13.

In resp
given. T

IVORINE

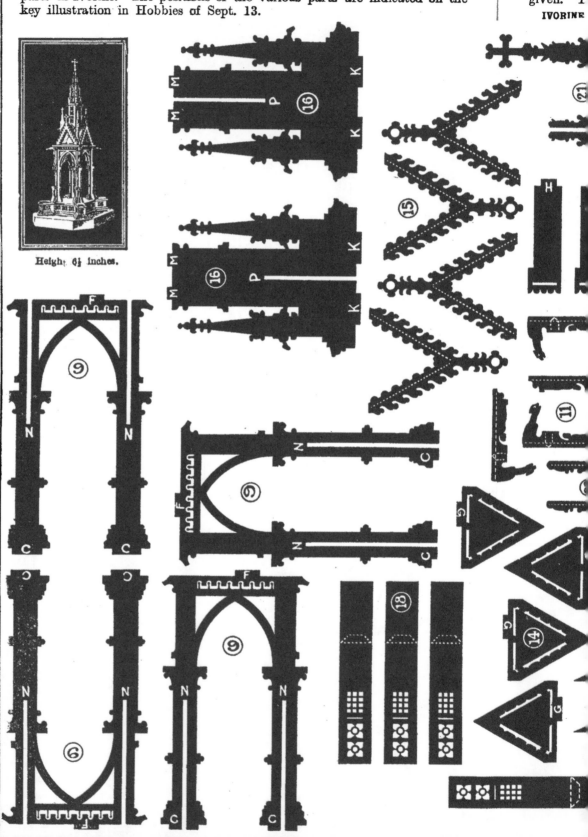

Height 6¼ inches.

sts we have reproduced this design to a larger scale than that in which it was previously
this pattern will be 6½in. high.
he of the correct thickness may be had from Hobbies Ltd., size 6in. by 12in., price 1/4, or post free, 1/6.

A TOY CROSSBOW

THIS toy crossbow is an ideal piece of equipment for boys playing at 'William Tell' and other characters from the Middle Ages. Although in the main the shape of the crossbow conforms to the original weapon, our version has been streamlined on modern lines.

Arrows are released by a trigger action and travel in a groove along the stock. The motive force is obtained from a length of elastic stretched from the ends of the bow.

Although the makeup described here is not powerful enough to do any serious damage, the usual precautions should be taken when using the crossbow. It should be fired out of doors, as with any other toy bow and arrow, and not pointed directly at any other person. Nevertheless, good fun can be obtained by aiming at trees or other targets. Parents should note that power can be controlled by the tension of the elastic, which should be adjusted accordingly. The tips of the wooden arrows should also be rounded as an additional safety precaution.

The makeup of the crossbow is on the sandwich or bread-and-butter principle. All the parts necessary are shown full size on the design sheet. Because of space limitations, some have been overlapped, but the shapes are clearly defined. They should be traced and transferred to their appropriate thicknesses of wood, and cut out with the fretsaw.

Chamfer one edge of each piece 1, and glue them to piece 2, as shown in Fig. 1, noting that the chamfered edges face each other. This will form the groove along which the arrow and flight travel. Next glue together pieces 3 and 4 as seen in Fig. 2, and continue by adding pieces 5 and 6 as shown in Fig. 3.

The trigger assembly is shown in Fig. 4 and an exploded version in Fig. 5. First

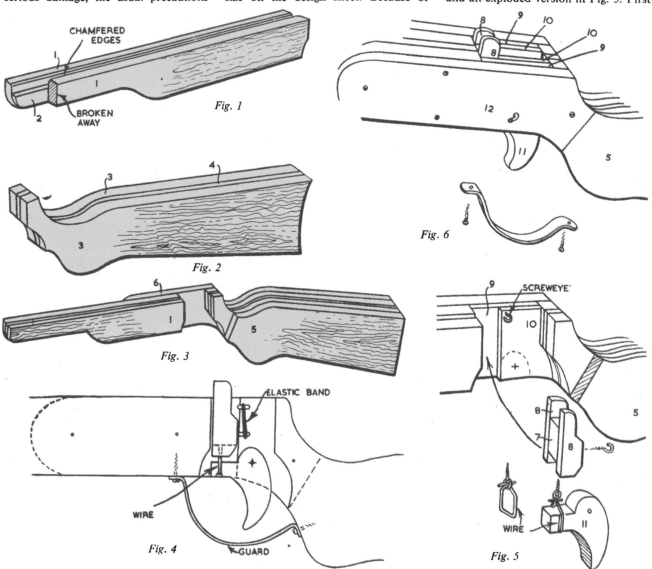

Fig. 1

Fig. 2

Fig. 3

Fig. 4

Fig. 5

Fig. 6

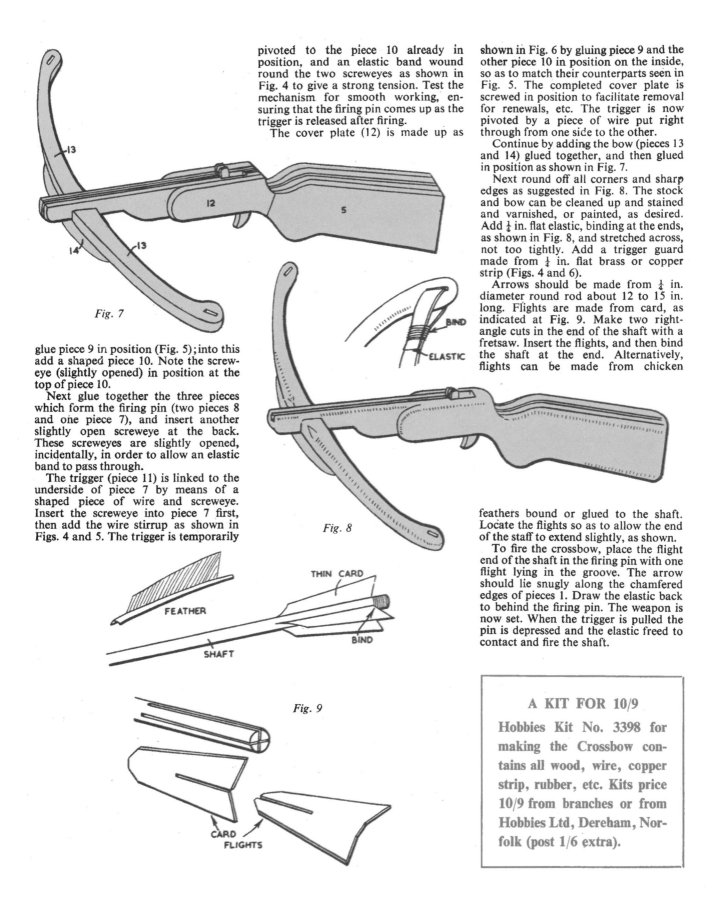

pivoted to the piece 10 already in position, and an elastic band wound round the two screweyes as shown in Fig. 4 to give a strong tension. Test the mechanism for smooth working, ensuring that the firing pin comes up as the trigger is released after firing.

The cover plate (12) is made up as

Fig. 7

glue piece 9 in position (Fig. 5); into this add a shaped piece 10. Note the screweye (slightly opened) in position at the top of piece 10.

Next glue together the three pieces which form the firing pin (two pieces 8 and one piece 7), and insert another slightly open screweye at the back. These screweyes are slightly opened, incidentally, in order to allow an elastic band to pass through.

The trigger (piece 11) is linked to the underside of piece 7 by means of a shaped piece of wire and screweye. Insert the screweye into piece 7 first, then add the wire stirrup as shown in Figs. 4 and 5. The trigger is temporarily

Fig. 8

BIND

ELASTIC

shown in Fig. 6 by gluing piece 9 and the other piece 10 in position on the inside, so as to match their counterparts seen in Fig. 5. The completed cover plate is screwed in position to facilitate removal for renewals, etc. The trigger is now pivoted by a piece of wire put right through from one side to the other.

Continue by adding the bow (pieces 13 and 14) glued together, and then glued in position as shown in Fig. 7.

Next round off all corners and sharp edges as suggested in Fig. 8. The stock and bow can be cleaned up and stained and varnished, or painted, as desired. Add $\frac{1}{4}$ in. flat elastic, binding at the ends, as shown in Fig. 8, and stretched across, not too tightly. Add a trigger guard made from $\frac{1}{4}$ in. flat brass or copper strip (Figs. 4 and 6).

Arrows should be made from $\frac{1}{4}$ in. diameter round rod about 12 to 15 in. long. Flights are made from card, as indicated at Fig. 9. Make two right-angle cuts in the end of the shaft with a fretsaw. Insert the flights, and then bind the shaft at the end. Alternatively, flights can be made from chicken

THIN CARD

FEATHER

SHAFT

BIND

Fig. 9

CARD
FLIGHTS

feathers bound or glued to the shaft. Locate the flights so as to allow the end of the staff to extend slightly, as shown.

To fire the crossbow, place the flight end of the shaft in the firing pin with one flight lying in the groove. The arrow should lie snugly along the chamfered edges of pieces 1. Draw the elastic back to behind the firing pin. The weapon is now set. When the trigger is pulled the pin is depressed and the elastic freed to contact and fire the shaft.

NOVELTY SHOOTING GAME

THE centre page patterns in this week's issue are for a novel pistol and target. The pistol is a very powerful little weapon and is remarkably accurate up to a range of 10 or 15 feet. The target itself provides the novelty, consisting of a wall on which are seated five cats of different sizes.

Each cat is hinged, so when it is hit, it falls back and disappears behind the wall.

The Pistol

It will be seen that the pistol comprises three parts, two sides and a centre piece, the centre piece fitting exactly between the two sides. After cutting these three parts, the trigger included, glue or screw the centre piece to one of the sides. A small fret-pin is knocked in and bent over at A, and in the trigger at B.

The next step is to make the plunger, which consists simply of a length of ¼in. dowel rod, rubbed down slightly with glasspaper, and notched to engage with the trigger. Two large screw-eyes are screwed in, one behind the other to prevent the screws touching, and allowing the shanks to project.

Now to fit the pistol together, bore a small hole

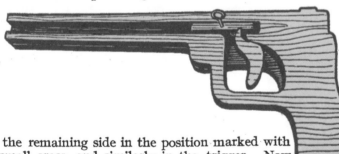

in the remaining side in the position marked with a small cross, and similarly in the trigger. Now put the plunger in the groove of the two parts which have been previously joined, lay the trigger in position and fit the other side in position.

Before screwing down, however, a pin should be knocked home through the hole already bored, and through the hole in the trigger.

The Elastic

This holds the trigger in place, and the side can now be firmly screwed down. The power is got from the elastic which is fixed on either side of the pistol, and tied around the screw-eyes in the plunger and the small eyes in the muzzle of the gun.

The trigger is held forward by a small piece of elastic which is tied through the pins A and B.

The main part is a piece of 3/16in. plywood 12ins. by 4ins. and the buttresses are of ¼in. by

¾in. stripwood, three being required each 4ins. long. Glue or pin these to the wall in the positions indicated, and glue the beading on the top as shown in the section. Next cut the hinge flaps and glue firmly in position on the back of the wall.

The Cat Figures

The cats must next be cut, but with a fine grade fretsaw, because the fretted parts are particularly delicate. Two of them must be reversed and the five of them hinged on to the hinge flaps.

The positions can be seen from the sketch of the finished thing.

Now for the finishing touches. The missiles should be made as shown, from ¼in. dowel rod, and rounded off at the ends. The pistol itself should be varnished or given a coat of jet black paint, but be careful not to get any in the grooves or the plunger will not slide freely.

The Realistic Wall

The wall should be finished off with Hobbies brick paper and an odd piece of rough cast on the buttresses.

The beading on the top should be painted bright red to add a splash of colour.

The cats should be painted red and black as shown on the centre page. With the addition of the wire stays, and the scoring numbers the game is complete.

The great feature of this shooting game is that it is great fun either indoors or out.

FITTINGS REQUIRED

1 piece beading 1ft. long.
1 piece stripwood 1ft. long.
1 piece 1/16th. brass wire 18ins.
1/16in. elastic 1 piece 18ins. long.
2 small screw eyes.
2 large screw eyes.
5 small brass hinges.
1 piece brick paper 12ins. by 4ins.

For particulars on making up the Patterns for a Novel Shooting Game turn to page 63

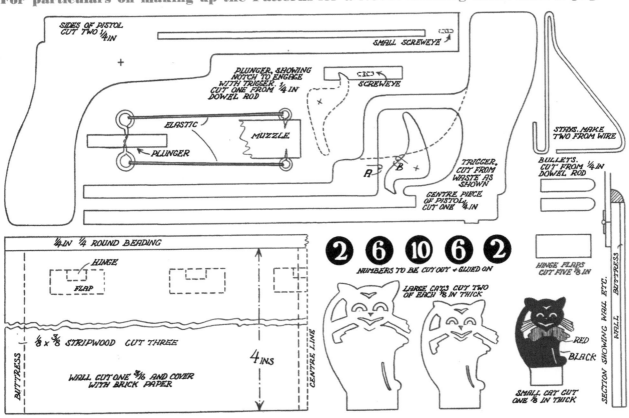

SIDES OF PISTOL CUT TWO ¼ IN

SMALL SCREWEYE

PLUNGER, SHOWING NOTCH TO ENGAGE WITH TRIGGER. CUT ONE FROM ¼ IN DOWEL ROD

SCREWEYE

ELASTIC

MUZZLE

PLUNGER

STAYS. MAKE TWO FROM WIRE

BULLETS. CUT FROM ¼ IN DOWEL ROD

TRIGGER, CUT FROM WASTE AS SHOWN

CENTRE PIECE OF PISTOL CUT ONE ¼ IN

¼ IN ¼ ROUND BEADING

HINGE

FLAP

HINGE FLAPS CUT FIVE ⅛ IN

② ⑥ ⑩ ⑥ ②
NUMBERS TO BE CUT OUT + GLUED ON

BUTTRESS

⅛ x ⅜ STRIPWOOD CUT THREE

LARGE CATS CUT TWO OF EACH ⅛ IN THICK

RED

BLACK

WALL CUT ONE ⁵⁄₁₆ AND COVER WITH BRICK PAPER

4 INS

CENTRE LINE

SMALL CAT CUT ONE ⅛ IN THICK

SECTION SHOWING WALL ETC.

WALL

BUTTRESS

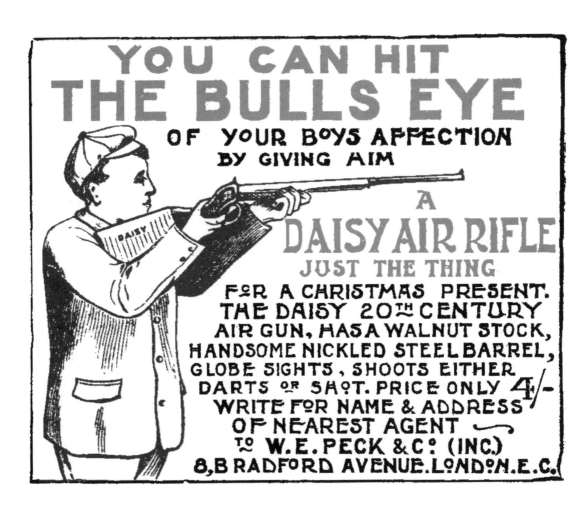

Amusing Novelty—The Dancing Skeleton.

THE effect of this little novelty is surprising. A small wooden skeleton is shown to be free from all preparation. It is laid on the table in full

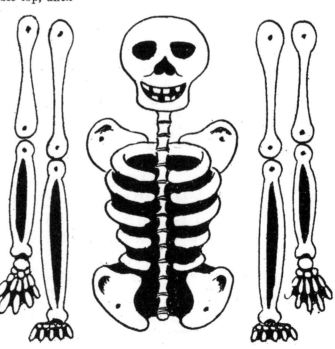

Black   Thread

Hook on back of head

view of the friends who have visited you, when, to their great surprise, the skeleton is seen to rise slowly from the table top, until it stands quite upright. Nor is this the most amazing part. A friend is asked to play a lively tune on the piano—or a gramophone will do, should there be one in the house—when the skeleton figure will immediately begin to dance in a very laughable manner.

Simple When You Know How to Make it.

Like most of the baffling things one sees, it is really a very simple business when you are "in the know." All that is required is a length of black cotton. Paste the pattern of the skeleton on a piece of three-ply, then cut carefully round the outside of the body, legs and arms, taking pains not to damage the pattern, as this can be left on

the wood, and will save painting the ribs, etc.

Having cut out the pieces, they can be pinned together with brass panel pins, which can be turned down at the back of the model.

It is very necessary to see that the arms, legs, and body work freely, otherwise the figure will not dance so funnily. Having joined the arms and legs to body, fix a small hook to the back of the skull (as illustration). Now all is ready for the fun.

The best way to show this novelty to your friends is to fix a piece of cotton on to the back of a chair near the table you are going to use. Bear in mind that the cotton (thread preferable) must be at least 12ins. above the table when pulled taut.

Lay the cotton across the table, with the free end hanging over the opposite side to the chair. Next show your friends the skeleton is only a piece of wood (taking care to hide the hook with your fingers).

Full size patterns for a simple
BALSA GLIDER

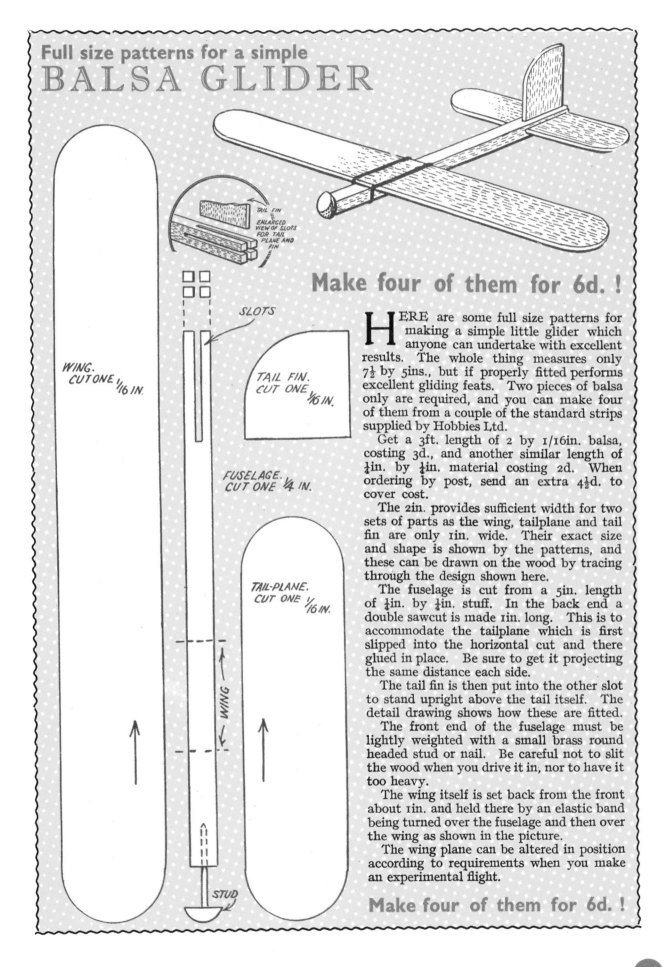

**WING.
CUT ONE ¹/₁₆ IN.**

*TAIL FIN
ENLARGED
VIEW OF SLOTS
FOR TAIL
PLANE AND
FIN*

SLOTS

**TAIL FIN.
CUT ONE ¹/₁₆ IN.**

**FUSELAGE.
CUT ONE ¼ IN.**

**TAIL-PLANE.
CUT ONE ¹/₁₆ IN.**

WING

STUD

Make four of them for 6d.!

HERE are some full size patterns for making a simple little glider which anyone can undertake with excellent results. The whole thing measures only 7½ by 5ins., but if properly fitted performs excellent gliding feats. Two pieces of balsa only are required, and you can make four of them from a couple of the standard strips supplied by Hobbies Ltd.

Get a 3ft. length of 2 by 1/16in. balsa, costing 3d., and another similar length of ¼in. by ¼in. material costing 2d. When ordering by post, send an extra 4½d. to cover cost.

The 2in. provides sufficient width for two sets of parts as the wing, tailplane and tail fin are only 1in. wide. Their exact size and shape is shown by the patterns, and these can be drawn on the wood by tracing through the design shown here.

The fuselage is cut from a 5in. length of ¼in. by ¼in. stuff. In the back end a double sawcut is made 1in. long. This is to accommodate the tailplane which is first slipped into the horizontal cut and there glued in place. Be sure to get it projecting the same distance each side.

The tail fin is then put into the other slot to stand upright above the tail itself. The detail drawing shows how these are fitted.

The front end of the fuselage must be lightly weighted with a small brass round headed stud or nail. Be careful not to slit the wood when you drive it in, nor to have it too heavy.

The wing itself is set back from the front about 1in. and held there by an elastic band being turned over the fuselage and then over the wing as shown in the picture.

The wing plane can be altered in position according to requirements when you make an experimental flight.

Make four of them for 6d.!

Hobbies WEEKLY

CONTENTS

March 31st, 1948   Price Threepence   Vol. 105   No. 2735

SOME time ago we included in these pages an article dealing with the making of a model of a Roman instrument of war known as the Ballista. In this article, we now deal with a similar kind of weapon, differently controlled, with the mechanical movement stronger in effect.

In Roman days, the foot soldiers and horsemen were backed up by the artillery which then consisted of catapults—huge implements for hurling large rocks into the ranks of

A ROMAN BALLISTA

the enemy, and the Ballista, a device working on the same principle, for throwing quantities of arrows.

In each of these the propelling force was produced by the sudden releasing of a great beam or a tree trunk which had been bent by means of ropes and winches to form a huge spring.

A shower of arrows hurled from a Ballista must have created as much havoc in the ranks of the enemy of those days as the bursting of a shell of modern warfare. It was said, too, that the great stones thrown by the catapults of the Romans were often as large as and as heavy as the shells of the modern ones.

So, now to talk of the interesting model we give this week, we will first briefly describe it. Looking at the illustration on this page we see that there is a framework which stands firmly spread on the ground. At the rear of this frame there is a platform upon which slides the back end of the inner frame carrying the spring mechanism and the windlass for winding and bending it.

This inner frame is pivoted between the head cross bar and the sill piece of the fixed framework. The windlass is fixed to the lower member of the inner frame, as can be plainly seen in the side view Fig. 1. The rope running from the windlass is carried round a sheaf block and pulley and up to the top of the laminated spring which is located between the two sloping side members, M, of the inner frame.

The spring consists of three or more thin members of wood secured together only at the lower extremity,

and bound here to the middle member of the inner frame with cord. It will be apparent that when the forward member of the spring is drawn back, the other members are allowed to slide, as it were, one upon the other to get the forward throw of the whole spring.

Two or more arrows lodged in

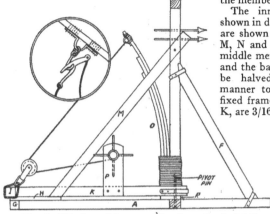

Fig. 1—Sideview of frame with release hook detail

retaining holes in the upright of the middle frame are thrown forward at great speed when the spring is released, after having been bent backward by the windlass and rope. The type of release hook to be fixed between the pulley block and the head of the spring is shown in the enlarged detail in Fig. 1.

Both frames, the fixed ground frame and the inner moving frame, are almost entirely made up from ⅜in. square wood.

The Fixed Frame

In commencing to make the fixed frame, which is shown in detail in Fig. 2, the sole pieces, A, and the cross piece, B, are taken up, halved together and glued and nailed with fret pins. Note the distance of 2½ins. between the members, A. Now cut and fix the end member, G; this should be halved into the pieces, A, as shown. The uprights, C, and the cross head piece, D, are next cut and fitted and nailed in place. These members are firmly held by the sloping struts and supports, E and F.

It is doubtful if anything in the nature of a true woodworking joint was made in those far-off days, but if our craftsman so desires, he may

make a really strong framework by introducing the joint shown in the enlarged detail in Fig. 2. Further strengthen it by adding a stirrup of brass or "tin" bent up and pinned on as our detail suggests.

When the frame shown in Fig. 2 has been completed, a platform, H, must be added and glued or nailed to the members, A and G.

The inner or moving frame is shown in detail in Fig. 3. All members are shown full with the exception of M, N and the spring pieces, O. The middle member, J, of this framework and the back cross member, I, should be halved together in a similar manner to pieces, A and G, of the fixed frame. The two side members, K, are 3/16in. wide and are nailed and glued to, J.

Between these side pieces, K, are glued the upright, N, and its spring pieces, O, as seen by the dotted lines in Fig. 3. To make this frame perfectly rigid, the two upright sloping members, M, are added,

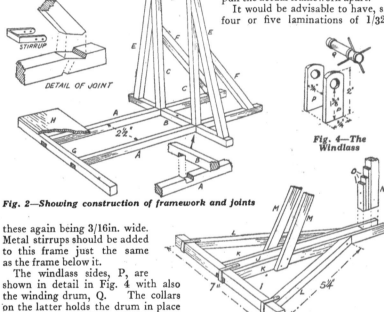

Fig. 2—Showing construction of framework and joints

these again being 3/16in. wide. Metal stirrups should be added to this frame just the same as the frame below it.

The windlass sides, P, are shown in detail in Fig. 4 with also the winding drum, Q. The collars on the latter holds the drum in place between the uprights and they may be of stout brass or other metal bent round and pinned on securely.

The cross handles for pulling the drum round may consist of stout wire driven through tightly. The side view Fig. 1 gives sufficient detail for making the sheaf and pulley which is held by cord to the rear member, I, of the frame.

The pulley should be of wood cut to a disc ⅝in. diameter and grooved round the edge with a rat-tailed file. This wheel is then inserted in a stirrup made from "tin" with an axle pin firmly held at both sides.

The finished block is held by a loop of wire passing through the stirrup

which is in turn held to cross beam of the frame by several strands of cord bound round neatly and coated finally with varnish.

Release Hook

A detail of the release hook is given in Fig. 1 and this can be filed to shape from a piece of stout brass, the two holes necessary, one for the release cord and the other for the sustaining rope running round the pulley, being drilled before the shaping is undertaken. A loop of wire bent up as shown and lashed with cord to the top of the wood spring will take the metal ring connected to the hook, or a length of cord may be carried from the top loop and the hook then fastened further down the rope as seen in Fig. 1.

A word of advice should be added, perhaps, regarding the make-up of the laminated wood spring. Do not attempt to make this too powerful by having too great a number of laminations or having the wood composing them very thick. Too great a strain, that is if the model is wanted for demonstration purposes, will not only break up certain parts of the model, such as the windlass sides, but will pull the actual framework apart.

It would be advisable to have, say, four or five laminations of 1/32nd

Fig. 4—The Windlass

Fig. 3—Triangular frame for platform

wood in preference to three stouter ones as pictured here. A useful tip to the constructor of this model, too, while making up the actual framing of ⅜in. wood is to get the correct angles for the ends of those struts and sloping members where they meet the square framing.

Having, say, the square frames made, and it is desired to proceed with those members such as E, F, L, etc., lay the latter in their true positions on the framing and mark across in pencil exactly where the frame member comes below it.

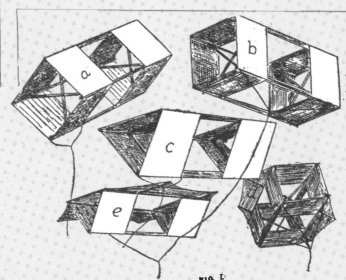

FIG. 1.

KITE flying is a very old pastime, and nearly everybody has had some experience with the old-fashioned flat, and diamond-shaped kite. The box kite is of comparatively recent origin, having been invented by an Australian, Hargreave, and it may be said to have given an impetus to the designs of the flying machine. Santos-Dumont invented a flying machine, which was really a series of box kites attached to a framework and driven by a propellor.

The simplest form of box kite is shown at a and b, Fig. 1, and is composed of 4 long strips covered in at each end, and kept in place by cross pieces. The covering material may be ordinary manila paper, either used alone or strengthened by pasting muslin over it; cotton, or linen fabric, or silk. The timber used should be strong enough to stand the strain which is often considerably, and may be of birch, mahogany or stiff American whitewood.

The kite shown in side and end elevation at Figs. 2 and 3 is 34in. long, with cells 16in. square and 7in. deep. First of all prepare the long strips, 34in. by ½in. by 3-16in., and then cut the material for cover-

ing, two strips 65in. long and 10in. wide. An overlap of 1in. has been allowed for, so join the two ends and glue them together. The edges must now be strengthened with thread or string, as shown at Fig. 6, the hem on each side being ½in., and should be glued down tightly.

The long strips should be glued to the material, as shown at Fig. 4, the edge of each piece touching the fabric being glued. Stretch the material well so that the fabric adheres to the stick, and when set glue on the other two, as shown at Fig 5. taking care that they are exactly in the middle. We have now to provide the cross pieces, as shown in the end elevation, Fig. 3. These are shorter pieces of the same stuff, and are each 22in. long, each piece has a slot cut in the end to fit over the long sticks, as shown at Fig. 8, and this slot is bound over with glued thread, to prevent it splitting, as shown at Fig. 9. Both the cross pieces are

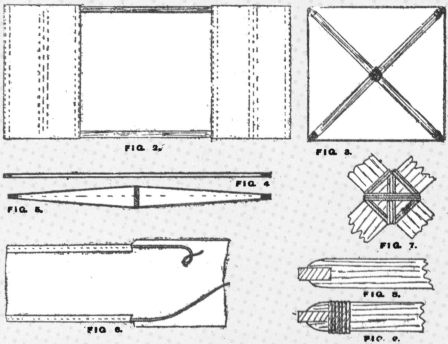

FIG. 2.

FIG. 3.

FIG. 4.

FIG. 5.

FIG. 6.

FIG. 7.

FIG. 8.

FIG. 9.

1. Some types of box kites. 2. Side elevation of simple box kite. 3. End elevation of simple box kite. 4 and 5. Method of attaching the long strips. 6. The method of strengthening the covering material, showing the hem and string. 7. The method of lashing the cross-pieces. 8 and 9. The method of fitting and strengthening the ends of the cross-pieces. 10. Side elevation of a triangular box kite. 11. End elevation of triangular box kite. 12. Method of attaching pieces of tin to triangular strips to hold the stays. 13. Enlarged details of triangular box kite.

lashed together with thread as shown at Fig. 7, and are then placed in position in the centre of each cell. The bridle is attached by either of the two methods shown.

The triangular box kite shown at c, Fig. 1, is another form which is very often seen, but it is not quite so easy to make. Three triangular strips should be prepared, as shown at Fig. 12, and then at each end a piece of sheet tin is tied on as shown. The stays, which in the triangular kite take the place of the cross pieces in the box kite, are fitted against these plates as shown in the enlarged detail at Fig. 13. The pieces are easily put in place, the third being sprung into position, and tightens up the whole thing.

A combination of box kite and flat plane is shown at d, Fig. 1, and with a little ingenuity this may easily be made. One method is to carry the cross pieces right through the material at each corner, and join the extremities with the ends of the long stick, and then

cover with fabric. This prevents the kite from being taken apart so that to make it portable a method of joining on the wings must be used; tubing or lashing are two methods easily adapted, and may be made quite strong.

The old-fashioned diamond shape forms a good type of lifting kite, if made as shown at e, Fig. 1. The triangular box kite, it will be seen, is used in conjunction with it. It is most easily made as may be seen from the illustration.

Considerable skill has been devoted from time to time to the design of kites, and it is a very interesting subject to work at. With the suggestions given above many readers will no doubt be able to make some high flying and good lifting kites and experience the fascination of kite-flying.

MAKING A BOX KITE

FOR the construction of this box kite provide four strips of wood 5/16in. by ⅜in. and 30ins. long. A planed blind lath cut into strips will do for the wood, but choose one with a straight grain and free from any knots.

For the cells of the kite, strong coloured tissue paper is the material to be chosen. This should be cut into two strips 9ins. wide and 4ft. 8½ins. long. The ends are pasted together to form two bands.

A ½in. of each edge is then pasted and a length of thread or fine twine laid along the pasted edge which is then pressed over to form a hem, enclosing the thread. Each band is then folded into four equal parts, the creases being guides for fixing the long strips of wood.

These are glued to the paper edgewise, and after the paper has been well pressed down, left for awhile.

The cross bars are strips of the blind lath cut 19½ins. long and fastened together in pairs by a fretwork nail through the centre. At the end of each cut a notch 5/16in. by ¼in. and pare the ends to a bevel. The cross strips are then pressed gently between the long strips to stretch them apart and

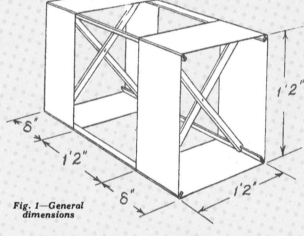

Fig. 1—General dimensions

Fig. 2—The threaded edge

bring the kite to shape. A small notch can be cut into the long strips for the ends of cross strips to set in.

Fig. 1 shows the main dimensions of the kite and Fig. 2 a detail, showing the thread inserted in the pasted hem and one end of a cross strip showing how it fits across.

It is important not to cut the cross strips too short or they will not fit tightly enough, and be useless. It is best to cut the length rather on the full side and trim the notches up as desired afterwards until the fit is satisfactory. It is easy to cut a piece off as required.

Care should be taken to get the fit right; if too tight, the paper cells may split under the strain, so go easy with the job until satisfactory.

No bridle line is needed for a box kite, the kite line being attached approximately where shown in the general view of the completed kite.

A box kite is not difficult to fly. Let out twenty to thirty yards of line and get a friend to launch the kite in the air for you, a good breeze will do the rest.

As ship lovers and modellers we like to recognise the ships we see in photographs, illustrations and old drawings and, when on holiday, we get the opportunity of seeing one of the fast disappearing types around our coasts. A knowledge of the wide variations of types of hull form and rig will, moreover, open wide a wonderland of ships from which to choose our next

Fig. 3 is a caravel of the time of Columbus. Two of his ships on the famous voyage of discovery were of this type, the *Pinta* and the *Nina*. The *Santa Maria* was converted to square sail for the voyage.

Fig. 4 is a Spanish treasure frigate. This is one of those out-of-the-way ships that I am surprised more modellers have not attempted. I made one myself

Fig. 6 is a naval cutter of the nineteenth century, being in use during the first half of the century. It is an ideal scale model as even to a large scale, say, standard museum scale of ¼in. to the foot, it allows very detailed modelling and at the same time does not result in a model that is too large for the average home.

Fig. 7. In this example we come to the latter part of the nineteenth century and find that the number of types of sailing craft is legion, so many and varied are the types of rig, each and every one designed for its own special purpose.

SAILING TYPES
By Whipstaff

The one illustrated by the sketch is a fishing vessel and even this one type has numerous variations, according to the type of fishing and the locality.

Fig. 8. In this we have a topsail schooner, a very graceful and picturesque ship and one which would grace any home. Again there are many variations of type, both in the number of masts and individual rig.

Fig. 9 is a distinctive type, it is an American fishing schooner of the Blue-

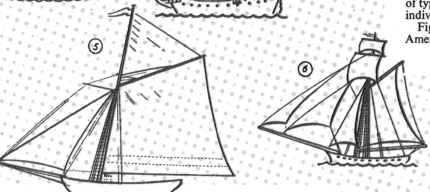

model. Many really worthwhile models have been made because the model maker saw an illustration, or, perhaps, had a family connection with some particular vessel.

Fig. 1 shows us a vessel similar in type to those used by William the Conqueror to transport his troops to the shores of this Country and is a very good prototype for the model maker.

Fig. 2 is a ship of the thirteenth century. An interesting item is that it shows the double paddle rudder still in use.

and found it a very fascinating model indeed. It represents a ship of about 1600 A.D.

Fig. 5, a naval sloop, would make a very interesting subject for the ambitious model maker and I am in fact commencing a detailed scale model based on the contemporary plans of an actual vessel of 1750 A.D.

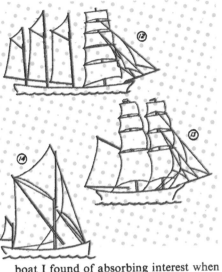

experience of seeing racing yachts in full sail will know, the 'fore and aft' is a most satisfactory sight and makes a graceful model.

Fig. 11. This is one of the variations of the square-rigged sailing ship, in this case it is a barque. One of the most famous of this type was the celebrated *Achibald Russell*. These are models that if well modelled are really satisfying to make and are the aim of the serious modeller.

Fig. 12. The four-masted barquentine is a variation of the square-rig ship, all these variations being very intriguing to make.

Fig. 13 is a brig of the nineteenth century and these are again many and various in type, the prototype not being a large ship, we again have a type that can be modelled in a large enough scale to show all the detail without the finished model being over large. This is also a very suitable type for those who want to make an actual sailing model.

Fig. 14 is an example of what is, perhaps, the last surviving type of sailing vessel to be in trade, namely the Thames sailing barge, always an interesting model to make.

nose type, popularly known by the term 'Gloucester Fisherman'. This is again a

boat I found of absorbing interest when modelling.

Fig. 10. In this we see a type of vessel that has a very large number of variations in masts and rig, it is the very beautiful fore and aft schooner. As anyone who has had the delightful

For Handymen and Craftsmen

October 29th, 1941   Vol. 93. No. 2402

A Working Model
AUTOMATIC PISTOL

THIS is not just an *automatic* pistol in name, but in working principle, in a sense. You see, there is a chamber, or loading aperture, at the front of the barrel which holds five wooden bullets. Before putting these in the chamber, the trigger is pressed and the plunger rod drawn backwards, then both released.

Plunger rod and trigger lock together, it will be found. When loaded, all one has to do is to press on the trigger—and out pops a bullet in a realistic manner.

To fire another shell, the trigger is again pressed and the plunger rod drawn backwards, whereupon the pistol is ready for firing another bullet and so on until the supply is exhausted.

Firing Five at Once

Simple, but automatic, and far better than having to load each bullet singly all the time. You can put in five projectiles at once and fire them quickly in the manner

explained. The whole idea is clearly shown by the diagram at Fig. 1.

As one bullet pops out, another one drops into the vacant space. As to the force and accuracy of the bullets, much depends on the elastic power and the construction of the model. It is imperative that the elastic tension is less strong than the spring actuating the trigger.

Therefore, use a good, strong spring in order to have the driving force as strong as possible. An ordinary steel hair clip of large size will provide an excellent spring, by the way.

Patterns and Wood

Patterns of the pistol parts are printed full-size on a sheet obtainable from the Editor for 2d. All parts are, with exception of an additional cover piece, shown; you can easily mark out a repeat shape from the cover piece when cut out.

Note that the plunger rod is cut from 3/16in. plywood. The other shapes are cut from fretwood. The reason for cutting the plunger rod from plywood is to have it strong where short-grained. The trigger, also, should be cut from plywood, if possible and in fact, it would not be a bad idea to cut all central parts from this material.

Consequently, if you can manage to do this, trace or paste the centre parts on the wood and cut them out with the fretsaw. While you are at it, cut out all the other parts shown and glasspaper them lightly on the reverse side to remove roughness and trimmings.

Assembly

Assemble the model by gluing the four centre pieces neatly on one of the cover pieces. The trigger is fixed in position with a panel pin (see Fig. 1) which serves as a pivot. Tap the pin in temporarily, for it must be remembered that the pin must go through both cover pieces.

Having fixed the trigger in place, obtain a large hair clip and bend it to the shape shown (a full-size drawing is given on the pattern page). It is necessary, of course, to cut the clip to length and bend up with the pliers. The right-angle bend fits tightly, or should do so, into the saw kerf.

Have the spring bent forwards to press against the trigger with some amount of force. Proceed by taking away the trigger and seeing that the plunger rod moves backwards and forwards easily.

Preparing the Plunger

When moving satisfactorily, drill holes for panel pins in the plunger and centre part. The elastic band fits over these pins. The detail at Figs. 4 and 1 will be helpful in showing what has to be done.

Two ½in. long elastic bands should be fitted over the pins, or alternatively a 1in. long band doubled would suffice. The trigger, after rounding the edge as shown (Fig. 4) is fixed in place, this time with the pivot pin entering from the opposite side.

Proceed by gluing the cover piece in place, taking care not to have any glue smudging the plunger or filling the plunger aperture. Drive the trigger pivot pin right through and file the point flush, then test the mechanism as explained.

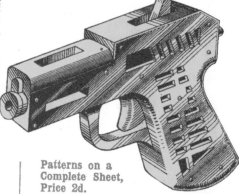

Patterns on a Complete Sheet, Price 2d.

If the elastic tension is too strong for the trigger spring, try using a single band. If the spring is not strong enough, try bending the end outward a trifle more, using long-nosed pliers. The circular aperture cut in the covers is provided for this reason.

Shaping Up

If working to order, level up the three pieces of wood forming the pistol, so far, by glasspapering. The top, fore end of the barrel is rounded

---

AUTOMATIC PISTOL MATERIALS

1 centre piece, 6 by 5ins. by 3/16in.
2 cover pieces, 6 by 5ins. by 3/16in.
2 overlay pieces, 6 by 5ins. by ⅛in.
1 piece dowelling, 6ins. by 3/16in. diam.
Other small odds and ends as mentioned.

over as shown at Fig. 3. Do this with a penknife, rasp, file and glass-paper.

Try to get a true semi-circular shape as shown by the fore-shortened view at Fig. 2. The overlay pieces can now be attached. We advise using small roundhead nails, these being driven in as per illustration of the finished work.

Do not use glue, as you might want to adjust the trigger spring, so the

Clean up the work with glasspaper, then attach the barrel nose pieces, including the plunger rod washer. You should now make five bullets from 3/16in. dowel rod. To ensure that there is some amount of freedom, a suitable length should be glass-papered and tried down the bullet aperture, following which the bullets are cut to length and one end of each pointed as shown.

Fit the five bullets in the bullet

manner, ejecting the "ammunition" with some amount of force and accuracy.

Regarding the finish, most auto-matic pistols are finished black, with some parts nickel. You could stain and polish the pistol ebony black and dull the high gloss by rubbing over with a boot brush dipped in powdered pumice or emery—in other words, knife powder.

Decoration

The heads of the roundheaded nails could be tipped with silver paint, including the trigger guard. The trigger itself is best given a coat of stain and rubbed with boot polish Even if you cannot get this model pistol to work, remember that it makes a good imitation automatic. The bullet aperture could be filled up with a piece of wood and finished off with the rest of the work.

Use a hardwood in its construction to withstand usage and if you happen to have any odd pieces of plywood, this forms the ideal material. Take pains to clean the article thoroughly with glasspaper before using.

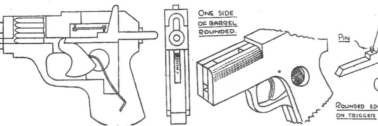

| Fig. 1—Side view showing mechanism | Fig. 2—Front view | Fig. 3—Constructional details | Fig. 4—Parts of plunger and trigger |

covers would have to be removed. This isn't necessary when you wish to fix in new elastic bands, for an aperture is provided.

chamber and try out the pistol as previously described. If you have followed the instructions carefully. the pistol should work in a realistic

Fly with the RAF
What young men of 16 and upwards can do about it NOW!

Scenes from the stirring life that awaits you in the R.A.F.

The R.A.F. have made it possible for every young man who is 16 and not yet 33, who is physically fit and keen to fight in the air, to start right now and get on with his job of preparing to be a pilot or observer, or to serve on technical duties. Even if you cannot be accepted at once for air crew duties, you can enrol for preliminary training in your spare time. By doing so you can fit yourself for R.A.F. service on reaching 18. Fill in the answers to the questions shown and the R.A.F. will advise you what immediate steps you can take.

Cut out this coupon and post to: Air Ministry Information Bureau, Adastral House, Kingsway, London, W.C.2. *Note:* By completing this coupon you do not bind yourself in any way whatsoever.

AGE............ YEARS
.... MONTHS

What R.A.F. duties do you wish to undertake?

NAME

ADDRESS

A.T.C. 18/5

The R.A.F. will give the young man his chance

K7940

AILERON

FLAP

Fretting on the
Home Front

You will be smitten with these novel ideas

A WOODEN GAS MASK

A SPLENDID ELECTRICAL GAME OF SKILL

A PORTABLE FIREFIGHTING UNIT

HOMEMADE SAUCEPANS

You will feel more secure if you build
AN A.R.P. SHELTER

THOUGH we all hope that war will never come, in these days the need for an air raid shelter is very important. Quite likely in time to come an A.R.P. shelter will be an essential part of every house, but in the meantime it is wise to be prepared by building one ourselves.

The type of shelter shown is of the trench dug-out kind. It is deep enough to afford protection from the effects of explosion and blast, and has a covering overhead to shelter the inmates from falling shrapnel.

The size of the shelter will, of course, depend on the number of people likely to use it, so though definite dimensions are given in the article it will be understood these can be extended to suit requirements.

Suitable Small Size

For the sake of this article, the size of the sheltered part of the dug-out is 4ft. by 6ft.

Estimating the size of the trench, add the distance A-B to that of B-C (whatever the latter may be) for the length, and say 4ft. for the width. Mark this carefully on the site and dig out to a depth of 4ft. 3ins.

Fig. 1 shows a view of the wood lining of the trench. Very important this, as if no lining is provided the sides of the trench will gradually fall inwards.

Preservative Paint

The sizes of the timbers used (red deal, unplaned) are given in Fig. 1. After cutting each piece give it a coating of creosote. Apply a second coat to all parts before placing in position in the trench.

Cut the ground rails to length and on these fix the uprights, skew nailing them as in Fig. 2. The ground rails being 3ins. by 4ins. stuff are laid with the broad side down to leave 1in. outside the uprights for the boarding to rest on.

For the boards use 1in. deal, and nail to the uprights. The end boards should be cut to length and nailed to a centre post of 3in. sq. wood. Drop this into place and lower the two sides into the trench. Force the sides into close contact with the end boards and in the angle at E screw brackets.

Instead of brackets, short stakes of 2in. sq. wood can be driven into the ground to keep the bottom or ground rails pressed flat to the sides of the trench.

Across uprights B & C

lay the bars shown, letting them be long enough to rest on the sides of the trench. Where they come over the uprights cut grooves to receive the ends of the longitudinal bars, F, and nail in place.

The Cross Bars

Bars F are then cut to length, halved at the ends to fit in the grooves, as in Fig. 3, and nailed along. These being 3ins. by 4ins. stuff cover both uprights and boarding.

To mark out the rafters, measure across G-H, these points being 2ins. away from each side. Draw a line this length on a sheet of paper, and in the centre draw line I, perpendicular to it.

From point G, draw line G-G1 at 45 degs. to meet line I. The length of G-G1 will be the length of each rafter measured along the inside after cutting the ends to 45 degs.

As the rafters have to bear some considerable weight, they should be placed at 2ft. centres at least.

To Take Weight

Fix each pair together by a tie board, J, Fig. 4, cut from 1in. by 6in. board nailed across at 4ins. below the top. Above this cut out a slot the thickness of the ridge board, K, for the latter to enter, where it will rest upon the tie board.

Lift the rafters, and nail to the bars F, noting that the tie boards are all facing towards the end. Now drop the ridge board in its place and nail the rafters to it.

Across the end, fill in the space between tie board and end boarding with more boards. The woodwork will then appear as in Fig. 1, with tie boards purposely omitted.

Across uprights D lay a bar of 3in. by 4in. wood, as across B, and cover the space between it and B with boards, nailed across. To the outer face of

this bar nail a board 8ft. long firmly in position.

Earth Covering

This board should be rather wide, say 9ins. to stand up above the bar. Its object is to support the earth covering of the dug-out. It is seen in Fig. 5, which shows a section through the forward end of the shelter, after earthing up.

A similar board is laid across just 2ft. away from

pipe end should be provided with a perforated zinc cover to exclude rats and insects.

Now cover the rafters with stout gauge corrugated iron to roof in. Along the top of the ridge boards nail a length of 1in. by 6in. board to cover the openings of the corrugations and prevent earth falling in the trench.

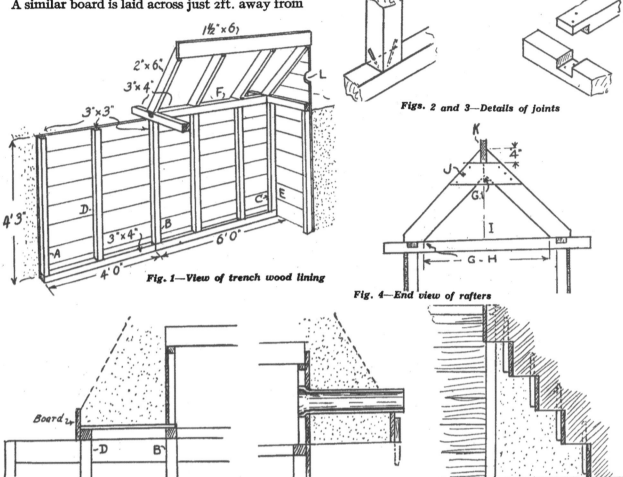

Fig. 1—View of trench wood lining

Figs. 2 and 3—Details of joints

Fig. 4—End view of rafters

Fig. 5—Section through forward end

Fig. 6—Section through rear end

Fig. 7—Section through steps

the end rafters for the same purpose. Both are joined together with side boards.

You now have a rectangle of boards just 2ft. away from the rafters on each side. It is perhaps needless to add that all these boards should be well creosoted. They are easily secured in position by driving short stakes of 2in. sq. wood into the ground, and nailing the boards to them.

Some form of efficient ventilation is vitally important, especially in the unlucky event of a fall of earth or rubbish choking up the entrance to the dug-out.

Should this happen, with no ventilation, you might be suffocated before anyone could dig you out.

To provide against this, a hole should be sawn out at the end below the tie board, where shown at L in Fig. 1. Make this large enough to admit a length of 6in. earthenware drain pipe,

The outer end of the pipe might rest upon the end board, as in rear section, Fig. 6, or, if the board is not high enough, upon a few bricks. The

The Trench

This will also prevent any rain water dripping in after soaking through the earth covering. The whole roof should now be covered with a 2ft. layer of earth, or sand, well flattened down.

To enter the dug-out, a series of steps should be cut. These are shown in section in Fig. 7.

Probably five will be enough, making each roughly 10ins. high and 8ins. broad. The steps should be faced with boards or they will soon be trodden down.

Lay the first board across uprights A, nailing it to them. Then dig the earth away to form the next step, and so on. The remaining boards are nailed to stakes of 2in. sq. wood driven into the earth each side.

If a middle stake is desired, drive this on the inside of the board to be out of the way.

The bottom of the dug-out should be covered with a layer of gravel, or cinder, well rammed down, and made slightly sloping towards the steps.

To keep the interior as dry as possible, unless a wooden cover is made to place over the entrance to keep out rain, a "soak away" should be provided in the trench for the exit of water. This may be a drain pipe, sunk into the earth level with the bottom and filled up with cinders.

In the interior a board might be nailed to brackets, to sit upon. As far as lighting is concerned, if the house is fitted with electric current wires can be run from the house supply to a small lamp suspended from the roof, or attached to one of the uprights.

If this is not possible, an electric lamp can be provided with current from an accumulator or long life dry battery.

In either case candles, or a small oil lamp, should be handy in case of the electric light failing.

A dug-out of this type can be utilised in peace time for other purposes, such as mushroom growing or a tool shed. The earth covering can be rendered less unsightly if covered with turf, or sown with grass seed.

In fact there seems no reason why the mound should not be planted with small rockery plants, or anything which would utilise the space and make it attractive instead of a garden eyesore.

For all weathers you need A WOODEN GAS MASK BOX

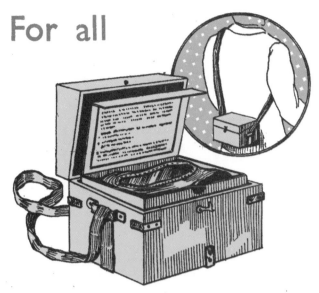

IN wintry weather it will be obviously necessary to consider the best type of case to make, for carrying your gas mask. We learn that it is detrimental to the mask itself to allow moisture to get at it, and that it should be folded carefully to prevent damage to the rubber.

The cardboard container supplied with the mask is ideal for size, but it affords no protection against rain and snow, and the wet would soon penetrate it and in time the mask would probably be ruined.

Hold the Whole Container

A light wood case seems to be best for protection, and we describe here how to make one up from fretwood, ¼in. thick. It will hold the cardboard container within this wooden case, and the only part to be cut away from it is the side flaps which fold down underneath the top cover.

The instructions on " Packing the Respirator " can therefore be retained, and this inner lid will form a further protection against dust, etc.

The box has a hinged lid, the front of which is made a little deeper than the back to allow quick and easy handling.

The Construction

The construction of the case is shown in Fig. 1. The two sides (A) are nailed or screwed to the ends (B), and over these are fixed the top and floor (C). The holes for the screws—these should be used in preference to nails—must be bored and the tops countersunk so the heads are flush and neat.

```
                    CUTTING LIST
A.—Two pieces 7½ins. by 4¾ins. by ¼in.
B.—Two pieces 5¼ins. by 4¾ins. by ¼in.
C.—Two pieces 7½ins. by 6ins. by ¼in.
D.—Two pieces, ¼in. triangular fillet 7ins. long.
D.—Two pieces ¼in. triangular fillet, 5¼ins. long.
```

When all six parts are fixed thus, the two measurements shown in Fig. 2 one at the front and one at the back of the case should be drawn on and a pencil line made all round the case. Grip the box in a vice and use a small-tooth tenon saw for sawing round the lines.

The case will need to be moved from time to time so the saw does not bind and is prevented from clearing itself during cutting.

Care must be taken when putting the case together in the first place to see there are sufficient screws to hold all parts securely together during cutting and afterwards when the lid portion is severed altogether.

Hinges and Catch

It is now only necessary to add a pair of 1in. brass hinges to hold the parts together. The hinges should have their flaps " let in " so that the two parts of the case fit closely together.

The lid should be strengthened inside by gluing around some strips of ¼in. triangular fillet (Fig. 2).

Two stirrups should be made by angling up some pieces of brass strip about ¼in. wide, and drilled for receiving the round-head fixing screws.

The case might be also strengthened by adding four or six angles plates (No. 101, sold by Hobbies at 6d.).

A stout hook and eye completes the case excepting for the paint which should be applied in two coats.

A tough wood such as beech or Spanish chestnut would be best for making up the case.

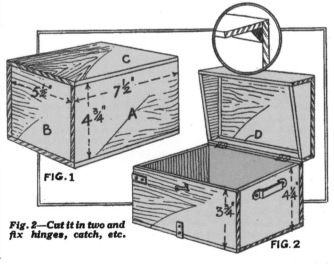

FIG. 1

Fig. 2—Cut it in two and fix hinges, catch, etc.

FIG. 2

Look out for details how to make a complete Home Cinema shortly. Don't miss it!

February 24th. 1940　　　　　　　　　Vol. 89. No. 2314

Patterns for miniature
MODEL BLENHEIM BOMBER

THOSE readers who have followed our articles for making miniature model planes, will by now be getting quite a respectable Air Force, with which to manoeuvre and play with great realism. Although small, these planes are true to type, and provide you with an excellent model for identification purposes as well.

We have already had fighters and bombers, and now add what is possibly one of the most used in the present war in the air raids taking place over the sea.

What It Can Do

This is the Bristol Blenheim which is a medium bomber of all-metal construction and one of the fastest in service anywhere. It is fitted with Bristol Mercury engines and with three-bladed controllable pitch airscrews.

It carries a crew of three and has a maximum speed of 295 miles per hour at 15,000ft. The range of flight is about 1,900 miles with duration of over 8½ hours. The machine has a wing span of 56ft., and stands nearly 10ft. high.

This plane has already won much commendation

carefully to the various angles and curves marked.

This shaping must be done patiently with a knife and finally glasspaper to get a smooth surface, carefully balanced wings and body.

A side view of the fuselage and a plan from above is shown on the left of the patterns, and the lines leading from these details give the outline of a template to the shape required.

Notice that at the nose (see Fig. 1) the shape varies on the two sides. On the left-hand side looking at the machine, the cabin is rounded, whilst on the right-hand side the roof of the cabin is lower. This can be seen also in the picture of the finished machine herewith.

Body and Wings

The body, of course, is cut from wood, and the cabin can be made by pasting on some transparent paper as imitation glass with the framework painted on.

The wings are made up in three pieces but joined finally as one. The centre piece—the root—

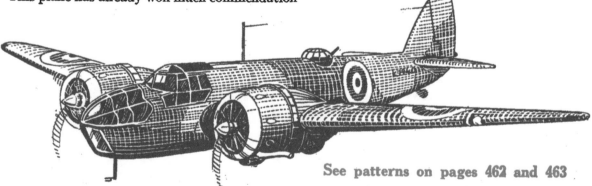

See patterns on pages 462 and 463

in the war, and is the outcome of an earlier and slower model with a shorter nose.

The patterns provide for a model of the same scale as the others. It has a wing span of 7ins., and a fuselage 5ins. long.

Those who have made up our earlier models will find no trouble in following the instructions and the particulars given with this one. The various parts are cut from thin wood shaped up

passes through the mortise or slot cut in the fuselage mid-way. Immediately the wing root leaves the fuselage, it is shaped to the sections and diagrams shown as far as the engine portion.

The outer portion with the flap, numbers, etc., is then shaped down to the taper and when replaced must be tilted slightly upwards towards the wing tip. A front view of the wing is given, showing this lift to be about 5/16in. at the tip.

When the two parts are joined again as shown at the dotted line, the inner edge is chamfered to provide the necessary angle and a short double-ended pin or nail is driven in to aid the glue and prevent breakage.

The tail portion is made up of a tailplane and a fin and rudder. The last two are in one piece fitted to the rear end of the fuselage. The flat plane portion is glued on to the flat recess at the top of the fuselage, then the fin and rudder pressed up to it and glued to the rear end vertically.

The engines are cut from ½in. piece of wood shaped bull-nosed at the front and tapering at the back. They drop into place and are glued in the hollow cut out of the wing, the position being shown by the light line on the pattern of the engine itself.

The actual shape of the engine when finished is given herewith, and the various rings are added to the front according to the lettered parts.

The main engine is 1in. long, then the wider rim C is added, followed by the thick portion B (¼in. wood). Then glue on the actual printed front of the engine shown in solid black, and over this add the rim A from which the centre is cut.

The Landing Gear

The wheels can either be made with the model standing, or as though retracted. One is shown on the underside of the engine and this portion only is glued on.

If you are having a complete carriage, the landing gear itself is made up with little wire struts cottoned across and the wheel pinned in between the bottom. Notice these little details in the right-hand corner of the pattern sheet because these tiny additions will make all the difference to the realism of the model.

The gun turret, for instance, is a piece of ⅜in. wood cut to the shape shown circular, and dropped into the hole bored 3/16in. deep into the top of the fuselage at the point shown.

The framework of the gun turret itself can be painted on, and a piece of wire stuck out for the muzzle.

A similar piece of wire is added for the aerial

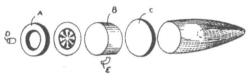

How the engine is made up

between the gun turret and upper cabin, whilst a wind indicator made of a similar piece of wire is dropped from the front and beneath the fuselage. This has two tiny pieces of cotton glued to stiffen as shown on the side view of the fuselage pattern.

The completed model must be thoroughly cleaned up, then painted with a camouflaged marking of brown and green.

The drawing shows you also the marking on the top and underside of the wings. Notice the numbers, the ailerons and flap are on the underside with only the shorter flap and the circular targets on the top. The target or cockade and the small number is also painted on the side of the fuselage as shown.

No. 4 in our popular series of patterns of
MINIATURE MODEL PLANES
A BRISTOL BLENHEIM FIGHTER-BOMBER

For complete
instructions
see page 453

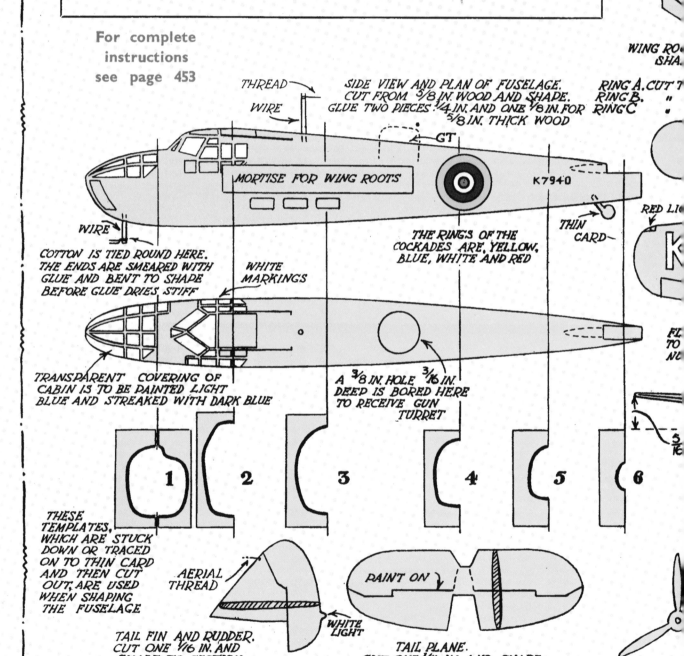

THREAD

WIRE

SIDE VIEW AND PLAN OF FUSELAGE.
CUT FROM ⅝ IN. WOOD AND SHAPE.
GLUE TWO PIECES ¼ IN. AND ONE ⅛ IN. FOR
⅝ IN. THICK WOOD

WING RO●
SHA●

RING A. CUT T●
RING B.   "
RING C   "

GT

MORTISE FOR WING ROOTS

K7940

WIRE

THE RINGS OF THE
COCKADES ARE, YELLOW,
BLUE, WHITE AND RED

THIN
CARD

RED LI●

COTTON IS TIED ROUND HERE.
THE ENDS ARE SMEARED WITH
GLUE AND BENT TO SHAPE
BEFORE GLUE DRIES STIFF

WHITE
MARKINGS

TRANSPARENT COVERING OF
CABIN IS TO BE PAINTED LIGHT
BLUE AND STREAKED WITH DARK BLUE

A ⅜ IN. HOLE ³⁄₁₆ IN.
DEEP IS BORED HERE
TO RECEIVE GUN
TURRET

FL●
TO
NU●

1   2   3   4   5   6

THESE
TEMPLATES,
WHICH ARE STUCK
DOWN OR TRACED
ON TO THIN CARD
AND THEN CUT
OUT, ARE USED
WHEN SHAPING
THE FUSELAGE

AERIAL
THREAD

PAINT ON

WHITE
LIGHT

TAIL FIN AND RUDDER.
CUT ONE ¹⁄₁₆ IN. AND
SHADE TO SECTION

TAIL PLANE.
CUT ONE ¹⁄₁₆ IN. AND SHAPE
TO SECTION

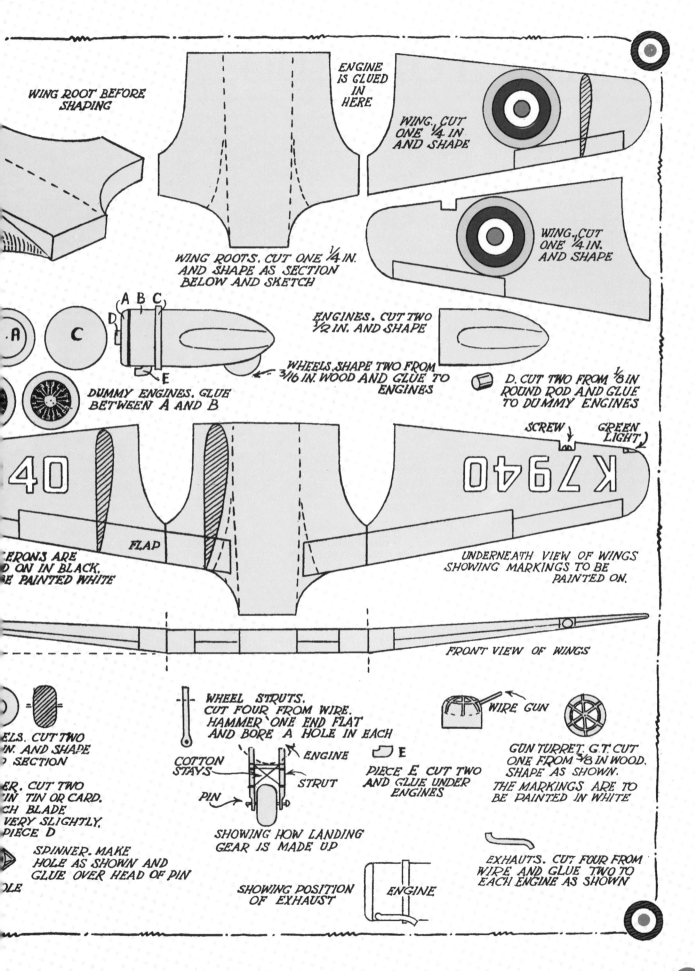

WING ROOT BEFORE SHAPING

ENGINE IS GLUED IN HERE

WING. CUT ONE ¼ IN. AND SHAPE

WING ROOTS. CUT ONE ¼ IN. AND SHAPE AS SECTION BELOW AND SKETCH

WING. CUT ONE ¼ IN. AND SHAPE

A B C

D

C

A

E

ENGINES. CUT TWO ½ IN. AND SHAPE

WHEELS. SHAPE TWO FROM 3/16 IN. WOOD AND GLUE TO ENGINES

D. CUT TWO FROM ⅛ IN ROUND ROD AND GLUE TO DUMMY ENGINES

DUMMY ENGINES. GLUE BETWEEN A AND B

SCREW   GREEN LIGHT

40

K7940

FLAP

ERONS ARE
ON IN BLACK.
E PAINTED WHITE

UNDERNEATH VIEW OF WINGS SHOWING MARKINGS TO BE PAINTED ON.

FRONT VIEW OF WINGS

ELS. CUT TWO
IN. AND SHAPE
SECTION

WHEEL STRUTS. CUT FOUR FROM WIRE. HAMMER ONE END FLAT AND BORE A HOLE IN EACH

WIRE GUN

ER. CUT TWO
IN TIN OR CARD.
CH BLADE
VERY SLIGHTLY.
PIECE D

COTTON STAYS

ENGINE

STRUT

PIN

E

PIECE E CUT TWO AND GLUE UNDER ENGINES

GUN TURRET. G.T. CUT ONE FROM ⅜ IN WOOD. SHAPE AS SHOWN. THE MARKINGS ARE TO BE PAINTED IN WHITE

SPINNER. MAKE HOLE AS SHOWN AND GLUE OVER HEAD OF PIN

OLE

SHOWING HOW LANDING GEAR IS MADE UP

SHOWING POSITION OF EXHAUST

ENGINE

EXHAUTS. CUT FOUR FROM WIRE AND GLUE TWO TO EACH ENGINE AS SHOWN

MODEL TORPEDO BOAT

THE excellent little model of a torpedo boat illustrated here is cut out in wood with the fretsaw, and the patterns for all parts required are given on the inside covers of this issue. The model is a miniature one 11ins. long and 1in. wide.

The patterns provided allow for building it as a complete solid model in wood which can be made to float in water if suitably balanced.

On a Baseboard

If, of course, you wish to have it as a waterline model like many of the others we have produced, it is a simple matter to leave off the two lower pieces of wood (A. & B.) and glue the whole thing to a suitable base. This baseboard can be 12ins. long and 1¾ins. wide, with a "sea" put upon it with putty or plastic wood or even just painted on the board.

If it is being built, on the other hand, as a floating model, you will have to arrange for it to lie in the water at the correct depth.

The waterline is indicated by the mark on the side view which you will see passes out at the stern.

This is a general line of a dot and dash and indicates the depth in the water at which the boat should ride.

Test for Buoyancy

If when completed it happens it is not far enough down, you can add little lead strips on the underside to get the effect required. Put the model into a bath or tub and then lay little pieces of lead or even weights on the deck in the position which you find is needed to get the correct buoyancy. Having weighted the boat down to its proper position you can then fix the weights.

If you do not want them nailed under the keel you should bore or groove holes in the wood and fix the lead or metal inside that—re-covering it and painting it afterwards.

Another method is to make one of the parts hollow, as will be mentioned later, and put the weights in the hull itself.

The boat should be painted all over, and the battleship grey provided by Hobbies in small

pots is quite suitable. The complete hull is finished in this rather drab colour, but relief is provided by the addition of the portholes, the guns, funnel lining, etc., which can be marked out in black.

In making the portholes, by the way, do not get the little dot of black any larger than that shown on the pattern, or it will look out of proportion.

Apart from the wood you require a few odd pieces of wire and some thread to make up the masts, rigging, flagstaffs, etc.

Deck Details

The success of the whole thing largely depends on the care and patience you put into making the various small pieces on the deck.

Cut these very carefully, then shape them up with penknife and glasspaper until you are satisfied you have got a perfectly good shape.

Have a good look, too, first of all, at the complete design and notice where the various parts come. They are shown in the side view and lettered corresponding to the small patterns provided.

The hull is the first thing to make up, and this is composed of four complete outlines to the shape

recess into which you can add the various little pieces of lead or metal previously mentioned, to provide the buoyancy for the whole model.

Shaping the Hull

You must, of course, remember not to glue the parts together if you are going to do this, until you have fitted up the necessary weights.

When all the parts (A, B, C, D) are glued together, you must shape them up carefully. A half section of the hull showing these shapes is given by the outline templates in the bottom righthand corner of the pattern sheet.

These templates correspond with the shape shown at the various cross markings at A, B, C and D, and if you cut a piece of card and hold it against the shaped hull as shown in the detail herewith, you will then be sure of getting a balanced and correct form.

Spend some time to get this correct, and notice that both bow and stern cut away downwards and inwards. When you have finished, the outline should be the same as that shown on the side view.

Various other little parts—guns, searchlights, torpedo tubes, etc.—are made from tiny bits and pieces

Complete Patterns are printed on the inside cover of this issue

given. The bottom one (A) is 3/16in. thick, the one above it (B) is ⅜in. thick and the one above that (C) is again 3/16in. thick. The part D forms the upper deck forward and is ½in. thick.

By the way, in the hull piece (B) there is an interior line given which can be cut out if you wish if you propose to make the whole thing a floating model. With this centre cut away you have a

and you will probably require small pliers, large pins, etc., to hold them whilst shaping up. Hints on making these tiny pieces have already appeared in these pages, and the ingenious worker will no doubt be able to complete them satisfactorily.

The guns themselves can really be tapering, nails suitably cut short and driven into the turrets. The little davits are turned pieces of tin or wire on which the boats are hung or fixed by further pieces of wire.

The main mast is driven into the block I glued on the upper deck and notice both this and the rear mast are sloping slightly backwards. The wireless aerials trail from a cross spar of wire down to the deck. A tiny Ensign astern can be painted on a piece of paper, whilst card can be also

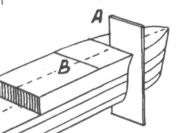

used for various other small thin pieces.

When the parts have been completed and before the hull has been painted, glue them in place. Notice the actual position of the parts according to the dotted lines drawn on deck C and D.

The funnels stand on part H with a gun between them on the turntable. These funnels, by the way, are made to slope backwards by cutting one end at a slight angle. Before cutting the length of the funnel, get it the right

How the hull is built, and a detail showing template card in place

shape, thus having a longer piece of wood you can hold one end whilst you shape up the other to the ellipse shown by the section above the design. Then having got it nicely rounded, you can cut it off to the length ready for gluing.

The same hint applies in the making of the boats, torpedo tubes, etc., where a long piece of wood can have one end cut and shaped as needed before being sawn off last. See all parts are

glued firmly in place, and if necessary add a little headless pin between to make a firmer joint.

Then paint the whole thing very carefully applying the first coat of grey or a priming coat evenly, and allowing it to harden into the wood firmly before giving the final coating. Get a matt finish paint because glossy would look out of place. Paint the hull and the various parts before you add the masts, rigging, etc., otherwise these parts will get damaged.

Additional Detail

Readers who are conversant with naval boats may suggest that this model does not follow out the lines of the particular Class they know. We have purposely made it a general model of a destroyer rather than follow too slavishly the lines of any particular Class.

Whilst, therefore, the armament and super-structure may be altered in some of the boats now iu commission, you can confidently make the model as a replica of those boats which are so uncomfortable for any aboard them, but so necessary as fast scouts for the larger ships.

The "TENSION" CUT-OUT
CALENDAR PICTURE

Supplement to Hobbies Weekly Dec. 4th 1946

This quaint picture forms an ideal gift for Christmas and involves very little work in its making. It is made to stand as a cut-out picture and provided with a Calendar date pad for 1947 supplied by Hobbies. First of all cut out round the coloured picture with scissors. Then paste the picture to a piece of $\frac{1}{8}$in. or $\frac{3}{16}$in. wood — plywood for preference. Now cut round the actual outline with a fretsaw, taking care not to break off the goat's horns or tail. Give a light rubbing of glasspaper to the back edges to take away any saw burr.

To make the picture stand, glue a long $\frac{1}{2}$in. square block of wood along the bottom. Do not have it actually in line with the edge, but about $\frac{1}{16}$in. upwards to prevent the picture falling forward. Apply glue thinly and evenly to the strip of wood, and weight or cramp to the picture part until set. The strip of wood can be cut short $\frac{1}{2}$in. each end. Paint the edges and back a jet black, and leave to dry before handling. A more realistic effect is obtainable by painting the edges the same colour as the picture on the front. A date pad suitable is obtainable from Hobbies Branches for 1d or 3½d., post free from Dept. C.P. Hobbies Ltd., Dereham, Norfolk.

Paste Calendar Pad here

TENSION!

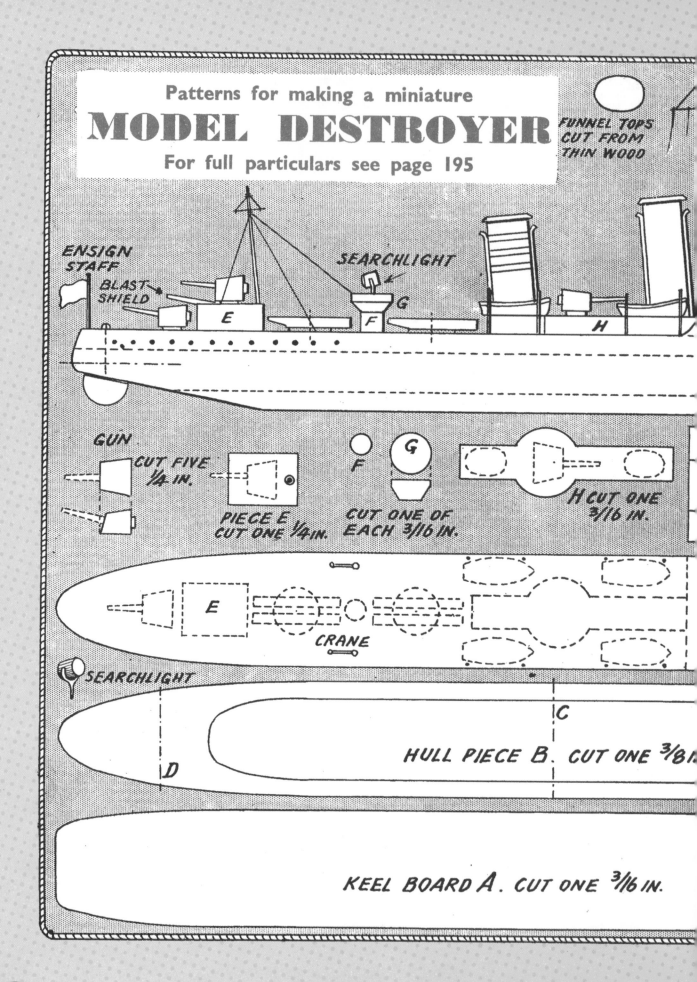

Patterns for making a miniature

MODEL DESTROYER

For full particulars see page 195

FUNNEL TOPS CUT FROM THIN WOOD

ENSIGN STAFF

BLAST SHIELD

SEARCHLIGHT

E

F G

H

GUN

CUT FIVE ¼ IN.

PIECE E CUT ONE ¼ IN.

F

G

CUT ONE OF EACH 3/16 IN.

H CUT ONE 3/16 IN.

E

CRANE

SEARCHLIGHT

C

D

HULL PIECE B. CUT ONE 3/8 IN.

KEEL BOARD A. CUT ONE 3/16 IN.

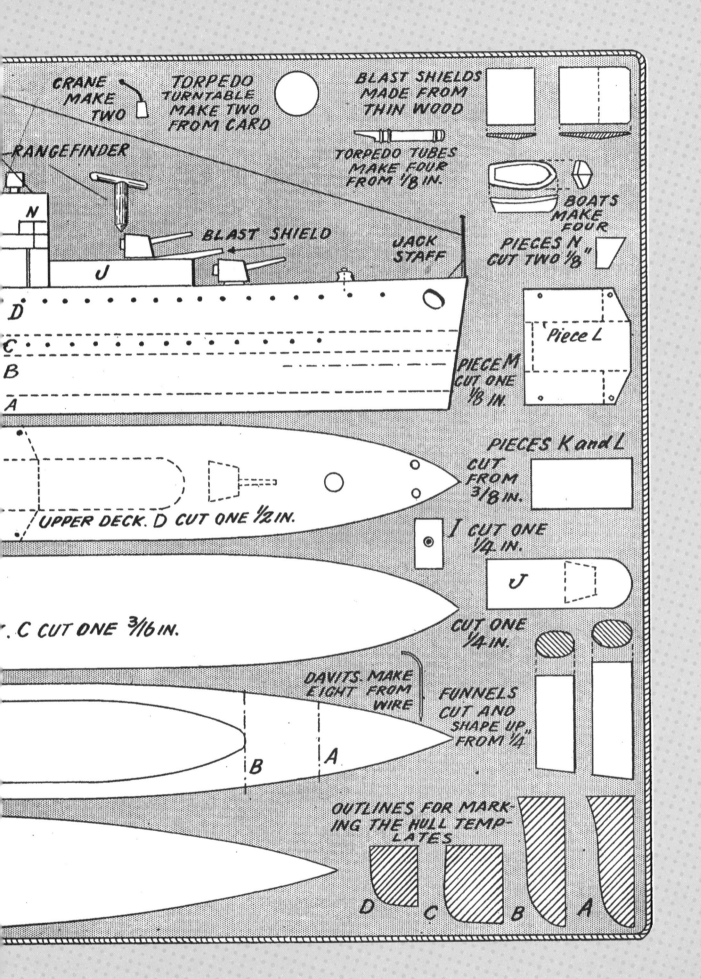

CRANE MAKE TWO

TORPEDO TURNTABLE MAKE TWO FROM CARD

BLAST SHIELDS MADE FROM THIN WOOD

TORPEDO TUBES MAKE FOUR FROM 1/8 IN.

RANGEFINDER

BOATS MAKE FOUR

N

PIECES N CUT TWO 1/8"

J

BLAST SHIELD

JACK STAFF

Piece L

PIECE M CUT ONE 1/8 IN.

D

C

B

A

UPPER DECK. D CUT ONE 1/2 IN.

PIECES K and L CUT FROM 3/8 IN.

I CUT ONE 1/4 IN.

J

.C CUT ONE 3/16 IN.

CUT ONE 1/4 IN.

DAVITS. MAKE EIGHT FROM WIRE

FUNNELS CUT AND SHAPE UP 1/4" FROM 1/4"

B

A

OUTLINES FOR MARKING THE HULL TEMPLATES

D

C

B

A

"BOMBING THE BASES"

THIS game of Bombing the Base is full of skill and enjoyment, excitement and interest, so everyone should make it and get it going as soon as possible. Complete patterns and details are provided on this week's Design Sheet, No. 2349.

Here is a novel, mechanical and topical electrical game for *all* the family. It is easily and cheaply made. Then you can modify it indefinitely, from a full electric driven transmission to realistic scale models, a miniature aerodrome for a target, etc.

The necessary patterns are provided on the sheet with this issue and full instructions follow here as to the construction, for which the necessary wood is supplied as a complete parcel.

A Game of Skill

The two planes revolve round the central pylon, and at a given signal, drop their bomb on to the target beneath. The skill is proved by timing when to release the bomb, in order to score a "bull."

The planes are made to revolve by a simple elastic drive, whilst the bomb is held by electric contact and released when the appropriate switch is operated.

Altogether a fascinating model to make and to use. Just the thing indeed to prove a "good seller" if you want to make pocket money.

The construction is very simple, but it should be executed carefully. The four sides are cut out from ½in. wood. It is best to

The swivelling arm is cut out of ⅜in. wood and in the diagram is 30ins. long. We would suggest that if you can spare the room and wood, a longer one would make the game harder and more intriguing to all players.

Bore a ⅛in. hole in the centre to take the shaft, and two ¼in. holes, one either end, to mount dowels to support the actual planes.

The Pylon Assembly

Join the parts together with glue, and thin nails, after the top pieces have had small tinplate "tubes" fitted to bush them to take the shaft.

For the time being only assemble the two sides on the top, middle and base. The other sides are better left off to allow the shaft and contacts to be fitted, also the 'motor.'

The Contact Drum

Now cut out the 2in. diam. circle which forms the

contact drum. Around this fix with tiny nails, filed off very smooth afterwards, a strip of tin or brass. The sealing band on a paste pot will do well for this.

Make this very clean and shiny, and as smooth as you can—that is with no projections such as nail heads—and solder up the seam. Drill a 3/16in. diam. hole exactly in the centre and mount on the top of the pylon, between the top and where the arm will eventually go.

For the shaft, a motor cycle spoke will do. Heat each end to blood heat and allow to cool to anneal it. Then form a hook on one end to take the motor.

Slip the shaft through the two bearings, the hole in the contact drum centre, thread on several washers and finally the arm. Bend over with pliers to 90 degrees and fix to the arm with a small staple.

draw the patterns out full size on a sheet of paper, noting the tenons on two sides only and trace them on to the wood with carbon paper, or then again with tracing paper.

Making the Main Tower

One piece each of the base, middle and top platforms of ⅜in. wood will be needed. Notice the mortice in the base. In the two upper pieces, bore holes to take the shaft and bushings, in the exact centre. Draw diagonal lines across corners to determine this position.

The shoe which engages the contact drum can now be fixed to the arm underneath.

This consists of a strip of thin brass, drilled to take two small screws about ½in. apart at one end, screwed to a small block of wood about 1in. by 1in. by 1in. This is in turn fixed to the arm with two very thin panel pins and glue.

The brass must, of course, make a good contact with the drum. Adjust to make this so, and see that a good spring is on this part to assure plenty of pressure on it.

The other contact must be made with a plate of brass bent to a half circle, in the form of a saddle. It is held tightly against the axle by a spiral expansion spring fixed to the inside of the pylon (see sketch). Clean the axle well with emery paper before fixing.

Bomb Release

For the actual bomb release, the method chosen is simple, effective and straightforward. A more professional way could be used, but we feel sure that the majority will prefer this type.

It consists of a piece of soft iron sheet—nothing else will do—bent to form a tube about ⅜in. or ½in. diam. It is wrapped with a piece of brown paper and on top ½ to ¾oz. of No. 24 S.W.G. copper enamelled wire. This forms the solenoid or electro-magnet.

The bomb is made as follows. The shaft is a piece of the same material as the core of the solenoid, and should be bent to a tube. It is a near fit, but is sufficiently loose to fall out of the core. A rounded hardwood block weights the bomb, while a compass or an old dart point forms the needle.

Fix the solenoid to the end of the arm, with a strip of brass bent round the coil and fixed at either end with small nails or screws to the arm sides.

Wire up as follows and as seen in the diagram. The positive lead from the coil goes to the shaft. A spot of solder is advisable to hold. The current is picked up at the 'saddle' contact (inside pylon) where it goes to the battery.

The other battery lead goes to the switch (a 6 volt toggle switch as used on cars is best). The other switch terminal is coupled to the contact drum at the top of the pylon. The current is picked up by the brass shoe, where it is connected to the other coil lead.

Thus, while the current is on, it retains the bomb, but when you switch off the current, the bomb is allowed to fall.

Fix a cup hook in the base and a loop of elastic to the shaft and hook. Now test the bomb-dropping and make this perfect by cleaning, etc.

Finish off the woodwork with the two remaining panels. Small screws would enable you to remove this part in an emergency.

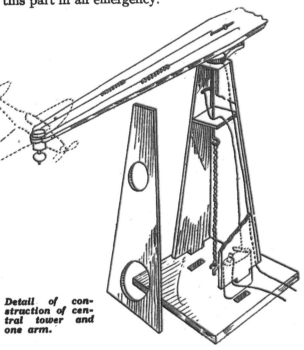

Detail of construction of central tower and one arm.

The model planes are not absolutely necessary, but they make the whole thing more realistic. Patterns are provided for this purpose and one who has already made up our designs for miniatures will have no difficulty in making these up.

Cut the parts to outline and shape to section with a rasp and small penknife. They could be finished in camouflage colours of Hobbies enamel to look excellent.

The whole model can also be painted in bright colours to make a professional finish and to make it more saleable.

As a final reminder for using the model, here are a few running instructions. Do not oil the contacts. Keep the bomb switch away from the range of the bomb! Do not run the arm too fast. Remember how fast these planes fly!

Use good batteries for safety!

To Remedy Damp Walls with Cement

THE handyman is called in to do all sorts of odd jobs, and one which sometimes arises is to remedy a damp wall. A good plan is to render it with cement, and here is the proper way to do it.

In cases where the dampness is caused by rain penetrating the wall, a remedy that is often effectual is to cover the whole of the exterior with Portland cement stucco. Sea sand is to be avoided on account of the saline matter and moisture it contains. River sand, although smoother than pit sand, is preferable, as it is free from clayey or loamy matter. The first coat is to be used as coarse as possible in the proportion of 3 of sand to 1 of cement, with a uniform thickness of not less than ½in. to ¾in.; the finishing coat is to be composed of sand of a finer grain, in the proportion of 2 of sand to 1 of cement, and to be ⅛in. to 3/16in. in thickness.

To increase the damp-resisting properties of Portland cement stucco, it should be painted six months later in dry weather.

A large Exhibition Model in wood of a
SPITFIRE FIGHTER

THE model illustrated herewith is built from the large design chart presented with this handbook, and the material provided as shown. It is built in wood, has a wing span of 18 ins. and is 15 ins. from tip to tail. This realistic exhibition model can be built with the aid of a fretsaw and a few tools if the reader follows out the instructions carefully and builds according to all the details provided.

The " Spitfire " itself is, of course, one of the outstanding fighters used in the war, and is an all-metal low-wing monoplane built to the plans of Vickers-Armstrongs, and carries four machine-guns in each wing and has a span of 37 ft. The speed is given as 362 miles per hour, although this, like much of its detail and shape, may have been subject to alteration and increase since war began.

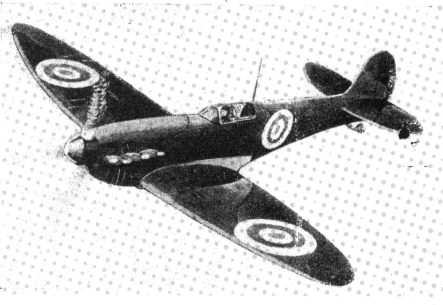

The interesting picture of the actual machine, which is reproduced by kind permission of *The Aeroplane*, is also helpful in many ways for finishing details. We are also indebted to Vickers-Armstrongs Ltd. for necessary details in the preparation of the model.

Check the Parts

First of all it is necessary to have the parcel of wood and check the parts up according to the illustration of the patterns on the sheet. Study the latter carefully in conjunction with the detailed drawings herewith so you get a good idea of how the whole thing is constructed.

In addition to the cutting there is a considerable amount of shaping to be done. This can be undertaken with a small plane, a rasp, a file and glasspaper. It is essential naturally to get the curves correctly balanced to get the streamline effect not only of the fuselage but of the wing itself.

Take your time in obtaining this and mark out as far as possible, being careful not to carry the shaping to excess. In this connection helpful templates are given, for instance, of the fuselage itself.

There is a side view with the lettered lines A to J. Below them are the shapes to which the fuselage must be completed on these particular lines.

A good plan is to mark this outline on to a piece

> Complete Parts shown on Sheet No. 219 Special presented Free with this Book.

of stiff card and cut out the inner portion. Then by holding this card close to the actual work you can gradually shape it down until the proper curve has been obtained. An illustration of this is shown in the detailed drawings at Fig. 1.

In other instances the shape of the parts is shown by a sectional drawing. The wings, for instance, have a fairly sharp curved front, but taper smoothly and gracefully to the back narrow edge. Notice, too, the similar tapering of the wheels, the tailplane, rudder, radiator, etc.

The building of the fuselage is the first consideration, and the sectional drawing at Fig. 2 illustrates how this is done. A good plan is to mark out on the wood from the design sheet so you may still have that part to which to refer as work proceeds.

Notice how the model is like the real plane shown below.

Photo by permission of "The Aeroplane."

Cut two ½-in. pieces of wood to the shape shown and glue the two pieces together. Draw a line round as marked "datum line", then cut out the two smaller pieces of the fuselage from ¼-in. wood. Note the position of the datum line on this and glue one each of these pieces so the line is a continuous one right round the model.

The front end of all four pieces is flush, then shape the whole thing down gradually tapering to the wing so where the ¼-in. piece meets the main portion it fades right away and will not be seen when the model is painted.

Where the wing and this extension piece join the fuselage, it will be necessary to add again a strip of plastic wood or putty to get the nicely rounded effect needed by the streamline lining of the machine. There must be no sharp angles which will catch the wind.

Wing Additions

The wings themselves have the addition of the four guns in the leading edge, and they are simply pieces of wire about ⅛ in. in diameter driven into the holes or recesses cut earlier.

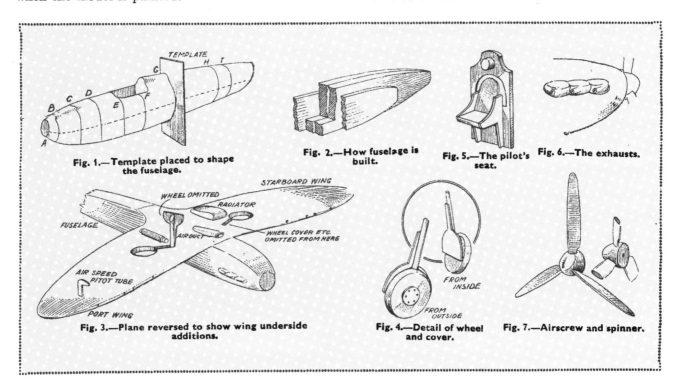

Fig. 1.—Template placed to shape the fuselage.

Fig. 2.—How fuselage is built.

Fig. 5.—The pilot's seat.

Fig. 6.—The exhausts.

Fig. 3.—Plane reversed to show wing underside additions.

Fig. 4.—Detail of wheel and cover.

Fig. 7.—Airscrew and spinner.

The wings are made in two separate pieces and dowelled on to the body at the point shown. This dowel hole must be cut straight through with a ³⁄₁₆-in. bit, but as the hole is bored into the ends of the wings, it must be slightly at an angle.

The wings tip up outwards and in consequence the dowels do not go in straight. This is shown by the drawing on the sheet and one must be careful to drill the holes for the dowels at the same angle in each case.

Be sure to get the wings lifting equally both sides. The actual angle is indicated in the front view. When glued in place there will be a slight gap between the wing and the fuselage but this can be filled with plastic wood or even putty to make a sound job.

At the back of the wing, too, there is a tapered piece which can be seen in the under view at Fig. 3. This is the wing extension cut from ¼-in. wood and let into the recess cut previously in the underside of the fuselage. The edges of this fade into the wing itself, and are rounded off to sweep back into the fuselage.

In the underside of the starboard wing is the radiator cut and shaped as shown, whilst on the opposite wing there is the shaped-up semi-circular strip set back as can be seen in Fig. 3.

The model is intended to stand on its wheels, and the retractable carriage is therefore down. A circular recess 1 in. in diameter is cut in the underside of each wing, and a groove run from it to the point where the wheel standard is let in. These wheel standards are 1⅞ in. length of circular rod.

The lower end of this is flattened so that the wheel when added slopes outwards at the angle

Another picture of the Spitfire, helpful for building the model

shown in the front view. On the inside of the rod or strut is fixed the cover, that part being merely glued as firmly as possible.

Each wheel is made of ¼-in. circle of wood rounded and provided with a cap on the outer side. A detail of these wheels is given in Fig. 4.

Returning to the top of the fuselage we must complete the cockpit with its little seat, head-rest and cover. The instrument board is added to the front in a semi-circular piece of wood, and to this

the actual panel is glued, on to the paper pattern provided. A detail of these parts is given at Fig. 5.

The cover of the cabin is cut in transparent material such as Rhodoid or celluloid. The template of the actual shape is given. Glue the tab under the other portion where shown to get the rounded effect, then glue the whole thing over the

Before fixing put in the short length of stiff wire to form the rear aerial of the wireless. As in the other instances, filling must be given in the angles where these parts join the fuselage, to make a nicely rounded shape for the streamline effect.

The three-bladed airscrew is fitted to the spinner which must first be made into a cone shape as shown at Fig. 7. The spinner is from a piece of 1-in. circular dowelling carefully tapered all round..

A good plan is to get a longer length of dowelling into the vice and shape the end as required before sawing it off. This allows you to hold it more easily than would be the case if you cut the correct length first. The blades are prepared to the shape shown, then fitted across the spinner at the angle marked in Fig. 7.

Cleaned and Coloured

The model is finally cleaned up, then painted, for which the little tins of enamel provided by Hobbies are suitable. You will require one tin each of green, brown, aluminium, black, yellow, red and blue. The whole of the upper portion of the fuselage and wings is in green with the camouflage marking across as shown in the colour picture on page 1.

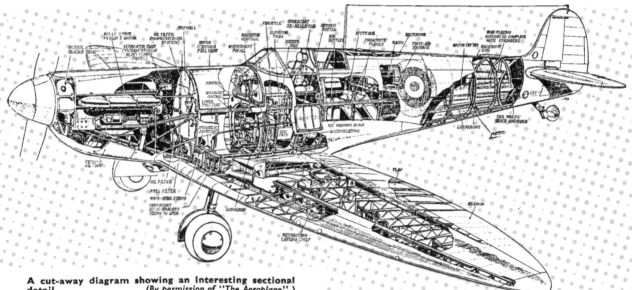

A cut-away diagram showing an interesting sectional detail. (By permission of "The Aeroplane".)

cockpit with either glue or Durofix. The actual lining is, of course, painted on in black afterwards, and a little strip of brass wire is sunk into the fuselage as the imitation runway upon which this top slides.

The rear wheel which is added is a circular-shaped piece pinned between two ⅛-in. parts, the centre stem being provided by a 3/16-in. piece of similar shape.

The exhaust ports are cut from ¼-in. wood rounded up as shown (see Fig. 6) and glued in the position shown in the side view on the sheet.

Tailplane and Rudder

The tailplane and rudder can be shaped up and added in a similar manner to the wings. The dowel passes through the tailplane 1⅝ in. from the rear and the projection of about ⅜ in. let into the tailplanes themselves after they have been shaped up.

The rudder and tail fin are erected vertically, being let into the fuselage and glued in place.

The underside is in aluminium. The targets are painted according to the circles indicated on the sheet, and you must notice which is on top and which is underneath. The upper ones are shown in colour on page 1, and those underneath are red, white and blue in that order from the inner circle.

Lettering and all lining up must be done with black paint or indian ink, and you will notice that a piece of card is required for lining along the trailing edge of the wings.

A base on which the model can be stood is also provided for in the parcel, and the construction of it is shown on the sheet. A piece of wood 15 × 4½ in. has a framework underneath it, and projecting just beyond it.

This frame is made of four strips of wood mitred at the corners, and the whole thing painted up in polished black or stained and polished natural colour.

BRITISH ARMY UNIFORMS

FOLLOWING the popularity of our recent Statuettes, we give below another series which will appeal equally strongly. They are of British Army uniforms and although, of course, some of them are not now seen, they are the peace-time dress of the regiments shown. The patterns are pasted to a piece of ⅛in. wood and then cut carefully round with a fretsaw. They can be made to stand by a short strip of ⅛in. square wood placed behind. This need not be longer than 1in. but must be glued level with the bottom edge.

Finish the back of the wood and the edges of the figures in a jet black paint to make them stand out stronger. Reprints of these are obtainable as a complete sheet at 4d. a dozen, no less quantity being supplied. They are obtainable only from the Editor. We should like to have suggestions, too, from readers as to other regiments which they would like, so we may be able to publish in due course the most popular.

INFANTRY T.A.

NORTHUMBERLAND FUSILIERS

ROYAL TANK REGT.

THE QUEEN'S OWN CAMERON HIGHLANDERS

THE LANCASHIRE FUSILIERS

INFANTRY BATTLE DRESS

LONDON IRISH RIFLES

THE BUFFS ROYAL EAST KENT REGT.

A MODEL TOMMY GUN

THIS is a very small, but realistic model Tommy gun in appearance, if not in working principle. It measures 16ins. long, the magazine being 3½ins. in diameter.

The latter holds ten tiny wooden bullets 1⅜ins. long by ⅛in. in diam. These are fed singly into the bullet chamber by the hand and are " fired " by means of two strong elastic bands and a plunger rod that is " locked " automatically by the trigger when drawn out to its fullest extent.

A touch of the trigger, and the bullet is projected with considerable force and accuracy. The gun will also shoot matchsticks and small peas or beads suiting the " bore " of the barrel.

Cutting the Patterns

The gun is made best from ⅛in. and 3/16in. plywood, although fretwood can be used. It is built up in layers and then rasped to shape. You will find the work entailed easy enough and interesting, and even if you cannot get the gun to work, you can make a good replica out of it.

Patterns are provided on the centre pages. Before pasting them to the wood or, better still, tracing them off, study them thoroughly and note the thickness of the wood from which certain parts are cut.

You will have to make repeats of the cover piece, face plate and hand grip, and owing to lack of space, you will see that the centre and cover pieces require to be extended. You have only to add the shape of the shoulder stock, and this can be done (by tracing over carbon paper) when the patterns are pasted down with sufficient allowance for the shoulder shape.

The magazine pattern should not be pasted on wood. From this single pattern you have to cut three separate discs which will form the drum. The front disc is ⅛in. thick and has a ¼in. wide aperture ; the central ⅜in. thick disc has a ⅞in. wide aperture ; the ⅛in. back disc has no aperture, but a top half-check like the other two discs.

Gluing the Parts

You could, at this stage, glue the drum discs together. Get them together neat and true as much as possible before hammering in three ¾in. panel pins at the points indicated on the pattern ; it is imperative that the half-check is dead square.

Now select the gun centre and cover pieces. To

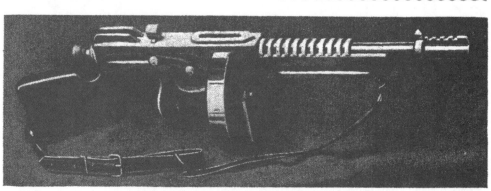

A photograph of the realistic model described here

one cover piece carefully glue the centre pieces and see that the 3/16in. wide channel is equidistant all along, as any inaccuracy here might interfere with the bullets.

The trigger must now be set in position (see Fig. 2). A ⅝in. long pivot, being either a piece of wire nail or ⅛in. dowel, is forced into the trigger to project evenly on each side. Having set the trigger in position, the other cover piece is added, after which the work is bound with strong thread until the glue dries, or you could use fretwork cramps or keep books on top.

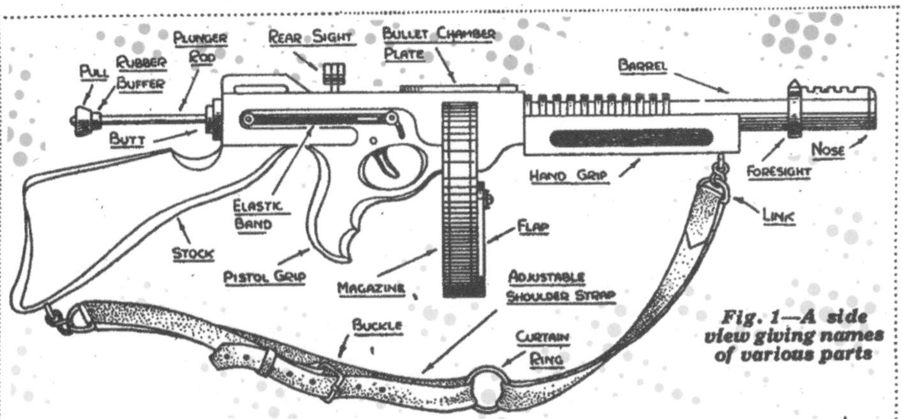

Fig. 1—A side view giving names of various parts

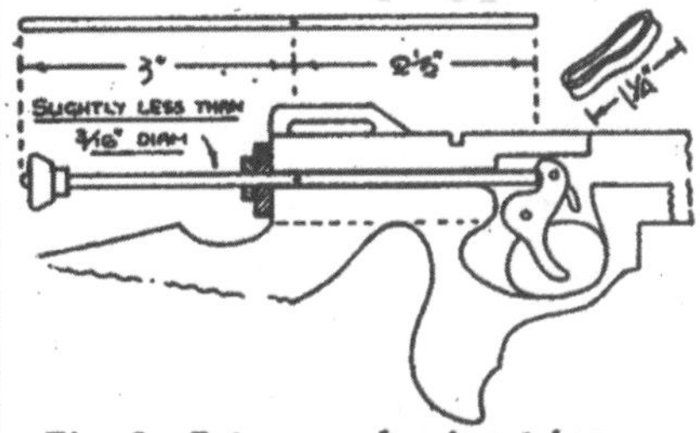

Fig. 2—Cut-away showing trigger and plunging rod

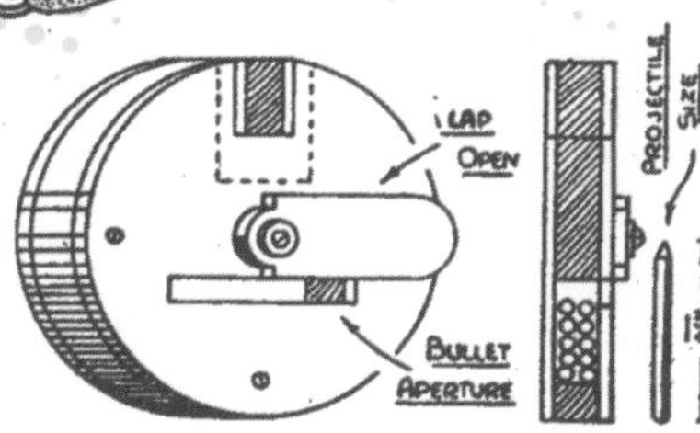

Fig. 3—The magazine with side sectional view

It is not advisable to nail these parts together. Owing to the shaping up, such would be greatly in the way.

Shaping the Work

If the glue has set, round up the gun barrel. It will be quite circular at the " muzzle " or nose and semi-circular along the barrel top. Much waste can first be removed with a sharp penknife and a small, iron block plane, after which the rasp and file (a flat file, by the way) is brought into use, then glasspaper (coarse and fine) to finally smooth the work.

Regarding the trigger grip and shoulder stock, the rounding is carried out as suggested by the view at Fig. 1. Here, again, the penknife and rasp will remove much of the waste—or failing a rasp, an ordinary half-round file will serve admirably.

Fixing the Magazine

Proceed by gluing the magazine in position, then the face plates and hand grip pieces. The top, flat part of the gun is levelled with the plane and glasspapered, including the underside of the hand grip portion.

When the " butt " or rear end of the gun has been levelled square, a couple of plywood discs (see Figs. 1 and 2) are glued centrally on same to cover the " bore " of the barrel, the holes being 3/16in. or slightly less.

Muzzle Parts

The barrel nose (muzzle) parts are now adhered. First of all, glue on the foresight piece exactly 1¼ins. from the end of the barrel. Follow this by attaching the nose piece; the nose end of the barrel must be made dead flat, if necessary, with a flat file so the nose piece fits on neat and secure.

Once the glue has dried, the nose piece is filed neatly with the diameter of the barrel, then the serrated-edged piece of wood glued between the nose and the foresight. Eleven semi-circular barrel rings are glued to rest on the hand grips ⅛in. apart.

The nose piece suggests the " gas compensator " fitted on Tommy guns. The raised " fins " at the butt give the shape of the " wind gauge."

Go ahead with the good work by attaching the bullet chamber plate and rear sight piece to the top of the model. The position of the former can be judged from the side view at Fig. 1.

The Plunger Rod

To make the plunger rod, refer to Fig. 2. Here you have the length and the distance of the hole that has to be drilled for the elastic carrier arm (see detail on pattern page), this being a piece of wire or a beheaded heel brad of adequate length.

You need two pins and four 5/16in. diam. plywood buttons ⅛in. thick. The edges of the buttons are rounded over to prevent them fraying the elastic. Drive the pins into the trigger and plunger rod and then attach the buttons.

(To be Continued)

MATERIALS

WOOD

1 centre piece	*17ins. by 5ins. by 3/16in.*
2 cover pieces	*Same size as above.*
2 hand grip pieces	*4½ins. by 1in. by ⅛in.*
2 face plate pieces	*6ins. by 2ins. by 3/16in.*
1 magazine piece	*4ins. by 4ins. by ⅛in.*
2 cover pieces	*4ins. by 4ins. by ⅛in.*
1 flap piece	*2½ins. by 1in. by ⅛in.*
1 scrap piece	*6ins. by 6ins. by ⅛in.*

NOTE.—Cut small parts not mentioned from scrap pieces.

FITTINGS

1 piece dowelling	*18ins. long by 3/16in.*
2 brass hook-eyes	*Eye about ⅛in.*

1 piece leatherette strap 36ins. long.
A ¾in. brass curtain ring.
Some brass wire, nails and elastic bands.

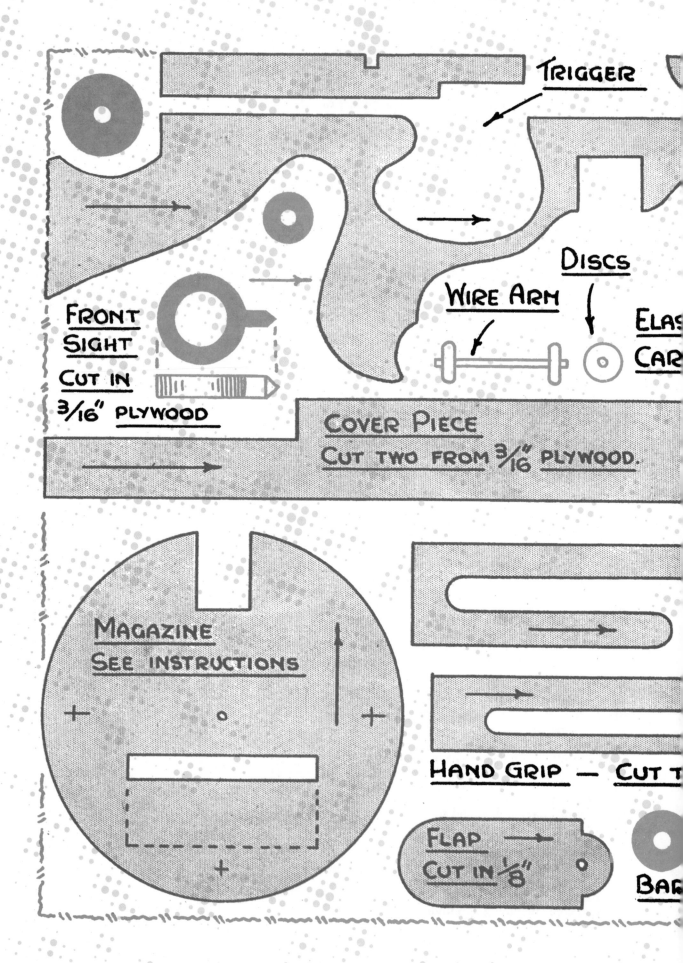

TRIGGER

DISCS

WIRE ARM

ELAS
CAR

FRONT
SIGHT
CUT IN
3/16" PLYWOOD

COVER PIECE
CUT TWO FROM 3/16" PLYWOOD.

MAGAZINE
SEE INSTRUCTIONS

HAND GRIP — CUT T

FLAP
CUT IN 1/8"

BAR

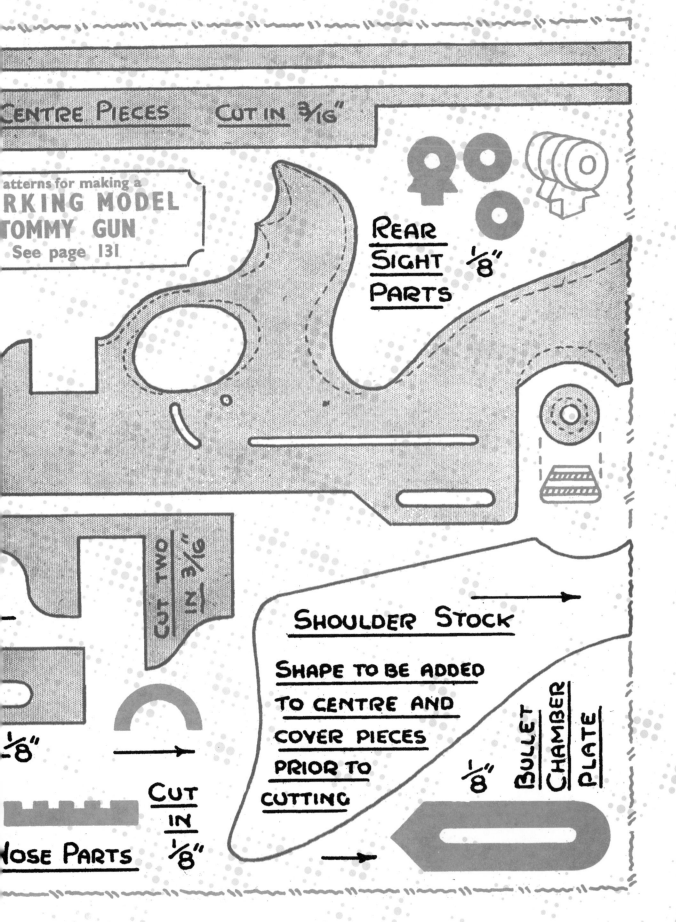

CENTRE PIECES   CUT IN ³/₁₆"

Patterns for making a
RKING MODEL
TOMMY GUN
See page 131

REAR
SIGHT
PARTS   ⅛"

CUT TWO IN ³/₁₆"

⅛"

CUT IN ⅛"

Nose Parts

SHOULDER STOCK

SHAPE TO BE ADDED
TO CENTRE AND
COVER PIECES
PRIOR TO
CUTTING

⅛"   BULLET CHAMBER PLATE

Here are some practical hints on the best way for
SHELTER DRAINAGE

IS water getting into your Dug-out or Air-raid Shelter ? If so, you are only experiencing the same trouble as scores of owners all over the country at this time of year. It is not as though dampness only was the bother, for this would soon be cured, but so often actual flooding takes place.

To clear water, the digging of a sump is generally suggested, but this unfortunately does not always solve the problem. Indeed, it is the writer's conclusion that in many cases these sumps, instead of draining water away are really the cause of its entrance.

Let us see just how water gets in. Shelters are, of course, all set below general ground level, with the result that in many places they cut through a soil covering to a clay or other water-bearing layer (see diagram).

Seeping Water

After rain, water sinks through the soil and then runs along the top of the lower layer in really considerable quantities, and at the bottom of slopes at quite a good pressure.

Thus, as indicated in the illustration, it finds its way through the sides of the sump (if unlined) which fills up like an ordinary well. Given that the hole was at ground level everything would still be all right, for it would just fill up to a certain height and the water would come no higher, but being below the level of the supplying area the water (in finding its own level) rises above the lip and floods out into the shelter.

In fact, if the refuge is set in a hollow we can get a very good example of " Artesian well," and it would be quite possible for the water released into the shelter to rise to general surface height.

Flooding from Below

That flooding comes from below can best be seen when the floor is cemented but the sump unlined, the water then easily being seen to rise and eventually run out into the shelter. It can often too be found forcing its way up between the cement and the corrugations at the sides.

How can all this be stopped ? Well, the solu-tion lies in treating the part of the shelter that is below ground level as you would a boat's hull and making it as water-tight as though it actually had to float. Fortunately this sealing is not too hard to carry out.

Cement Floor

The floor must, of course, be cemented. A sand and cement mixture of about two to one will do for this, and if laid on broken stone a layer of half an inch to one inch is quite sufficient for all general purposes.

A sump hole must be left to collect any water that does enter the refuge from above, such as drippings from the roof, rain driving through the door, condensation, etc., but it must be part of the floor, not a hole through the floor. The heavy black line in Fig. 3 showing what is meant.

Having cemented the floor, the lining of the sump may be carried out at once (also with cement) if the weather is dry, but if there is a period of heavy rain on, it will be found that the water seeping through the damp cement continually washes it away making the sealing impossible.

Bucket Sump

A good plan therefore (shown in the inset Fig. 2) is to sink a bucket into the hole and make it continuous with the floor by cementing round the top.

The sump being sealed and no leakage possible, the floor round the outer edges, that is between the base girders and side corrugations, should be made absolutely watertight, each little " bay " in the metal receiving individual attention, the cement being pressed tightly in, and if anything sloped down a trifle towards the general level of the floor.

The vertical joins in the metal must now be sealed. It is seldom that these can be got in absolutely tight contact when erecting a shelter, so they must each be given a cement filling, as far as ground level at least, but better still right to the top.

More sand and less cement can be put into this

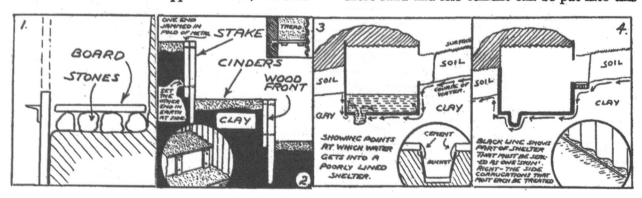

mixture and it must be pressed well in with the point of the trowel; be quite liberal with the mixture if it seems that some cavity behind the join needs filling, and finish each seam off neatly, flush with the metal surface.

When the shelter itself is dry, attention should be given to the approaches outside. This is very important, for no refuge can be kept dry if everybody enters wading through a sea of mud.

Any earth steps leading down to the entrance must be wood or brick fronted and the treads well cindered or cemented. Wood fronting is particularly simple, as the steps come down sideways to the shelter one end of the wooden front can be jammed in a fold of the metal and the other set a little into the earth wall opposite (see Fig. 2).

This, with the two stakes, makes the front very strong with a minimum of work and cinders can be rammed home very firmly behind. Paths should be edged with strong strips of wood and then cindered.

The lowest step (right in front of the door) is very important. It must be cut down to several inches below the sill of the door. Large stones of the rockery type should then be laid in position as shown in Fig. 1 and finally a well-fitting piece of thick board laid on these. This will keep the step well drained and if it eventually silts up everything can be taken out and the step relayed.

To drain away any water that runs down the covering earth it is good to cut a small trench round the bottom leading it away down the slope of the land, just as you would with a tent.

And finally, if you do not succeed at first in keeping out all water, keep on with the work, for perfection in jobs like this are more often obtained by the accumulative results of numerous small efforts rather than by one quick stroke.

For Handymen and Craftsmen

December 3rd 1941   Vol. 93. No. 2407

Special large Sheet of Patterns for a
MODEL SHORT SUNDERLAND FLYING BOAT

ANOTHER popular model is provided this week for making a non-flying type aeroplane which has been in great demand by readers. It is for the famous Short Sunderland flying boat which has done such marvellous work not only far out over the Atlantic, but over other waters.

The model shown is a replica in wood at a scale of 1/8in. to the foot, equalling 1/96th of the prototype, and all the required parts are clearly shown on the sheet. In addition we give a scale for these parts so that anybody who wishes can increase or decrease the size as they desire. The model has a wing span of 14ins. and a fuselage length of 10⅝ins.

The various parts are cut with the fretsaw to the outline shown and then shaped carefully either before or after being glued in position with each other. Finally the model is painted and if necessary a base stand provided for it.

A parcel of wood provides sufficient boards for all parts, and the first job is to mark out the various patterns. This can be done by pasting down the design, or, better still, laying the pattern over a piece of carbon paper and tracing off on to the wood direct.

Various useful sectional drawings are given, and these should be studied in conjunction with the picture of the finished boat. Then, too, if you have, as you can readily obtain, other pictures of the boat, they will be helpful to you for finishing touches in shaping, painting, fitting, etc.

The principal job, of course, is to get a nicely shaped and balanced hull and wings, and this can be only done by patiently carving and glasspapering down when the wood has been cut to the shape needed.

There is nothing monotonous about the work, for you will find it intensely interesting gradually to shape up and complete what will in the end be a striking replica.

First of all you should get out the two parts forming the hull or fuselage. This is from ½in. wood each piece being to the outline shown, and having the two openings cut to take the wing and the tail piece. Glue the two boards of the hull together and begin to shape it rounded and with its flat under edge for the water portion.

Lines are drawn across the pattern at A, B, C and D and above these are shown the exact sectional shape at that point. Notice that at D we have an egg-shaped hull but just behind it

the piece slopes up to form a flat platform to take the rudder and fin upright. A drawing of this is given herewith.

Notice, too, how the underside has a V sinking in it between the sectional line B and C. This and the way in which the float portion tapers off to the tail can be seen in the finished drawing, and must be cut carefully in the wood.

The wings are cut separately and in each two elliptical holes are cut to take the struts of the wing float.

Details of tail, rudder and rear gun turret

These holes need not be cut until the wing itself has been tapered down to its right curve.

Wing and Engine

The wing root itself—the widest part—will be the same shape as the hole cut in the hull, and from there it tapers gradually to the tip, the leading edge being more rounded than the trailing edge at the back. Before shaping the wing it is best to add the engine pieces.

The position of these is indicated by the two parts protruding on the wing itself, and the method of building up is shown on the pattern sheet. A piece forming the engine casing is glued above and below, the larger piece being on top.

The engine body itself is rounded and then fades away into the shaped wing. The wing in turn is shaped from front to back as previously mentioned. Get the whole thing nicely streamlined and maintain the balance of taper in both wings.

Forming the Engine

A picture is given here of the completed engine which is made up of the fixed piece to the wing, and then two rings on the front. The first ring is of ¼in. wood glasspapered down slightly thinner to be definitely to scale. On the front of this is the ring, the inner edge of which is rounded off.

The best plan is to cut this inner circle first, round it as required, and then cut the outer circle. In the centre of this ring is fixed the spinner

to which are attached the three blades of the airscrew. Their position can be seen on the front view and the shape of the spinner is also marked on the sheet.

The Tail Portion

The shaping and fixing of the tail is also given in the diagram herewith, most of the work involved being a question of getting the three parts down to their balanced curves. As in the wing, each portion of the horizontal plane sinks into the hull

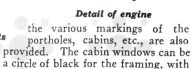

Two views showing how to shape the floats

opening half way there to be glued finally in place.

The rudder and fin which are, by the way, one of the distinguishing points of this boat, stand flat on the platform provided by that portion of the hull, and shown in the detail drawing on the design sheet.

This rudder and fin are cut from 3/16in. wood shaped each way as shown by the sections, then fixed upright. Strengthen the glue by putting in a headless nail partly into the hull and partly into the upright fin. Take care not to slit the wood in doing so.

Floats

The two floats can be added now, but not finally fixed in. Test them in place and then leave them until the remainder of the model has been painted. If you fix them altogether you will probably knock them off again when painting.

The shape of the float must be undertaken carefully with penknife and glasspaper, the side view and that shown on the front view giving an idea of the actual lines. Two further drawings of it are also given here which will be helpful.

These floats have about ¼in. or 3/16in. of the upright spars sunk into them at the point shown, the other end of the spars being driven into the holes cut in the wing itself.

Thin wire is also driven into the float and then stretched across to the underside of the wing as shown in the front view. As the part will be painted you can easily make a hole for this wire and fill it up with plastic wood or even hold the wire taut with tiny staples. All this fixing will be covered carefully with the paint after the final cleaning.

The actual work of making the

model is now completed, and it only remains to give it the final " once over " before painting. Do not be in too much of a hurry with this, and use the Hobbies enamels which leave a flat surface.

If you have used very soft wood it may be necessary to put a priming coat on to fill up the grain. The boats normally, of course, are white but now are painted a drab or camouflage of greens and grey-blues.

The roundels are painted on the hull and wing tips where shown and

Detail of engine

the various markings of the portholes, cabins, etc., are also provided. The cabin windows can be a circle of black for the framing, with aluminium paint for the glass.

Gunners Fore and Aft

The tail and front gunners are in a glass cage which can be similarly painted on, the actual lines being seen from the front and side views on

the design sheet. A couple of pieces of thick wire can represent guns.

If you want to fit the boat to a suitable stand, a base for it can easily be made although wood is not provided in the parcel. Get a piece 10ins. long and 3 to 4ins. wide. Round off the edges nicely. About 2ins. from each end raise a little upright support piece a little narrower than the width of the base and about 2ins. wide.

Into this cut the under shape of the hull near the bow and near the tail. Thus, when the model is stood in place, it will bed down comfortably on to these two upright pieces shaped to hold them.

It is advisable, by the way, to run a screw through upwards from the underside of the base to stiffen these uprights and prevent them falling over.

Another Miniature Aerodrome Model will be provided with Next Wednesday's Issue

A simple-to-make and easy-to-handle
PORTABLE FIRE-FIGHTING UNIT

THAT England is becoming 'fire-guard' minded is shown by the numerous items of 'home-made' fire-fighting equipment that handymen are turning out up and down the country.

The 'item' described here is a mobile pump unit, designed and made by a Cheshire party. It consists essentially of a light trolley upon which is permanently mounted a 60-gallon oil drum and a 'Pioneer' stirrup pump; the intake of the pump being connected to the drum by a short lead.

Pulled by Children

So easily does the unit run that a couple of children can move it, even when fully loaded, and it arrives at the scene of an outbreak with water for no less than 45 minutes of pump action, which should be ample for most jobs. A good long hose for feed-water, however, is supplied. The delivery hose also has been lengthened so all rooms in the area concerned can be reached from front or back door positions.

The unit is simple of construction and well worth copying. Certain parts, like the drum and pump, must of course be bought, but otherwise the unit is made throughout of wood. For quickness of manufacture and sturdiness, bolts have been used at all major joints.

The body consists of two main members (a) and (b), 3ft. 2ins. long and 4ins. by 2ins. section. On these rests the frame (A) which is built up of two side pieces 2ft. 9ins. by 2ins. by 1in. and end-pieces 1ft. 10ins. by 2ins. by 1½ins. Six cross-bars (f), of 2½ins. by ½in. section, are spaced down the whole frame as indicated, the ends being recessed into the lower edges of the sides.

At what will be the front-end of the main members goes the block (c), 10ins. by 5ins. by 2ins. Upon this the pump is fastened by the bracket (m), this being two angles of iron

which any blacksmith will make for a few pence.

To secure the pump, the usual 'foot' is removed, the end unscrewed and two bolts then dropped through the holes (then apparent) and through two similar holes in the cross-bar of the bracket.

Suitable Pump

The adaption is quite simple and should be made clear by the sketch (n). Any stirrup pump could be adapted, but the use of a 'Pioneer' is recommended, as on the unit illustrated.

For assembling the frame is laid on the main members spaced 2ins. apart, and holes for bolts drilled at the points of inter-section as shown. Ten 3in. bolts and four 5in. bolts are required for this part.

The 5in. bolts are for the front block (c), and for the back axle-block. Fit at this juncture the back-board (e) and the floor for standing on (d); the dimensions of each being given in the diagrams.

Steering

Steering is possible with the front axle, and a little studying of the sketches will show how this is effected. Under the main members (a) and (b), and right below the block (c), is the metal plate (k), 10ins. by 5ins., cut from any ¼in. material and bored in the centre and at points corresponding to the bolt-holes in (c); the main members, (k) and (c) all being held tightly together by the two 5in. bolts.

The swivelling part consists of the block (g), 4ins. by 3ins. by 1ft. 2ins., upon the top of which goes the plate (h), and below which the axle is secured by the same two bolts. A

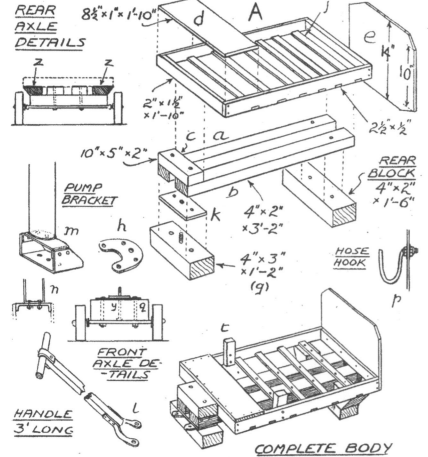

REAR AXLE DETAILS

8½" x 1" x 1'-10"

2" x 1½" x 1'-10"

10" x 5" x 2"

PUMP BRACKET

4" x 2" x 3'-2"

4" x 3" x 1'-2" (g)

2½" x ½"

REAR BLOCK 4" x 2" x 1'-6"

HOSE HOOK

FRONT AXLE DETAILS

HANDLE 3' LONG

COMPLETE BODY

A diagram of the various parts lettered for constructional detail

single 5in. bolt goes right up the centre to act as pivot.

Assemblage is effected by passing this centre-bolt through the centre hole in (k) and finishing by a large washer and two nuts for locking here is the fitting of the two blocks (z) which nearly double the effective bearing width of the complete assembly and some care in fitting should be exercised to see they actually take the weight of the outer sides of the frame.

It (the drum) is now prepared by screwing up any bung-hole it may have and chiselling off an end, so that when in position the top can be opened. A hook (p) made from any odd length of iron, and held by two nuts, is also fitted to take the delivery hose.

The lead to the intake of the pump is attached to the drum by the simple measure of using an ordinary tap. This attaches to the drum by drilling a suitable-sized hole, putting the end of the faucet through and screwing up tightly the collar supplied. The hose is then fastened to the tap by one of the 'tap connections' that can be bought at any ironmongers. The tap thus acts as the simplest of connections and as a stop-cock.

Beyond a coat of red paint and a length of cork or rubber matting on the foot-board (d) the unit is now complete. The delivery hose of the pump in the unit illustrated has been extended to 40 feet, but this length could be varied according to the special area the unit has to cover. The replenishing hose in this case is 60 feet.

The operator, it should be noted, stands on the trolley (i.e. on (d)), which gives him an excellent position well over the pump handle, and the complete unit should have on board sand-bags and scoops. A chunk of wood for scotching the wheels when in action should be carried also. Finally, it will be noted, that a good number of iron parts have been mentioned, but these can all be made very readily at any blacksmiths at a small cost.

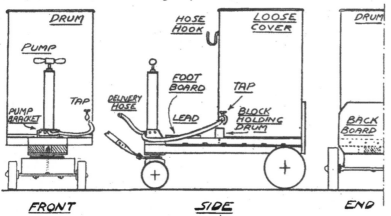

Three helpful details showing position of apparatus on the truck

purposes. The front elevation makes this clear.

For the handle it is best, if possible, to obtain one from an old lawn-mower, as the parts for connections are all there ready-made. If this cannot be done a handle can be built up as shown. The two lower strips (l), it will be noted, are heated and twisted to agree with the end of the plate (h), the two being held together by small bolts.

Back-axle assembly is somewhat similar, but here the two bolts which hold the axle go straight through the main members. An important point

Wheels and axles generally can be picked up from junk stores, and if they do not fasten to the axle-blocks as the ones described, suitable modifications will have to be made; but these should not be hard. The wheels, incidentally, must be of the fairly sturdy 'truck' variety, as 60 gallons of water plus the operator, who stands on the trolley, make a fairly heavy load.

The drum is of the usual oil variety and simply rests on the trolley. It is held from side movement by the blocks (t) and contact with the back (e).

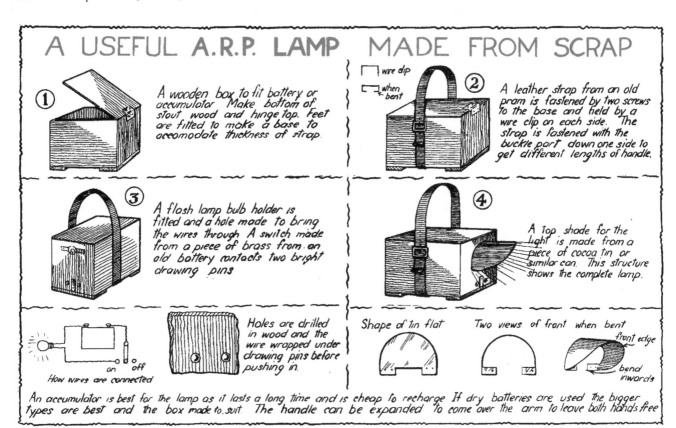

A USEFUL A.R.P. LAMP MADE FROM SCRAP

① A wooden box to fit battery or accumulator. Make bottom of stout wood and hinge top. feet are fitted to make a base to accomodate thickness of strap.

② A leather strap from an old pram is fastened by two screws to the base and held by a wire clip on each side. The strap is fastened with the buckle part down one side to get different lengths of handle.

③ A flash lamp bulb holder is fitted and a hole made to bring the wires through. A switch made from a piece of brass from an old battery contacts two bright drawing pins.

④ A top shade for the light is made from a piece of cocoa tin or similar can. This structure shows the complete lamp.

How wires are connected   Holes are drilled in wood and the wire wrapped under drawing pins before pushing in.

Shape of tin flat   Two views of front when bent   front edge   bend inwards

An accumulator is best for the lamp as it lasts a long time and is cheap to recharge. If dry batteries are used the bigger types are best and the box made to suit. The handle can be expanded to come over the arm to leave both hands free.

Everyone will be smitten with the novelty of a
DUG-OUT CIGARETTE BOX

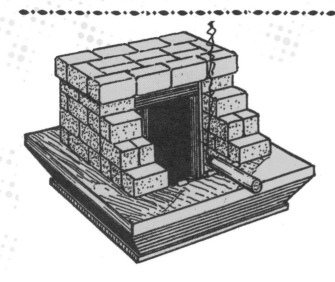

A FEW pieces of wood only are needed to make this little novelty, comprising a box for cigarettes or matches, and also an ashtray. It might prove a popular article to make for bazaars or to give as a present. Most of the topical novelties are.

The base, Fig. 1 can be cut from a solid piece of wood, or two or more pieces glued together. To make up the thickness saw out the rectangular opening, turn over and run a pencil line round the bottom, ¼in. from the edge.

Bevel the edges from a ¼in. down from the top to this line. For a bottom, glue over a piece of ⅛in. wood or a piece of stiff cardboard.

The Cigarette Case

The cigarette box, Fig. 2, is made of ¼in. wood to dimensions given. It is glued and nailed together with fine fretwork nails. For a space of 2ins. at the front chisel out a recess 1/16in. deep. Just a couple of saw cuts will do this, with a little paring with a chisel between.

Cut a piece of ⅜in. wood for a lid, 1/16in. larger all round than the box and hinge to it. Glue the box to the base in the position shown by dotted lines in Fig. 1, the recessed face being flush with the opening cut out.

Mark out the sides, ends and lid of the box to imitate sandbags.

These markings are cut in with a chisel to make them cleaner. Also rub off the sharp corners.

Just give a look at the finished view of the box and you will see what is meant. Inside the box two pieces of triangular fillet are glued lengthwise in the bottom angles to make it easier to pick out the cigarettes.

For the sandbags in front of the box cut some pieces of ⅜in. wood, as steps (see Fig. 3) and glue either side of the opening and to the front of the box.

Round off the sharp corners and glue in position, taking the view of the finished box as a guide. Now give the woodwork a good glass-papering.

Paint the box itself yellow, and the base green. The lintel, A, and side posts, B-C, Fig. 2, are painted in brown, the side posts being extended to the bottom of the opening. The door space can be painted black or green.

Making an Ashtray

The removable ashtray can be cut from thin sheet brass, or tinplate, to the dimensions given in Fig. 4. Bend at the dotted lines and solder the side strips to make a shallow tray, as in Fig. 5. The top ⅛in. is bent over to meet the base.

Take some care to make this tray a comfortable fit in the opening, as if it is tight it may not be possible to remove it for emptying out the ashes without distorting it. If the tray is made of brass it could be polished and lacquered, but if of tinplate, enamelled.

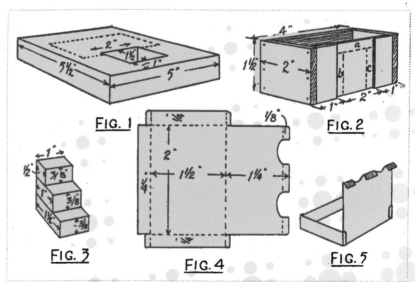

FIG. 1

FIG. 2

FIG. 3

FIG. 4

FIG. 5

Help Saving and the War Effort by arranging
MODELS FOR PROPAGANDA

THERE are many ways in which model enthusiasts can help the National Savings Movement. Models are admirable for showing the public the aim of any particular village, town or group. In every town and village there is a National Savings Committee and you can get the address from your Local Post Office. The Area Secretary will be delighted to get hold of someone to help him with his schemes, and he or she is bound to be a person who has ideas and gets things done.

A Special "Week"

First of all, find out what special campaigns the committee are likely to work on through the Winter months. They may be going to have a Tank Week, a Battleship Week or something similar, or saving to raise sufficient money to buy some particular War Weapon. Here is where you can come along and show your imagination and abilities.

If it is an effort to buy a Motor Torpedo Boat, then, perhaps, you can fret out a cut-out of this and paint it in suitable shades, so that it can be displayed in a local shop or the committee rooms of the Movement.

Window Dressing

Do not just pop it in the window so it looks as though it had got lost. Give it a little "atmosphere" by a nice realistic "sea" made of crushed crepe paper in sea green and blue and, of course, the finishing touches of wadding for the waves.

Now for the essence of your message. Write out a suitable poster, or get a friend to do it for you and let it tell, in plain words, the object of the show. "Our Aim—to raise enough for a Motor Torpedo Boat—Cost £55,000."

Models to Aim For

Now you see what a wonderful scope you model-makers have if you only try very hard. Here are some costs of War Weapons so that you can judge just what you, or your local model club can do to help in this great National Campaign. Approximate costs are as follows :—

Battleship	£8,000,000
Aircraft Carrier	£3,300,000
Cruiser	£2,000,000
Large Destroyer	£700,000
Corvette	£300,000
Flying Fortress	£60,000
Bomber Aircraft	£20,000
Medium Tank	£15,000
Naval Launch	£2,500
Searchlight	£1,500
Barrage Balloon	£700
Heavy Ambulance	£600
Light Ambulance	£300
Large Bomb	£45

Secretary's Help

Having outlined a few of the costs of War Weapons you can think out a scheme by which to use some of the excellent models which have been published in these pages in recent months.

Incidentally, try and get the local Secretary to let you see the very fine posters which are issued by the Movement, for in these you will find excellent material for making fret or cardboard cut-outs of the various War Weapons. Probably you are already familiar with some of them, but new ones are repeatedly being produced and give some fine outlines and details of boats and other articles.

Bomb Cut-outs

Bombs cut out in plywood and made to stand on a wooden block are always splendid propaganda because we are always saving for bombs and always sending them to Hitler.

Then those little cut-outs of the various services could be utilised, as you can tell people that it costs about £7 16s. 0d. to clothe a soldier. This might represent the effort of one street group.

There is no limit to what you can do, once you have got the idea, and by doing what you can, you will achieve interest, feel you are helping the country and feel more proud than ever that your models have not lost their value as show-pieces.

Firms and Plant

If you are employed in a firm, then plan them a blackboard with markings going up in hundreds of pounds chart-fashion, each week represented by a white line. Now you can find a small model fighter plane and let this indicate the amounts as they rise week by week.

Show your workmates what they save—show your firm what you can do in producing something original. Either at home, at work or at your club, form a little committee to help the National Savings Movement.

A Reader's Games Sets

TRYING to obtain a set of Chessmen to amuse my pal and I during firewatching at night, I found they were unobtainable now owing to them coming formerly from France. So we studied how to make a set.

The drawing explains and shows the set of chessmen we made out of plywood scraps. We painted one set yellow and one set brown, and they look real smart. The bottom two pieces are circles glued together and the figure has a tenon on to fit in so they can stand. Needless to add the board is a piece of plywood.

Making Draughts

Our set of draughts are also made from a piece of broom handle and the chessboard answers for either.

This is another instance where my handframe has helped me to make something I was unable to buy. Nobody need be without a selection of games for the blackout if he has access to a fretwork handframe and some scrap wood.

Dominoes can be made from plywood also. The black for them can be obtained by dissolving a piece of a gramophone record in methylated spirit, it gives a lovely ebonite effect.

Other Suggestions

Ludo, tiddlywinks, halma or table tennis, and scores of other games can be made by anyone able to use a fretsaw. I think other readers would be glad of particulars how to make themselves a set, so please pass it on. Once again, I give thanks to the friend who introduced me to fretwork some years ago.—(C. H. Ramsden, Bradford).

Castle (4) **Knight** (4) **Bishop** (4) **Queen** (2) **King** (2) **Pawn** (16)

A fine Animal Jointed Toy Design Sheet next week

HOME-MADE SAUCEPANS

THE appeal by the government for aluminium ware met with a great response, but it also created some difficulties. People gave many small pots and pans willingly, but often at some sacrifice and inconvenience. Moreover it did not much assist the national effort for economy if money had to be spent and labour expended upon some form of replacement of the bestowed utensils.

This led the writer to devise a little expedient which provides pots and pans thoroughly useful, yet which neither cost much money nor put any tax upon the labours of industry. The illustration shows the result.

Rolled Edge Opener

The form of tin opener, consisting of a cutter, guided round the tin by means of a toothed wheel gripping the outside ridge is now in fairly general use. It possesses the advantage of leaving a perfectly clean smooth edge. A tin so opened could not scratch the lips if used for a drinking cup.

Accordingly, a tin neatly opened in this way seemed quite suitable for a saucepan and the writer set about making some with conspicuous success.

The illustration shows a saucepan made from a tin which had held green peas, and the handle originally formed part of an old parasol. It is really only the handle which calls for any workmanship.

A piece of round wood is chosen for a handle, and a strip of tin is cut from some other can, long enough to go twice round the stick and about 2½ins. wide.

It is rolled into a tube to fit the stick, pushed on to it for ¾in. and secured by driving a nail right through and out the other side and bending the point down.

Beyond the end of the stick the tube is hammered flat or squeezed flat in the vice. The square points are cut off, leaving the flat metal three-sided, like the head of a coffin.

In this metal three holes are punched or drilled. A hole is made in the side of the can in a suitable position for the lowest hole, a rivet passed through outwards and hammered down.

Home-made Rivets

The projecting end of the vice or some other piece of solid metal must support the head of the rivet when the hammering is done. Rivets can be made by cutting off the heads of french nails, leaving about a quarter of an inch of the stem.

When one rivet is fitted, a second hole is made in the can, corresponding to one of the others in the handle, and this is riveted through. Then the third rivet is secured in the same way.

Handle Holder

Finally the flap of the handle is firmly clipped in the vice or a clamp and the handle is bent back to the desired angle. If not so clamped, an attempt to bend the handle may loosen the rivets.

Apart from various size saucepans frying pans can be made in the same way. Some kinds of fish, such as herrings or pilchards are put up in flat oval seamless tins which are excellent for the purpose, while shortbreads are packed in quite large flat tins, though these usually have seamed edges.

For Frying

The handles of frying pans are made from long tubes of rolled up tin, which may either be left cylindrical for the greater part of their length or may be more or less flattened if desired. This is because frying pans are so strongly heated that the wooden handles would char and drop out.

A convenient finish to the handle is to press it oval for the greater part of its length, but to flatten it at the hand end as well as the riveting end and finally to make a fair sized hole through this flat end for hanging the pan up. The square corners of this flap may advantageously be rounded off.

Measuring yourself for a Cycle

DO you know how to get the correct measurement of a cycle frame to ensure comfort and ease in riding?

The maker's measurement of the height of a frame is the distance from the edge of the opening where the saddle-pin is inserted to the centre of the crank axle. If you add the crank length of 6½ or 7ins. to this height, and also allow for the saddle and the saddle-pin above the frame, you may then arrive at a measure from the peak of the saddle to the pedal at its lowest point, which corresponds to the human measure—as taken by a tailor—from crutch to shoe-sole. A person with, say, a 31in. crutch measure, allowing a crank length of 6½ inches, could just about manage a 24in. frame, but would be much wiser to choose a 22in. to allow adjustment.

KLIPIT

MECHANICAL BUILDING OUTFITS

The extraordinary variety of Models which may be constructed from these Outfits is here illustrated. KLIPIT covers the building of Model Furniture, Mechanical Models, Models of Household Articles, Buildings, the foremost examples of Engineering—such as the Tower Bridge, etc.

The outstanding advantages of KLIPIT are:—
1. That the wood and clips may be used over and over again without damage.
2. The ease and rapidity of building the Models.
3. The naturalness of the finished Model.

No. 1 BOX, 5/-   Post Free 5/6

This Box contains:—252 sections of wood of varying sizes, 144 assorted clips, 4 pulley wheels, 2 spindles, crank, and pair of set collars, also a clip, lever and the 40pp. KLIPIT Book of Models with full instructions. The 36 page KLIPIT Book of Models will be sent post free to any reader on application.

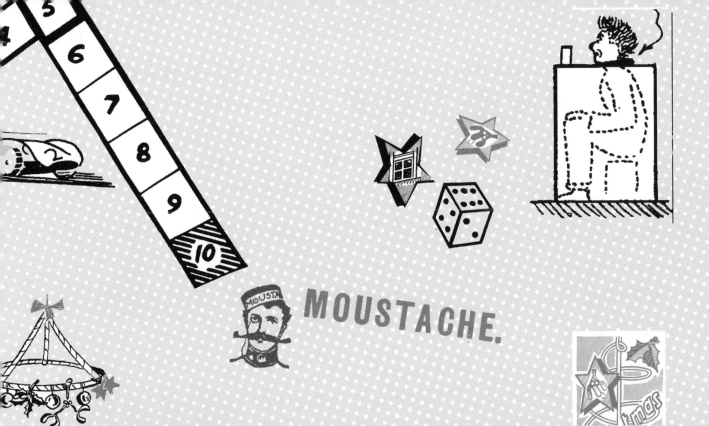

MOUSTACHE.

Home Entertainment

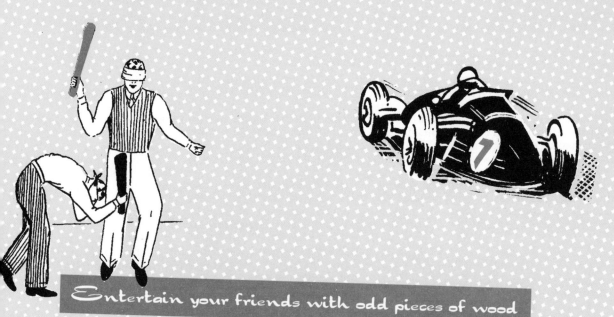

Entertain your friends with odd pieces of wood

PLAY SPOON HOCKEY!

HarrySecombe'scard

ACCELERATE

XMAS FUN and GAMES

GAMES and stunts are always in demand at Christmas time, but it is not always easy to get fresh ideas. Here are a good selection, and it is worth remembering that when you are planning a few games, they should not all be of the same type. There are so many sorts available—quiet, boisterous, games for a lot of folk, games for a few, games necessitating quick thinking, and those depending on agility. So in this collection are some of all sorts.

He Can Do Little—

Seat all the players in a ring, taking your place with them. Then hold a walking stick upright in front of you and tap its point on the floor, at the same time saying—" He can do little who cannot do this." Then pass the stick on to your left-hand neighbour, who tries to repeat your performance, and earns either " Right " or " Wrong " from you. Each player in turn round the ring speaks the same words, and taps the stick similarly on the floor.

A few, of course, may get the thing right by chance, but even they will probably go wrong when their turn comes round again. Keep on until all can give a correct performance—for those who have already found the clue take a lot of pleasure in pitying those who have not !

The secret of the thing lies here—during the repetition of the words, and for whatever taps accompany them, the stick must be held in the right hand. Then it must be passed into the left hand before being handed on to the neighbour. Most players instinctively pass the stick on with whichever hand they have used for the tapping.

What causes so much fun in the game is the tendency of the players to concentrate on making the tapping of the stick fit with the rhythm of the words—actually, of course, the tapping is of no significance.

Hip Hop

This game is very enjoyable if you have a large, mixed company, and a good-sized room. It consists of marching round the room in double file to music. The double file is of men and girl partners.

The games leader marches in front of the first couple—all partners hold hands as they go forward. Each time the leader gives a command, the leading pair turn about and march down the line of players, finally turning again and taking up their places at the rear, and so going forward once more with the rest. Only two orders are given by the leader—" Hip " and " Hop "

When he says " Hip " the leading couple turn inwards ; reclasp hands and, bending forward, go down inside the double line of players, underneath each pair of arms, which are lifted to make a high arch.

When the leader says " Hop " the leading pair release hands and turn outward, going down outside the double file and on opposite sides of it, until they rejoin at the bottom.

So there are always one or more couples going down the line, either inside or out, while the main body marches forward.

Rhubarb Race

Two " bundles of rhubarb " take part in this race game. Each bundle consists of three to six players. If there are just three they may squeeze through a hoop ; alternatively they may be held together by a rope tied round all their waists. The race should be up the room and back again— for there is additional fun when your bundles try to turn.

A group of players fastened into a bundle in this fashion find it no easy matter to get along even at a walking pace—and as it is a race they will all be trying to run !

Hands on Knees

Get all your players but one seated in a ring. The one, who is *It*, stands at the centre—and hopes to get a seat soon ! All those who are seated must keep their two hands flat on their knees in front, palms downward ; but they are allowed to slide them down the sides of their legs when they are in danger of being slapped by *It*.

It dashes about the ring as he likes, slapping there, here, and everywhere, until at last he succeeds in catching someone unawares. When he thus succeeds in slapping the hand of some player the two change places.

No hands are allowed to be off knees except at the actual moment when the slap is being made at them, and they must be replaced immediately the danger is over.

Lost Memory

When the rest of your party do not notice, take some person aside and ask him to turn all his pockets out on to a tray—if it is a girl the contents of her handbag will serve equally well. A little later bring the tray in and place it before all the others.

Announce that a person has been found suffering from loss of memory, and invite the players to deduce what they can from the exhibits on the tray, and so help to discover the identity of the unfortunate person. There is sure to be plenty of amusement as well as real ingenuity.

Life Stories

Players must know each other pretty well for this. Seat them all in two straight rows, facing each other, so that each has a player directly opposite. Supply all with pencils and paper.

Now announce that each person is to assume that the one opposite him has been made Prime Minister, and with this fact in mind he is to write a life story of him. The fun of the thing lies in making each life story as true as possible, yet in suggesting how various happenings have helped towards bringing the person to such prominence.

Instead of Prime Minister you may announce that life stories can be about quite different characters. Your players for instance, may be supposed to have become—convict with life sentence; film star, fattest man in the world, operatic tenor, champion weight lifter, cat burglar.

Forty Ways of Getting There

Have the players in two parallel rows down the room, facing inwards, with a broad avenue between them—this is to give them ideal seating as spectators.

Each player in turn now goes down the middle of the room. No method of " getting there "—that is to the bottom of the room, must be used more than once. Thus, if the first person walks in straightforward fashion no later player must.

The game is a test of ingenuity, each player trying to think of some new way of going down the room. If you like, those who fail to follow on can drop out of the game until only the winner remains.

There are innumerable ways of " getting there " —far more than forty anyhow. Here are some suggestions :—walking — forwards, backwards, sideways, with short steps, long steps, high lifting knees, stiff legs, on toes, running, jumping, hopping, somersaulting, rolling, crawling, pretending to— skate, swim, play a drum, carry a baby, use a crutch, waltz with a partner, and so on.

The Affectionate Penny

Tell your companions that there is one penny in your pocket which seems to know its owner.

It can communicate sensation to you through your fingers or palm so that you are able to pick it out from a number of other coins, even if you are blindfolded.

Let yourself be blindfolded. Then pull the penny from your pocket and place it on the table. Your friends can then strew a few other coins round it.

By passing your hand over them carefully you will have no difficulty in picking out your penny, The explanation is that for a minute or two beforehand you will have been holding it tightly in your hand, inside your pocket, and this will have made the metal warm so that it is readily distinguishable from the other coins which are cold by comparison.

Orange Battle

Two at a time take part in this humorous and exciting stunt. Each is armed with a dessert-spoon in each hand. On the right-hand spoon is balanced an orange, while the spoon in the left hand is available as a weapon of defence—and offence.

It is the aim of each player to knock off the orange of his opponent, so that it falls to the ground, while preserving his own safely.

If you like you can have players taking part in round after round, the beaten ones being eliminated each time until only the finalists are left. Or the winner of each bout can take on a newcomer, until all have had a turn.

Caveman's Bride

This is a strenuous, musical game, in which the players are gradually eliminated because they are caught on their feet when the music stops, until at last only the winner remains.

All sit in a ring, in couples, each man having a girl at his side. One man has no partner, and an empty chair is by him.

When the music—piano, radio, gramophone— starts, he jumps to his feet and dashes across the ring, seizing any girl he may choose by the wrist and dragging her over to be his " bride."

The man left without a partner must not move until the other couple are in their seats, but then he springs up and rushes to secure a new partner in similar fashion. The two who happen to be on their feet when the music stops drop out of the game.

Our Free Calendar Picture

The Coloured Picture presented with this issue is for a new and novel Calendar subject which anyone can make as a suitable gift for Christmas and the New Year.

It is well printed on strong paper and details for completing are printed with the picture. Date Pads for 1937 are obtainable from Hobbies Ltd., who can also supply you with further copies of the picture for 2d. each or 1/9 a dozen. You can easily make up a dozen or so quite cheaply as gifts for your friends.

Play Test Cricket at Home

WITH the aid of the Play Chart illustrated and some small pieces of white cardboard, it is possible to experience the thrills of a Test Match at home. The dramatic fluctuations of a struggle at the Oval, or the unpredictable course of the day's play at Old Trafford can be recaptured all the year round by using this simple chart and two packs of numbered and lettered cards which are easily made.

To prepare for this most exciting game of home cricket, cut out 54 pieces of plain white card. The size of each card is immaterial, but in practice, cigarette-card size has been found quite suitable. The first 32 cards are numbered 1 to 32 by printing in ink, or with coloured pencil, the relative numeral in the middle of the face of each card. The remaining 22 cards are lettered A to V in similar manner.

This game may be played by any equal number of players, up to eleven on each side, but it is usually played by two only, the solo player on each side assuming captaincy and control of the game from his team's viewpoint. We shall assume, therefore, that one player each side is to play. The two captains will chose a side each and construct their teams. Thus, if one is England and the other Australia, South Africa, or any team in the news at the time, or, coming down to County cricket, if one picks Yorkshire and the other plumps for Lancashire, each will write down the members of his team, as chosen by him, in the score book.

A score book can easily be ruled out in an exercise book. Having entered up details in the score book, the name of each player is written down on a small slip of card or paper, the chart set out on the table, the two packs of cards shuffled and placed face downwards on the table in front of the chart and all is ready for the toss to decide choice of first innings.

The batting side will place the slips bearing his opening batsman on the table at each end of the 'pitch' — that is, about 9ins. apart. The fielding side will place the card bearing the opening bowler's name in a line with and on the outside of batman No. 2, and bowler No. 2 will have his card positioned in a slip position behind and slightly to one side of the opening bat. It must be remembered that, to make this table game as realistic as possible, the non bowling member of the bowling pair will always be moved to a slip position between his overs, until finally taken off. New bowlers can be brought on at discretion.

To commence play, the fielding side will shuffle the two packs and replace on the table. The batting side, on behalf of batsman No. 1, will take a card from each pack and from the combination of letter and number find the square on the play chart which has decided the result of the first 'knock'.

Assuming, for instance, that the two cards drawn are N and 23. By referring to the chart we find that square N.23 (the 14th line down and the 23rd column across) is marked '3'. This means 3 runs for the batsman, and, as this is an odd number of runs, the batsmen's cards are changed from one end of the pitch to the other, and batsman No. 2 is brought into play for the next ball. The score is, of course, entered in the score-book, and the ball recorded in the bowling analysis. A 'blank', of course, indicates no score—and no wicket. And thus the game will proceed, in accordance with the rules of procedure for the real game.

The catches are numbered from 1 to 11 and, therefore, credit can be given to the successful fielder, according to his number in the batting order.

In actual practice, the chart has been devised to give an innings of 200–250 runs. The number of catches and other ways of losing one's wicket are based on analysis of a dozen first-class matches. The differing number of runs, byes, etc., are worked out on the same basis.

As the chart will be subject to much handling in the course of several matches it is advisable to mount it on a piece of stout card or fretwood.

It is astonishing how interesting each game can become as it progresses, especially if the score-book is faithfully and fully kept. One exciting possibility is permitted in this humble replica of the big match — a player may be his own Test selection committee and he may even include his own name in the England side. The feat of knocking up a century against the might of Australia's bowling is alone worth the little trouble involved in mounting the chart and preparing the cards for this attractive game.   (C.O'R.)

	1	2	3	4	5	6	7	8	9	10	11	12	13	14	15	16	17	18	19	20	21	22	23	24	25	26	27	28	29	30	31	32	
A	-	1	-	2	-	4	1	2	-	1	-	1LB	1	4	2	-	1	2	-	2	1	-	1LB	4	2	1	-	-	-	2	1	-	A
B	1	-	4	-	1	2	C1	4	-	2	1	-	3	B	1	-	2	1	C4	4	1	1B	2	RET HURT	1	-	2	1	4	2	-	1	B
C	-	-	2	1	2	-	3LB	-	1	C7	4	2	1	2	3	2	1	2	5	2	4	B	1	6	2	-	1	C2	3	1	-	4	C
D	4	1	2	B	6	1	2	-	4B	1	2	-	-	1	4	LBW	3	1	-	-	1	2	1B	4	C8	1	2	2	1	4	2	2B	D
E	-	-	2	1	1B	4	RUN OUT	3	1	2	1B	4	1	-	2	1	2	-	2	1	4	-	-	1B	1	2	3	1	-	2	C6	1	E
F	1	2	4	-	1	2	2	1	4	2	1	1	B	3	1	-	-	-	4	C2	1	-	3	1	2	4	B	1	-	2	1	2	F
G	2	1	C9	3	4	1	2	2	C8	1	-	2	1	2B	4	1	1W	-	2	1	2	-	1	LBW	2	1	2	3	1	4	-	1	G
H	4	2	1	2	1	B	2	1	1B	-	1	4	C3	1	2	C10	4	1	-	2	1	2	3	1	2	1W	1	4	C1	1	-	1LB	H
I	1B	1	2	3	2	4	1	-	2	1	2LB	2	1	4	2	1	1LB	2	1	4	B	1	INB	-	1	2	-	1	2	4	1	-	I
J	1	LBW	4	1	2	1	2	1B	4	C9	1	2	-	1	2	-	4	C11	3	1	2	2	1	2	4	C4	1	-	1	2	2B	1	J
K	2	1	2	-	1	C11	2	1	3	1	2	ST	4	3	C5	1	1B	2	1	-	4	1	RUN OUT	4	2	1	1LB	-	1	B	4	2	K
L	-	3	1	2	4	1	2	-	4B	1	2	2	1	2	1	4	2	1	6	B	1	2	4	-	2	1	1B	2	4	1	-		L
M	2	1	C2	4	-	-	1	B	4	1	6	2	1	3	2	1	C6	4	2	1	1	3	-	2	2	1	C10	4	1	2	3	1	M
N	1	2	4	1	-	1	2	4	1	2	C1	2	2B	LBW	1	2	4	1	-	2	1	2	3	C3	1	2	4LB	1	-	1	C7	4	N
O	1B	2	1	-	2LB	2	1	-	-	1	4	-	1	4	3	2	1	2NB	2	1	ST	4	1	2	2	1	1LB	4	1	2	1	-	O
P	4	C4	2	1	3	B	4	1	2	2	1	1LB	-	1	1W	4	C10	2	1	2	3	1	2	2	1	-	2	LBW	6	1	-	1	P
Q	2	1	4	-	2	1	2	-	B	3	1	2	-	1	2	4	1	-	2B	1	4	C6	3	-	1	4	1	2	1W	1	-		Q
R	1	-	1	4	2	4	1	2	-	2	2B	C7	4	2	2LB	1	-	4	C11	2	1	2	2	1	1B	3	2	1	-	-	1		R
S	-	1	2	2	1W	1*	LBW	4	1	-	-	1	6	2	1	B	4	2	1	3	1	1LB	4	1	2	4	C5	2	2	1	3	-	S
T	-	4	C5	1	-	2	1	3	-	1	2	1B	1	-	4	1	2	2	1	1B	2	1	2	C8	1	1LB	4	1	2	B	1	-	T
U	1	2	4	2	1	-	2	-	1	2	C3	4	-	1	2	4	1	2	1	C9	5	-	2	3	1	2	4	-	1	2	2	4	U
V	-	1	-	2	4	1	-	2	4	2	2	1	1LB	-	-	4	2	1	-	2	-	1	-	2	1	2	1	-	1	4	2	1	V
	1	2	3	4	5	6	7	8	9	10	11	12	13	14	15	16	17	18	19	20	21	22	23	24	25	26	27	28	29	30	31	32	

HERE are some new games guaranteed to make your party go with a real swing. The first is a good one to start with since it helps your friends to get together and become friendly.

MONEY FOR NOTHING

CUT out some discs of thin cardboard to the sizes of a penny, sixpence and a shilling. Write these values on the discs and for success you will probably require about four times the number of counters as you have players. The 'coins' are then scattered about the house or room as you wish but left so that they can be seen without disturbing the furniture. The game is started at a given time and at the end of a decided period — say five minutes — a halt is signalled. The winner is the player who has collected the highest value.

GUESSING THE MIME

FOR this game everyone goes out of the room except one who has to invent a mime (e.g. putting a coin into a slot machine, lifting the packet of chocolate out and opening). This little mime is performed to the first person who is called in. The solution is not revealed but this player has to pass on the mime to the next person who is called and similarly until everyone has seen and done the mime. Finally, the last player has to perform the mime before all and endeavour to guess the solution when a comparison is made by the originator. This is rather fun since the mime becomes more and more confusing as it passes from one to the other!

SHOPS

THIS is a fairly noisy game so you are warned!

Once again one person leaves the room while the others select a particular type of shop, say a grocery store. Each guest then selects some item sold in the shop such as tea, coffee, bacon, flour, rice, soap and so on. The player is recalled and the players shout out their different items, sharply and loudly on a signal given by the leader. It is best if the leader gives a count in, like a bandleader, and if the contestant can guess the type of shop after three attempts he is asked to indicate who gave the clue and this person then takes his place when another type of shop is selected.

TUNE TAPPING

WE have two teams for this game and each in turn must decide and tap out a tune which the other side tries to guess. It is best to have pencils and pieces of cardboard ready for this game and the winning team is the one which guesses the most tunes.

HOW ARE YOU!

THE guests should form a circle with one in the centre. The latter points to one player and says 'How are you today?' The correct answer is 'Quite well, thank you.'

But if the centre player points to someone and does not speak the player indicated should not reply. If he does reply — although never asked — he must take the centre. Or if the questioner merely says 'How are you?' — without the 'today' the one addressed is caught out and must take the centre.

MUSICAL GAMES

WITH the aid of a little music there are several other games at your disposal. First of all we have the popular Musical Chairs. When the music stops the players have to find a seat and the one without it 'out'. A chair is removed and the game proceeds to the last player.

For Musical Parcel, wrap up a small gift in lots and lots of paper and string. When the music stops the player holding the parcel is allowed to begin opening but must pass to his neighbour when the music starts again. The parcel is passed round in this fashion until the gift is finally revealed.

Musical mat is game where a mat is placed on the floor and the guests walk over this while the music is playing. When the music stops anyone on the mat is out and once again the last player to be in the game is the winner.

MEMORY TEST

THIS is another intriguing game to test the memories of your guests. You should have pencils and paper ready for the written answers. All you have to do by way of preparation is to arrange about 20 different articles on a tray and exhibit these before the guests for a minute or so. Do not allow too long for this. Small articles such as needles, pins, spoons, matchboxes, rubber bands, hairclips and the like may be used and the winner is the one who eventually proves to have remembered the most objects.

The tray may be exhibited again after an allotted time has elapsed and the lists checked with the articles.

BLACK MAGIC

THIS is a different type of game where the leader requires an assistant who goes out of the room for a moment or so. The remaining guests are asked to select some visible object which has to be guessed by the one outside. On returning the leader asks his assistant 'Is it this' or 'Is it that', pointing to some object at the same time. The secret of this game is between the leader and his assistant only and for your information when the former has pointed to some *black* object the assistant knows that the next will be the one selected. Note that by arrangement the colour can be changed and anyone who thinks he has guessed the secret is invited to test his skill.

These games should give a good selection for any type of party but to ensure success it is as well to make a programme, have some pencils and paper ready and a few prizes. And we do hope you have a happy time.   (S.H.L.)

ACCELERATE TO 29

OIL ON ROAD BACK TO 16

GEAR TROUBLE MISS 2 THROWS

SMALL CARS MADE FROM SCRAP WOOD PAINT DIFFERENT COLOURS

LOSE A WHEEL BACK TO PITS

STOUT CARD FORMED ROUND CIRCLE

R TO PAINT BRIGHT OLOURS

WELL POSITIONED EXTRA THROW

5 OPPOSITE 2.

3 OPPOSITE 4

OUT OF RACE

DICE CUT FROM STRIPWOOD.

1 OPPOSITE 6

WOOD CIRCLE

PRINTED IN ENGLAND.

THE TALKING HEAD!

HERE is an illusion easily arranged by any handy man and which is very suitable for Boy Scout shows, concerts or clubroom parties.

The idea is in no sense new, but the following is a description of how the illusion was prepared and carried out by a Birkenhead troop.

To an audience the illusion appears thus :—The curtain goes up on a stage containing near the front a small table. If at a party, the guests will be ushered into a room with the table standing in a suitable corner.

The Illusion

Professor Digemup, the famous Egyptologist, then appears and in a short speech tells how while travelling up the Nile he found a mummified head, which while not having any body attached, is quite capable of speech and indeed is something of an oracle, answering questions, etc. This head, he goes on to say, he has with him to-night, and it is his intention to give the audience a full demonstration of his marvellous find . . . . . and much more to this effect.

Having finished his speech an attendant brings on a box (very gingerly) marked " Head, with care."

This is placed on the table and the Professor asks for the lights to be lowered, at the same time lighting the two candles " floodlights " on the edge of the table, which lights illuminate excellently the table top and box. The Professor now makes a great fuss of undoing catches, etc., and then lifting the box reveals apparently lying on the table, a head, eyes closed, and most grotesque in appearance.

The Talk

He then proceeds to waken the head, which opens its eyes and begins to speak. A cross talk now starts between the head and Professor, which if carried out well, can be very funny and entertaining.

Finishing the " turn," the box is placed over the head, is apparently locked, and is lifted away showing a perfectly empty table top. Professor says " good night " and curtain falls.

The way the illusion is

worked is, of course, obvious from the sketches, but simple as the idea is the illusion of a head on the table is very complete.

The Frame Structure

The table is a framework made up of four uprights (A) 2ft. 6ins. by 2ins. by 1½ins., four side pieces (B) 2ft. 3ins. by 3½ins. by ½in., and eight strengtheners (C), carried from the mid point of the side pieces to the mid point of each leg, and shaped as shown. Thin material only is needed for these members (3/16in. or slightly less) as they have to sit outside the legs and inside the side pieces.

Further Strength

This is not sound carpentry as it leaves the pieces slightly askew, but the table thus made is very rigid and after all, in this case, this is all that is needed. Should a better finished article be desired the strengtheners can be sunk into line by slightly recessing each leg at (b). The table should now be made to stand square on the ground so the person inside will not cause it to rock by any inadvertent movement. Each joint is fastened by one screw only.

Next obtain two sheets of card (E) and cut out an oval just large enough for the " head " to come through. Place on top of the table and secure with short sprigs.

Cloth Covered

Now get two sections of cloth that are capable of fitting round the table (as F) right down to the ground, with a division across the middle, and over the hole. Two curtains will do admirably. Sew in, as shown, two lengths of elastic along the edges that fit over the hole and fasten all down with drawing pins.

Finally make two holders for the candles (H) out of white card curved and held to a rectangular base by a series of pins pushed up through the base into the card. All is now finished bar the head box, which is a large but solid hat box inverted and labelled as indicated.

Inside the Frame

It is carried with the

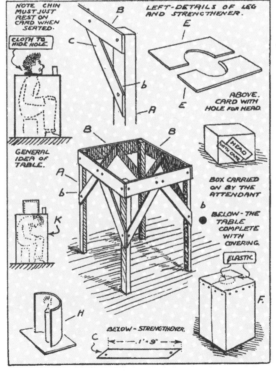

NOTE CHIN MUST JUST REST ON CARD WHEN SEATED.

CLOTH TO HIDE HOLE.

LEFT-DETAILS OF LEG AND STRENGTHENER.

GENERAL IDEA OF TABLE.

ABOVE. CARD WITH HOLE FOR HEAD.

BOX CARRIED ON BY THE ATTENDANT

HEAD WITH CARE

BELOW-THE TABLE COMPLETE WITH COVERING.

ELASTIC.

BELOW - STRENGTHENER.

1' 9"

open " bottom " slightly tilted from the audience. In working " the head," a smallish person is inside the table before things start (K). He should be comfortably seated, on a hassock or on something else just the right height. His chin when up should just comfortably rest on the edge of the card.

When the box is placed on the table the Professor gives a sign (say a tap) and the boy underneath very gently parts the elastics and pushes his head up into the box. The Professor the while keeps his hand firmly pressed on the box to prevent movement.

The box is lifted from behind slightly first, that is tilted forward on its front edge and while doing this the Professor pushes under a scarf or some ample piece of cloth close up to the neck. When the box is finally removed he carefully **arranges** this around the neck apparently to support the head in an upright position—but actually to cover any break in the cloth of the table top, and generally camouflage any idea of a hole. With a little care all this can be done quite naturally, but it should be practised quite a lot beforehand.

The Disappearance

Disappearing is just the reverse process. The head should be " got up " grotesquely, white powder all over, red tip on nose, arched eyebrows, etc. A wig helps but it must be firmly fixed.

We have given no indication of the dialogue to be employed, but if two people of the right type work this stunt, there will be no difficulty on this score.

A NEW PICTURE PUZZLE

Now then you sharp-eyed people, what's wrong with this picture ? A whole lot because our artist purposely omitted some essential parts. There are not hundreds of them nor any tricky silly ones. See if you can spot what he has left out. Prizes will be awarded the list sent in nearest to his official one. Good prizes will be awarded and all entries must be in by Saturday, October 14th., 1939 in accordance with the rules.

Read these Rules : Write your list in ink on one side of the paper one below the other. Number them consecutively and put the total at the end. Add your name and full address. Post in a sealed envelope using a 1½d. stamp. A stamp for ½d. or 1d. will not do. Entries in by October 14th, and the Editor's decision is final. In case of more than one correct entry, neatness will count. Names of winners will be announced in Hobbies as soon as possible.

PRIZES TO WIN

1st. Prize A1 Fretmachine value 52/6. Other prizes of Tools, Pin Tables, Fountain Pens, etc. and lots of Consolation prizes.

Overseas Section

Readers outside the British Isles (including Eire) can send in solutions up to December 2nd. and special prizes will be awarded them.

AMUSING NOVELTIES

HOW TO ENTERTAIN YOUR FRIENDS WITH ODD PIECES OF WOOD

WHAT AWFUL CHOCOLATE!

THE subject of this week's novelty, made from an odd piece of wood, is a very laughable joke, that takes the shape of an *imitation* piece of chocolate. Any odd piece of wood that measures 2½in. long by ½in. thick will do. Should a soft piece of wood be used, it will made no difference.

The writer of these amusing novelties has been " taken in " by one which the perpetrator of the joke confessed was made from a piece of batten off a packing case. From this, it will be quite clear that a careful selection is not necessary. If the following instructions are carefully followed, it should be practically impossible to tell the fake piece from a genuine piece of chocolate.

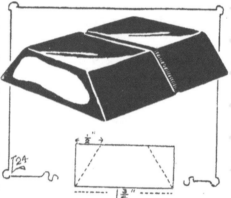

Cutting Out.

Mark and cut out your piece of wood to the sizes given, next proceeding to bevel off the two sloping sides (which should bevel to a line drawn ½in. away from the two outsides of top). Having done this with a hacksaw, or any saw, you may have that will give you a cut about ⅟₁₆in. wide, cut your groove round the two bevel sides and top. This groove should run across the middle of the length of wood, *i.e.,* 1¼in. from either end ; finish off groove with a round file, so that the cut does not look too sharp. It will be found wise to file the edges all round a little to prevent too harsh a result, as it will be noticed, by looking at a real piece of moulded chocolate, that the edges are not sharp like a knife, but slightly rounded.

Painting the Exact Colour.

After having sandpapered the whole quite smooth, the careful work of painting the wood must be tackled. Obviously, the block must now be painted a chocolate brown. A dark oak is the nearest matching colour to chocolate, but it must be very dark, and to ensure this result a little black paint can be mixed with it. Great care and attention is necessary to do this part of the work properly, and it will be found that two coats will be necessary to get a perfect colour.

As the Sketch.

When the brown has dried, the cream must be painted on one end with white paint (as sketch). Don't do this too regular, as the cream in chocolate very seldom follows exactly the outline of the chocolate.

If, on completion, the joke chocolate bar has not the glossy look of chocolate, a coat of varnish will remedy that. Don't get the white part glossy, or the real effect will be greatly diminished.

Aids to Future Work.

The writer of these novelties is eager to lay a training ground for the handyman or fretworker in the home. They are intended as a stimulus to larger and more useful work. Once create the desire to make, to mend, to restore any broken or unsightly fallen-away work, and the spirit of industry and handiness becomes a real, absorbing pleasure.

Not only is this so, but homes can be made to look really beautiful, through renovation and repair that comes in the handyman's way, and to crown the work with the last word in success the satisfaction lies in the knowledge that the work has been done in the home for which it is intended.

It must always be understood that beautiful homes do not necessarily belong to the rich man's purse ; the working man is often a shining light in his home which he loves to make happy and comfortable.

A glance at Hobbies' illustrated catalogue will tell him at once the tools and equipment that are necessary and of service to him in his work.—L.

DISC BREAK?

THE TEMPERANCE SEVEN

PRESENTING . . . the rage of radio, the terrors of television, the sensations of society, those popular gentlemen 'The Temperance Seven', who are now willing and able to conquer the world of the talking steam gramophone through the medium of their Parlophone recording of *You're Driving Me Crazy* and *Charlie My Boy* (45-R4757).

Let us first introduce individually the members of this remarkable ensemble, which owes its success to being forty years out of date — playing in the 'sixties the dance music of the 'twenties.

CAPTAIN CEPHAS HOWARD, leader, trumpet and euphonium. After a distinguished military career, during which he was awarded the Charing Cross (with bar), the Last Order (with bar) and the Alhambra Star (nothing barred), he was unhappily cashiered for gross misappropriation of five chassepot rifles and a billiard table.

ALAN SWAINSTON COOPER, clarinet, pedal clarinet, soprano saxophone, swannee whistle and phonofiddle. The only pedalling clarinettist still at large he is the holder of the tricycle record London–Brighton, 1903.

SHEIK HAROUN WADI el JOHN R. T. DAVIES, trombone, alto and personal bodyguard. Astronomer Royal to the late Kemal Attaturk and collaborator of Thomas Alva Edison. He has three times swum the Channel to the discomfiture of the Dover Customs and Excise Officers.

PHILIP 'FINGERS' HARRISON, alto and baritone. Renowned vegetarian and inventor of the clockwork hansom cab, steam harp and magnetic corkscrew.

CANON COLIN BOWLES, piano and harmonium. Formerly of the British Matchbox Label and Booklet Society, now unfrocked. Founder of the British and Empire Free-style Balloon Society.

DR JOHN GIEVES-WATSON, banjo. Formerly personal manservant to the Keeper of the Eddystone Lighthouse, he was chosen as Chief Druid and holder of the Bardic Crown, Llanfairfach Eisteddfod, 1902.

FRANK PAVERY (pronounced 'ffry'), sousaphone. An undischarged millionaire, famed for his feats on the high wire, the troop of performing sealions which he trained in three weeks, and his proficiency in the one-wheeled cycle race.

BRIAN INNES, grand jazz percussion kit. Professor Emeritus and formerly occupier of the Chair of Percussive Studies, Witwatersrand University.

WHISPERING PAUL MACDOWELL, megaphone vocals. Ambassador Extraordinary to the Outer Hebrides, A distinguished diplomat, sword-swallower and dancer, he is perhaps best known as an embezzler of international standing.

Having introduced the gentlemen of the orchestra, let us delve into the glorious past of the 'Temperance Seven' and draw back the shroud of secrecy which cloaks the days before that epic occasion at the Bournemouth Centenary Celebrations of 1910, when they were awarded the Prix d'Honneur for their original rendering of the new dance craze, *The Kaiser Rag*, following which they were hired for a record-breaking residency at the Balls Pond Cocoa Rooms.

Persuaded to remain serious for a moment, Brian Innes vividly recalls the band's formation:

'It was Christmas 1955, and I was at home doing nothing in particular when there was a tap at the window. I looked out and there was my friend Paul MacDowell. He talked me into allowing him in and announced that he wanted to form a band. He took me to meet Philip Harrison, the only other remaining founder-member, and with some other enthusiasts we became the Paul MacDowell Jazzmen — for one appearance only. By the time we played in public again we were known as 'The Temperance Seven'. Why did we choose the name? Well, I suppose it was

All types of fun for you in a selection of new
XMAS PARTY GAMES

YOU want some fresh fun for the party ? Then try these games : They are specially written for Hobbies and will create no end of fun and laughter.

Shoe Scrounge

A sort of rowdy ice-breaker to set the party going. Boys usually enjoy being players—you need four of them. These contestants—combatants is probably a better word—all have their shoes unlaced, or wear slippers.

They stand at opposite corners of the room, until the starting signal is given. Then they dash to the middle, each intent on securing as many shoes as he can.

A reasonable time should be allowed for the scrimmage. Finally, the one who emerges with most shoes is declared the winner.

Survivor Plane

This, if performed impressively, is a good trick, and one quite easy to perform.

Get your audience seated in a ring. You sit at the centre with slips of paper. You ask the others to tell you, in turn, the name of enemy planes—Junker, Heinkel, Messerschmitt, Caproni, and so on—and they see you write down a name on every slip.

But they do not know that on each paper you are putting the same name, the one that was first given you.

When all have given names, adding English ones if necessary to make up the number, you mix the papers together and invite any person to come and draw a single one—being careful not to let you see which is drawn.

Then you burn the remaining slips ; stir the ash, examine it closely, and finally announce that you know n o w t h e name of the plane which has survived.
Simple enough !

Black-out Scrap

Two at a time take part. They a r e blindfolded, and each is equipped with a cudgel made from a couple of rolled-up newspapers.
They are allowed

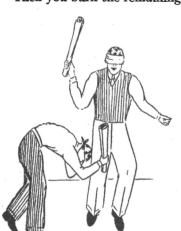

The black-out scrap

to move freely about the room, the aim of each being to belabour the other.

Or if there is little space they can sit in easy range. Allow them a couple of minutes, then have the next volunteers.

Reporting the Party

You write out beforehand a " press report " of the party. Names of people present can be mentioned. Spaces for adjectives can be left blank.

Then, for the game, you ask each person in turn for some adjective, which can be pleasant or uncomplimentary and write these into the blank

How the game of spoon hockey is played

spaces in proper order. When all the blanks are filled the " report " is read aloud.

Animals or Birds

This is a game which demands quick thinking. A box of the familiar little letter cards or blocks, or scraps of paper with letters written on is required. This is put near the middle of the table.

Each player in turn must stir up the letters, then draw one and declare what it is. Instantly all begin trying to think of an animal or bird whose name begins with this letter.

The one who first calls out a name, which has not previously been used, scores a point—and draws next time from the box.

Blind Bombing

For this you need a large piece of brown paper a pin and slip of paper for each player. On one side of the large piece draw a number of small circles, writing the name of a " military objective " in each. Each has a definite value, thus: oil dump, 5 points; aerodrome, 4 points; factory, 3 points; warehouse, 2 points; railway, 1 point. Now hang the paper up with the drawings towards the wall.

Players write their names on their paper slips. Then each in turn sticks his pin, with the slip attached, through the wall paper—hoping to hit an objective. When all " bombs " are used up the paper is turned over and scores reckoned.

Spoon Hockey

Six players is the best number for this and a large table with smooth top is needed. For hockey sticks teaspoons are used with the rounded side kept downward. Instead of a ball have a wood draught or checker, cotton reels make good goal posts.

With six players, arrange a goalkeeper at each end, and one player of each team on each side of the table, the two players side by side being therefore opponents. Start with a " bully off " at the centre, and follow the normal rules of hockey as closely as possible.

Neat passing is better than hard hitting. Hands must not be put on the table. And remember to keep the spoons right way up so as not to scratch the surface of the " field."

Card Pack Pass

This is for teams which stand or sit in straight rows. The end player of each has a pack of cards. As soon as the race starts he begins to pass on the cards one at a time to his neighbour.

So they all travel along, always one by one. The last team member must get the whole pack together and laid tidily on the floor in front before his opponents in order to win.

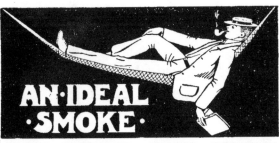

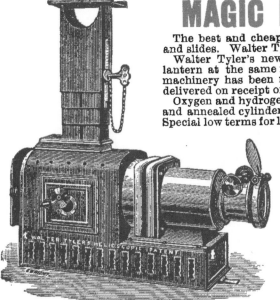

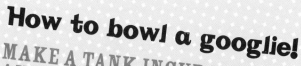

How to bowl a googlie!

MAKE A TANK INCUBATOR
AND A PAIR OF SKIS

THE GREAT
OUTDOORS

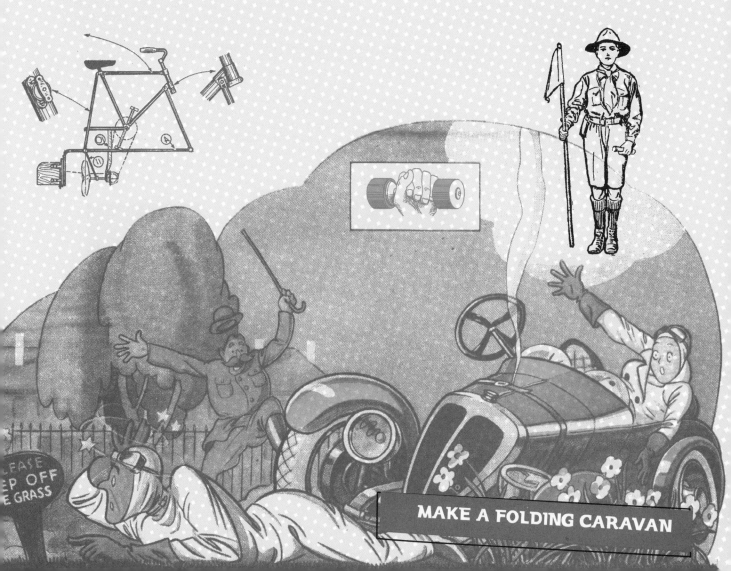

MAKE A FOLDING CARAVAN

SOME PRACTICAL HINTS ON CRICKET

The first of two excellent articles full of helpful illustrated tips. This one deals with bowling and fielding.

HERE are some helpful hints which will enable you to pile up a score like those dreams of imaginary centuries and taking wicket after wicket.

Begin with bowling. Erect your stumps, mark your crease, pace out your pitch and begin. Hold the ball in your fingers, not in the palm of your hand, and get your third finger round the seam. Circle your arm from the shoulder several times to loosen your shoulder joint. Next, one or two preparatory runs to the wicket, with an imaginary delivery, until you have got back comfortably into your stride. The first important points to concentrate on are :—

1. Let go of the ball when the body and arm are at the highest stretching point. See photograph 1.

2. Make a good delivery by completing the circular movement of your arm, and continue your run one or two steps over the crease. The pace at which you deliver the ball depends upon the speed of your preparatory run, and the speed of your arm action in delivery. A fast bowler uses a longer, faster run, and has a swifter arm action than a medium or slow bowler. He also likes a dry, hard pitch and a new ball.

Bowling Tips

A good length ball deceives the batsman into thinking that he can step forward to it and hit it for four. He does, only to find it has pitched just short of his reach. He has edged it and is caught, or he has played either inside or outside

it and his stump is somersaulting into the wicket keeper's hands.

Every bowler must be able to keep a good length ball, and the best way to practise it is to put a mark just where the batsman cannot reach, and try to make an average of ten out of ten balls pitch on the mark.

Having got your length now learn to " spin " your ball. You can use either a leg break or an off break. A leg break is the term given to a ball pitching off the wicket on the leg side, but breaking on to the leg stump. To get the ball to do this you must hold it with your fingers round the seam and, as you deliver the ball, twist your wrist so that the thumb turns from right to left.

Your wrist action finishes with the little finger side of your hand uppermost. To make the ball break in on to the off stump from the off side of the wicket, you must hold the ball with your fingers round the seam and, as you deliver the ball, twist your wrist so that the thumb moves from left to right, finishing with the palm of your hand uppermost.

In break bowling a good length is important, so again find the spot outside the leg and the off stumps where the ball must pitch, and keep up that average of ten out of ten when you practise. Remember also that the ball must come off the pitch at a good pace ; a sure sign of a tired bowler is loss of pace off the pitch.

A Googlie

To bowl a googlie you must deliver the ball from the palm of the hand. Twist your wrist, as for a leg break, and the ball will perform an off break. You will find this needs considerable practice.

Try bowling one or two fast yorkers. These bound on the crease and, if your batsman takes one of these to be a half volley (as you hope), the ball will go underneath his bat and you will have another wicket to your credit.

Slow and medium-paced bowlers will find it useful to get variation in height of the ball. This is done by loosening the grip on the ball. Every bowler, no matter what his pace, will want to be considered a cunning bowler, and this will come only with practice and some thought.

The Break

For instance, do not use too much break. The batsman will watch your hand and, seeing the obvious twist, will not be deceived. When you can be sure of sending up a good length ball you can try one or two not such good lengths to encourage your batsman to step out before you send him your best break.

A word here about fielding will be helpful. Go into the field prepared to do a great deal of work. Therefore keep your weight balanced more on your toes than on your heels.

In the deep field be ready for a quick sprint in towards the wicket, keeping your eye on the ball so that you can gather it up as you run, and go on running as you throw in. The photograph will show you a good position of the hands and body as you pick up.

Throwing In

For throwing in keep the ball in your fingers, not in the palm of your hand. Your left arm must give you the direction in which the ball is to be sent. Throw the ball in a sideways, upwards direction—(see the photograph)—it is not good enough to let the ball bound before it reaches the wicket keeper or bowler. You must aim into his hands level with the bails on the wicket.

When you are running in for a high catch do not rely on your hands only, but hug the ball to your chest, when you have grasped it, and immediately throw in. The fourth photograph shows this clearly.

The Slips

For fielding in the slips you will find it necessary to be well on your toes, with your feet a little apart, and your hands cupped down ready to hold the ball. Catches glancing off the bat are upon you here in a moment. You need to watch the ball right from the bowler's hand, on to the bat, and off again into your hands.

As a wicket keeper you take much the same crouch as in slips. Perhaps a little more so, since you must watch the ball just over the level of the wicket. For a fast bowler the wicket keeper will stand a longer distance from the wicket ; but do not overdo this. Get to know the type of bowling you are backing up.

"WATCH OUT FOR WHAT GOLF —(GULP!)— BALL?"

SAILING ON CYCLES: A NOVEL SPORT

THE accompanying photographs, kindly lent by the editor of the *Bournville Works Magazine*, represent a sailing bicycle which was made for use on the sands at Rhos Neigh, on the west coast of Anglesey, during the holiday season last year. The writer of the article says "it took some time to develop the idea even to the perfection shewn. The first trial would not allow us to return back along the sands on the opposite tack without getting off and adjusting the sails; but eventually, after we had re-built the framework for the fourth time, success justified our efforts.

As will be seen from the illustrations, the main framework consisted of two boards, each about sixteen feet long, bent in the shape of a boat to give plenty of room for turning the front wheel; on this was built up a triangulated mast of most unorthodox appearance, which

SAILING.

at which one rode made a fall seem inevitable, and it was some time before one learnt to trust the supporting power of the breeze. Going about at the end of the tack was exciting work, and we got the best results by turning out of the wind, instead of, as in ordinary sailing, into it; the boom supporting the bottom of the mainsail then swung over for the opposite tack, when one was travelling at a good speed. If, however, the speed was slow, this swinging over of sail and boom was sufficient to upset the equilibrium of most, and a fall was the result. This we soon found to be the critical point of cycle sailing, and if one can survive the going-about the rest is comparatively easy. Naturally the best results were obtained with a sea breeze at right angles to the shore, and often a speed of from fifteen to twenty miles an hour back and fro along the shore was made, and this was maintained once for

MOUNTING.

carried a main sail and jib having a combined area of about forty square feet. The framework was securely fastened to the bicycle by numerous pieces of rope and an occasional tourniquet for adjustment.

It cannot be said that the craft had a very boat-like appearance, for it leant up against instead of heeling over with the wind like an ordinary boat. The first sensations of riding on it were decidedly unpleasant, as the angle

over half an hour without a dismount.

Visitors were very much interested, and we enjoyed letting them try their hand, as falls were frequent, especially when they steered into the sea or on to soft sand.

It only remains to add that the whole outfit, including sails, cost from 5s. to 7s.

My object in writing on this subject is partly a selfish one, as I should much like to hear the experience of others who would care to follow my example ; and there may, also, be others who can refer me to such information as will lead me to build more perfect sailing arrangements another time.

Yachting on Wheels.

Grand sport is also being enjoyed by youngsters on Tooting Common with a ship on wheels. As seen by the illustration, the idea is a very simple one. The sails are fixed to a framework; to which are attached four perambulator wheels, and when there is a good wind the quaint vehicle will travel at a rate of twelve miles an hour. The boys when photographed were managing their land ship as skilfully as does a most expert yachtsman with a proper boat on the water Whenever the boys bring their ship upon the Common for a " jolly sail "

BATTERSEA BOYS ENJOYING THE SPORT.   [*Photo by J. Babburn.*

they are watched with keen interest by a huge crowd of people. Boys, especially those in the country, should try this exciting sport. A ship on wheels is neither a hard nor an expensive matter. The picture is enough to show how the thing can be made.

A FOLDING
TRAILER CARAVAN

THE caravan illustrated, though presenting quite an imposing appearance, is yet within the scope of any fellow capable of reasonably good woodwork. It is of the folding type, the sides being removable and the front and back hinged to fold over on to the floor. This is most handy where space for storing is limited.

A few words as regards the wheels are necessary. A complete trailer chassis can be purchased, but costs about £21 0s. 0d. Such a chassis, having a narrow wheel base, does not lend itself so well to the folding type of caravan and as it is proposed in a future article to deal briefly with the fixed type of caravan, further reference to the chassis mentioned will be deferred until then.

Cost under £12

For the kind of caravan now to be dealt with, the wheels from an old motor car will be about the best to use. These can be bought from almost any garage for a very few pounds, and should be furnished with axle, brakes and springs complete.

With the cost of wood and fittings, the whole affair need not cost above £10 to £12 and may well total less.

If the distance between the mudguards is not less than 6 ft. 2ins., the general measurements given in the article can be strictly adhered to, otherwise it may be necessary to amend the width of the caravan to suit.

The sizes of all timbers used are given in the cutting list, and it is advisable to order the wood planed to those sizes. The wood chosen, especially that for the joists and under-frame, must be free from knots and shakes. For the under-frame, oak or ash is preferable but good quality deal may be used. In any case deal is used for the remainder.

Make a start with the underframing shown in plan view from underneath Fig. 1. The ends B are tenoned into the sides A, while the joists C are stub tenoned into B. The latter tenons should be about ½in. deep, no more, so as not to unduly weaken the ends.

The Floor Fixed

The under rails D are bolted across, and the longitudinal bars E, which carry the springs, bolted to D. Fix these the same distance apart as the springs. The whole frame, glued and nailed, can now have the floor fixed.

Along the upper surface of sides A run a pencil line down, just 1in. from the outer edges. The flooring is cut and laid on the frame to come to these lines only, therefore the boards are cut 5ft. 10ins. instead of the full 6ft. and nailed across.

Just a tip. Do not lay all the full length boards first and then finish off with the short ends, but work the latter in between as you go along. The flooring extends the full length of the frame.

The Front

At this stage you can bolt the springs to the bearers E, and support the floor at both ends to keep it from tipping up.

The front of the caravan, Fig. 3, is framed up as shown, 6ins. angle blocks of 1in. thick wood being glued and nailed in each corner.

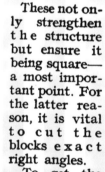

These not only strengthen the structure but ensure it being square— a most important point. For the latter reason, it is vital to cut the blocks exact right angles.

To get the door posts truly parallel, cut ½in. deep grooves in the top and bottom pieces in which the posts can be housed. Nail strongly in place. The horizontal above the door, should also be grooved into the posts.

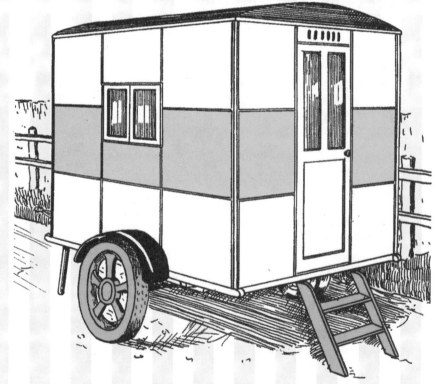

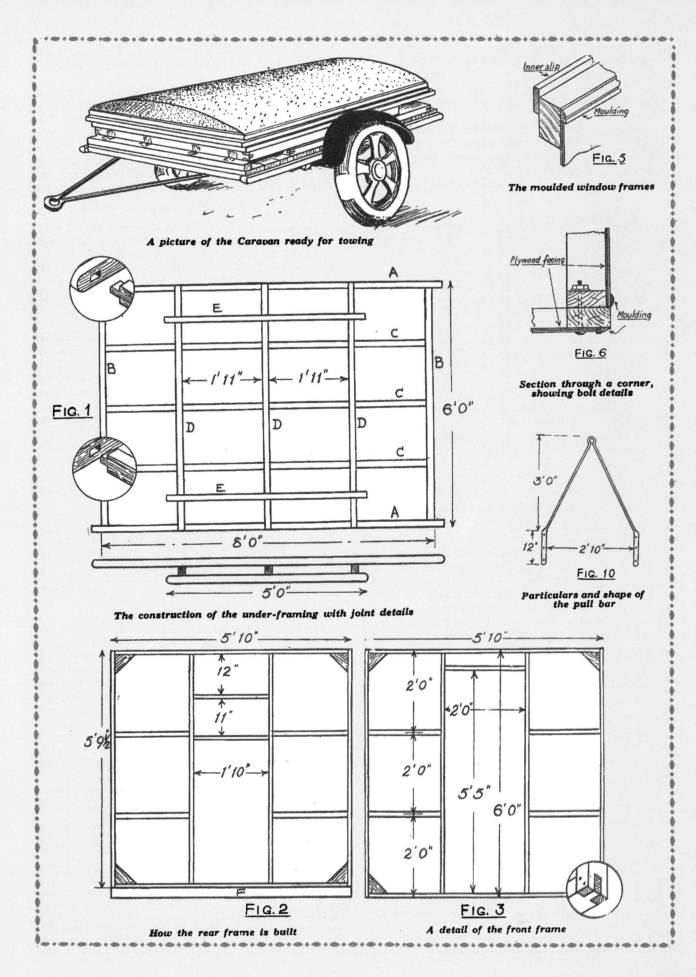

A picture of the Caravan ready for towing

FIG. 1

1'11"   1'11"

6'0"

8'0"

5'0"

The construction of the under-framing with joint details

Inner slip

Moulding

FIG. 5

The moulded window frames

Plywood facing

Moulding

FIG. 6

Section through a corner, showing bolt details

3'0"

12"

2'10"

FIG. 10

Particulars and shape of the pull bar

5'10"

12"

11"

1'10"

5'9½"

FIG. 2

How the rear frame is built

5'10"

2'0"

2'0"

2'0"

2'0"

5'5"

6'0"

FIG. 3

A detail of the front frame

The remaining horizontals cut from 1½in. sq. wood, can be simply nailed across.

Now cover the frame, except the door opening, with plywood panels and nail the half-round moulding down each side and down against the edge of the door opening.

Similar moulding should also be nailed horizontally to cover the joints where the panels meet. Use 1in. wire nails to fix the panels, and glue and panel pins to fix the moulding.

For ventilation, in the narrow panel above the door cut six slots like those cut in Fig. 7. These slots are 3ins. by 1in. and are spaced 1in. apart. The front can now be turned upside down and two pairs of 2in. iron back-flap hinges let into the bottom bar, knuckles of the hinges inwards.

Lift the front into position and screw the hinges to the floor so that the front can be folded over. Fix so that the plywood covering comes level with end B, and is exactly 1in. short of each side.

The Back

The back, Fig. 2, is constructed the same way, and covered with plywood finished off with half-round moulding down each side as before. The window space, 11ins. high, is left open. It will be seen that the height of this frame is 2½ins. less than that of the front, as it is hinged to bar F instead of to the floor.

Bar F is firmly screwed or bolted to the floor first, the back being afterwards hinged to it so as to fold over inwaid and rest upon the front. The panel, above the window is provided with ventilating slots like the front.

The sides, Fig. 4, are framed up from 2ins. by 1in. wood, only the wood is laid broad face outwards so that the thickness of the frame is only 1in.

FIG. 4

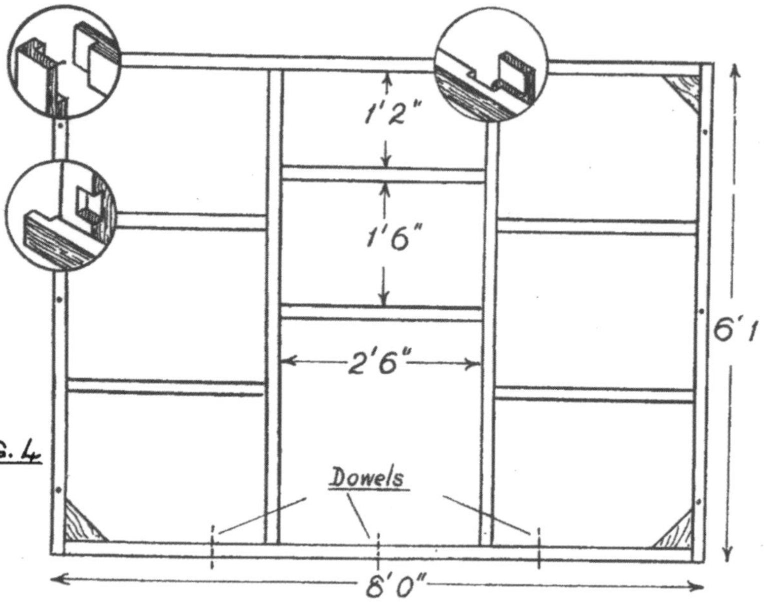

The side frame with details of joints used

The Side Frames

The height is given as 6ft. 1in., the extra being the nominal thickness of the flooring, but as this flooring will probably only be ⅞in. actual, the loss of ⅛in. due to planing, should be taken off the height. Join at the corners with closed half-lap joints as shown, and stiengthen with angle blocks. The uprights are halved into the top and bottom bars and the horizontals notched across. These joints are shown in the insets.

A ⅜in. by ¾in. moulding is now nailed against the edge of the window opening, and down tbe sides, and on the inside of the window opening a 1½in. by ⅜in. planed slip is also nailed round. This is to exclude draughts when the windows are closed.

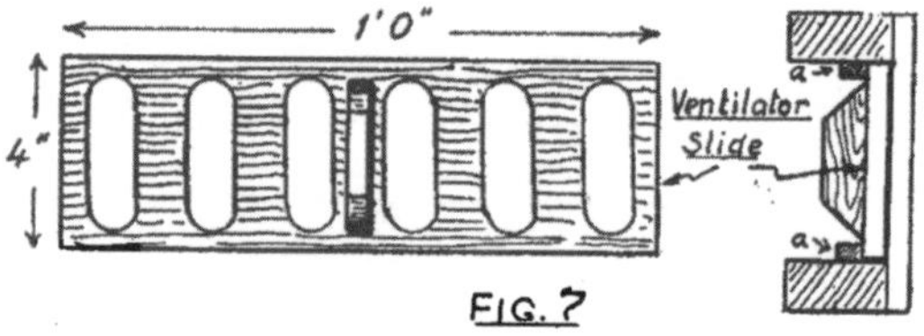

FIG. 7

The shutter ventilator

The detail, Fig. 5, shows this and also the moulding and how the plywood butts against it.

Now raise the frame in position and with a ¼in. bit bore dowel holes at the points indicated in Fig. 4. Bore right through the bottom bar and about ½in. into the sides A. Remove frame and glue in the holes 2½in. lengths of ¼in. dowel rod

(To be continued)

CUTTING LIST

Description.	No.	Long.	Wide.	Thick.
Floor Frame—				
Sides A	*2*	*8ft. 6ins.*	*2ins.*	*2½ins.*
Ends B	*2*	*6ft.*	*2ins.*	*2½ins.*
Joists C	*3*	*8ft.*	*2ins.*	*2½ins.*
Rails D	*3*	*6ft.*	*2ins.*	*2½ins.*
Rails E	*2*	*5ft.*	*2ins.*	*2½ins.*
Front and Rear Frames—				
Uprights	*8*	*6ft.*	*2ins.*	*1in.*
Horizontals	*4*	*6ft.*	*2ins.*	*1in.*
Horizontals	*3*	*2ft.*	*2ins.*	*1in.*
Horizontals	*8*	*2ft.*	*1½ins.*	*1½ins.*
Hinge bar F	*1*	*6ft.*	*2ins.*	*2½ins.*
Panels—				
Front	*6*	*2ft.*	*24ins.*	*¼in.*
Front	*1*	*2ft. 0½ins.*	*6ins.*	*¼in.*
Back	*6*	*2ft. 0½ins.*	*24ins.*	*¼in.*
Back	*1*	*2ft.*	*14ins.*	*¼in.*
Back	*1*	*3ft. 9ins.*	*24ins.*	*¼in.*
Side Frames—				
Uprights	*8*	*6ft. 1in.*	*2ins.*	*1in.*
Horizontals	*4*	*8ft.*	*2ins.*	*1in.*
Horizontals	*12*	*2ft. 9ins.*	*2ins.*	*1in.*
Side Panels	*12*	*2ft. 9ins.*	*24ins.*	*¼in.*
Side Panels	*1*	*2ft. 9ins.*	*18ins.*	*¼in.*
Side Panels	*1*	*3ft.*	*33ins.*	*¼in.*
Roof Sides	*2*	*8ft.*	*2ins.*	*1in.*
Roof Ends	*2*	*6ft. 1in.*	*2ins.*	*1in.*
Curved Supports	*4*	*6ft. 1in.*	*6ins.*	*¾in.*
Curved Supports	*1*	*6ft. 1in.*	*6ins.*	*1½in.*
Centre Bar	*1*	*8ft.*	*1½ins.*	*1in.*
Plywood Panels	*4*	*4ft.*	*39ins.*	*⅛in.*

Incidentals—Flooring, 1in. T. & G. boards, ⅞ square.
Planed strip 1½in. by ⅜in. for roof, etc., 50 ft.
⅜in. by ¾in. moulding, 60 ft.
½in. half-round moulding, 112 ft.
Note that allowance for trimming is made in mos cases but wood for windows, door and steps is not included.

HOW TO MAKE A KAYAK

HOW pleasant it would be to have a canoe and explore the many waterways with which this country is seamed ! You have doubtless envied those lucky fellows with shop-bought canoes, and thought that boat ownership was beyond your slender means. Well, why not make yourself—not a flimsy toy, but a genuine bit of boatbuilding, which will soon pay for itself by money saved in boat hire ? The one about to be described is based on a type used by Sea Scouts, and if well made, is thoroughly reliable. It is a single-seater, about 10ft. 6ins. long, and 2ft. 6ins. in the beam.

Red deal is a cheap and useful wood, and if well painted afterwards, will serve well. If one can afford it, we would recommend oak for the stem pieces, and ash for the side ribs. Brass screws MUST be used, as a canoe framework may literally fall to pieces owing to the rapid rusting of iron screws. Where nails are used, galvanized ones are indicated.

General Hints

The canoe (or kayak, as the Sea Scouts call it), is the same shape both ends, and is built in its preliminary stages upside-down on a "building timber", which is exactly 10ft. 10ins. long, and about 3ins. by 2ins. section. It must be dead straight, otherwise the canoe will be unsymmetrical. Screw it, each end, to a couple of strong

MATERIALS (to present stage)

1 part building timber (deal) 11ft. by 3ins. by 2ins.
4 part frames (2, 3, 4 and 5), (deal) total—25ft. by 4ins. by ⅜in.
2 part frames Nos. 1 and 6 (deal), total—4ft. 6ins. by 5ins. by ⅜ins.
3 part keel and side plates (deal), each 11ft. 6ins. by 3ins. by ⅜in.
2 part stem pieces (oak), cut two from 2ft. by 3ins. by 2ins.
2 inner coaming strips (ash), each 5ft. by 1in. by ⅜in.
10 side strips (ash) each, 10ft. 6ins. by ⅜in by ¼in.
2 coaming pieces, (oak) each 5ft. by 5ins. by ⅜in.
1 back rest (deal) 1ft. 6ins. by 5ins. by ⅜in.
5 floor slats, (ash) each 5ft. by 2ins by ⅜in.
2 rubbing strakes (oak), each 11ft. 6ins by 2ins. by ⅜in.
1 outer keel, (oak), built from 3 pieces each 11ft. 6ins. by 1½ins. by ⅜in.
2 stem capping pieces, Cut from 2ft. of 1in. beading. (1in. dowel planed down).
Odd strips of ⅜in. by ¼in. (ash), for decking.
Odd pieces for fillets, paddle, etc.
1 packet ½in. No. 6 brass screws.

(NOTE :- The whole can be made in red deal and spruce, but for a really good job, some better woods are indicated. Note also, that owing to the curved work, it is not convenient to give exact lengths. Neither is it desirable to cut the wood too fine, and all lengths are approximate. The building timber should, if possible, be borrowed, or hired.)

boxes, sawing trestles, etc., and bevel each end (bevel on top) to 60°. The distance between the bevels should now be 10ft. 6ins.

For the stem pieces, take a piece 3ins. by 2ins. and 2ft. long, and plane to the wedge-shape shown in the detail. Then saw in two. These pieces are fastened to the ends of the building timber in such a way that their ends (which are cut back to 80°) are 8ins. above the foundation. (see diagram).

The moulds, or "shapes" are now tackled. There are six of them, but as Nos. 1 and 6 ; 2 and 5; 3 and 4 are the same (except for certain slots to be mentioned), only three distinct templates are required.

Take a piece of paper, and fold it down the centre. Keeping the fold on the right, rule 1in. squares on one half, and in turn, copy each of the three shapes on three pieces of paper. If the outline is cut with scissors, a perfectly symmetrical shape is obtained when opened out.

The small end shapes are composed of two horizontal pieces of 14ins. by 5ins. by ⅜in. deal joined with cross battens. The shapes can be pasted flat on them, and cut round with a pad or bowsaw. The other " open shapes" are composed of two vertical 4in. by ⅜in. strips laid over two horizontal ones.

Full Size Shapes

It is an advantage to paste the paper shapes on cardboard, and use the cardboard template to arrange the strips to the best advantage. Be very careful where the screws are placed. Reference to the drawings will show that much of the wood is cut away afterwards, but the screws must still remain, and hold the frame together strongly. As the corners are cut away, a nail will serve here. After the outlines of frames 2, 3, 4, and 5 have been cut, mark a line 2ins. inside each, but do not cut this yet.

Notice that the 1in. by ⅜in. slots for the coaming strip occur in different positions on each frame. The reason for this is obvious, but don't make any mistake. The slot in the middle of No. 2 is 1in by ⅞in.

Divide the building timber up into seven equal 18in. divisions, and on either side of each, mark nail blocks, a shade under ⅜in. apart, so that the moulds can be set up in them, upside down.

Note that under frames 1 and 6, an extra piece ⅞in thick is first laid. It is of utmost importance that the frames are all in exact alignment, and square with the building timber and stem posts. An unbalanced craft is dangerous.

Now take the keel plate. This is of 3in. by ⅜in. section, and about 10ft. 6ins. long. It is screwed, (brass screws, don't forget!) to the tops of the frames (or rather the tops as they appear upside down), using two screws to each shape.

The Keel

Take great care not to disturb the moulds. Taper off the keel plate at the ends. The side plates, which are the same size as the keel plates, are also screwed on. If they are allowed to assume a natural curve, it will be found that they come half-way up the stem between the building timber and the keel plate. Screw them there.

Between the keel and side plates, five side strips are spaced each side. These are ⅜in. by ¼in. stuff, without any knots worth speaking of. Where they meet the stems, they can, with advantage, be bevelled so as to make them fit snugly. As with the side plates, it is as well to make them rather too long, and then trim off afterwards.

Interior Work

At this stage the canoe can be removed from the stocks, by unscrewing the stems from the building timber. The interiors of the four middle shapes are cut away with a padsaw. This could not have

been done before as it would have seriously weakened the whole structure.

Take the coaming strips, which are each about 5ft. long, and 1in. by ⅜in section. They terminate at Frame 5, and meet in the middle of Frame 2, where they must be mitred. Cut away the tops of Frames 3 and 4, inside the coaming strips, and screw the strip to the frame edges.

Fixing the Coaming

Inside the coaming strip, the coaming proper is fixed, but it is only screwed temporarily, as it has to be removed whilst the boat is being canvased, and then refixed permanently. It is of two pieces, 5ins. wide, but tapering to 3ins., so that it flares towards the prow. It is about 5ft. long and ⅜in. thick, and projects 2ins. beyond Frame 5, so that a notch must be cut to enable it to slip over Frame 5.

It may be tricky to make a neat joint at the point. The best way is to chisel the bevel as accurately as possible, and then, clamping the sides together, run a fine tenon saw down the joint.

A triangular block is screwed inside the point, and the lot screwed together. A copper or brass cap outside, is a good idea.

The Backrest

At the other end of the cockpit, a backrest with a curved top is screwed against the top of Frame 5. The projecting ends of the coaming are rounded off for neatness, as shown in the drawings, and triangular fillets fitted where deemed necessary. Four or five floorboards of 2ins. by ⅜in. deal, 5ft. long are fitted, but it is as well to defer screwing them down until the other framework has been painted.

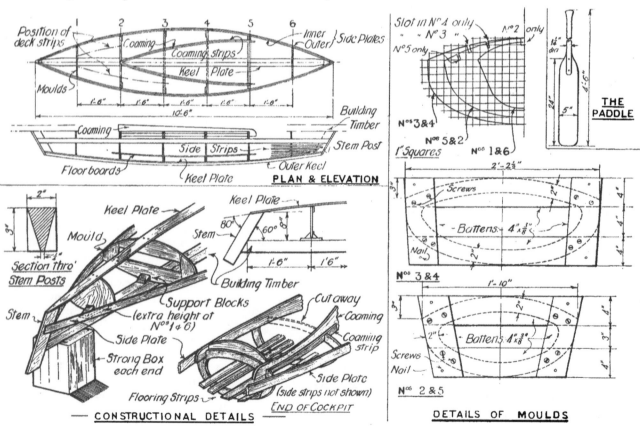

— CONSTRUCTIONAL DETAILS — DETAILS OF MOULDS

The stem capping pieces, the side rubbing strakes, and the keel proper, can be made now and held in readiness until the canoe has been canvased. The stem capping pieces are lengths of 1in. wide beading, formed by planing down 1in. dowel.

The side rubbing strakes are precisely the same as the side plates, to which they are afterwards screwed, through the canvas.

The keel proper is 1½ins. by 1in. section, but as it has to be bent, it is as well to form it of three pieces of 1½in. by ⅜in. stuff, all well painted *inside*, before being screwed to the keel plate. Where the keel and stem caps, and the side strakes and stem caps join, they should be neatly bevelled.

The front stem (prow) is left projecting 3ins. and rounded off at the top. The other one is sawn off flush with the deck. A few strips of ¾in. by ¼in. stuff are fitted more or less concentric with the coaming strips, to support the canvas deck. Cut notches for them.

Go all over the framework with coarse, and then finer glasspaper, to remove all sharp corners. Bad joints, if any, should be now stopped with putty. Then give two good coats of paint, or better still, a wood preservative. Tar is sometimes used.

To Cover the Canoe

The work just described will keep you busy, and another article will tell you how to cover the canoe and make the paddle. If you have any difficulty don't forget that we shall be pleased to help you if you will write to the Editor, enclosing a stamped addressed envelope.

MODERN means of keeping fit would send some of our ancestors unfit if they saw how it was done. The modern girl, dress and suitable shoes (see illustration). The great points are freedom of action and elasticity, and suitable clothing.

GOOD HEALTH BRINGS THE SMILE. BY MEANS OF PHYSICAL CULTURE THESE CITY GIRLS KEEP FIT.

Skipping.

This is a great asset, especially for girls, for both arms and legs are brought into action, and including as it does jumping, it is one of the best forms of training. This is well-known, especially by cricketers and footballers.

You would be surprised if I had to tell you the name of a famous International cricketer who every morning goes through a course of skipping all the year round ; it keeps him very fit. You know his name if you are anything of a cricket enthusiast.

Physical culture does not mean that your exercises are of the non-stop kind.

without becoming masculine, can adopt exercises which make her a more healthy, human being.

Relaxation is very good and singing improves your breathing powers. The full development

The stronger sex have many games they can play which help to keep one in health. To-day we rely too much on transport ; walking is becoming almost a thing of the past, and if we are not careful the degeneration of our race is bound to follow.

It would have shocked our forefathers to see girls jumping and leaping about and doing pyramid stunts, and, shall I add, playing tennis and cricket. Now, the athletic girl has come to stay and rightly, too, she has her place.

For physical culture you require very light

CHARMING DISPLAY BY GYM. GIRLS, SHOWING ONE OF THE METHODS OF PHYSICAL CULTURE.

of the body does not mean that you must be always jumping or doing some form of pyramids. I have in mind a pianist who, during his spare time, does fretwork; also Clough, the Bradford Second Division football goalie, for relaxation finds fretwork a keen fascination. All forms of handwork help in physical culture and dexterity, for what is development after all but the building up of the body along with the brain.

Lopsidedness.

This with some is a disease. You meet such individuals everywhere—persons who think of nothing but cycling; persons who go mad on swimming; and those poor mortals who never see anything outside the reading of a novel. To use their hands would be the last thing in the world, whilst to use tools might soil them.

The lopsided individual who cannot join in tennis, cricket, physical culture, football and swimming is to be pitied, whilst those who cannot use a hammer without knocking their fingers are even in a worse plight. Physical culture helps the handy man or woman. It fits them to take their part in the world's great struggle for existence—for the fittest survive!

O.W.J.

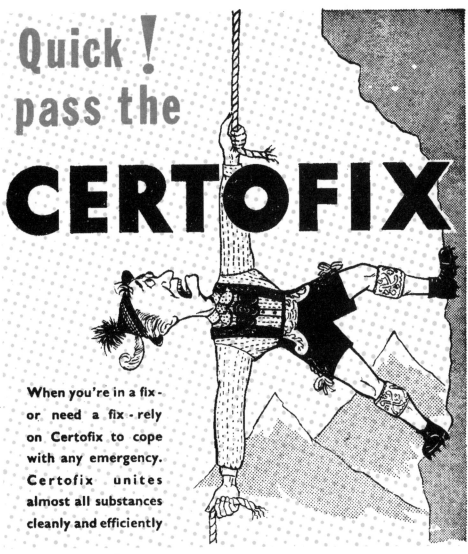

A FOLDING TRAILER CARAVAN

The concluding portion of a straightforward article of practical interest. The first part was in April 4th. issue.

IN the earlier article we completed the construction of the framework, and gave illustrations of the various parts. The frame had been put in place, and holes bored for the dowels.

The projecting ends of these dowels act as guides when frame is in position.

Now, starting from the top, fix the panels and finish off the lower edges of the bottom panels with a length of moulding. This will break up the sides into panels as shown in the general view of the caravan.

Raise the sides in position and where shown by small circles drill ¼in. holes right through, also through the side framing of the front and back. Bolt together with ¼in. bolts. Detail, Fig. 6, shows how the sides are thus bolted and should make this clear. Now for the roof.

length of fillet, planed up from a strip of ¾in. sq. wood, is fitted along near the edges between the supports to nail the bottom edges of the roof covering to (see detail, Fig. 9). Now raise the roof in position and bore holes through the framing, the holes going right through the top bars of the side, front and back. Three holes each side and two each back and front will be enough.

The fixing bolts should be inserted from below. A planed strip of wood, ¾in. by 1½ins. is now nailed round the edges to exclude possible draughts. Nail these strips to the roof only, not to the sides or you will not be able to lift the roof off as required.

The thin plywood panels for the roof can now be nailed over. The grain of the plywood should run lengthwise, and the cheaper quality should be used as it bends easier.

Windows

No details of the window frames or door is given—it is scarcely necessary. The window frames, cut from 2in. by 1in. wood, are just mortised and tenoned together in the usual way and hung with 2in. iron butt hinges.

The glass is fitted in with beading. No frame is needed for the rear window, the glass being

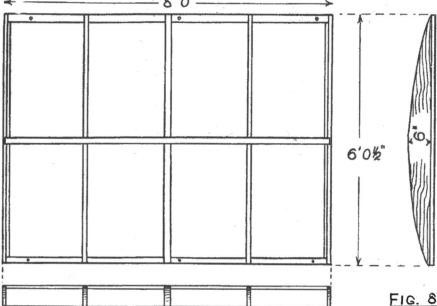

Plan and details of roof frame

Plan, side, and end views of the roof, without top covering are given in Fig. 8. Make up the frame of 2ins. by 1in. wood, halved at the corners, and cut to rather full dimensions, in fact if 1/16in. in excess of both width and length all the better.

Roof Supports

Four of the curved roof supports are cut from ¾in. board, and glued and nailed across. The middle support should be cut from 1¼in. material. The bottom edges of the three intermediate supports are best cut curved to allow a little more headroom.

The centre bar is notched into the supports. A

beaded in the opening.

The door can be made up in the usual manner with 3in. stiles and rails

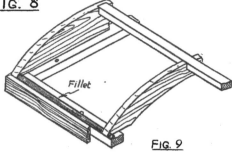

The construction of the roof

and a 2in. centre bar. Wood 1¼ins. thick should be used. Glass is beaded in the upper panel openings, and a plywood panel in the lower. Hang with 3in. iron butt hinges and fit a suitable lock and handles.

Round the door opening at the back of the door, nail round a planed slip of wood as a jamb.

To regulate the ventilation, cut two plywood panels as in Fig. 7, and saw out the slots as before. Glue in the centre a wood slip as a finger grip. Now arrange these panels on to inside so as to slide sideways, alternately closing and opening the slots in the outer panels. The illustrations will make this quite clear.

The Pull Bar

The pull bar, Fig. 10, is bent to shape from a length of ¾in. iron rod and bolted to the under framing. Any blacksmith will do this job for you.

The short pair of steps are simply made and hinged to fold under the caravan when not required. Support struts of 2in. dia. wooden rod are hung either end to keep the floor level when the caravan is at rest.

Give the completed caravan a coat of priming colour as a start. When this is dry, coat the ply-wood roof with thick paint, and lay calico thereon pressing it well down to the surface, and rubbing out all creases.

When dry, give the calico two coats of lead colour paint.

The remainder of the caravan can be painted any colour desired. Green is a good choice and looks well, especially if the moulding is painted black or dark green to show up the panels. The interior can be painted white or varnished, it is just a matter of personal choice.

Some form of braking must be used. This will have to be determined largely by the pattern of brakes already fitted to the wheels.

Another Type Coming

In case of difficulty, the advice of a friendly motor mechanic should be sought. It scarcely comes within the scope of this article, but we will make some suggestions to overcome any difficulties when dealing with a fixed form of caravan in which will be given as a future article.

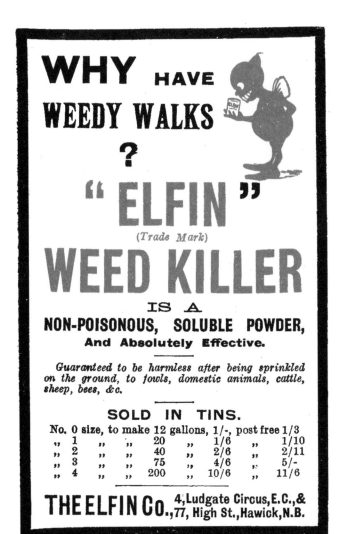

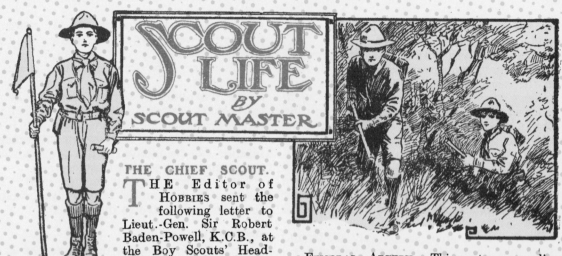

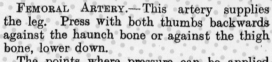

THE CHIEF SCOUT.

THE Editor of HOBBIES sent the following letter to Lieut.-Gen. Sir Robert Baden-Powell, K.C.B., at the Boy Scouts' Headquarters, on the occasion of his birthday.

"Dear Sir,—On behalf of the readers of HOBBIES, many thousands of whom are Boy Scouts, may I be permitted to offer you on your birthday heartiest congratulations upon the success of the great movement you have inaugurated, and also to wish you ' many happy returns of the day.'—Faithfully yours, "EDMONDS SEARS."

The Chief Scout has replied cordially thanking HOBBIES and its readers for their good wishes.

FIRST-AID REMINDERS.

Arresting Bleeding or Hæmorrhage.

IT is necessary, when arresting hæmorrhage, to know whether it is an artery, a vein, or a capilliary that has been cut, so that you may know whether it is trivial or serious.

When an artery is cut, the blood is scarlet in colour, and spurts out in jets from the end of the cut nearest to the heart.

When a vein is cut the blood is dark-red in colour, comes out in a sluggish stream, when the wound is big, and comes oozing out when it is a small cut.

When a capillary is cut, the blood is bright red in colour and comes in a brisk, smart, free stream.

Where to Stop the Bleeding.

The following are the three main points where the largest blood vessels, after leaving the trunk, may be compressed against bone.

SUBCLAVIAN ARTERY.—Through this artery the blood passes to the arm. To compress it, use your thumb or padded door key and press on the first rib and behind the collar bone.

CAROTID ARTERY.—This artery supplies the interior of the skull, face, neck, and head. Press inwards at a point 1½in. from the collar bone (inner end) and against the neck-vertebra with one thumb. The large jugular vein runs alongside this vein. Do not press on the windpipe.

FEMORAL ARTERY.—This artery supplies the leg. Press with both thumbs backwards against the haunch bone or against the thigh bone, lower down.

The points where pressure can be applied are shown by little crosses. The other points where pressure can be applied are as follows :—

OCCIPITAL ARTERY.—Compress at a point two or three finger's breadth from the centre of the back of the ear.

TEMPORAL ARTERY.—Apply pressure at a point one finger's breadth in front of opening of ear.

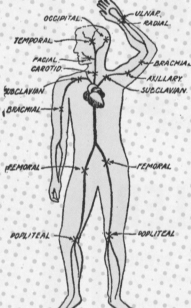

FACIAL ARTERY.—Compress where the artery crosses the lower jaw, about two finger-breadths in front of angle of jaw.

ULNAR AND RADIAL.—(*Inner and Outer Sides*). Compress one inch above the wrist on each side.

FEMORAL, POPLITEAL AND BRACHIAL ARTERIES.—Put a firm pad in the joint, bend the arm and bandage in this position. The joint must only be kept in this position for a *short time* only, as the pain and discomfort can't be borne for long.

AXILLARY ARTERY. — In addition to putting pressure at the subclavian artery, a firm pad can be put in the arm pit and then bind the arm to the side.

HINTS ON PITCHING AND STRIKING A BELL TENT.

THE first point in pitching a tent is to fix the centre or point on which the tent is to rest. When there is more than one tent being pitched the points will be marked off.

Having got the centre, the proper front should be ascertained, and the point for the four guy rope pegs must be fixed before anything else is done.

The manner in which the points are fixed will be easily understood by referring to the diagram shown. A is the centre and X is the front or door of the tent. From A lay the pole in the direction A B, which should be half a right angle (or 45 degrees) from the direct front. Drive a peg in at point B, then place the pole in the direction A C, which should also be 45 degrees from the front. Drive in a peg at C, and continue the line to D, and drive in a peg at point D. Now continue the line C A to D and put in a peg at D. The points, C B D E should form a complete square. Before proceeding further, see that the pegs do form a complete square, as the success or failure of your pitching depends on that.

Unfold the tent now and pass the round end of the pole into the cap, or top of the tent, and place the other end of the poles on point A. If five boys are at work, four will take a guy rope each, which are marked red, or should they not be, take the first, sixth, and 11th rope, counting from the door, round each side.

Now raise the tent and place the four guy ropes on the four pegs, C B D E, and tighten the ropes so that the pole is perfectly upright.

To drive in the other pegs is quite a simple matter, taking care that each rope runs down in a perfect line with the seam of the tent. Do not pull the ropes too tight until you get the screen of skirting pegged down.

When striking the tent, one scout will get inside the tent, and after all the pegs, with the exception of the guy rope pegs have been drawn, he will lower the pole. The pegs should be put in the peg-bag, together with the mallet, and the pieces of pole should be tied together. The ropes are now wound up and secured, and the tent is folded and rolled tightly from head to foot and put in the tent bag along with the peg bag.

If your tent has been hired, see that you do not strike the tent when it is wet, or should you require to do so, advise the firm of its condition, so that they may open it out and dry it. Also put the pegs in the bag and not down the side of the tent, a practice which makes the tent very dirty for the next hirer.

THE TROOP MASCOT.

You all know what a mascot is, it is something that brings you luck. Well, wouldn't it be nice if your troop had a mascot, a real live luck bringer.

Some troops I know of have adopted a little cripple as their mascot, others have a boy who is deaf and dumb or otherwise afflicted.

The little mascot is looked upon by the troop as a sacred trust and the scouts all vie with each other in making their little luck-bringer happy.

It is not possible for your cripple scout to take part in the more boisterous outdoor games, but his life can be made bright by following the scouts at their indoor instruction and games.

If your little mascot is deaf and dumb teach him how to signal so that he may be able to follow your messages when outdoor. Signalling will also act as a means of intercourse between himself and the scouts who do not know the deaf and dumb alphabet.

The East Park Home for incurables (Glasgow), have had a patrol of cripple scouts for some time now, and there is a troop of 50 cripple scouts at Carshalton in Surrey, with Doctor Griffen as their Scoutmaster.

Your mascot can be enrolled as a scout and try for any badge that is within his power.

A CAMP FILTER.

As explained in our issue of February 11th, it is necessary to have a good wholesome supply of water, and in some cases your supply of water may be all that is required from a wholesome point of view, but it gets muddy at times and requires filtering. If your camp is to last for a week or so, it is best to rig up a camp filter, as shown in our sketch. To do so you get two small barrels and connect them with a piece of piping.

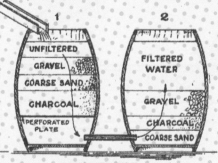

CAMP FILTER

Into barrel number one you put a piece of sheet iron, through which a lot of small holes have been punched. On the top of this perforated plate you put a layer of charcoal, then a layer of coarse sand, and on the top of that a layer of gravel.

We now come to barrel number two; into this barrel put a layer of coarse sand, a layer of charcoal, then a layer of gravel in the proportions shown.

Your filter is now ready, and by studying the arrows you will see the course that the water takes from the time it enters barrel number one until it reaches the top of barrel number two. The process that the water goes through makes it clear and takes away many objectionable properties from it.

To make the charcoal, dig a pit and fill it with wood and light up; when full of embers, put earth on the top. After 24 hours remove earth, and the pit will be found full of charcoal.

MAKING A PAIR OF SKIS

WHITE ash, birch and spruce are good woods to use for the making of skis, but pine or cypress may also be used. Use only straight grained pieces that may be easily shaped up and bent.

Skis are made from 4ft. 6ins. long to 9ft. long, depending upon the weight of the bearer. A boy weighing 100 lbs. would require skis about 5ft. in length and a man weighing 150 lbs. or over would have skis 8 to 9ft. long. The width of the skis would be a trifle wider than the sole of the shoes which are to be used with the skis.

Having chosen the wood from which the skis are to be made, plane the two pieces to the required width

Plane the wood down to those lines. Draw lines from F to B on each of the edges and plane the faces of the outer ends to these lines.

The skis are now the required thicknesses of ¾in. just under the foot, ½in. thick at the rear end and towards the front it is reduced to ½in. thick where it begins to curve, while the thickness along the curve is from ½in. to ¾in. thick at the front end (Fig. 2).

Next check out the notches shown at Fig. 4. The length of these are made to fit the breadth of the straps for fixing to the foot. Usually the depth of notch would be about 3/16 of an inch, but the better plan is to buy the straps and the piece of leather for foot grips and then to make the notches to fit the weight of the leather.

Bending the Wood

To bend the skis at the front some kind of frame is needed so that when the wood has been bent to the shape it can be held securely in that position until it has dried and set. The ski bender shown at Fig. 7, Fig. 8 and Fig. 9 is quite a good idea and is made up of two pieces of wood 34ins. long and framed apart with two rails 9ins. long.

These four pieces are nailed strongly together and then have the four shaped ribs shown by dotted lines at Fig. 8 and spaced as given at Fig. 9. These ribs are securely nailed to the cross rails. One might perfect the ski bender

Although you may think the winter is over, remember we had frost in May last year. Have them ready for any time.

and thickness. Draw the centre line (A, Fig. 2). Then lay out the thickness of the end at N, ½in. from the bottom and square across.

Draw the lines E to N on the edges of the wood and plane down to those lines. Lay out the line D 6ins. towards the front from the centre line A. Lay out the line B 12ins. from the front end on each of the pieces and square the lines down on each edge. Mark out a point ½in. from the bottom at B and draw the lines on the edges from these points to D.

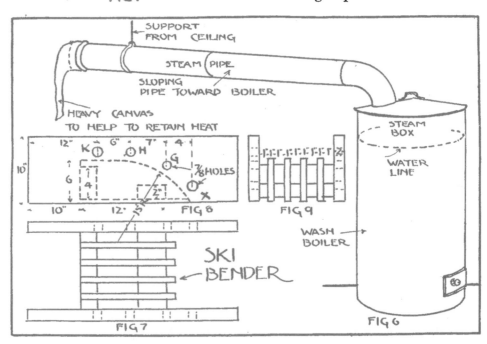

by covering the ribs with narrow strips of thin wood.

The sides of the bender is then bored with four holes in each, spaced as shown at Fig. 8. The holes should be just sufficient to allow a ½in. diameter piece of iron gas pipe to pass through easily, and the distance between the underside of each hole and the shaped ribs should be equal to thickness of the ski to be bent.

To bend the front end of the ski, steam must be resorted to, and Fig. 6 shows a home-made steam box which may be used.

The heating medium is the wash boiler with a piece of a stove pipe fitted into the lid, Fig. 6. The piece of wood for the skis having been planed and shaped at the end as given at Fig. 3, are now placed in the steam pipes and the outer end of the pipe sealed up with heavy canvas to retain the heat.

The time that the timber should be steamed depends somewhat on the nature of the wood and the intensity of the currents of steam in the pipe. One hour would certainly not be too long and it would be better to have the process of steaming well done rather than insufficient steaming with possibly a bad bend.

In bending the skis, when the two pieces of wood are taken out of the steaming box, the two skis are placed on the bender with their points at X, Fig. 8. Then the first piece of gas pipe is struck through above the skis to hold them in place.

The skis are bent backwards and the next piece of pipe introduced at G and finally the ones at H and K are put into place holding the ski in position on the forms. After allowing the skis to remain in the bender for several days, they are removed and finally touched up with the plane and sand-papered.

The skis are then given two coats of spirit varnish. During the time the varnish is hardening, prepare the leather for fixing. For the front toe piece, shape a piece of wood the size and shape of the front of an average shoe.

Take the strip of leather and soak it well in water, lay it over the wood mould, then hammer and rub it well on to the shape and tack it down at both ends.

When the leather is dry take out the tacks, then trim the ends to fit into the notches in the ski. In fixing, pierce the ends for a screw nail and complete the fixing with brass screw nails and copper washers. The ankle straps are fixed in much the same way.

Pedal along the cool rivers on a
NOVEL WATER CYCLE

WHEN it gets too hot to cycle along the roads, why not cycle on the cool waters of a river? Impossible? Not with the Water Cycle you see here!

It is not intended to be a serious contribution to the shipwright's art, and it is not intended for long river trips.

What it *is* intended for, however, is to give lots of fun and exercise, so that if you live by a river, or, being Scouts, have a lake at your campground, here is just what you want.

By looking at the illustration (Fig. 1), you can see at a glance what the thing looks like and how it works. (The propeller is hidden by one of the floats; it is seen in Fig. 3).

You can also see that the thing is partly made from an old bike. Part 12 (Fig. 3) is a gear box, so that when you twiddle the pedals, the propeller revolves, and off you go.

How to Steer

Steering is effected by means of a rudder controlled, by cables, through the handle bars.

Now, before we get down to brass tacks, there are one or two things which should be made clear. In the first place, you'll want an old bike.

The writer of this article is not too proud to say that he got his from a village "old-iron" dump, having noticed it on a ramble. Use your own ingenuity as to where you get your old bike (you need only the frame, not the wheels).

Secondly, you'll need a propeller and a gear box. This latter has two geared wheels arranged so that as one revolves vertically, the other revolves at right angles to it. The gears are enclosed in a case which has a flange with bolt-holes in it.

For these two items—the gears and the propeller, the writer paid several visits to boat-houses and such - like along the Thames and eventually found what he wanted. One might also try firms and garages which deal in second - hand motor parts. The propeller should be roughly 16ins. diam.

It should next be understood that as the size of the bike frame, the propeller, the gear box and other parts, vary, all dimensions shown on the drawings are approximate, and lastly it should be pointed out that though there is a fair amount of welding to be done, there are few towns, if any, without at least one welder who will do the job at a reasonable cost. Enquire at garages, etc.

Begin on the Frame

Now presume you are ready to start. Take the bike frame, and cut off the front fork. Cut off, also, the back fork which leads from the saddle bracket to the back hub, but leave on the horizontal fork which leads from the bottom bracket (by the pedals), to the back hub.

Prepare parts (4), which are two tubes 51ins. long and 1½ins. outside diam. They are connected by a similar tube (6) about 39ins. long, so that the three tubes form an H, welded together. The front stays (2) are ¾in. diam. and about 26ins. long.

Their upper ends are flattened rounded off at the ends, and drilled to take a small bolt which passes through the front down tube of the bike frame, and so holds the lot together at this point. The lower ends are welded to part (4), at a point 11½ins. from the end. (See Fig. 2).

Now the Back Stays

Somewhat similar stays are fitted at the back (3). There is already a drilled lug at the back of the seat bracket to which one can attach the upper ends of these stays.

Part (9) is a pipe bent into a square U shape, roughly 8ins. high and 10ins. wide. Its purpose

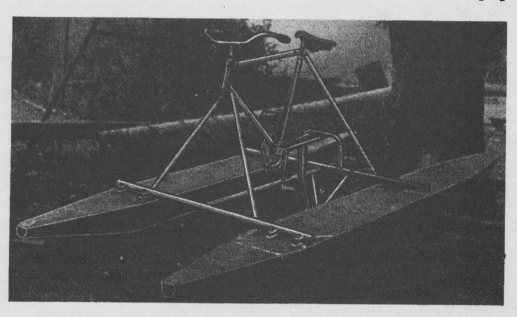

Fig. 1—A photograph of the complete cycle ready for "launching"

is to support the ends of the back fork of the cycle frame. These ends are welded to it.

The part we cannot describe in great detail is the gear box and its supports, since everything depends on what size box you get, and what sort of a flange it has.

In general, however, the shaft of the propeller should be 10ins. below part (4). Part 10 is a strip of iron, about 1½ins. by ⅜in. welded to the back fork, and so adjusted that the gear box can be bolted to it. Part 11 is a V-shaped piece of pipe about ½in. diam. welded to the rear (4), and its lower end supports one of the bearings of the propeller shaft.

The back sprocket from the bike is, of course, fitted on the gear box, and the chain suitably adjusted.

The Rudder

In line with part (4), is a right-angled piece of ½in. pipe welded on to take the rudder. This rudder is shown in a separate detail (Fig. 5). In the writer's cycle-boat, a ready-made rudder taken from an old wrecked boat was used, and this is the one shown in Fig. 3.

A new one can be made from a piece of oak about ½in. thick. The rudder is 8ins. square, but to this must be added the tenons by means of which it is joined to the post which is 1½ins. thick.

The tenons are waterproof glued, and as an extra precaution, small pegs may be driven in as shown. The blade is not ½in. thick throughout, but is tapered off at the edges, so the whole has a long oval section.

A square or round bar, about 9ins. long is passed through the top of the post, and this bar has holes drilled in each end so that rings can be attached to take the cables, or steering lines.

Steering Line Guides

Two large screw-eyes are inserted in the post, as shown, and another two are welded to the iron tube. A long thin bolt connects the two parts.

On the top tube of the frame, a ring is brazed on each side to guide the steering lines. A pulley, of the type shown, is also fitted to the back struts, about half way up. The lines are attached to the handlebars, and as these are turned, the rudder moves accordingly.

This completes the upper part, except for the clips welded to part (4) to take the floats. The detail shows everything, so no further description is necessary.

Making the Floats

The floats are made entirely of wood. Get two planks, about ½in. thick and just over a foot wide. If you cannot get them this width, glue up two narrower boards with *waterproof* glue. Taper off the two ends as shown in Fig. 4, and then make

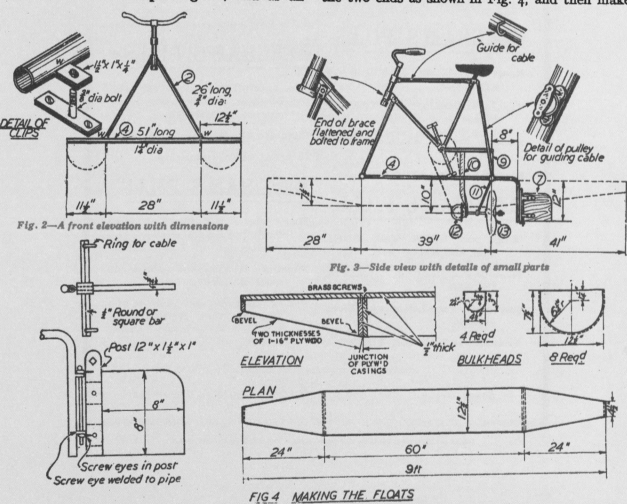

Fig. 2—A front elevation with dimensions

Fig. 3—Side view with details of small parts

Fig. 5—How the rudder is fitted

FIG 4   MAKING THE FLOATS

Fig. 4—Plan and constructional details of the float

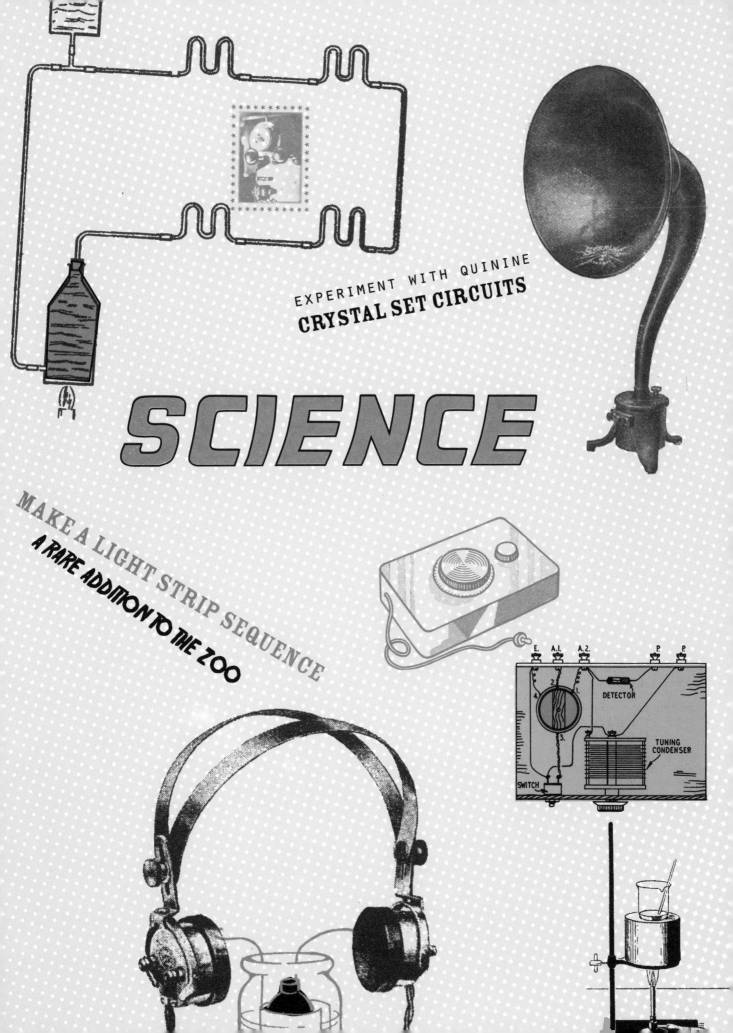

SCIENCE

EXPERIMENT WITH QUININE
CRYSTAL SET CIRCUITS

MAKE A LIGHT STRIP SEQUENCE

A RARE ADDITION TO THE ZOO

DETECTOR

TUNING
CONDENSER

SWITCH

E. A.1. A.2. P P

MAKING SPARK-INDUCTION COILS.

A SPARK induction coil is a favourite exercise with amateur electricians.

Its construction, principle, and outward appearance are almost identical to a shocking or medical coil, but it must, however, be made with much more care as to detail. All these belong to the same family of induction coils, that is to say each have an iron core working inside coils of wire, through which an electric current passes, thus inducing magnetism in the iron core. They each have an apparatus for automatically breaking the continuity of the electric current, and then alternately magnetising and demagnetising the core.

Further, they each have a secondary coil of fine copper wire wound over a primary coil of thicker wire, and a secondary current of high tension is induced in the outer coil by the interrupted current of low tension in the primary coil.

The main feature in constructing a shocking coil is to make an apparatus to give electric shocks, whilst the principle of the medical coil is to graduate the force of the electric current to suit the individual receiving the current.

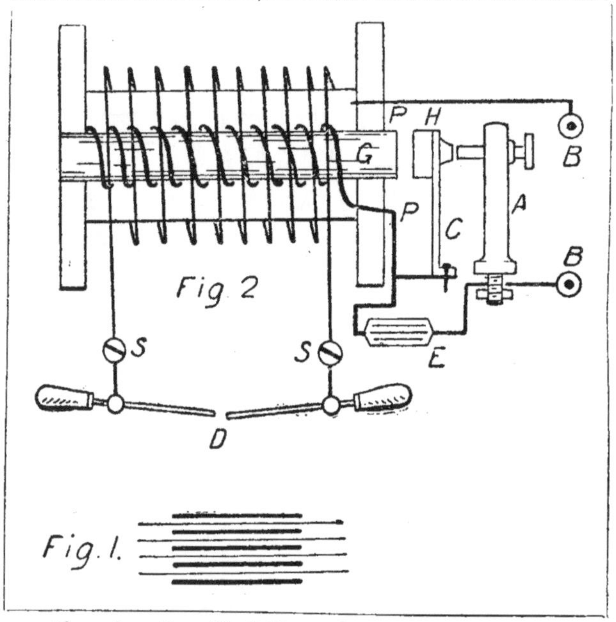

In making a spark coil, however, much greater attention is necessary in putting the various parts together, otherwise it will fail to give the length of spark for which it is designed.

The reason may be clearly seen if we think for a moment that the tension of the secondary current in a shocking or medical coil must be low, on account of human beings not being able to stand alternating currents of high tension. A low tension current can easily be confined to its own conducting wire by ordinary insulation, but the tension of the secondary current in a spark coil must be high, and the tension increases with each layer of the secondary wire, the length of which materially determines the length of spark obtained from its terminals. Consequently each layer and turn of secondary wire must be thoroughly insulated from its neighbour, in order to prevent leakage of current from one to the other, with a corresponding loss of power. The popular insulating compound used for silk covered wire is melted paraffin wax, and by increasing the thickness of this coating a very effective insulating is secured.

The best method of obtaining this is to melt the wax in a vessel—glue-pot fashion—in order to allow the liquid to be easy of application with a brush. Another method, and that which is perhaps the best of the lot, is to run the silk covered wire itself through the hot liquid.

The best insulator for the heads and body of the coil is ebonite, the next best being hard wood soaked in melted paraffin wax for the heads, and similarly soaked paper for the body. Each layer of the secondary coil should be separated from the under layer by a thick coating of the wax, or better still, a fold of thin paraffined paper. A layer of thin ebonite should also separate the primary coil from the core as well as the secondary from the primary coil, the object of the last precaution being to prevent the sparks from passing from one coil to the other and so break down the insulation. For coils giving three inch sparks and upwards, the whole coil should be immersed in melted paraffin wax for a few hours after it is wound.

Knots and bare places should be thoroughly examined and attended to before it is wound, the former being cut out, and the ends soldered together, whilst the latter should be coated with fine silk. As a guide in the construction of spark coils, the following dimensions will be found useful :—

Length and diameter of Bottom.	Length and diameter of Core.	Primary Coil.		Secondary Coil.		Condenser.		Cells of Battery.		Length of Spark.
Inches.	Inches.	No.	Layers.	No.	Weights.	Sheets.	Area.	No.	Size.	Inches.
3 × 1½	3¼ × ¼	23	2	40	2 oz.	25	2″ × 1″	1	Pint.	⅛
3½ × 2	3¾ × ⅜	22	2	40	4 oz.	40	2″ × 1½″	1	Pint.	¼
5½ × 2½	5¾ × ⅝	20	2	40	8 oz.	50	2½″ × 2″	2	Pint.	½
6½ × 2¾	6¾ × ¾	18	2	40	12 oz.	60	4½″ × 3½″	3	Quart.	¾
7½ × 3	7¾ × 1	17	2	38	1 lb.	100	7″ × 5″	6	Quart.	1
8½ × 3½	8¾ × 1⅛	16	2	38	2½ lb.	100	9″ × 7″	6	Quart.	2
10 × 4	10¼ × 1¼	16	2	36	4½ lb.	150	9″ × 7″	6	Quart.	3

It may be here mentioned amateurs will have much difficulty in constructing a three inch spark coil, as sooner or later the enormous tension between the two terminals (30,000 volts) of the secondary coil in one continuous length will break down the insulation and reduce the length of the spark. All coils to give sparks of over one inch in length should be built in sections to distribute the pressure, and reduce the chance of the insulation breaking down.

As the potential in the secondary coil is proportionate to the density of the current in the primary coil, and this is determined by the resistance of the primary wiring, as well as the voltage of the current from the battery, care must be taken to keep the before mentioned resistance low. No more current can go through the primary circuit than the contact breaker will pass, therefore the contact surfaces must be large in big coils—No. 14 gauge platinum answering very well—and they must fit each other squarely. If this is not secured when the coil is new, the surfaces will be burnt by sparks, and consequently, the resistance materially increased. The contact breaker works quietly, and if this is made of very soft iron there is enough time between each movement to magnetise and demagnetise the core.

The action will be reluctant, and the coil will retain an electric store, even after contact is broken, which will emanate as a spark at the contact surfaces. It is here that the use of a condenser underneath the coil becomes necessary to utilise this static store and minimise the sparking. This detail consists, as indicated, in Fig. 1, by sheets of tin foil between which sheets of paraffined paper is put. The relative sizes of each can be gauged by the figure, wherein the thick lines represent the tin foil and the thin the paper.

In making a condenser two sheets of the paper are first laid on a clean surface, then a sheet of the foil, followed by another sheet of paraffined paper. Another sheet of foil is now placed on this, so as to project over the end of the other for a distance of half an inch. Another sheet of paper is now put on top, followed by another sheet of tin foil projecting over at the opposite end for half an inch, as before, and the whole pile built up in this manner. Three or four sheets of paper are then put on top, and the pile pressed down for some time, until quite solid, and then bound tightly with string. The connections are made with copper wire to the projecting ends of the foil, and this is done by rolling the foil round the wire and soldering. Damp is an enemy to a condenser, and therefore, if any signs of this be suspected, the condenser should be put in a warm oven before the connections are made.

Normally, the condenser is placed in a wooden box under the coil, and its wires fitted up, as shown in Fig. 2, in the direction to the foot of the break pillar A, and on to battery terminal B, whilst at the other side the wire is brought to the foot of the break spring C. The other letters of this Figure are as follows: D represents the path of the electric discharges, E being the condenser, G the core, H the hammer of the contact breaker, whilst P and S represent the ends of the primary and secondary coils. Of course the wiring in this figure is shown very loose, in order to give the amateur a better idea of the construction.

The ends of the secondary coil are brought out through the bobbin heads, one on one side and one on the other, and then connected to suitable terminals on the heads. The handles of the discharging rods should be made of ebonite, in order to protect the worker from receiving the electric discharges in the form of shocks. The last item is an important one, as a shock from a spark coil may be dangerous.

A RARE ADDITION TO THE ZOO.

THE Zoological Society has just received and placed on exhibition at the Gardens in Regent's Park, London, a fine young example of the Takin, which, next to the Okapi, is the rarest and least known of the ruminants. The Takin comes somewhere between Goats and Antelopes, and its nearest ally is probably the Serow. Takins are heavily built and powerful animals, an adult male standing three and a half feet high at the shoulder. They are thickly clad with long and coarse dark-coloured hair, which forms a thick fringe round the neck. The muzzle is hairy, the profile convex and sheep-like, and the tail short. The horns are powerful sharp weapons, in the adult nearly meeting across the forehead where they rise from the skull, as in the African Buffalo, then bending outwards and backwards to end in sharp points. Very little is known of their habits, as they are natives of the highlands of Tibet, and have been seen by very few white sportsmen, whilst no example has hitherto reached Europe alive.

The Society owes its present specimen to a Corresponding Member of the Society, Mr. John Claude White, C.I.E., late Political Officer of Bhutan and Tibet. Mr. White interested the Maharajah of Bhutan in the matter, but great difficulty was experienced owing to the inaccessible haunts of the animal. Several years ago a single animal was captured, after it had killed one hunter and wounded another. It was brought down to India, but died as the result of eating aconite. Its skull and skin were sent to the British Museum. The example which has now reached the Gardens belongs to the same race, and was captured by the Maharajah's men in N. W. Bhutan.

A WIRELESS TELEGRAPHIC INSTALLATION
ITS CONSTRUCTION & WORKING.

Hobbies Special

4. THE AERIAL.

THERE are so many different types of aerial that it is somewhat difficult for the amateur to know which is the most suitable for his purpose. There is the cone form of antennae used by Marconi, the rectangular form known as the Lodge-Muirhead, the four wire aerial used by

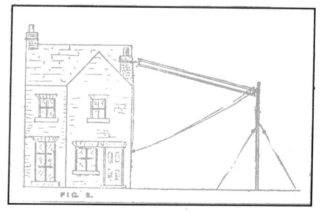

the Admiralty, and the single wire. The first-mentioned type is quite out of the question for a small station, but either of the others may be used and no doubt one of the latter two, or at least a modification of them will be most suitable.

The main point to consider is that it is essential that the aerial at the sending station and at the receiving station should be as far as possible alike; their efficiency depends on them being thoroughly well insulated, and in such a position that they can easily pick up the ether waves. It is not proposed to send further than a few hundred yards; in fact, the coil at our disposal will not be powerful enough to create ether waves to travel more than half a mile. This will be quite sufficient for ordinary purposes, especially when it is remembered that the same aerial used for sending such a short distance, may be employed in receiving messages from a station at least 25 miles away.

If it is desired to confine the experiments to different parts of a house or large building, there is no need to set up a wire aerial at all, but to use either a pair of Hertz oscillators or two stiff wires attached to the spark gap.

So much depends on the facilities that each experimenter has for erecting an aerial, that it is practically impossible to give exact length, but if the construction of the antennae is clearly shown it will not be a difficult matter to fix one up. It has already been stated that the Admiralty type of aerial is one of the most suitable for the amateur, and as will be seen at Fig. 1, it is composed of four wires. A suitable length for our purpose will be from 10 to 20 yds. but there is no reason why this length should not be exceeded; in fact, it is a great advantage in a receiving station to have a much longer aerial than this. The wire to be used in the aerial should be No. 12 or No. 14 S.W.G. aluminium, costing 2s. 3d. per lb. (there is, roughly, about 50yds. in each lb.).

One of the most general methods of fixing the aerial is to attach one end to a convenient chimney or tree, and bring the other end to a pole or flag staff. It is a good plan to have the aerial entirely on the roof, but for a simple installation it will be enough to use the first plan. We will suppose that it is possible to fix up an arrangement as shown at Fig. 2, the chimney being about 35ft. from the ground, and the garden post about 20ft. high. It should be possible in this case to get a length of at least 60ft. The other arrangement is shown at Fig. 3, and here the ends may either be attached to posts fixed to the chimneys, or to uprights securely fastened to the walls, and properly stayed, as shown at Fig. 4. Whichever method is followed it will be necessary to make the aerial in the same way, so it will be as well if this is described at this stage.

Making the Aerial.

First of all provide four lengths of oak, each 2ft. by 1¼in. by 1¼in., and in the middle of each piece make a 1¼in. by ¼in. groove, as indicated at Fig. 5. Bind two pieces together with stout cord, as shown at Fig. 6, and bore a ¼in. hole at each end as shown, thus completing the two frames. Next provide two 6in. lengths of 1in. diameter vulcanized fibre rod, and drill a ¼in. hole 1in. from each end, as shown at Fig. 7, and tie one end to the frame as indicated. Having decided on the length of the aerial, it will now be necessary to cut off four lengths of the wire and attach the ends to small porcelain insulators, and then tie these to the frames, in the manner indicated at Fig. 8, with strong cord. The result is the aerial shown at Fig. 1, and it is now ready to fix in the most suitable position, and to attach the

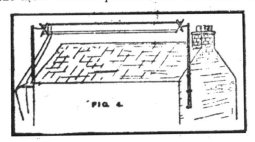

"leads" or connecting wires leading from the coil. These are two lengths of the same gauge wire twisted together for a few feet from the coil, and then separated out and connected to the four wires of the aerial, as shown at Fig. 2. It is advisable to have as long a lead as possible, and in the present case it should be as long as the aerial, if possible longer, and it is also most important, as in the case of the aerial itself, to have the leading in wires perfectly insulated, as well as to have good contact where they do touch.

Fixing the Aerial.

Three methods of supporting the aerial have been shown, using the house roof to get to a serviceable height, but, of course, there is no reason why convenient poles should not be used alone, or even trees, providing that no part of the aerial touches the branches. It will be seen that there is practically unlimited scope in the methods which may be utilized, and if only the antennæ is properly insulated it does not very much matter where it is, either outside or inside ; in fact, the writer has seen a very neat installation where the aerial was stretched across an attic ceiling, the wires being carried through a division wall and passed through glass tubing ; this particular aerial

was capable of receiving messages from a station 10 miles away. It is necessary that the aerial wires should be stretched, and so secured that they may be easily taken down, thus necessitating the use of pulley blocks at both ends. In attaching a pulley to a chimney it is not

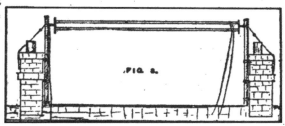

advisable to trust to an iron bracket, but to have an iron band encircling the brickwork, or to attach a post to the brickwork with stout holdfasts. Posts attached to the wall, as shown at Fig. 4, should be securely stayed with stout cord ; galvanized wire is often suggested, but much better insulation is effected by using cord. Poles situated some distance from the house should be well bedded in the ground, and the lower part either creosoted, charred or tarred, and in this case it is allowable to use galvanized wire properly insulated with porcelain insulators, for stays, as the aerial is some considerable distance away and not likely to touch it ; and besides, the wire will hold the pole so much better.

Ordinary pulley blocks, as indicated at Fig. 9, may be used to run the cord through, and where it is possible to obtain wooden blocks, similar to those used on sailing boats, they will be found much more suitable. We will now assume that the posts or other method of hoisting the aerial have been fixed, and will proceed to attach a length of cord to each of

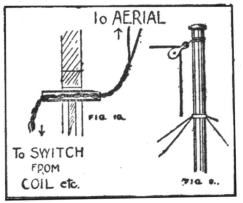

the vulcanite rods, the edges of the holes being rounded off to prevent chafing, and then the aerial may be hoisted in position with the wires fairly taut. Finally arrange matters so that the leading in wires are spread out so they neither touch each other or anything else ; this may be effected with suitable lengths of bamboo or

ILLUSTRATIONS.

Figs.
1. The Admiralty type of aerial.
2. A convenient method of fixing the aerial.
3. The best way of attaching the aerial to chimneys.
4. A suitable arrangement for an aerial on the roof.
5. One of the pieces for the frame.
6. The two pieces forming the frame bound together.
7. The vulcanite insulator attached to the frame.
8. The method of attaching the antennæ to the frame.
9. The method of fixing the pulley block to the top of the pole.
10. The position of the insulating tube to carry the leading in wires.

wood. To carry the end of the lead into the instrument room it will be necessary to utilize either a length of thick glass tubing or a stout piece of vulcanite tubing, as shown in section at Fig. 10, remembering that the whole efficiency of the aerial depends on the efficiency of the insulation.

The Earth.

Quite as important as the correct fitting of the antennæ is the fixing of the earth, and this is done most conveniently by soldering a length of stout copper wire to the nearest water or gaspipe, not only in one but two or three places. The wire may be fastened to a copper bands encircling the piping or soldered to any suitable part, the main point being to ensure that the current is properly conducted to the ground. In positions where it is impossible to make use of these ready-fixed earth connections, it may be possible to use iron railings, and failing that it will be necessary to bury a plate of iron, some old iron railings or wire-netting in the ground, and properly secure the earth wire to it. The important part about the earth connection is to have it as close to the instrument room as possible, and to use as thick wire as is practicable.

(To be continued.)

INTERNATIONAL MORSE CODE *(See page 235)*

A	· —	B	— · · ·	C	— · — ·
D	— · ·	E	·	F	· · — ·
G	— — ·	H	· · · ·	I	· ·
J	· — — —	K	— · —	L	· — · ·
M	— —	N	— ·	O	— — —
P	· — — ·	Q	— — · —	R	· — ·
S	· · ·	T	—	U	· · —
V	· · · —	W	· — —	X	— · · —
Y	— · — —	Z	— — · ·		
1	· — — — —	6	— · · · ·		
2	· · — — —	7	— — · · ·		
3	· · · — —	8	— — — · ·		
4	· · · · —	9	— — — — ·		
5	· · · · ·	0	— — — — —		

Learn it with
a pal and
practise together

Learn the code with this

Morse Practice Oscillator

Says F. G. Rayer

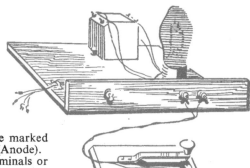

A KNOWLEDGE of the Morse code is useful in various boys' group activities or for signalling with friends. It may also be studied in order to pass the G.P.O. transmitting licence examination, or for interest only, in reading amateur, shipping, and other code signals. A buzzer is often used for Morse practice, but has the disadvantage that the note does not resemble that of radio signals. This can be overcome by using a valve oscillator, with headphones, and Fig. 1 shows a very simple circuit which is perfectly satisfactory.

Very few components are required. Any small switch is suitable for switching the Low Tension supply. The transformer is of the ordinary intervalve coupling type, and can have a ratio of anything from about 1:2 to 1:7. If a number of old transformers are to hand, each can be tried, as some provide a more satisfactory note than others.

sockets. Other holders may be marked 'P' (Plate) here, instead of 'A' (Anode).

Some transformers have terminals or tags in different positions from that shown. If so, they should be wired up to suit. The switch and key terminals are mounted on a strip of insulating material.

The beginner can check wiring to see that it is as follows:—One L.T. lead to valve filament, transformer secondary, and H.T. negative. Second L.T. lead to

Symbols for the International Morse Code are given on page 234

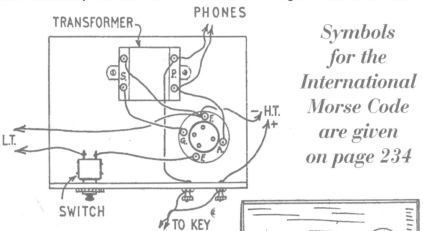

Fig. 1—Wiring plan

Almost any type of valve may be used. The wiring shown is for a triode with English 4-pin base, and these are obtainable for a few shillings from ex-service stores. If to hand, a pentode or screen-grid valve can be used, anode and screen-grid being wired together. The valve can be of detector, L.F., or Power type. It is also possible to use one of the small 'all-dry' type valves, if available.

Wiring Up

This is very simple, but one or two points must be watched. If a different type of valve is used, a suitable holder is necessary, correctly wired. If the valveholder does not have the sockets marked, the anode socket of the English 4-pin type can be identified because it stands farthest from the remaining three

Fig. 2—An easily made Morse key

switch. Second switch tag or terminal to remaining filament terminal. Grid valveholder terminal to transformer secondary. Valve anode to transformer primary. Second primary terminal to key circuit. Key circuit returned to H.T. positive.

Using the Oscillator

The 'all-dry' type of valve will have a 1·4 V or 2·8 V filament. For this, use a single dry cell (for 1·4 V) or two cells in series (for 2·8 V). The 4-pin type of valve may be operated from a 2 V accumulator, or a single dry cell may be used instead.

Only a small H.T. voltage is required —a 9 V grid bias battery will usually be sufficient, or two such batteries wired in series. The H.T. must be connected in the polarity shown, but the L.T. polarity is not important.

On switching on and shorting the two key terminals, a continuous oscillation should be heard in the phones. If not, the two leads going to the secondary of the transformer should be reversed.

Key

Though a proper Morse key is desirable for much work, the simple key shown in Fig. 2 will be satisfactory for practice. The baseboard is about 2½ins. by 4ins. When the knob is pressed down the circuit is completed.

The tone of the note heard in the phones can be modified, if desired. Changing the valve, or H.T. voltage, will change the note. So will wiring the phones in series with the transformer primary, instead of in parallel, as shown. Again, if the note is too high-pitched, it can be lowered by wiring a condenser in parallel with primary or secondary. Values from ·0005 to ·005 can be used—the larger the capacity, the lower the note. If necessary, the note can be increased in pitch by wiring a resistor of about 10,000 to 100,000 ohms between transformer secondary and valve grid.

After initial practice to learn the code letters, one person should send while the other writes down the message. A dash should be the length of three dots, and each letter should be clear and separate.

BUZZER, BELL and SWITCH

MAKE a wooden base about 3ins. by 7ins. and glue into holes made in the base small upright pieces of wood (A), (B) and (C) or fix them with brass screws from underneath as in Fig. 1. Fix an iron nail, with a large head, into the upright piece (B) and wrap about 10yds. of No. 22 D.C.C. wire carefully round this nail to make an electro-magnet. Fix two terminals to the base, and a strip of tin plate to the upright (A) with two small round-headed screws. Under one of these screws fix one end of the wire from the nail from which the insulation has been removed near the end. The other end of the wire from the nail is fixed to one of the terminals. A short length of insulated wire connects the other terminal and a long brass screw, in the piece of wood (C). Adjust until the pointed end just touches the tin plate strip when it is about an ⅛in. from the head of the nail.

tubing. If you wish, you can improve your buzzer and bell by using a U-shaped electro-magnet instead of the single iron-nail magnet. A method of doing this with a single U-shaped iron core, or better still, a bundle of U-shaped iron wires is also shown, using a larger piece of wood in place of the small upright (B) (Fig. 6). The core

~~~~~~~~~~~~~~~~~~~~~~~~~~~~
Contributed by T.A.T.
~~~~~~~~~~~~~~~~~~~~~~~~~~~~

should be wrapped with a little paper before winding on the insulated wire, and you must note carefully the method of winding the core. Why is the U-shaped core better than the single nail and why must it be wrapped in this way?

Notice what happens near the point of the brass screw. How is this avoided in an actual electric bell?

A Battery of Miniature Leclanché Cells

THIS battery consists of a number of small glass jars (Fig. 8) in each of which is placed a little ammonium chloride solution and pieces of zinc and carbon rods, with their surrounding black powder contained in muslin bags, taken from worn-out high-tension batteries. One such 120 volt battery will supply you with 80 such cells for this and other experiments. The zinc cases from these old cells can be removed by cutting them along the joints with an old knife, but do take care lest the knife slips, and do not break off the connecting wires from the pieces of zinc and the carbon rods. Each one of these cells will give an electro-motive force of about 1½ volts and you can connect up any number in series to

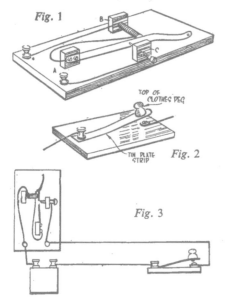

Fig. 1

Fig. 2

TOP OF CLOTHES PEG

TIN PLATE STRIP

Fig. 3

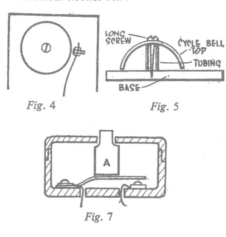

Fig. 4

Fig. 5

LONG SCREW

CYCLE BELL TOP

TUBING

BASE

Fig. 7

A Home-made Bell Push

IF you wish to improve on the simple switch you can make one which is more like a real bell push (Fig. 7). For this you require a small cylindrical wooden box. Drill two small holes in the base for the insulated wires to pass through, and a small circular hole in the lid. Shape a cylindrical piece of wood (A) and fix a short piece of tin plate strip to the inside of the bottom of the box with a screw and a washer as shown. Fix another screw and washer so that when the tin plate strip is pressed down by means of the piece of wood (A), it touches the head of this screw. Fasten the ends of the insulated wire under the washers and tighten the screws. Fix the lid of your model, push in position and it is now ready for use.

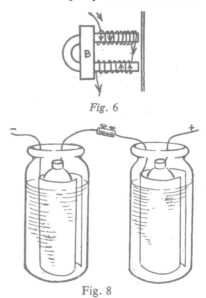

Fig. 6

Fig. 8

build up a battery strong enough to work your models.

PARAFFIN AIDS

ADD a drop of paraffin to the water when washing floors, paint-work and windows. This facilitates drying and cleaning, promotes a high polish and helps to keep down insects.

To remove rust from the rims of bicycle wheels, rub them with wire wool soaked in paraffin. The wool will not scratch, and the rust soon disappears leaving the rims bright and shiny.

To keep iron bedsteads and springs free from rust, paint them occasionally with paraffin. (R.L.C.)

Next make a simple switch as shown in Fig. 2 and then connect the terminals of the model electric buzzer to the switch and battery (Fig. 3). Note carefully how the buzzer works. Try the effect of adjusting the brass contact screw.

You may now convert your buzzer into an electric bell as shown in Figs. 4 and 5. A small hole is drilled in the end of the tin plate strip and a nut and bolt are fixed through to act as a clapper. Fix the bicycle bell top to the wooden base, using a long screw and a length of

Home Chemistry
Experiments With Quinine

WHEN the Spanish conquerors penetrated into South America they found a more valuable article than Inca gold. This was the bark of several species of a handsome tree which grew high up in the mountains of Peru. The Jesuits who accompanied the conquerors came to know that the bark would cure fevers. The bark first came into real prominence when a famous Spanish lady in Peru was cured of malaria by its use.

When chemists got to work on it, they found that the medically active principle contained in the bark was a white substance to which they gave the name quinine. It was found to be a base and consequently formed salts with acids. Some of its salts are now used instead of the bark.

Fig. 1

Quinine sulphate is the most convenient form of the drug for use in our experiments. It is a light white powder and sparingly soluble in water. Take up a little on the point of your penknife blade, drop it into a test tube half full of water, close the tube mouth with your thumb and shake. The powder does not all dissolve. Now add a few drops of dilute sulphuric acid and shake again. The powder goes completely into solution. Quinine acid sulphate has been formed and this is much more soluble than the normal quinine sulphate.

You will be astonished to see that something else has also happened. The solution has acquired a magnificent blue fluorescence. Fill up the test tube with water. The fluorescence is still visible. This fluorescence with sulphuric acid is a delicate test for quinine.

You might like to make a specimen of this interesting salt quinine acid sulphate. Stir 1 gram of quinine sulphate with 11 c.c. of cold water and drop by drop stir in dilute sulphuric acid until the powder dissolves completely. Pour the solution into a small evaporating dish and drive off the water on a water-bath until only a thin syrup remains.

If you have no water-bath, you can make one quickly and easily from a syrup tin. Wash out the tin and cut out a disc from the middle of the lid (Fig. 1). For small dishes use it with the lid, for larger dishes use it without.

Remove the dish from the water-bath and let it cool and stand awhile. The syrup solidifies to a moist white fibrous mass of quinine acid sulphate. Scrape this out and place it on a clean porous tile or brick to drain and dry. This salt of quinine, too, has found considerable use in medicine to reduce the temperature in fevers and as a tonic.

Another striking reaction of quinine is the thalleioquin colour reaction, and which is much used in the analytical detection of quinine. To try it out, pour some freshly made chlorine water into a test tube to the depth of about 1 in. Drop in some quinine sulphate whose

Fig. 2

volume is about that of a peppercorn. Now add one drop of clear household ammonia (ammonium hydroxide). A brilliant green colour will appear. This reaction is so delicate that it will detect one part of quinine in 20,000 parts of water when carefully applied.

You can make some chlorine water for this test by acting on bleaching powder ('chloride of lime') with dilute hydrochloric acid and leading the evolved chlorine gas into water until the latter has a distinct greenish-yellow colour. Use the apparatus shown in Fig. 2 and conduct the operation in the open air, for chlorine is poisonous if breathed in any quantity.

A modification of the thalleioquin test gives a useful confirmatory reaction for the presence of quinine. Mix chlorine water and quinine sulphate as before and then add one or two drops of potassium ferrocyanide solution so as to give the liquid a yellower colour. On adding one drop of household ammonia a fine ruby red colour makes its appearance.

Quinine belongs to a class of carbon compounds containing nitrogen, which are known as alkaloids. As such, quinine gives certain other reactions which are typical of alkaloids. Dissolve a pinch of quinine sulphate in half a test tube of water by adding dilute sulphuric acid drop by drop and shaking. Now add some Dragendorff's reagent. A lovely orange-red precipitate will appear. When you carry out this experiment you are seeing a typical reaction for alkaloids.

Another typical reaction is that with tannic acid. Shake a pinch of tannic acid with half a test tube of water until it has dissolved. Make a solution of quinine sulphate as in the last experiment and add some of the tannic acid solution. An off-white precipitate forms.

A curious compound of quinine sometimes known as Herapathite also serves for its detection. Herapathite is known chemically as quinine iodo-sulphate. To prepare a specimen, mix 1 gram of quinine sulphate with 10 c.c. of methylated spirit and add enough dilute sulphuric acid to give the liquid an acid reaction — which may be ascertained by testing a drop on blue litmus paper, when it will turn red. Stir in portions of a solution of iodine crystals in methylated spirit as long as a brown precipitate continues to form. The precipitate is Herapathite, but to see it in its characteristic form it must be recrystallised.

Heat up a water-bath, turn out the flame and warm the vessel containing the Herapathite in the water. If the Herapathite does not entirely dissolve when the liquid is boiling, add more meths. until complete solution is effected. Remove the vessel from the water-bath and let it cool and stand some time. Bronzy, scintillating spangles of Herapathite separate as the liquid cools.

Before the liquid cools place a drop on a glass slip. As the drop dries out, the Herapathite takes on a green metallic appearance — but only in reflected light. If you have a small student's microscope, look at the Herapathite with the light passing through it on the slip. The crystals now look red in the transmitted light. A strong hand magnifier will also show the red colour.

After standing some hours the Herapathite can be filtered off, washed with cold water and dried at room temperature for your specimen collection. (L.A.F.)

ALUMINIUM belongs to an important group of metals known in commerce as the " light metals." These metals are used extensively in the construction of aircraft, and aluminium and its alloys are the most important members of the group. The many interesting properties of this metal make it a most engrossing subject for the home chemist to study.

Aluminium does not occur naturally in the free state, but it is found abundantly in such minerals as clay, bauxite and feldspar. In fact, the earth's crust contains a larger proportion of aluminium than of any other metal.

The metal is prepared by an electrolytic process. A current of electricity is passed between carbon rods in a graphite-lined furnace containing aluminium dissolved in molten cryolite.

The current density is so high that the furnace requires no external heating, since the electricity generates sufficient heat to keep the mixture of alumina and cryolite in the fluid state.

The process is continuous, since the aluminium is removed and fresh supplies of aluminium oxide are added without interrupting the working of the furnace.

Properties of the Metal

Aluminium is a silvery-white metal which will take a very high polish. It is remarkable for its extreme lightness; its density is about 2.65. When exposed to normal atmospheric conditions the metal soon acquires a thin coating of aluminium oxide, which protects it against further attack.

This coating of oxide is such an effective protection against corrosion that many aluminium articles are superficially oxidised by an electrolytic process. This process is known as anodising.

Let us now investigate some of the chemical properties of the metal.

In separate test tubes try the action of dilute hydrochloric, nitric and sulphuric acids on aluminium. You will find that, while the metal dissolves readily in nitric acid, it is only attacked very slowly by the other acids.

A Simple Test

In a similar way, test aluminium with a strong solution of caustic potash or caustic soda. The metal will dissolve, giving off hydrogen and forming a solution of potassium or sodium aluminate. Add a little potassium nitrate solution to this liquid while the hydrogen is still coming off. You will soon notice the familiar odour of ammonia.

This gas is formed by the reducing action of the hydrogen on the potassium nitrate. A test based on this phenomenon has been used to measure the amount of nitrogen in drinking water.

An important compound of aluminium is aluminium oxide, or alumina. This compound occurs naturally as corundum and emery. Ruby and sapphire are composed of impure alumina the colour of these gems being caused by the impurities.

A Preparation

You may prepare a specimen of alumina from alum, which is a compound of the sulphates of aluminium and potassium. Prepare a solution of this salt and add a slight excess of ammonia solution.

A slimy precipitate of aluminium hydroxide will be thrown down. Filter off this precipitate, dry it, and then heat it strongly in a crucible. The white residue will be pure aluminium oxide.

Alumina finds its chief use in the dyestuffs industry, where it is used as a mordant, or fixing agent. This use may be demonstrated on a small scale in the home laboratory. Add some litmus solution to a solution of alum and then add a few drops of ammonia to the mixture. The precipitated aluminium oxide will carry down the dye in the form of a lake.

In the dyeing of cotton the lake is precipitated on the fibres of the fabric. Any substance which combines with an organic dye stuff in this way is known as a mordant.

You may prepare lakes from dyes of various substances by substituting the dyes for litmus in the above experiment.

Preparing Aluminum Chloride

Aluminium chloride was formerly the chief source of the metal. This salt may be prepared either by heating aluminium in chlorine, or by passing chlorine over a strongly-heated mixture of alumina and powdered charcoal.

Aluminium chloride is a white solid, which, when kept in an open vessel, absorbs so much water from the air that a solution is formed.

This property is called deliquescence, and a material which exhibits the property is known as a deliquescent substance. If this solution is evaporated to dryness it will not yield anhydrous aluminium chloride, for the salt will be " hydrolysised " to hydrochloric acid, water vapour and aluminium oxide.

For Waterproofing

An important salt of aluminium is aluminium acetate. Fabrics impregnated with a solution of this substance become water-repellent. Because of this, aluminium acetate is often included in compositions for dressing and water-proofing tents and sails.

Aluminium acetate was one of the first metal compounds to be used for this purpose, but it is now being replaced by metallic soaps such as aluminium naphthenate and zinc stearate. These extremely interesting substances, which are beginning to find fresh uses in many great industries, will be described more fully in a later article.

Making Alum

Aluminium and a few other metals form an unusual series of double salts known as the alums. These compounds form crystals which are composed of the sulphates of two metals.

Common alum, for instance, is a double sulphate of aluminium and ammonium, while chrome alum contains chromium sulphate instead of aluminium sulphate.

Getting Exhibition Crystals

The alums may contain the sulphates of sodium or potassium in place of ammonium sulphate. Although ammonia is not a metal, its salts behave so like those of the metals that ammonium sulphate may quite reasonably be classed with metallic sulphates.

You may prepare excellent exhibition crystals of great size and brilliancy from the alums. Prepare a saturated solution of alum and put the vessel on a shelf where it will not be disturbed.

Now take from your stock of alum a small, well-formed crystal, attach this by means of a tiny speck of sealing wax to the end of a hair. Now suspend the crystal in your saturated solution and do not disturb it for several days. At the end of this time you will find that a large, perfectly symmetrical crystal has been formed.

As Big as Your Fist

This experiment may be varied by first growing a large crystal of chrome alum and then suspending this in a saturated solution of common alum.

In this way you will obtain a huge crystal with a translucent exterior and a violet heart. With patience you should experience no difficulty in growing crystals as large as, or larger than, your fist.

An Ideal Christmas Gift.

WILL this be a Radio Christmas in the fullest sense of the word ? In the author's opinion, no one should be without a radio set this Christmas, since its value from both the entertainment and educational points of view is practically unlimited. Paterfamilias will probably have some difficulty in selecting a suitable present for his offspring, and it is suggested that the purchase of a radio set would help him out of the difficulty. In fact, one could present a radio set to practically any relative with the certainty of it being appreciated.

For the man who already has a set, probably a few accessories, or a book on the subject, would form a suitable gift.

If the reader happens to be one of the few who have not joined the ranks of radio listeners, he will probably be at a loss as to what kind of set to buy, and it is hoped that the following notes will be of assistance to him.

It is necessary first of all to obtain from the local Post Office a Broadcast Licence, which costs ten shillings, and remains in force for one year. Other licences are issued to qualified applicants, but these are only obtainable from the Secretary, General Post Office.

Crystal and Valve Sets.

The reader may already know that radio dealers sell what is known as a crystal set, and what is known as a valve set, but which he should buy presents a real problem to him. When choosing a radio set, one should select a crystal or valve set which will give at the required range a good factor of safety in signal strength ; that is to say, one should be able to hear the quiet passages of music or speech at a comfortable strength. The

STERLING " AUDIVOX " LOUD
SPEAKER.

next point is, whether the broadcast transmissions are to be rendered audible through the medium of telephones or a loud speaker. A loud-speaker will mean a multi-valve set, for, except in the case of the " Crystavox," there is no other satisfactory means of working a loud speaker on a crystal set, and even to use this efficiently the signals must be of sufficient strength to be heard in telephones at least twelve inches away from the ears. Under average conditions, quite good telephone reception can be obtained on a crystal set fifteen miles from a broadcasting station, whilst for twenty-five to fifty miles a single valve receiver with re-action would suffice ; and for over fifty miles, a two-valve set, one of the valves being a high frequency amplifier and the other a detector. It should be explained at this point that high frequency amplifiers will increase the range of a set, and low frequency amplifiers the volume to be obtained from a set. The range of a set, however, cannot be pre-determined precisely, as various considerations are involved. It has been stated that the two-valve set is suitable for distances over fifty miles. The author receives on a set of the type named Continental telegraphy regularly, and Madrid, eight hundred miles away, comes through with remarkable clearness and strength. One or two American stations have also been received, but such reception should not be expected when a set is first placed in the hands of a beginner. Of course, these are ranges over which telephony can be satisfactorily received. Telegraphic signals may be received over much greater ranges. With a crystal set, however, the Chelmsford high power telephony station, or the one which is to take its place, should be capable of reception at least one hundred miles from the source of transmission. In purchasing a set, it will be found that it pays to buy the best, and that simple apparatus will give better reproduction of speech and music than the more complicated instruments. It is well known, too, that a crystal set gives a better tone than most valve sets, and therefore it often pays

THE DUCON ADAPTER.

to have a crystal set and amplify the signals received by means of a low frequency amplifier. At ten miles from a broadcasting station, a crystal set will, in the ordinary way, give very good signals on the telephones, and practically all the power that is wanted for a loud speaker by introducing two stages of low frequency amplification.

When a set has been purchased, some difficulty may be experienced in setting up the station, but a few hints on the matter may be gleaned from the articles entitled "Chats on Efficiency," which appeared in Nos. 1511, 1512, 1513 and 1515 of HOBBIES. The ranges of the receivers referred to are the results to be obtained on outdoor aerials of the average length, conforming to the Postmaster General's regulations; but the sets will work at somewhat shorter ranges by the use of indoor aerials, which some people, through lack of choice, are forced to adopt. For the man who has to use an indoor aerial, it may be said that electric bell systems and electric lighting mains may be used as aerials, the latter being adapted for use by means of a small device known as the "Ducon" adapter, which is obtainable from most radio stores.

The kind of earth which is to be adopted will vary according to circumstances, and your dealer should be able to give you some advice on this matter, as well as a few hints on operating your set.

Accessories as Gifts.

As already intimated, to the man who is offering a gift to a radio enthusiast, probably a few accessories would be acceptable. For example, if your radio friend is using an indoor aerial, he probably finds that tuning is extremely critical, and would welcome some means whereby tuning may be made easier. To overcome the difficulty, there has recently been placed upon the market what is known as a "True Wave Form" aerial wire. This presents a comparatively large surface to incoming waves, and, as a matter of fact, enables one to get into a given space an additional length of aerial one-third as long

again as is possible with straight wire. Fittings are supplied with the aerial for attaching to the corners of a room. When *in situ*, the aerial, owing to its springy nature (due to its being constructed of hardened phosphor bronze) does not sag, and looks very neat.

Another accessory of utility is known as a coil-holder, and if one of these is purchased, care should be taken to see that a substantially constructed article is obtained, which permits of fine adjustment, and is of such construction that flexible leads are not required to place it in circuit with the remainder of the apparatus.

The man who is using a valve set, and experiments a great deal with valves, would probably find a dual rheostat of service, inasmuch as such a device enables him to place in circuit a variable resistance up to, say, seven or up to 30 ohms, which resistance valves are suitable for bright and dull emitter valves respectively. "Dull emitter" valves are suitable for use in remote country places, as they consume but little current, and will work for a long period off dry batteries. One particular dull emitter valve consumes only one-tenth of a watt, compared with about two watts consumed by the average bright emitter valve.

Then again, good quality (value about 25s.) head-phones may be of service, but before

STERLING LIGHT-WEIGHT HEAD-PHONES.

presenting these, it will be desirable to ascertain what resistance phones are already being used by your friend, and to purchase phones of the same resistance. It is usual, however, to buy what are known as 4,000 ohm phones.

Why Not a Loud Speaker?

Loud speakers may be worthy of consideration, and apart from the one named, the "Crystavox," for the crystal user, there are a multitude of others suitable for use in conjunction with valve sets. Care should be taken to purchase a properly designed loud speaker, and to be prepared to pay a good price for one. One of the new comers on the British market is known as the Sterling "Primax" loud speaker, and differs from the usual type of instrument, in that there is no trumpet, sound being emitted by a pleated parchment diaphragm. The author personally uses one of this type, and can testify to its being of good tone. One of its principal features is that there is no " out-of-the-hole " effect.

Your friend may have a splendid set accommodated in a cabinet which lacks a good finish because the requisite tools are not available. Here a glance through Hobbies' Catalogue should prove of assistance.

Should the foregoing suggestions not be of use, a book dealing with Radio is almost sure to prove an acceptable Christmas gift. There are various books now upon the stalls, some dealing with the subject from the beginner's point of view, others of a more abstruse character for the experienced operator, and there are various books on Radio of the popular variety.

An Ideal Radio Cabinet.

By the way, why not present a copy of Hobbies' 1925 Catalogue ? To say the least, it contains a design for a bureau which, when completed, is a splendid piece of furniture, incidentally forming an ideal Radio Cabinet.— H. J. H.

SYNCHRONISM.

WE have traced in fair detail how the Baird "Televisor" performs its task of presenting to the eye images which are faithful replicas of all that is happening before the transmitter in the far off studio. Although sharp corners or edges show a tendency to be softened somewhat, everyone who sees a television image is struck by the amount of really intimate detail that is revealed.

chronism? Two conditions must be fulfilled, namely, that of speed and phase. Suppose you had two pendulums of equal length and suspended them from a beam. If set moving they would execute swings in exactly the same times and the magnitude of their respective swings would be equal. Unless they were both set in motion at the same instant, however, the position of each pendulum relative to the other would be different, say as indicated in Fig. 1A.

A BAIRD COMMERCIAL TELEVISOR INSTALLED IN A HOME COMPLETE WITH MAINS DRIVE WIRELESS RECEIVER.

The next stage to be examined is the all important one of automatic synchronism, for this is the part of the process which makes the images hold steady behind the lens without any tangible medium connecting receiver and transmitter.

The Meaning of Synchronism.

First of all then, what do we mean by syn-

In other words, their speed or time executions would be identical, but they would not be in step or phase. The condition which Fig. 1A has fulfilled is known as isochronism and must not be confused with synchronism. This latter condition is only complied with when the pendulum movements are in step as shown in Fig. 1B.

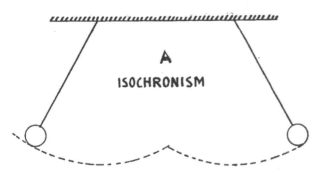

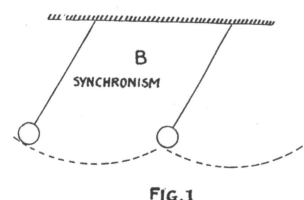

FIG. 1

A Further Example.

Let us take another case to make the position quite clear. If there are two accurate clocks, one of which was situated in your own home and the other in, say, Bombay, you would know that their accuracy ensured both the minute and hour hands performing equal angular movements. It is obvious, however, that they would not register the same time at the same instant owing to their different positions with reference to the Greenwich meridian.

Here again we satisfy equal speeds and establish isochronism, but synchronism between the two clocks will not be fulfilled until the hands not only move at the same rate but point to the same time at every instant.

Always bear this fact in mind, therefore, for it is particularly important. Isochronism can be established without synchronism being present, but it is impossible to achieve synchronism without first of all bringing about sochronism.

Several Unpractical Schemes.

With the Baird television system we establish isochronism through the agency of the ingenious mechanism incorporated in the receiving apparatus, and this is done automatically. The phasing or bringing into step of the transmitter and receiver disc holes is accomplished through one of the controls provided, an operation presenting not the slightest difficulty.

Many and varied have been the proposals put forward to bring about this question of equal speeds. Obviously, one method would be to employ alternating current synchronous motors. This applies only to a restricted area, however, for it is essential to have both transmitter and receiver motors run fron the same mains supply. A moment's reflection will show that for this country at least, with its varying voltages, frequencies, etc., the suggestion is out of the question for commercial use.

There are several other methods eminently suitable for laboratory working where the experiments are confined to one building or are under expert supervision, but it would be out of place to deal with them here.

Simple, yet Effective.

Something simple and inexpensive had to be devised to bring television within the scope of the ordinary domestic user, and this was accomplished by Mr. Baird and his engineers, but only after months of patient research work. It was first shown in operation at the September 1928 Radio Exhibition in London.

No separate synchronising signal was sent out, but the picture itself was made to provide the necessary impulses required to keep the receiver in a state of isochronism with the transmitter. It is important to note that no

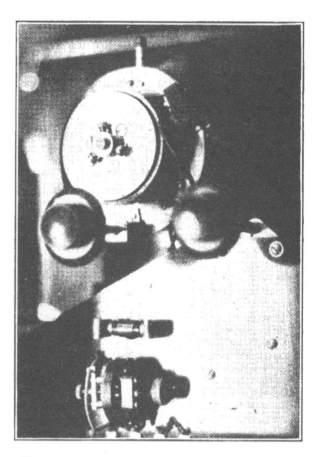

THE FIRST AUTOMATIC SYNCHRONISING MECHANISM DEVELOPED BY BAIRD, AND KNOWN AS THE RELAY SYSTEM

additional communication channel is required, whether by wire or by wireless, over and above that necessitated by the actual television signals.

This factor is of extreme importance and ensures that everyone in possession of Baird apparatus, no matter where situated (that is, in England or abroad, provided they are within service range of the wireless station sending out the vision signals), will be able to synchronise automatically.

A Light Strip Sequence.

It is fairly obvious that for this to occur there must be some component part of the television signal which varies exactly in accordance with the transmitter disc and is uninfluenced by the type of scene or object which is being televised.

Remember that the spotlight at the transmitter creates light strips in its bottom to top movement, thirty of these strips being built up, side by side, in this way owing to the special positioning of the holes in the scanning disc. The actual strip sequence is the

PORTION OF TRANSMITTER AT 2 T.V. LONG ACRE, FROM WHICH EXPERIMENTAL TRANSMISSIONS WERE CARRIED OUT.

fundamental component which is employed, for this is unvarying. Based on the standard transmitter speed of twelve and a half pictures per second it produces a signal three hundred and seventy-five times per second with a well defined beginning and ending, and of course an intervening period. How this signal is made to carry out its synchronising function in a simple yet ingenious manner is extremely interesting. —H.J.B.C.

Show a copy of *Hobbies* to your friends.

Simple Science Experiments

IN his previous article T.A.T. described simple experiments which can be made at home to determine what causes water pipes to burst. Continuing this theme he shows what takes place in the

Domestic Hot Water Supply and Central Heating

Required:—a flask; some glass tubing; a lamp chimney and a Bunsen burner. If a Bunsen burner is not available you can make quite a good methylated spirits burner from an old tobacco tin filled with cotton wool saturated with methylated spirits (Fig. 9).

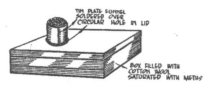

Fig 9

WHEN water above 4°C. is heated its density is diminished. If only part of the water is heated the difference in density thus produced causes currents to be set up. The action of these convection currents is to carry the warm water away from the point at which it is being heated, whilst its place is taken by colder water from surrounding parts.

Fill the lamp glass, tubes and flask with water after you have arranged them and supported them in some way (Fig. 10). Add a little ink to the water in the lamp glass. Heat the water in the flask and the path of the convection currents set up will be indicated by lines of coloured water.

Make a small paper box with drawing paper as shown (Fig. 11). The flaps may be stuck down with glue.

Suspend this box with thin string and half fill it with water. You will find you can boil this water by holding the box over a Bunsen flame or a methylated spirit burner, while the paper will not be scorched where it is in contact with the water. The water conveys the heat away from the paper as quickly as it is communicated to it.

[Fig. 10

This experiment also illustrates the great heat capacity of water; that is, the

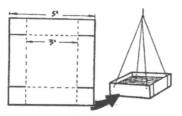

Fig. 11

great amount of heat required to raise the temperature to boiling point and then to change it from water, at the boiling point, into water vapour.

* * *

Model Domestic Hot Water System

FIG. 12 shows a method of making a simple model domestic hot water system. You may like to try to adapt this to fit into a simple model house if you can obtain or make one.

(A) is an empty metal polish tin which acts as the boiler. A small hole is drilled near the bottom of this tin and over this a short piece of copper tubing is soldered. A length of glass tubing (B) is connected to the copper tubing with a short piece of rubber tubing. (C) is a larger tin can which has three short pieces of copper tubing soldered over small holes near the bottom, as shown. (D) is an empty treacle tin with a short piece of copper tubing soldered over a small hole on the base. (A), (C) and (D)

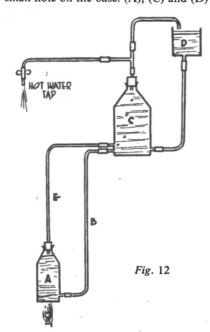

Fig. 12

are connected with glass tubes fixed to the copper tubes with short pieces of rubber tubing and a glass T-tube is fitted through a cork in the neck of (C). This T-tube is connected to other pieces of **glass** tubing as shown.

The whole apparatus is filled with water by pouring it into the treacle tin (D) which serves as the cold water storage tank, which you usually find at the highest point in the bathroom. Heat the water gently in (A). Small air bubbles will show the path of the hot

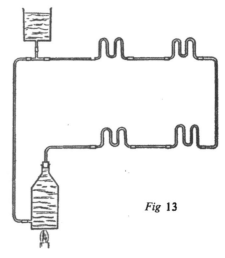

Fig 13

water up the tube (E) into the can (C). Cold water will descend down the tube (B) and enter at the base of (A). When the upper part of the can (C), which serves as the hot water storage tank, becomes really hot, place a little ink in (D), run off some of the hot water at the tap and watch carefully the path of the coloured water through the 'pipes'. You should learn how cold water is automatically fed into the system when water is run off at the hot taps, and how to prevent water in the hot water storage tank from losing heat.

You can adapt the apparatus used for the last experiment to make a simple central heating system for a model house, as shown in Fig. 13. The radiators consist of pieces of glass tubing heated in a Bunsen flame and bent into shape. The radiators, glass connecting tubes and tin cans are connected with short pieces of rubber tubing.

The apparatus is filled with water by pouring it into the treacle tin and it is gently heated in the boiler. You should note the direction of movement of the water by watching the small air bubbles in the tube.

For medium and long waves

BEGINNER'S CRYSTAL SET

By F. G. Rayer

MANY constructors begin with a crystal set, and that described here is ideal for a beginner, as there are no snags or difficulties, and good results can be anticipated. The set tunes both Long and Medium Waves (like the average domestic radio).

Readers who have never built a crystal set may appreciate a few details of the results to expect. To begin with, such a receiver requires no mains or battery supplies whatever, which helps to account for the popularity of sets of this kind. Its chief limitations are lack of sensitivity, and rather flat tuning — which means that a crystal set is really intended for listening to local stations only. The actual maximum range from a major B.B.C. station is around 100 to 150 miles or so, though it is occasionally possible to hear some overseas stations, at low volume, after dark. (Wave propagation is reduced by daylight).

It is also very desirable to provide a good aerial and earth or volume will be reduced. There is no amplification, as in valve sets, so that a very short aerial, and using the set with no earth, will not be very satisfactory.

Crystal detector and other parts are almost 'everlasting' and no further licence is required if the householder has a licence for an existing receiver. Running costs are thus absent.

Circuit and Parts

The circuit (Fig. 1) is of the usual type which proves best for general results. The .0005μF tuning condenser should be air-spaced, though a solid-dielectric one *can* be used, if to hand. A knob will be required for it. Condensers of less than .0005μF will reduce the wavelength coverage, so that only part of the

Medium and Long wavebands can be tuned. The full .0005μF condenser will usually have twenty to thirty plates, half fixed and half moving, the exact number depending upon the area of the plates, and distance between them.

An on/off switch is used for wave-changing, and can be of any type. Any kind of crystal, germanium diode, or crystal diode is satisfactory. Some crystal diodes have wire ends, and these can be taken directly to the terminals. Others require clips for the ends, or need to have connecting wires twisted on. Leads must on no account be soldered in place, or the detector is likely to be ruined.

Five bolts with nuts or terminals, and a strip of paxolin or ebonite 1in. by 6ins. will be required, and a wooden baseboard 6ins. by 4ins. by $\frac{3}{8}$in. thick. The panel can be of 3-ply, 4$\frac{1}{2}$ins. by 6ins.

Making the Coil

This is shown in Fig. 2, and requires an insulated tube about 1$\frac{1}{2}$ins. in diameter. A Paxolin tube may be purchased, or it can be made by winding glued card or brown paper round a suitable object, removing, and allowing to dry. When dry, such home-made tubes should be varnished to exclude moisture, and to stiffen them. The tube needs to be at least 3ins. long.

For the M.W. section, eighty turns of

28 SWG enamelled wire are used, wound closely side by side. When about forty turns have been wound on, a loop long enough to reach the one aerial terminal is twisted in the wire. This is point (2) in Fig. 2, (1) being the beginning of the winding, and (3) the end.

A space of about $\frac{1}{4}$in. is then left, and some 32 SWG cotton-covered wire is joined to the end of the M.W. winding. One hundred turns are then wound on, in a compact pile about $\frac{1}{4}$in. wide. A $\frac{1}{4}$in. space is left, a further hundred turns wound on, and the wire finished off at (4). All turns throughout the whole coil must be in the same direction, and the ends can be anchored by passing them through pairs of small holes in the

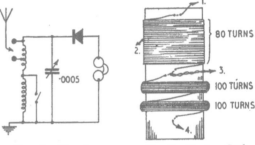

Fig. 1—*Circuit*   Fig. 2—*Tuning Coil*

tube. End (3) will be two wires, as in Fig. 2.

The coil is mounted by cutting a strip of wood upon which it can be pushed, and screwing this to the receiver baseboard, as in Fig. 3. The finished coil

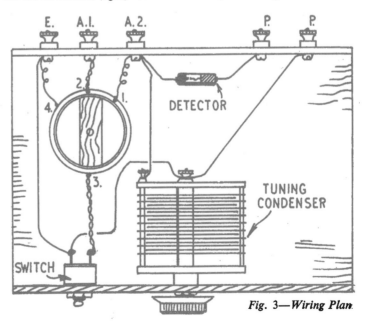

Fig. 3—*Wiring Plan*

must not be painted with varnish, wax, or any other substance, though a touch of varnish or wax will help to hold the ends secure. The turns will not move, if tight. It is in order to fit large cardboard 'washers' to the tube, if desired, and to wind the two 100-turn piles between these, to keep them compact. Slight modifications in the coil diameter, wire gauge, or number of turns will not significantly influence results, but *very* thin wires and small tubes are not satisfactory.

Wiring Up

Some of the 28 SWG wire will be satisfactory for connections in the set, all of which will be seen in Fig. 3. Insulation must be scraped from the ends of the connections, and a tight clean joint obtained. Leads from the coil are numbered to agree with Fig. 2.

Some tuning condensers will be different from that shown, and may have tags or terminals situated in different places. However, one will go to fixed plates, and this tag or terminal is wired to A2 in Fig. 3. Similarly, the moving plates terminal, tag or contact strip (or frame, with a metal-framed condenser) is connected to the terminal marked (P).

Failure to obtain proper tuning may arise from a broken coil winding or shorted condenser. This can be tested for with phones and a dry cell. Continuity through the coil windings will be shown by a loud click in the phones. There should be no contact between fixed and moving plates of the condenser. Examination or testing with a battery and bulb will check for this.

Volume obtained can be greatly influenced by the type of headphones, and those suitable for crystal sets are necessary. These will be of medium or high impedance. Low impedance and moving-coil phones are sold by some ex-service stores. These are designed for other equipment, and are not satisfactory with crystal sets.

In the event of no signals being heard, the phones or their leads must be suspected if they are old. The phones should click loudly if the leads are momentarily touched on a dry cell. If not, they cannot function. Testing up at each ear-piece will show if the fault is in the flex leads or phones themselves.

Using the Set

The phones are wired to terminals marked (P) in Fig. 3. The Earth lead is taken to the terminal (E). The best earth consists of a metal spike or other metal object buried in damp soil out-of-doors. Sometimes a lead may be clamped to a descending water pipe. Gas pipes are not suitable, nor are rising water pipes, or any connection which only goes to earth by a round-about path. Fair results with no Earth will only be obtained up to twenty-five miles or so from a station.

For maximum volume, a long high out-door aerial well away from walls, trees and any earthed object is best. It can be of 7/22 wire, which will also do well for the Earth connection. One or two small egg insulators should be fitted at suspension points. About 60ft. of wire will provide an efficient aerial, carried in one length to form both aerial and down-lead. The latter should

be kept a few feet from walls, etc., for maximum signal strength.

Sufficient volume will often be obtained with less effective aerials, or even with an indoor aerial. The latter should be near the ceiling, and can be carried round two walls of the room. With such an arrangement, an Earth becomes very necessary. Indoor aerials are not suitable in metal buildings. Short rod aerials are not satisfactory.

An average aerial can be taken to terminal A1. Using terminal A2 will slightly increase volume, but flatten tuning. It is thus most suitable for a relatively inefficient aerial. Medium Waves are tuned with the switch closed, and Long Waves with it open.

It is possible to sharpen tuning to almost any desired extent by providing a tapping nearer to point 3 on the coil, or by using a pre-set condenser in series with the aerial lead-in. Such modifications will result in a loss of signal strength, and this limits their practical use, except when a local station is very near.

★ ★ ★ ★ ★ ★ ★ ★ ★ ★ ★ ★ ★
★   ★
★   Next week's free de-   ★
★   sign will be for a novel   ★
★   Weather House and   ★
★   Thermometer. Make   ★
★   sure of your copy.   ★
★   ★
★ ★ ★ ★ ★ ★ ★ ★ ★ ★ ★ ★ ★

Radio Valves

For battery valves 150 volts is maximum. 120 volts is usual, and even 60 volts will give reasonable results.

The grid bias should also be adjusted to the voltage which gives best results (usually from 4·5 to 9 volts). As was seen, this voltage governs the current flowing. Consequently as high a voltage as possible should be used, as this will greatly increase the life of the high tension battery. Too much grid bias will so reduce the current, results will be poor.

Fig. 3 shows a complete three valve set. The decoupling condenser (about ·1 mfd.) prevents unwanted signals remaining on the screen grid. Sometimes a resistor is added at the

point "X" to prevent these signals flowing into the H.T. battery. Except in critical sets, this condenser can be omitted.

The choke allows the H.T. to reach the anode, but prevents the flow of the signal, which passes through the coupling condenser (about ·0002 to ·0005 mfd.) to the second tuning coil. The signal is then built up across the grid leak and amplified by the detector.

The second choke prevents the radio part of the signal passing, which goes through the reaction coil and condenser, increasing volume because the reaction coil is coupled to the tuning coil. The audible part of the signal cannot pass through the anode resistor (about 30,000 to 50,000

ohms), which nevertheless allows H.T. to reach the detector anode.

The signal consequently goes through the second coupling condenser, to build up across the second grid leak and be amplified by the last valve, which is connected to the speaker. A transformer could be used for coupling, as in Fig. 2.

The output valve screen grid is connected directly to maximum H.T. 40 to 75 volts is ample for the detector, however, or it may tend to oscillate too violently.

Sometimes the lead marked "G.B.1" goes to a potentiometer so that anything between zero and 9 volts may be applied. This acts as a volume control.

Helpful details for the amateur on types and use of
RADIO VALVES

IT is hoped this article will help readers both to understand the valves they use, and to employ them in the best way. Although there are scores of different types, three of the most popular (the triode, screen-grid, and pentode) are used almost exclusively in straightforward one-, two- and three-valve receivers intended for home construction. Thus excessive complication is avoided.

How a Valve Works

The bulb is evacuated and a filament is heated until it emits electrons. These form a small electric current flowing through the empty space inside the valve. The first valves made (the diode) had a metal plate a little distance from the filament. When this was charged positively the electrons flowed to it.

However, no electrons could flow from the plate (usually called the anode) to the filament, because the plate was not emitting electrons. In consequence, the internal current could only travel one way. Such valves are used for rectifying (chang-

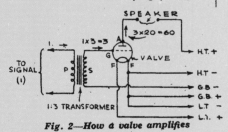

Fig. 2—How a valve amplifies

ing alternating current to direct current).

If a metal grid is placed between the filament and anode, the electrons must flow through its mesh. If this grid is slightly negative, it tries to stop the flow. When it is not negative the flow is uninterrupted.

Thus small changes in grid voltage produce large changes in the current flowing to the plate (anode current), just as raising and lowering a sluice controls the flow of water under it. This increase is what is meant by amplification.

Screen-Grid Valves

When two metal objects are near, a capacity exists between them. As the capacity between grid and anode was bad from a radio point of view, a further grid was put between them. This is called the "screen grid" because it screens the first grid from the anode. Valves with this are called Screen-Grid Valves.

This extra grid had to be positive to attract electrons, and it was found some bounced back off the plate, which was not wanted. In con-

sequence, a further grid was put between the screen grid and anode. This was called the "suppressor grid", and its inclusion made the Pentode Valve.

The first grid is called the "control grid" because it controls the electron stream initially. A "bird's eye view" of the electrodes in a pentode is shown at "E", Fig. 1. In screen-grid valves the suppressor grid is absent. In triodes both suppressor grid and screen grid are omitted.

The Triode

The symbol and pin connections for a battery triode are shown at "A" in Fig. 1. These valves are good for detection and low frequency amplification. They are little use for high frequency amplification because of the capacity between control grid and anode.

As the size of the electrodes and the distance between them governs the power the valves will handle, certain valves work best for certain purposes.

For detection, the Mazda HL2, Ever-Ready K30C, Mullard PM1HL, Cossor 210HF, or Osram HL2 are all very good. For low frequency amplification, the Mazda L2, Ever-Ready K30E, Osram L21, and Cossor 215P are suitable. Power output requires a Mazda P220A, Mullard PM202, Osram P2 or Cossor 220P to provide good speaker volume.

Screen-Grids

Connections for the Mullard PM12M and Osram VS24 are shown at "B". These valves have a top cap for the anode connection. Pentodes such as the Osram VP21 and Cossor 210VPT have the same connections and can be used instead. Where possible, 120 volts should be applied to the anode, with about 60 to 80 volts to the screen grid.

These valves can also be obtained with seven-pin bases, when connections, *looking at the bottom of the*

valve, are as shown in "D". Four-pin pentodes have the metallising on the outside of the valve and the suppressor grid joined internally to one filament pin. Except for very

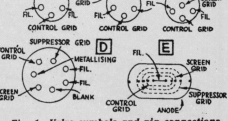

Fig. 1—Valve symbols and pin connections

special circuits this is satisfactory.

Low Frequency Pentodes do not have a top cap, but an extra pin, as shown at "C". Valves of this type are: Mazda PEN220, Ever-Ready K70B, Osram PT2, Cossor 220HPT and 220PT, and Mullard PM22A.

With these, a voltage of 100 to 120 should be applied to the screen grid if it is available. Some old valves have a side terminal instead of the extra centre pin.

All the valves mentioned have 2-volt filaments for operation from an accumulator.

How Amplification Takes Place

Fig. 2 shows a typical amplifier with batteries connected. Electrons flow from the filament, through the grid to the anode. A transformer is used, because if it has more turns on the secondary than are on the primary, the voltage of the signal will be stepped up. If the signal is called "1" a 1:3 transformer increases it to about "3".

This is applied to the grid, and if the valve amplifies (as described) twenty times (an average figure), the signal will be sixty times as strong when it reaches the speaker. (In practice, losses actually prevent quite such good results).

For best results, the anode voltage should be as high as possible.

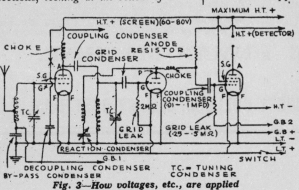

Fig. 3—How voltages, etc., are applied

How to take a dent out of a bowler hat
CANDLE HOLDERS FOR YOUR TENT

DID YOU KNOW?

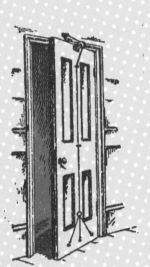

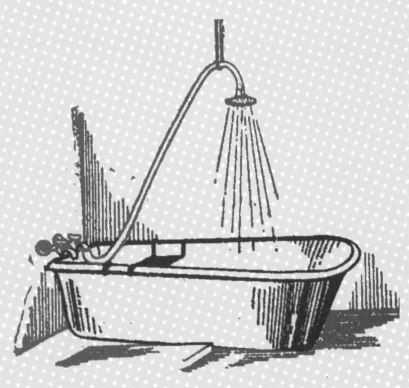

**MAKE A USEFUL TRAPDOOR
FOR PIGEONS**
MORE HOBBIES FOR HANDYMEN

ALL PARAGRAPHS PRINTED ARE PAID FOR AND A PRIZE GIVEN FOR THE BEST.

The Editor offers a Prize of 2s. 6d. every week for the best paragraph submitted. In addition the sum of 1s. will be paid to all others whose paragraphs are printed. Address "Kinks" to the Editor HOBBIES, 125, Fleet Street, London.

THE prize is this week awarded to MR. E. WILSON, W. Norwood, for the following "Kink."

Making a Pencil Gauge.

THE drawings show a pencil gauge made from a broken ruler, fitted into a block so as to run easily, and made secure at any distance

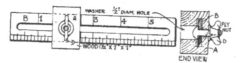

(as indicated by the ruler edge) by means of a thumbscrew. A is a block of birch, 1½in. by 1in. by 1in., mortised so as to receive the ruler. B is a 5in. length of an ordinary ruler, with a slot, C (which could be cut with a fretsaw) just large enough to admit the screw, D, which is fixed in the block A. The thickness of the wood between the washer and the ruler should only be ⅛in., to allow a little pliability.—E. WILSON, W. Norwood.

Straightening Wire.

A VERY useful device for straightening wire can be made from a block of wood, 3in. deep,

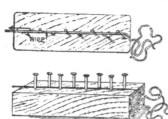

4in. wide, and about 15in. long, in the top of which is inserted a number of nails placed as shown. To straighten the wire it should be pulled right through the middle of the two rows of nails. —E. WILSON, W. Norwood.

Bath Fed from Copper.

THIS is an arrangement for applying hot water to a bath which can be used in a Bungalow or other small house. The bath is placed in a room on the ground floor next to the scullery. An iron pipe having a top at one end is connected to the copper and taken through the wall. The copper is filled, and the water made hot; then it is run off into the bath.—L. BLANCHARD, *Leatherhead.*

Useful Egg-Beater.

To make this egg-beater it will need about ten inches of wire about the thickness of the top of a drill. After that is got cut the centre wire to whatever length you like, and then twist the outer wires to centre, as shown in the illustration. Last of all fasten wire across. After all is finished remove the bit from a drill and fix top into the hole. There you have got your egg-beater. — N. WILCOCK, *Accrington.*

Useful Trapdoor for Pigeons.

A VERY useful trapdoor for pigeons can be made out of a piece of strong wire. In the door of the cage or box, cut a rectangular hole, 3½in. by 5½in. Now obtain a stout piece of wire and bend it to the shape of a U as A in Fig. 1. This loop should be 2in. by 7in. Now obtain two staples, and nail the loop to the top of hole 1½in.

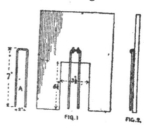

above, at the back of the door as in Fig. 2, so that it may be able to swing backward and not forward, just touching the bottom of the box. When a pigeon goes in it pushes the wire back and easily gets in, but when it wants to get out it is easily stopped by the wire.—G. V. SHORTER, *Windsor.*

To Take a Dent out of a Bowler Hat.

A USEFUL, yet very simple "Kink" is that of taking a dent or any number of dents out of a bowler hat. To do this, take a lighted match and hold it inside the hat. By the time the match has burnt out, the dent will have become quite soft. It can then be carefully and easily pushed out with the hand, without any fear of damaging the hat.—H. PINCHBECK, *South Bank, Yorks.*

Selling Fretwork.

IT will be found that fretwork sells a lot easier and at a greater price with the buyer's monogram on it. This is simply, but very effectively accomplished. Some nickel or silver plated nails of the required length are driven into the wood to form the required letters. Transfers of different letters can be obtained from drapers' stores, which, when heated, will print a copy on the wood.—A. L. COLLINS, *Birmingham*.

Handy Bread-Toaster.

WHEN you are toasting bread with a fork, it makes your arm ache, and the heat of the fire burns your hand. This difficulty can be overcome by an easily-made substitute. It consists of a round strip of iron, ⅛in. diameter, and 27in. long, bent with pliers to the shape

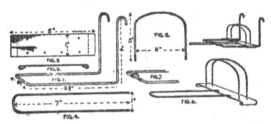

given in Fig. 1. Next get a piece of tin, 4½in. long by 1⅞in. wide, and bore holes with a bradawl, as in Fig. 2. The dotted lines, as shown in diagram, are to be rounded over as in Fig. 3. When finished get a piece of wire 1-16in. diameter and 11in. long, and bend to shape, as in Fig. 4. Then we shall want two pieces of the same kind of wire, each 12in. long, and round as in Fig. 5 to the bread. Now take the piece of tin you have already made, and fix the wire shapes into the holes as in Fig. 6, and lap ends over the tin. Now take the wire for the handle as shown in Fig. 1, and fix in the remaining two holes. Now for the last fixture: Get a piece of wire 1-16in. thick, and 2in. long, and twist as in Fig. 7. Round end of iron marked with a cross in Fig. 1. Now fix together, and the result will be astonishing, as will be seen in our remaining sketch. It will hook on the bars and toast quite easily.—S. SERJEANT, *Ipswich*.

Home-made Fountain Pen.

WITH a piece of thin wire about 3in. long make two small coils, as shown in sketch. These coils may be made by winding the wire round a pin. When this is done, take the piece of wire from between the two coils, A, and pass it over the points of the pen, bringing the coil into the hollow of the nib. Then take the two ends, B, B, and fasten them at the back of the nib. The pen is now finished, and will write a letter with only one dip in the ink. Another method is to cut a thin strip of tin, and bend it as C. Let the top rest against the hollow, and the bottom into the holder.— C.E. SOUNDY, *Clapham*.

Handy Print-Trimming Knife.

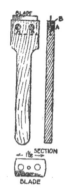

CUT out a handle from ¼in. fretwood to size, and shape shown. Next make a fine saw cut about ¾in. deep, as indicated at B (Fig. 3). Bore two holes to take the wood pegs, A, A, and by their means fix an old "Gillette" blade into the saw-cut B. The ends of the pegs should be cut off, and sandpapered smooth, and all sharp corners and edges on the handle should be rounded with sandpaper. — FRANK M. MARSHALL, *Glasgow, W.*

To Discover Small Hole in Cycle Tube when Water is not Available.

TAKE out tube, light your pipe, and blow in the tube as much smoke as possible; then watch for the smoke coming from the puncture. Another way is to take out tube, inflate with pump, light cycle lamp, and then run tube round close to the flame; when puncture is opposite the flame the flame will waver. This is a good plan when on the road at night. —W. LONG, *Chichester*.

Substitute for a Wrench.

IF in need of a spanner, and one is not at hand, take a bolt, and run on two nuts, allowing a space between them to fit over the nut to be turned.—E. LANHAM, *Eastleigh*.

Candle Holder for Tents.

THIS method is useful in tents and outhouses, &c. Dig one blade of an ordinary penknife into the tent pole, and half open the other in the manner illustrated, and upon it fix the candle in an upright position. — W. ANNISON, *Wells-next-Sea, Norfolk*.

Boring Holes Similar Depth.

THE woodworker often finds it necessary to bore holes of the same depth with a brace and bit. The illustration shows a method of accomplishing this. Take a cylinder of wood and with the bit to be used, bore a hole lengthways through the wood, holding the latter upright in a vice. Cut off such a length of this hollow cylinder as will leave the required length of bit uncovered. By slipping this cylinder over the bit, the holes will be all the same depth. By making a plug to fit the end of the cylinder, the latter may be used as a guard for the point of the bit.—M. DOBSON, *Matlock*.

Door Opener.

BEND a piece of $\frac{1}{8}$in. thick wire round the door knob, and the other end at right angles to the door. It should be supported by a hook or screw eye at A. Then hinge together two pieces of hard wood, one 2in. long by 1½in.

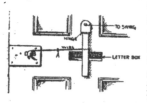

wide by $\frac{1}{4}$in. thick, and the other 1in. wide by $\frac{1}{4}$in. thick. Screw this above the letter-box, as shown, and see that it swings loosely. When hanging, it should just touch the end of the wire. A little push to the left against this from outside the door will at once open the latter. This arrangement will not interfere with letters, &c., which come through the letter-box ; because as soon as the letter is pushed through, the hinged piece of wood will rise, and fall back into its original position when the letter is through.—LEO. WHITE, *Cardiff.*

Door Curtain Lifter.

IT is extremely difficult to open a door on which a curtain is fixed, as the curtain gets jambed between the door and the floor. This difficulty can be overcome by the following

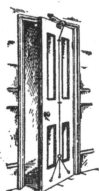

method :—On the top of the door fix a pulley, which can be bought at small cost. If this shape cannot be obtained, a small screw pulley can be used, but this must be put in at an angle so that it does not prevent the door from closing. Over this pulley place a cord which is to be fastened to the top of door frame and also to the bottom of the curtain. It must also pass through the long screw eyes or staples shown in the centre of door. When the door is open, the cord is pulled at right angles, thus lifting the curtain. The length of cord and position of pulley, &c., can be found by different experiments.—B. W. LACEY, *Moseley, Birmingham.*

A Simple Shower Bath.

GET some rubber tubing and attach one end firmly on to a tap. From the ceiling

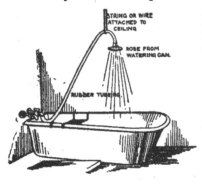

above a little to the right, hang down a loop of string, through this put the rubber tubing, making it come down again. On to this end fix an ordinary watering can rose. Where the string supports the tubing ; it must be kept round, or else the water will not flow easily. Turn the water on, and it will descend through the watering can rose.—R. E. EMMETT, *Bedford.*

To Duplicate a Design.

PROCURE a piece of ordinary glass, and the piece of clean white paper. Stick the latter on to the design to be duplicated, and fix the whole on the glass and hold up to the light, artificial or otherwise. You will then see the design quite plainly ; trace and remove. It matters not how you want the duplicated design, for in some cases one wants it reversed ; in that case you have to stick white paper on *back* of design, but in both cases the design is next to the glass.—J. HILL SINCLAIR, *Enfield.*

Electric Light and Bell.

THE illustrations show how an alarm clock can be made to switch on your light at the time the alarm rings. The alarm winder is fitted

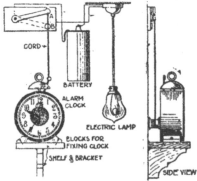

with a round piece of wood (such as a cotton reel) to which some thread is attached, and the other end of thread fixed to connector of switch. It must be arranged that when the alarm is set the thread is unwound, but tight, so that when the alarm goes off the reel winds up the thread which pulls down switch form, terminal A to B, which forms the complete circuit, and the lamp is lit.—T. GIBBS, *Fulham.*

A Ceiling Clothes Airer.

MAKE the ends of battens, the joints of which should be mortised. The rails are laths, and a pulley strong enough can be obtained for 2d. or 2½d. A is the ceiling and B the wall. The large screw eye, C, should be well screwed into

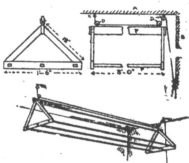

the rafters. D is the pulley wheels. E, the cord, should be stout blind cord. The four rails, F, are 8ft. or more in length.—R. PESTER, *Brighton.*

HOBBIES LTD.

Hobbies are still thriving after supplying modelmakers since 1895 and are looking forward to supplying the hobbyist for the next 100 years. Although no longer based in Dereham, they are still located in Norfolk at The Raveningham Centre, just a few miles from Norwich.

Hobbies have a large shop that is crammed full of wonderful craft and modelling ideas.
The mail order side of the business goes from strength to strength, with orders received from around the world.
Why not take a look at their website www.alwayshobbies.com

Contact Hobbies at:

Units 8-11

The Raveningham Centre

Beccles Road

Raveningham

Norfolk

NR14 6NU

Telephone: 01508 549330

Website: www.alwayshobbies.com

TO REQUEST A FULL CATALOGUE OF AMMONITE PRESS TITLES, PLEASE CONTACT:

AE PUBLICATIONS LTD. 166 HIGH STREET, LEWES,
EAST SUSSEX, BN7 1XU, UNITED KINGDOM
TEL: 01273 488005 FAX: 01273 402866
WWW.AE-PUBLICATIONS.COM